LAST TRAINS
Dr Beeching and the Death of Rural England

CHARLES LOFT

Biteback Publishing

This edition first published in Great Britain in 2014 by
Biteback Publishing Ltd
Westminster Tower
3 Albert Embankment
London SE1 7SP
Copyright © Charles Loft 2013

ISBN 978-1-84954-712-3

10 9 8 7 6 5 4 3 2 1

A CIP catalogue record for this book is available from the British Library.

Set in Caslon

Printed and bound in Great Britain by
CPI Group (UK) Ltd, Croydon CR0 4YY

To Elaine, Billy, Sid and Ron

Contents

Chapter 1

Introduction: a wound that has not healed

O n a September evening in 1964, a branch line terminus in the north of England waited for the Beeching Axe to fall. As the last train from Carlisle pulled into the tiny terminus at Silloth, the usual diesel replaced by a steam locomotive for the occasion, passengers in the packed coaches gasped to see a crowd of between 5,000 and 9,000 people spilling across the tracks and a group of folk singers performing 'The Beeching Blues'. The police had already ejected the local Labour Party candidate from the platform. With the train preparing to return to Carlisle, officers repeatedly removed a placard which read, 'If you don't catch this you'll never get another one – unless you vote Labour', from the front of the locomotive, which was also adorned by a wreath. The final departure was delayed, first while the police removed detonators from the rails and then as they removed 'dozens of "teenagers"' sitting on the line to shouts of, 'Remember it's your train they're stopping as well as ours' from the crowd. As the locomotive inched forward, the driver released hot steam and then hot water to clear the last of the demonstrators sitting on the tracks before the train pulled away to the sound of Brian Poole and the Tremeloes' 'Do you love me?' playing

on the crowd's transistor radios. As it pulled into Abbeytown,
police cars raced to the station in response to a bomb hoax. Such
desperate acts may stop a train, but they cannot make it run; the
line had closed, the crowd departed, some in tears. The following Friday, the *Carlisle Journal* reported this 'great train robbery'
in uncompromising terms. 'With one swift cut of your scalpel,'
it warned Beeching, he had deterred holidaymakers and new
industry from coming to 'once booming' Silloth, and 'severed a
vital lifeline … that can mean the difference between prosperity
and poverty'.[1]

A few weeks earlier the local MP, Willie Whitelaw, had
been accosted by a constituent whose farm bordered the line.
The farmer complained that if he was no longer able to see the
branch train passing in the afternoon he would not know when
it was time to go home for his tea. He was advised to get a watch.
This was not just the loss of a local amenity, it was a fundamental
alteration to a pattern of life; the old certainties steamed away to
the soundtrack of the new Britain. This convenient symbolism
was less significant, however, than the fact that the 'teenagers'
(the account in the *Railway Magazine*, founded in 1897, felt the
word still required inverted commas) were as unhappy at the loss
of their railway as the watchless farmer.[2]

The atmosphere in which the last train left Silloth was unusu-
ally politicised and rowdy (the 1964 general election was only
a month away), but similar scenes took place all over Britain
during the 1950s and 1960s, as the passenger railway network
contracted from around 17,000 miles in 1948 to under 9,000 in
1973. The fall in the number of stations open to passengers was
even more dramatic, from over 6,500 to 2,355. Sometimes there
were protests but more often the last train was mourned like the

passing of an old friend, albeit one the mourners had lost touch with lately. It was not unheard of for someone who had travelled on a line's first ever train to travel on its last; people would wave from level crossing gates and enthusiasts would descend from far afield. It was not uncommon either for the last train to be barely marked, perhaps an epitaph chalked on the locomotive by its crew and a dreary sense of resignation among the few remaining passengers. The name of Dr Richard Beeching has become so indelibly associated with this process that over thirty years after he left the British Railways Board (BRB) the BBC could use it in the title of a sitcom set on a rural branch line in the early 1960s, *Oh Dr Beeching!*, and be confident the public would recognise it.

Beeching joined the British Transport Commission (BTC), the publicly owned body with responsibility for the railways, in March 1961 and became chairman on 1 June. When the BTC was replaced by the BRB on 1 January 1963, Beeching became its chairman, remaining in the post until 1 June 1965. The context for Beeching's appointment was the railways' burgeoning deficit. Operating profits had declined steadily since 1952, becoming losses in 1956. In 1962 that loss was more than £100 million and interest on the railways' debts added some £50 million to that figure (even though interest payments on much of their debt had been temporarily suspended). Under Beeching's chairmanship, the BTC and BRB closed 2,479 route miles to passengers (less than a third of the total contraction). In March 1963 the BRB published *The Reshaping of British Railways*, or the *Beeching Report* as it soon became known. At great length the report expounded what was in essence a very simple message: the railways had to concentrate on carrying the traffic for which they were best suited with increasing efficiency, while cutting out that which did not pay. This meant investing in the transport of large loads over long distances, while withdrawing many stopping-train passenger and pick-up freight services (in other words local services stopping at every station), and closing lines on which no other traffic was carried. In short, the railways should behave like a business. Beeching made a number of positive recommendations, most notably investment in freightliner trains, which he hoped would allow rail to retain some general merchandise traffic by offering a long-distance service combined with collection and delivery by road. Nevertheless, the parts of the report which attracted the most attention were the list of 2,363 stations to be closed, 266 services to be withdrawn and seventy-one to be modified, and the accompanying map which showed that roughly a third of the passenger network's route miles would go. By 1973, 31 per cent of the route mileage open to passengers in 1962 had closed; slightly more than half of this was achieved by the end of 1965. By this time, studies set in motion by Beeching had identified a network of 7–8,000 miles, less than 5,000 miles of it open to passengers. This implied nearly twice as many closures again as Beeching had presided over. These proposals were never implemented.

As a literary text, the *Beeching Report*'s pages of alphabetically ordered stations to be closed have the mournful look of names on a war memorial. This sombre list immediately inspired a *Guardian* editorial, entitled 'Lament', which utilised some of the more interesting station names and ended 'Yorton, Wressle, and Gospel Oak, the richness of your heritage is ended. We shall not stop at you again; for Dr Beeching stops at nothing.'[3] In a similar vein, later the same year Flanders and Swann produced their valedictory song for the passing of the 'Slow Train', which to a large extent involved setting to music the list of stations to close. It wasn't only professionals who put pen to paper. The Ministry of Transport's files on railway closures are stuffed with letters of protest, ranging from the bizarre and misguided to the eloquent anger of Mrs Joan Price of Cavendish, Suffolk, who attacked 'this inhuman plan' as a 'monstrous embodiment of ruthless disregard' for those affected by closures: 'it is like cutting off the nation's feet in order to save the cost of shoe leather'.[4]

The contraction of Britain's railway network was well underway before the *Beeching Report*. Between 1950 and 1962 the passenger rail network shrank by over 3,300 miles, the rate of contraction accelerating from 1958. But the concentration of so many closures in one slim volume associated Beeching with the entire process. No other nationalised industry chairman is so well remembered: at the Lord Beeching's pub in Aberystwyth; at Beeching's Folly, the former Southern Railway station in Tavistock; at, among others, Beeching Close and The Beechings, housing developments on the site of the former stations at Halwill Junction, Devon and Henfield, Sussex, respectively.

These are not fond memorials but infamy. The name Beeching still arouses passion, at least in men of a certain age. When I tell people I study transport policy their eyes glaze over; when I tell them I study Beeching I am often treated to a brief lecture on my subject. By the end of the twentieth century, Beeching was typically seen as having callously ignored the social consequences of closures, falsified figures, studied the railways in isolation from transport as a whole, and was variously accused of cooperating with an anti-rail conspiracy or simply being wrong.

One historian calls Beeching's appointment 'a tragedy for the nation' and refers to his 'dismantling of the railways ... as one of the major aberrations of the Macmillan government'.[5] The late Robert Adley, MP and railway enthusiast, saw Beeching's legacy as the 'mass decimation' of the railway network.[6] Ian Marchant describes Beeching's 'brutally simple task' as being to make the railways pay '[n]o matter what it cost in social terms'.[7] Most recently Richard Faulkner and Chris Austin, echoing David Henshaw's 1991 *The Great Railway Conspiracy*, claim that there was 'clearly a conspiracy between ministers, senior civil servants and the road lobby' to cut investment in rail and that Beeching's report was part of 'a determined attempt ... to diminish the role played by rail in meeting the nation's transport needs'.[8] In the introduction to Henshaw's work, Stan Abbott of the Railway Development Association wrote that praising Beeching for his achievements in improving railway management 'is rather like praising Hitler for helping create the VW Beetle while conveniently forgetting his other more notorious deeds'.[9]

It is perhaps worth reminding ourselves that Richard Beeching never killed anyone; indeed, he did not close a single railway line. Individual closures had to be approved by the Minister of Transport; all Beeching did was to put forward for closure those lines which were, in his view, irretrievably unremunerative. The prioritisation of financial criteria evident in the *Beeching Report* was founded upon the BRB's terms of reference set out in the 1962 Transport Act. Beeching's critics have generally recognised that their barbs must equally be aimed at Ernest Marples, Conservative Minister of Transport from October 1959 until October 1964, who appointed Beeching, implemented many of the closures he proposed and presided over both the 1962 Act and a shift in investment resources from rail to road which preceded it. Both contemporary and more recent commentators have tended to see the apparent shift in emphasis from rail to road as a direct reflection of Marples's influence, and – for some – the result of an unjustified anti-rail prejudice on his part. But whether it is Beeching, Marples or the 'road lobby' that gets the blame, Bruce Grocott's reference in a House of Commons debate in February 1996 to the 'vandalism of the Beeching era' typifies the lasting resentment over railway closures. They are, as Stewart Francis, then chairman of the Rail Passengers Council, wrote in 2002, 'a wound that hasn't healed'.[10]

Why should this still be so, decades later? Some obvious explanations are available; the most obvious of all being the bitter memories of those directly affected. In 1976, British Rail (BR) commissioned a study which concluded that rail closures had a significant adverse effect on the quality of life of many former passengers. Only a third of people who had travelled beyond their line's junction with the main line on a reasonably regular basis continued to do so and those without cars tended to abandon non-essential travel altogether. Even when the loss on a service clearly outweighed its social value, those who depended on the railway suffered when it was removed. Take, for example, Melton Constable, a tiny Norfolk village distinguished from its neighbours until 1959 by the fact that it was the hub of the former Midland and Great Northern Railway, the point at which a duplicate route from the Midlands divided into lines to Norwich, Yarmouth and Cromer. It was once the site of a locomotive works and a railway-owned concrete works, producing everything from fence posts to prefabricated offices. By 1963 only a sheet-metal works and the line to Cromer via Sheringham remained. A total of 189 people used the ten daily trains on the Sheringham–Melton section in the summer, 166 in the winter. Closure was expected to save £26,700 net and only thirty-one objections were made. The fact that the taxpayer appears to have been paying over four times as much to operate the service as its passengers and that such expenditure could not be justified when so few benefited was undoubtedly no consolation to those marooned in a village that had lost its purpose: the two school-teachers and a pupil who would have to wait until 6.45pm for a bus back to Sheringham; those reliant on the train to reach doctors, dentists and chemists in Holt; and those seeking new jobs when the railway's last remnant, the sheet-metal works, closed the following July. A local councillor, Miss M. Gray, suggested that Beeching and Marples should 'come out here for a month, leave their cars at home, and see how they would like it. That is the way to prove what hardship means... With no station and no trains we might as well be dead.' It is significant that her letter implied she used the line not to get to work, but for 'little outings by train' which gave her 'something to look forward to'; even for those who did not depend on the railway in absolute terms, its loss had an appreciable effect on the quality of life.[11] Miss Gray's rhetoric may have spilled into hyperbole, but for those with no cars rural life would be significantly bleaker without the railway and they were unlikely to meekly accept the argument that, from a national perspective, there were too few of them to be worth subsidising.

Such complaints might not have resonated for so long had *Reshaping*'s claim that 'if the whole plan is implemented with vigour, much (though not necessarily all) of the railways' deficit should be eliminated by 1970' had been achieved.[12] Professor Terry Gourvish's thorough business history of British Railways concludes that the amount saved through closures was 'anybody's guess', but that it was less than expected during the late 1960s.[13] In the early 1970s BR concluded that there was no size to which the railway network could be reduced that would render it profitable. If this suggests that Beeching was fundamentally on the wrong track, there is little doubt that, in some cases at least, the figures offered in support of individual proposals were vague calculations in support of a general principle that rural railways did not pay. Certainly, closures were not subject to detailed social cost–benefit analyses. Nor can there be any doubt that the 1962 Transport Act prioritised financial criteria and changed the procedure for considering closures to speed up the process. The reopening of some 180 route miles by 1991 supports Henshaw's claim that they should not have closed in the first place; and further reopenings have followed. One can make a case, therefore, for seeing this as a policy that failed, based on data that was at best flawed and at worst faked, bludgeoned through in the face of popular opposition, ignoring the need to consider transport as a whole and with scant regard for the wider picture of social costs and benefits or the suffering endured as a result, possibly as a deliberate attempt to benefit the road lobby at the expense of rail users.

These views, however, are open to dispute. Most people did not suffer like Miss Gray suffered and most places did not lose like Melton lost. If the sweeping away of almost all rail services has done lasting damage to the economies of the Scottish borders or east Lincolnshire, it did not prevent quality of life improving significantly for most people in the ensuing half-century.

For many, the 1960s were the time they bought their first car or took their first foreign holiday and the overwhelming majority of them did not do so because their station had closed or because they could not get to Bude by train. They chose to. When I told a student of mine from Cirencester, who had been born in the late 1970s, that Ernest Marples had been burnt in effigy outside her station when it closed in 1964, her response was one of amazement: 'But it's only five minutes to Kemble [the town's railhead] in the car.' Even Beeching's harshest critics accept that many of the lines closed before 1966 had to go; any assumption that full-scale cost–benefit analysis would have prevented many of the more controversial closures needs to be treated with caution, given the results of those studies which were carried out, as we shall see in Chapter 8. As for reopenings, with fifty years' hindsight is it really surprising that the contraction of the rail network went further than we think it should have done, when the construction of it so obviously did? It is one thing to believe Beeching got things wrong or that this or that line should still be open, but the passion with which many people continue to revile Beeching cannot simply be explained by the difference between what the railway was and what it is; we need to look also at what it means.

In his survey of the place of the railway in English culture, Ian Carter shows how having once been the 'epitome of modernity', the 'railways' historic role as modernity's spear tip is [now] blunted to the point of fatuity' and that the association of the railway with main line speed has given way to the prominence of the rural branch line 'at home in the English landscape' as a cultural reference point, a process he traces back to Arthur Quiller-Couch's *Cuckoo Valley Railway* of 1893, which 'invented a new way of writing about railways in Britain ... *nostalgic memory*, a conservative and yearning regret for lost days'.[14] Could anything illustrate the place of the railways in the landscape more clearly than the name ascribed to the line that was the subject of the most controversial closure of the 1950s and the first standard gauge passenger preservation project, the Bluebell Railway in Sussex? Carter stresses the place of the quaint and whimsical in the nostalgic memory he describes; it was precisely the loss of the quaint and the whimsical, of Trouble House Halt and Midsomer Norton, which lay at the heart of Flanders and Swann's lament.

When David St John Thomas wrote in his survey of *The Country Railway* that such a line 'was always part of the district it served' he was straddling the ground between history and nostalgia, as does Henshaw's reference to rural lines 'ingrained into the communities they served; integral and indispensable threads binding the rich tapestry of rural life'.[15] This idea resounds, too, in a letter pleading the case for Bridlington station sent to the Minister of Transport in 1967. Having complained bitterly of the effects of bus sickness, the correspondent emphasised that the local station was not simply a functional place but a 'beloved ... [and] precious landmark' where in two world wars 'countless servicemen said "farewell" forever':

> Its lights at night mean a good deal to us who live nearby. We are never lonely when we look out at the back of our cottages and see those lights. Please, please do not have them taken from us.[16]

The branch line railway ran through the heart of the place where the English, or many of them at least, imagine they live; an essentially rural nation onto which urban modernity has been rudely imposed.[†] The image of the steam-operated branch line as an integral part of this imagined land is reinforced by the almost obligatory appearance of a pristine steam train at a beautifully kept rural station in just about any recent film set in England between 1850 and 1960. The essentially rural nature of imagined England encourages the English to preserve the countryside – a desire which at the time of the railways' construction was often confined to those who owned it, but which is now almost universal. Consequently, nostalgia for the rural branch line railway is fuelled by the association between its demise and increasing traffic, road building and other unsightly modern developments.

The most perfect evocation of the place of the railway in the countryside is Edward Thomas's poem 'Adlestrop', in which an express is stopped at a wayside station on a hot summer's day and nothing happens. Contemplating the song of a blackbird the poet seems transported to a higher plain, aware of 'all the birds of Oxfordshire and Gloucestershire'. Noticing the station on Dr Beeching's list of closures in 1963, a *Times* correspondent reminisced about his visits to it before linking Beeching's work to environmental destruction: 'the economy axe is breaking the spell for hundreds of Adlestrops throughout Britain as we move into the era of the coach crawl and (if Miss Rachel Carson's

---

†   I have not ignored Scottish and Welsh closures in this book in as much as they relate to the overall development of policy, but it is no coincidence that only English cases are discussed in more detail. The significance of railways as part of an imagined rural England cannot be simply superimposed on to the way in which the Scots and the Welsh imagine their countries; perhaps the general lack of preserved steam railways in Scotland and the distinctive nature of the preservation movement in Wales as 'the Great Little Trains of Wales' reflect a different role for the railway in Scottish and Welsh imaginations. In any case, for both Scottish and Welsh nationalists, railway closures could be depicted as indicative of the negative effects of living in a 'united' kingdom, and their significance as part of the development of nationalism and its narrative seems to me to be a question worthy of its own study.

warning is not heeded) the silent spring' (Rachel Carson's 1962 book *Silent Spring* was a global catalyst for the environmental movement).[17] Surveying the contrast between Thomas's evocation of the English countryside and the modern site of the closed station, past which 'sleek bullet-nosed machines thunder', the poet Richard Medrington asks 'when was it that we came to equate success with speed and mobility' and to devalue the experience of being 'fully present'?[18] In a similar vein, the writer and architectural critic Jonathan Glancey, when asked what was lost when the railways closed, answered 'everything that matters: the poetry of the English landscape'.[19]

Where Beeching closed rural railways, Sir John Betjeman – whose writing on railways Glancey has edited – eulogised them in poems such as 'Dilton Marsh Halt' and complained of the 'Inexpensive Progress' that was creating a world 'where motor car is master' (a line which the Council for the Protection of Rural England took as the title of its 1992 pamphlet on transport policy). As Vice-President of the Railway Development Association, Betjeman wrote to the Minister complaining of the 'diesel-scented traffic jams' which would be created by railway closures in Cornwall.[20] His celebration of the Great Central Main Line is not concerned with its fine engineering but the farms, woods and village churches past which it runs; when the train passes a modern housing estate the poet makes a pointed reference to the regimented 'cars of parked executives'. The whimsically inappropriate name of Rugby Central station, the whereabouts of which 'does only Rugby know', is an asset as far as Betjeman is concerned.[21] As the champion of branch line closures, therefore, Beeching is not simply the man who vandalised the railways or deprived communities of a valuable service, but the man who drove the dagger of soulless modernity into the heart of Englishness. He is the anti-Betjeman.

This impression is bolstered by the removal of steam locomotives from Britain's railways by 1968, a process Beeching did not start but did accelerate. Steam often returned to branch lines for final services and, for all the suggestions of cost-saving methods involving alternative traction put forward by opponents of closure, the steam locomotive was fundamental to the romantic appeal of a branch line and vital in attracting visitors to those reopened by the preservationists. In 'Dilton Marsh Halt' Betjeman looks forward to the day when, the world's supply of petrol having run out, 'the horrible roads are finally done for ... [and] steam trains will return.'[22] When the penultimate scheduled steam service on BR pulled into Blackpool South on 3 August 1968, small boys flocked to the cab to get the autographs of the driver and the fireman. Preserved railways and the continuing popularity of Thomas the Tank Engine, including personal appearances on preserved lines, have transmitted nostalgia for steam to a generation who never experienced it first-hand.

In *The Titfield Thunderbolt* – an Ealing comedy released shortly before the Isle of Wight provided the first major closure controversy in 1953 – the sort of archetypal English community that had put paid to Nazi invaders eleven years earlier in *Went the Day Well?* thwarted the attempts of the Ministry and the BTC to close their local line and ran it themselves. The squire and the vicar played leading roles and overcame the spiv-like bus operators with the help of a train-driving bishop. Screenwriter T. E. B. 'Tibby' Clarke was inspired to write the script by a visit to the Talyllyn Railway, the first to be preserved (although, unlike Titfield it was not saved from the Ministry and the

Commission, having escaped nationalisation, possibly because the Ministry did not realise it was still operating). Although the film was not a huge hit on its release, the best part of half a century later critic Leslie Halliwell considered it 'among the best' of the Ealing comedies, in particular because of its 'immaculate colour production, showing the England that is no more'.[23] The film opens with an express crossing Midford Viaduct on the Somerset and Dorset line and then pans to the 'Titfield' branch train running beneath (on the Camerton branch of the Great Western which had closed not long before). A series of shots of the train making its way through the countryside establishes it as almost a natural feature, while we see the village come to life as it approaches (albeit that coming to life produces only a handful of passengers). The most revealing line in the film is the heartfelt appeal preached to Ministry of Transport officials by Squire Chesterford (whose grandfather had, in true patrician style, 'built the line for Titfield'):

Don't you realise you're condemning our village to death? Open it up to buses and lorries and what's it going to be like in five years' time? Our lanes will be concrete roads, our houses will have numbers instead of names. There'll be traffic lights and zebra crossings.[24]

The squire (who owned a car) was wrong, the growth of road traffic was happening irrespective of railway closures, but his appeal illustrates the strength of the branch lines' perception as the sinews of imagined England.

'It's rather a relief to be drawn by steam through this uneventful countryside and just to hear the noises we heard as children… How nice to see it without a foreground of villas and petrol stations,' Betjeman said in a televised pilgrimage along the Somerset and Dorset's branch to Highbridge, broadcast in the month of the *Beeching Report's* publication; but the poet knew his defence of 'comfortable travel' had to acknowledge the spirit of the times: 'I am not just being nostalgic and sentimental and impractical about railways. Railways are bound to be used again; they are not a thing of the past.'[25] It was a point he must have felt needed to be made because by 1963 the railways had come to symbolise two discernible strands in political debate and cultural commentary: decline and modernisation. This period saw the emergence of a sense that Britain was in decline which, Jim Tomlinson argues, was widely propagated and instilled assumptions in the public mind 'with sustained and significant consequences for public debate about Britain's situation, which in turn had a major impact on the tenor of British politics'.[26] These concerns centred on the belief that the British economy was growing less quickly than that of its European neighbours and was bolstered by Britain's apparent decline as a world military and political power. This mood was expressed in such works as Michael Shanks's *The Stagnant Society* and came to focus on what Anthony Crosland called 'a dogged resistance to change [that] now blankets every segment of our national life' and Anthony Samson referred to as 'a loss of dynamic and purpose'. Such complaints went hand in hand with an attack on the amateurish nature of British government and management. A variety of answers was offered to the much-debated question 'What's wrong with Britain?', but by the general election of 1964 modernisation had emerged as a popular solution and both major parties sought to present themselves as modernisers.[27] The use of modernisation as a panacea for decline reflects the wider national fascination with modernity that stretched from politics to the young men and women who would lead British popular culture in the coming decade, a phenomenon which Christopher Booker castigated as a kind of mass psychosis in his 1969 book *The Neophiliacs*. The contrast between the apparently inefficient railways in the last days of steam and the motor car's encapsulation of the spirit of individual freedom, speed and excitement that so concerned Booker, identified the railways with 'Old England' and all its problems.[28] The rising standard of living, expressed through increased car ownership, and the growth of new industries more suited to road transport than rail were important factors in the railways' decline; but this did not prevent that decline from being presented as indicative of a national problem.

Politically, the response to this mood in the early 1960s included the attempt to join the Common Market, the creation of the National Economic Development Council, the development of an incomes policy, a renewed emphasis on planning and the control of public expenditure and a new expectation from 1961 that the nationalised industries should behave more like nationally owned businesses and less like public services. These moves reflected not only the concerns of politicians and voters but of Treasury officials attempting to come to terms with modern conditions. The Treasury's ultimate responsibility for the investment programmes of nationalised industries fostered a belief that it needed to develop a picture of future needs against which to judge those programmes. Efforts to apply this principle to transport spending were central to the policy behind the *Beeching Report*. In turn, the report was one of a series of measures the Conservatives hoped would convince the electorate that they were the standard-bearers of modernisation, and Labour's opposition to closures sat uncomfortably with Harold Wilson's attempts to present himself as the moderniser *par excellence*.

This book argues that the *Beeching Report* was the outcome of a genuine modernisation of Whitehall's management of the economy. Its form and presentation were a reflection of what was imagined to be wrong with Britain; its limitations reflected the difficulties of modernising Britain. It occupied the space in which the nation's enthusiasm for modernisation collided with its, or at least England's, self-image and was the point at which a superficially attractive term had to be transformed into a clearly less attractive reality. This last point was emphasised by the contrast between its emphasis on contraction and the more positive tone of the BTC's 1955 *Modernisation Plan*. If Beeching attacked a myth of England, his report also punctured the 1955 dream of what modernisation might mean. The *Beeching Report* represented a recognition that England was not a nation of villages bound together by field and rail but an economy threatened by decline and, in attempting to avoid that decline, the nation could not afford dreams of rural idylls or chromium bullet trains, but would have to take unpleasant decisions. It was 'the first full-dress statement' of what modernisation might mean for industries that appeared to be obsolete; and as enthusiasm for modernity waned, Beeching, like the motorway and the high-rise estate, became a symbol of its destructive nature.[29]

The starting point for many of Beeching's critics is their dissatisfaction with the transport system. Whether or not that dissatisfaction is coloured by a sense that something more fundamental than a transport service was lost when railways closed, they would like a larger and better rail network than we have. Convinced that this is what should have happened, they then seek an explanation for the past's failure to bequeath it. Beeching and Marples are obvious targets because they were the public face of an apparently proactive period of transport policy-making – a time when government actually seemed to be shaping the transport network rather than breathlessly attempting to keep pace with its development. Add in the secrecy and dodgy figures and it is all too easy to lay blame at the feet of a cabal of anti-rail officials or a conspiracy of pro-road interests. This book is not a defence of the outcomes of the Beeching era, but it is something of a defence of those responsible for it. By looking at the years that preceded the *Beeching Report* and trying to appreciate the perspective of those charged with solving 'the railway problem', it attempts to explain how government and the railways arrived at a point where the policies of the early 1960s seemed right and the manner of their implementation justified. It goes on to look at why the conclusions of Beeching's studies were not implemented and how the seeds were sown of the popular memory of Beeching today. The chapters that follow take a chronological approach to the development of government policy around the contraction of the railway system but are generally structured around individual cases, because it is impossible to make sense of either as history without the other. The closure of railways throws into sharp relief the relationship between the individual human beings charged with making and implementing government policy and those challenging and opposing it. I hope the reader will emerge with some sympathy for both.

Chapter 2

Colonel Stephens's lost causes: the railway problem 1914–51

The great railway age effectively ended in 1914, but the railways were still the most important form of transport in Britain. It is the inter-war period of the 'big four' companies, the Southern, the London Midland and Scottish (LMS), the London and North Eastern (LNER) and the Great Western (GWR), the age of the *Flying Scotsman* and Auden's 'Night Mail' that encapsulates the golden age of steam in popular memory today. It was to this period that some, John Major among them, looked when considering the merits of a privatised railway in the early 1990s. If all the romance of the inter-war railway could be distilled into a single day, 3 July 1938 would do well. It being a Sunday, the 'silence and peace which once characterised so many branch termini' would have been even more pronounced than usual.[30] Sundays were the best time for irregular workings and, on the LNER main line just north of Grantham, a small group of railwaymen prepared to take the next step in their struggle of engineering and public-relations expertise with the rival LMS. Almost three years earlier, the LNER had launched a new *Silver Jubilee* high-speed service between London and Newcastle using streamlined locomotives and coaches. Their modern look caught the imagination of the public and the LMS felt obliged to respond, even though its west coast main line was less suited to high speeds. In 1937 a train hauled by the LMS *Coronation* broke the steam speed record at 114mph before careering to a halt in Crewe station where the broken plates in the dining car could be cleared up. The following year, under the cloak of 'brake trials', one of the LNER's newest express locomotives, *Mallard*, was sent out to win back the title. The locomotive's aerodynamic casing was not just for show, it produced the extra speed required to approach the record as it accelerated southwards from Grantham. Germany had already achieved speeds of over 120mph with diesel and electric traction but, while Sir Nigel Gresley, *Mallard*'s designer, was influenced by streamlined German trains, Britain had rejected proposals for a twenty-year programme of main-line electrification in 1931 and *Mallard* was the best steam could offer. Its limit was reached that Sunday in July 1938, shortly after roaring down the long, straight descent of Stoke Bank and through the quiet wayside station of Little Bytham at 120mph, when driver Joseph Duddington smelled violets, a scent given off by a safety device installed to warn him that the big end was overheating. Nevertheless, he decided to push on and, during a three-mile run at over 120mph, reached 126mph for a few hundred yards. The Mallard's fame was ensured and the LNER regained its crown. In presenting this brief, unsustainable glimpse of main-line speed as their public face, the LNER were playing to the railways' strengths, a point Dr Beeching would reiterate in his report some twenty-five years later. Two-and-a-quarter hours were cut from the London to Edinburgh journey between the wars; the high-speed trains of the 1930s were real technical achievements, operated by skilled men and providing an excellent service; however, they were the proud face of an empire in decline.

Much of the rail network in 1938 consisted of lines that had completely failed to fulfil the hopes of those who financed them. The Clayton West branch, which survived until 1983 due to the difficulty of operating a replacement bus service, earned annual receipts of £1,811 in 1881, against expenses of £2,500. The bitter competition between the South Eastern and London, Chatham and Dover companies ruined both shareholders and services alike. When the Manchester, Sheffield and Lincolnshire company, whose initials were jokingly said to stand for 'Money Sunk and Lost', built an extension to London and renamed itself the Great Central, the wags justifiably re-dubbed it 'Gone Completely'. The 'railway king', George Hudson, central figure in the 'railway mania' investment boom of the 1840s, built a railway empire that exceeded a thousand miles and shaped the network permanently on imaginary profits and false promises that ruined many an investor as well as himself.

Railways had never been guaranteed financial successes, but in the inter-war years no one was making much money from them. The assumption that earnings would return to pre-war levels, on which the Southern, LNER, LMS and GWR had been created from a host of smaller companies in 1921, proved to be wrong and, although the industry was by no means bankrupt, earnings on ordinary stocks ranged from little to nothing. The LNER paid nothing on its deferred stock after 1925 and even preferential stockholders could not always count on a return. In 1938, ordinary shareholders of three of the big four received no dividend while those of the fourth got half of 1 per cent. These results prevented the companies raising investment capital on the stock market, resulting in a net disinvestment of £125 million between 1920 and 1938. What investment did take place (including the Southern Railway's major programme of electrification) had been largely dependent on government incentives, such as grants to cover interest payments, since 1929.

While the causes of the industry's financial performance between the wars should not be oversimplified (and a major factor was a decline in heavy-freight traffic, especially coal, which was caused by general economic conditions), both the railway network and the legal framework in which it operated reflected the virtual monopoly of inland transport the railways had enjoyed prior to 1914. Not only the number of lines, but the number of competing separate networks, the short distances between stations and the complex framework of regulations protecting passengers and businesses from ruthless exploitation by the railways' monopoly made less and less sense once significant numbers of buses and lorries existed to rival the stopping train and the pick-up goods. When a small consignment of merchandise needed to be taken to or collected from a railway siding by lorry, the greater convenience of simply taking it to its final destination in one road journey was fairly obvious. The First World War kick-started the road haulage industry, as the government ordered large numbers of lorries for use on the Western Front and at the end of the war sold them off at a time when large numbers of men who had been trained to use them needed work and possessed demobilisation grants with which to purchase vehicles. Railway freight charges were governed by regulations that required the approval of charges schemes by the Railway Rates Tribunal and obliged them to carry any traffic offered, to provide a reasonable level of service, to publish charges and not to give undue preference to one customer over another.

One consequence of these regulations was that railway charges bore little relation to the cost of specific services; another was that, as hauliers could pick and choose traffic and quote whatever price they liked to individual customers, it was a simple enough matter for them to undercut the published railway rate for a job by enough to win the traffic. General merchandise traffic fell by more than a quarter between 1924 and 1937, largely as a result of transfers to road.

Just as a certain class of freight traffic was almost inevitably lost to road, so buses proved devastating rivals to rural railway services that were not particularly fast and served stations that were often inconveniently sited (by 1950, branch line operating costs were 25d per passenger mile against 2d for a bus). Peter Butterfield's study of the north-east shows that, between 1921 and 1925, rail receipts for journeys under ten miles declined by a quarter; 1926–7 saw an even greater expansion of bus services and a parallel fall in rail passengers and, at some stations, traffic had fallen to less than 10 per cent of its pre-1914 level by 1929. Service improvements sometimes helped restore it, but not by enough in the long term to justify the additional cost. Attempts to win back traffic by lowering fares produced mixed results. It was not only branch lines that suffered, but wayside stations on the main line like Little Bytham (although it was not until the withdrawal of all local trains between Peterborough and Grantham in 1959 that Little Bytham closed). By 1938, 50 per cent of passenger revenue in the LNER's north-eastern area was being earned by just seven stations while 53 per cent of stations earned just 2 per cent of revenue – an imbalance that persisted into the 1960s and not just in the north-east. The rise of road transport has been estimated to have cost the railways as many as 300 million passenger journeys a year by 1937. While total land passenger journeys increased by nearly half between 1920 and 1938, rail passenger traffic increased only slightly and this was more than offset by a decline in earnings per passenger mile as the railways cut fares to compete.

In the face of this onslaught the big four argued for greater restrictions on road transport and fewer on rail. In 1928, they won the right to expand into passenger road transport and to establish a royal commission, the findings of which led to the imposition of a licensing system on bus operators. In 1932, further lobbying saw the establishment of the Salter Conference on transport, which led to legislation increasing the railway's commercial freedom (a little) and imposing a licensing scheme on road hauliers. Both licensing schemes involved an examination of the need for a service and the existence of alternatives – including rail – before a new licence was granted. But if these Acts restricted road transport, they did not solve the railway companies' difficulties, and in 1938 they launched a new 'Square Deal' campaign for increased commercial freedom. Although the government accepted their case, legislation had not been passed by the outbreak of war. By the late 1930s the railways' general merchandise and short-distance rural passenger traffic had no real commercial future unless some overriding reason could be found for eliminating road competition. This was precisely what happened when Britain went to war: petrol was rationed and the railways were busier than ever before.

The author of *Railways To-day*, published in 1938 as part of a series entitled *Pageant of Progress*, introduced his subject with the observation that 'we are so accustomed in these days to take railways as a matter of course, like the hills, that it may be a surprise to some of us to be reminded that, until a little over

a century ago, railways were not in existence as public carriers'.[31]
The idea that railways might not be as permanent as the hills was
equally surprising. When, a few months before the *Mallard*'s run,
Douglas Macdonald Hastings of the *Evening News* stumbled
across the deserted Singleton station in Sussex, which had lost its
passenger service three years earlier and was now available to let,
he gave his readers an account of his exploration of this strange
phenomenon, 'too incredible for invention'. Singleton station
was quite an extensive affair, as it was the station for Goodwood
racecourse and had been built with both the capacity and style to
accommodate Goodwood's well-heeled clientele (the patterned
glass was still in the windows of the goods shed in 1981, when the
platforms were being used as a scrapyard). There was a carpet of
leaves in the booking hall and the ticket office hatch closed with
a 'ghostly bang'. A generation ahead of the preservation movement, he concluded that he might take the lease:

> I wanted to play with it. I wanted to fill the racks in the book-
> ing office with bright green tickets and stamp them with a date
> stamp… I had even made up my mind to buy a second-hand train
> so that I could drive it and shunt it in and out of my station with
> clouds of steam and blasts on the whistle.[32]

By 1938 some railwaymen appreciated that the 'small wayside
station has in most cases outlived its usefulness',[33] and in Britain,
as elsewhere, the rail network had begun to contract. The LNER
withdrew passenger services from thirty branch lines and
closed two others outright in 1930–34, generally blaming bus
competition for rendering the services unsustainable. In 1929, a
deputation from Allendale, where it was rumoured that the

branch service from Hexham was to be withdrawn, lobbied the railway's passenger manager for its retention. But this level of protest was rare and the company gave it short shrift. Passenger numbers had collapsed in the previous six years and the deputation was told that, unless they picked up, no assurance could be given about the future. The decline continued and the service was withdrawn in 1930. The LNER was not alone in closing lines: in the summer of 1937 Gainsborough pictures took over Cliddesden station on the recently closed Basingstoke and Alton line to film Will Hay's classic railway comedy *Oh, Mr Porter!*, and across the country the 1930s saw the final passenger services leave Devil's Dyke, Loch Tay, Knott End, Ditton Priors and Durham Elvet among many others. Even London Transport drew in the Metropolitan Line's horns from Brill and Verney Junction. Dolphinton could consider itself particularly unfortunate to lose two lines. Some 1,200 miles of route were closed to passengers between 1923 and 1938, three quarters of them in just five years from 1929, without significant protest, so low was their usage. Nevertheless, by 1934 the LNER had concluded that 'there are probably not many cases left where the company will benefit by cancelling services'.[34]

In the early 1930s, the LNER also investigated the possibility of fighting fire with fire by turning two of its branch lines into private roads, along which it would run its own bus and haulage services. The Wivenhoe–Brightlingsea line served a small resort near Colchester, with a healthy summer traffic, not too much bus competition and a route far enough from any road to offer the possibility of charging tolls for cars to use it after conversion. The Mid-Suffolk Light Railway between Haughley and Laxfield was a very rural affair which – being the remnant of a grander,

unfinished, plan – didn't really go anywhere and had suffered
from the depression in agriculture and the rise of the bus. But
any hope the LNER had of road conversion as a business propo-
sition stumbled at the first hurdle. In both cases the junction
stations made little sense as freight railheads; it would be simpler
and cheaper to distribute freight from Colchester or Ipswich. The
cost would also be prohibitive, particularly on the Mid-Suffolk,
where it was estimated at over £200,000. Single-track railways
would need significant widening for use as a road, which meant
converting even minor cuttings and embankments would entail
significant expense. Road maintenance and operating costs did
not seem attractive either, although in the case of Brightlingsea
this partially reflected the LNER's determination to cater for
even the highest peak of summer traffic, requiring nineteen
52-seater buses, whereas only three were needed in winter. It
would be another thirty years before the railway abandoned high
peak summer traffic as fundamentally unprofitable.

By the time the LNER attempted to tackle the inter-war
decline in rural passenger traffic by replacing its rails with a road,
the tiny independent group of railways controlled by Colonel H.
F. Stephens had already tried – and failed – to solve the problem by replacing trains with a bus on rails. A world away from
the glamour of the east and west coast expresses, Holman Fred
Stephens exemplified the eccentricity the English like to believe
is a national characteristic. His clipped moustache and military
title – acquired in the Territorial Royal Engineers – belied his
background as the son of one pre-Raphaelite artist, named
after another. Having qualified as a civil engineer and worked
briefly for the Metropolitan Railway, at the age of twenty-two
he oversaw the construction of the South Eastern Railway's

Hawkhurst branch on the Kent–Sussex border and by the turn of the century had set himself up in a small office in Tonbridge from where he built a Heath Robinson empire of rural railways with such names as the Hundred of Manhood and Selsey Tramway, the Shropshire and Montgomeryshire Light and the Welsh Highland. Typified by their tendency to connect 'places with little demand for transport via country with none at all',[35] using worn out second- or third-hand equipment, the locomotives often saddled with the names of Greek gods, Stephens's lines pioneered the art of running railways on a shoestring. His work was his life; he lived in hotels and clubs and visited at least one of his projects in a lorry to which flanged wheels could be fitted, enabling him to inspect those parts of the line too remote to be reached by road. Early aficionados of railway whimsy were attracted by his practice of retiring broken-down or unwanted stock, most of which had been relatively ancient when purchased, to some corner of an overgrown yard deep in the sleeping countryside, just in case part of it came in handy. The 1896 Light Railways Act eased many of the regulations governing railway construction in return for imposing speed and weight limits (it is this Act which allowed preservationists to begin reopening lines in the 1960s). The Act helped Stephens to engineer most of the lines he controlled (and others) cheaply, avoiding major works in favour of harsher gradients and numerous level crossings. On one of the rare occasions he had to build a tunnel – on the East Kent Light Railway – he built it to take double track in the hope of future expansion, but cut costs by only excavating enough chalk inside the tunnel to allow for one line.

Economy of construction was increasingly matched by economy of operation as Stephens responded to bus competition. The

Light Railways Act had been passed specifically to help the rural economy by opening up areas to railway development that would never support conventionally engineered lines; unfortunately, within a quarter of a century of its passing, the prospects of such lines had taken a significant downturn thanks to the bus and the lorry. Stephens's lines were particularly vulnerable, operating as they did on routes that were often paralleled by roads but with inconveniently sited stations. His best-known innovation was the introduction of petrol railmotors: two lorry chassis fitted with flanged wheels and specially made bus-type bodies coupled back to back, which was cheaper than having a reverse gear.[36] These were first introduced on the Kent and East Sussex Railway (K&ESR), which ran between Headcorn on the Tonbridge–Dover line and Robertsbridge on the Tonbridge–Hastings line, via Tenterden. Passenger numbers had fallen by over a third between 1913 and 1922 when the new machines arrived, cutting costs and providing a more intensive service that led to a temporary stabilisation in traffic. But while the railmotors slowed the descent towards bankruptcy (and inspired similar efforts elsewhere), they could not prevent it. The fact that they were not always able to cope with the gradients, could not pull freight and provided an uncomfortable and sometimes fume-filled journey didn't help, and by 1926 the K&ESR was in the red. When, in 1930, the directors sought advice from Sir Herbert Walker, chairman of the Southern Railway, he told them the position seemed hopeless:

> There is absolutely no chance whatever of being able to effect sufficient economies to enable the line to be run at a profit and even if the line were closed down for passenger traffic and worked

only as a goods line it is very doubtful whether the receipts would more than cover working expenses.[37]

By this time passenger numbers were around two-fifths of the 1913 figure. Results elsewhere on Stephens's lines in 1930 were no better. On the Shropshire and Montgomeryshire, passengers were nearly 80 per cent down on 1923, the Ffestiniog had ceased carrying them altogether except in summer and the East Kent had already abandoned passenger services on its Sandwich extension – a line of which the railway's historian writes 'its future had looked bleak ever since its opening'.[38] In 1931 Stephens succumbed to a series of strokes. The strain of it all may have been a factor, but he never lost the determination and optimism that made him something of a model for the preservationists who have rescued some of his lines and many others. When he fell ill he was still working on plans for a new electric suburban light railway south of Croydon and ballast had been laid on further extensions of the ever-optimistic East Kent.

Stephens's assistant of some forty years, William Austen, took over the business and while some lines closed and others went into receivership, remarkably the K&ESR and the East Kent were open to passengers when the railways were nationalised, as was the Sheppey Light Railway in north Kent, which Stephens had engineered but never owned. All three lines would soon come under the scrutiny of the newly formed Railway Executive of the British Transport Commission (BTC), as the nationalised behemoth pursued the 1947 Transport Act's dream of 'an efficient, adequate, economical and properly integrated' national multi-modal transport system 'to provide most effectively and conveniently for the needs of the public, agriculture, commerce and industry'.

With well over 600,000 employees and assets which included trams, buses, lorries, canals, docks, hotels, depots, offices, a travel agents and a film company, the BTC typified the vast public corporations that ran much of Britain by the end of the 1940s. The nation may have been on the winning side in the Second World War but the spoils of victory were freedom and survival, not prosperity. Facing levels of austerity that make the modern use of the term ring hollow, with petrol and many foodstuffs still rationed in 1949 and cities disfigured by bomb sites, the central control and communal enterprise that had secured Britain's survival were now expected to make good its future. Along with the British Electricity Authority, National Coal Board, the NHS and the planned Iron and Steel Corporation, the BTC was brought into being by the Labour government elected by a landslide in a general election sandwiched between the defeats of Germany and Japan in 1945. These centralised, nationalised near-monopolies joined the General Post Office, the BBC and state-owned airlines in a centrally planned economy. It is hard to imagine anything more different to the network Colonel Stephens had run from Tonbridge, but in its death throes, the remnants of Stephens's empire hinted at the difficulties the new railway order would face in the 1950s.

While public ownership of the railways was the long-held aim of a labour movement that wanted to see railwaymen working for the public good rather than private profit, integration, the other guiding principle of the 1947 Transport Act, had been a feature of debates about transport policy throughout the 1930s. There was more than a little truth in the allegation that the railways' enthusiasm for the concept was based on a desire to handicap road transport. However, the example of the London Passenger Transport Board, established in 1933, demonstrated the manner in which different modes could be made to work together, and the licensing systems imposed on buses and lorries in the 1930s rested on similar principles. The idea that competition leads to a wasteful duplication of facilities may appear outlandish to those readers who have grown up in a country where politicians have, for twenty years, appeared to broadly agree that competition drives efficiency. In a country where rationing still persisted and which had just spent six years of war treating waste as an enemy and imposing central control on all forms of transport (and much else), things looked very different. The plethora of competing railway lines the Victorians had bequeathed to the BTC only lent support to the concept of wasteful competition.

The integration (or coordination) of transport is often treated – in particular by critics of Beeching – as being synonymous with better rail services and restrictions on road use. The most obvious form of integration by 1951, however, was to replace rural railways with bus and road freight services; or rather to close the rail services that had already lost most of their traffic to road. Progress was slow; the Commission was feeling its way and was wary of imposing a particular mode on its customers. Charged with integrating rail, canals, bus services and public long-distance road haulage in the national interest while making enough money to cover its costs 'taking one year with another', the BTC had been given an enormous task. A small body whose members were generally past the peak of their professional abilities, it oversaw a vast undertaking, the structure of which, divided into executives responsible for railways, docks and waterways, hotels, London Transport, road haulage and buses, was hardly conducive to either inter-modal coordination or central direction. In particular the Railway Executive, which accounted for around 80 per cent of the business, was eager to go its own way. Establishing the new organisation was a complicated process and by 1951 the Commission had yet to complete the acquisition of road haulage companies. Just keeping services running in the post-war economic environment was a significant challenge. The railways had endured six years of wartime overuse, bomb damage, under-maintenance and little investment; now fuel, labour and materials for reconstruction were often in short supply. They were still subject to the restrictive regulations the industry had been trying to reform when war intervened, including 'common carrier' obligations that hindered attempts to turn away uneconomic freight traffic and the existence of a Transport Tribunal to which the Commission had to apply if it wanted to increase its charges. The costly delays the latter process imposed on increases in charges were a source of persistent complaints by the Commission.

From the start, the new organisation was burdened with the requirement to pay interest on British Transport Stock that had been used to purchase the nationalised assets. There can be little doubt that the railways were overvalued and the big winners from nationalisation were the compensated shareholders in an industry whose prospects were gloomy (although in the immediate post-war period, with petrol rationed and rail use higher than ever, the full extent of the gloom was less apparent). Whether one uses the Commission's published accounts or the recalculations made by Terry Gourvish, which make some allowance for this overvaluation, the surplus earned on rail operations in the Commission's first three years was not enough to cover their contribution to the BTC's central charges (primarily interest on British Transport Stock) and this was only partially mitigated by the results of the rest of the business. In March 1949 the Railway Executive, under pressure from the Commission, had decreed that each region should set up a committee to investigate branch lines that might be losing money, the whole exercise to be overseen by the Executive's own branch line committee. By the time the Executive was abolished in 1953, 1,420 miles had been cut from the passenger network (253 miles closing completely) and a further 359 miles of freight-only line had closed. From a post-Beeching perspective, this looks like mere tinkering around the edges of the problem. Several of the early cases were not so much closures as recognitions that a service had ceased to be. Early 'schemes' put to the committee included the Old Ynysybwl branch (half a mile of freight line that had seen no traffic since 1944), the Port Talbot railway ('Traffic: Nil'), the Acton Central–Kew Bridge shuttle (suspended since 1940) and a horse tramway in the Forest of Dean.[39]

Unsurprisingly, the remnants of the Stephens empire were soon in the committee's sights. The East Kent owed its existence to the local coalfield; however, this had not developed to the extent Stephens had hoped. Only one successful colliery, Tilmanstone, was served by the line and most of the numerous extensions Stephens proposed never materialised. The railway stabilised – if that is the right word – around a line that headed east from the Canterbury–Dover main line at Shepherdswell, passed Tilmanstone, threw off the Richborough branch at Eastry, and then gradually turned back on itself towards Canterbury. It terminated six miles from the city at Wingham

(Canterbury Road) station, the location of which appears to have been decided on the basis that this was as far as the line had got when the money ran out. In 1948, passenger traffic on the remaining service from Shepherdswell to Wingham was so light that the Railway Executive could name the five 'regular' passengers affected by closure:

> Mr and Mrs Tritton of Upper Eythorne travel once a week or once a fortnight from Eythorne to Eastry... Mr and Mrs Oates of Approach Rd, Shepherds Well ... travel to Elvington less than once a month and use the train when the weather prevents them cycling... Mr Lovell of Wingham visits Shepherds Well about once in three months.[40]

The line closed to passengers in October, before the committee had even begun its work.

In the whole of 1948 the only traffic carried on the East Kent's Richborough branch had been twenty wagons of sugar beet from Richborough Castle siding and ten wagons of manure and beet pulp the other way. Given that this could be dealt with by a siding on the Dover–Ramsgate line about a mile away, its closure in October 1949 was a formality. It must have raised hackles in the area, however, given the response when the branch line committee turned its attention to the freight service on the remaining section beyond Tilmanstone to Wingham. Here, two trains each way six days a week had carried just under 15,000 tons of freight in 1949, less than a ton-and-a-half per train – not much work for twenty-one staff. Closure would save an esti-mated £9,150. It should have been a simple case, but there was already significant concern at the effect of branch line closures on agriculture. In March 1950 the National Association of Corn and Agricultural Merchants met the Railway Executive to set out the 'apprehension and fear' of its members about closures.[41] The NFU had also been active and, together with Eastry Rural District Council and the local chamber of commerce, it went to the local MP to complain. The MP went to the minister, who sent him to the Central Transport Consultative Committee (CTCC) to convey 'the very strong feeling' locally that the line should remain open.[42]

The CTCC had been established under the 1947 Act along with area Transport Users Consultative Committees (TUCCs), consisting of appointees representing 'agriculture, commerce, industry, shipping, labour and local authorities', with an independent chairman and BTC representatives. TUCCs could make recommendations to the Commission and the CTCC; the CTCC made recommendations to the Commission and the minister; the minister could direct the Commission to follow these recommendations. However, as with much of the 1947 Act, little thought appears to have gone into the way consultative committees would function in practice. They had not been set up to deal specifically with objections to closure proposals and procedure was established on the hoof, with the CTCC exerting pressure on the BTC on the basis of what would look proper. As no TUCC had been established for the southeast as yet, the CTCC felt it ought to allow the objectors to make their case at its next meeting and asked them to collate all their points into a single paper. The Southern Region agreed to produce answers to a 41-paragraph memorandum setting out the details of the objectors' case, arrange a visit to the line by the chair of the CTCC, postpone the closure (which had been arranged for 1 December 1950) and send a representative to the CTCC meeting.

A delegation of objectors, Messrs Bones and Stythe of the local National Farmers Union, Baynton, a coal merchant, and Parker, the manager of Hamill's brickworks, took their case to the CTCC in early January 1951. Arriving at the shabby, bomb-damaged offices in the shadow of Euston's doomed, soot-blackened Doric arch, they saw themselves as fighting for their community against an unaccountable and often dishonest state. The railways, they alleged, were acting unreasonably in divorcing the profitable line to the colliery from the loss-making section beyond it, because they had a duty to serve the area as a whole. The original East Kent company's reserves and its share of the funds provided by government in return for wartime use had been swallowed up into the BTC's general funds instead of benefiting the line they belonged to. The BTC, they felt, was in posses-sion of all the facts, but could choose to reveal only those which supported its case. The delegation raised issues that would soon become familiar to the CTCC: the line was overstaffed (staff had been increased on nationalisation, in accordance with union agreements); money had only just been spent on new track (the track was in a dangerous state and the line would otherwise have had to close immediately); the figure of £80,000 on renewals in the next decade seemed too high (the rest of the track had not been renewed since 1912); the service was not properly advertised. Their key question, however, was how industry and agriculture could be expected to meet national needs without the railway? The point was rather undermined by the 'untrammelled grass on the track' and generally unused stations CTCC chairman, Major Edgar Cadbury, director of the confectionery giant, had seen on his visit.[43] The delegation agreed that, generally, they found road transport much more efficient, but in future they might need to go back to rail. The CTCC approved closure, aware that it was setting a standard for future cases. All that Bones and his companions took home was a request from the CTCC to the Commission that it keep the line open until March, so that the last of the year's sugar beet could be sent by train and to allow farmers to stock up on manure. Months later, the farmers' union was still complaining about the increased cost of transport in the area. The case did, however, generate some internal questioning at the Commission. Was it right, some asked, to include as a saving interest on the £80,000 of expenditure required to bring the line up to scratch if it remained open? It was an issue that would dog the BTC for years to come.

At the same time as it had approved proposals to close the East Kent, the branch line committee had also approved closure of the former Sheppey Light Railway. This meandered along the largely unpopulated north of the Isle of Sheppey on the Thames estuary in the hope that its terminus, Leysdown on Sea, would become a major holiday destination rather than the 'straggling resort of bungalows and bus bodies' that it had turned into by the outbreak of war.[44] In its final summers, the route offered an Arcadian journey: lineside trees and shrubs 'all bowed in the wind created by our passing and in several places bloom-laden blackberry bushes ... brush[ed] the train'.[45] None of its intermediate stations were conveniently sited – two of them were nowhere near anywhere – and a better bus service was available on the parallel road. The average passenger-train load was less than five and each passenger journey was subsidised to the tune of about a pound. Nevertheless, the closure proposal produced demands for a public inquiry, threats of legal action, letters to the minister, a suggestion from a parish council chairman that he take it over and make it pay and accusations that branch lines lost money because fares were too high. Surveying the furore, the BTC's public relations department warned 'these closures of branch line services are going to give us plenty of trouble'.[46]

Even at the start of the 1950s, the extent of losses being made on branch and other stopping-train services was becoming clear to some at the BTC, but this realisation took time to displace the long-standing railway practice of maximising traffic in order to maximise gross revenue. When a derailment on the K&ESR line in March 1949 raised the question of whether track renewals had been deferred pending its closure, the Southern Region insisted that far from planning to close it, the line

> has considerable agricultural traffic ... passenger traffic has suffered because of the lack of enterprise of the former light railway company and [the region is] bringing into operation a new and improved service... They say that there is more potential traffic capable of being fostered on this line, than many other secondary lines in the Southern Region.[47]

They were not saying this for long. By mid-1951, as the BTC exerted pressure to find more savings from closures, the region was coming to the conclusion that the line should close to passengers. However, the preparation of closure cases was already proving an administrative burden and the Southern Region's commercial superintendent responded to demands for more closures with the complaint that no machinery exists within the commercial department for the ascertaining of revenue on a branch or at an individual station and this results in all such information having to be obtained from the accountant, in whose department all cases fall to be assessed by one group of staff who have their ordinary work to do... A somewhat similar position exists on the expenditure side.[48]

It took the region until early 1954 to implement closure of the K&ESR, nearly a quarter of a century after Sir Herbert Walker had found its situation hopeless (the line's southern section remained open to freight until June 1961, when the Colonel's first commission, the Hawkhurst branch, also closed).

The 1896 Light Railways Act represents the high-water mark of railway development in Britain: a time when, in the absence of an alternative, it seemed necessary to stimulate the extension of railways into the most rural parts of Britain, so that they too could enjoy the prosperity brought by modern transport. It is ironic that Stephens, who began his career as a pioneer extending the boundaries of the modern world, is now remembered as a staunch defender of the quaint and outdated, holding back the flood of modernity with his dogged refusal to surrender to the lorry and the bus. What the story of his lines shows is that, even in cases where services had been losing money for a decade or more before the war, their users could be relied upon to fight for their retention, and that the work involved in closing individual lines was stretching the resources of the BTC and the machinery of the consultative committees. When the little party of objectors took the fight for Eastry to Euston, they blazed a trail that would be regularly followed in the 1950s; yet their expedition can seem almost comical when viewed across six decades that have seen Hawick, Padstow and so many others lose similar battles. An obvious modern parallel with the closure of rural railway lines is the closure of rural post offices; a more accurate one, in terms of understanding the reaction that these early closures produced, may be to imagine that the Royal Mail has refused to deliver letters to a swathe of rural east Kent because it cannot do so profitably. The authorities point to the fact that so many local residents prefer electronic communication to writing a letter that it collects from near-empty pillar boxes and sends postmen out with empty sacks. Villagers are offered PO box addresses in Canterbury or Sandwich instead, to which they must also travel to post a letter. It is this kind of universal service, always available when desperately needed, however little one uses it the rest of the time, that was being taken away. It was a service that businesses had grown used to, run by an organisation that was supposed to take the rough with the smooth. Passenger closures could be seen in the same light, especially by a generation that had grown up accustomed to branch lines with much lower passenger numbers than were common before the arrival of buses.

As the first case to be considered in such detail by the CTCC, the East Kent closure occurred at the start of an ad hoc development of procedure which became increasingly burdensome for the railways without ever satisfying critics. Much of this dissatisfaction stemmed from the disparity between what objectors wanted from committees and what they had been set up to do. The committees existed to provide a forum for the Commission to discuss issues with transport users and find a consensus (for example, in its first year the CTCC took a great interest in the adequacy or otherwise of services to Hastings). However, objectors expected them to act as impartial tribunals, sitting in judgement on the Commission's closure proposals, and were understandably dissatisfied to find one of the parties in the case – the BTC – had a seat on the bench, while passengers were only indirectly represented via local government. The railway official commenting on the Sheppey case probably had no idea how right he would be proved, but by 1950 it was already becoming clear that almost any contraction in the rail network would be controversial. Within a few years closures would dominate the work of the committees almost to the exclusion of everything else and their original conception became increasingly impossible to sustain. The consistent and growing friction between committees and objectors from 1950 provides the context for the way in which Beeching and Marples went about closing railways, and the same controversies they provoked are evident in these long-forgotten minor cases.

The Sheppey Light Railway has vanished almost without trace, so insubstantial was its construction, and the parts of the East Kent and K&ESR that closed before 1960 are equally hard to find, but these two railways have demonstrated the sort of pig-headed refusal to accept defeat that allowed them to survive until nationalisation. A preservation society was quickly formed to save the K&ESR in 1961 and after a somewhat fractious history involving a battle over the legality of the minister's refusal to grant a light railway order, trains ran south from Tenterden again in 1974, although it was another twenty-six years before they reached Bodiam. Initial plans to reopen the final section on to Robertsbridge had to be sacrificed to official objections over the delays to cars at level crossings; however, now that steam railways are a recognised part of the tourist industry, there is hope that a way may be found to accommodate the line and a separate charity is slowly rebuilding this section. If the project succeeds, according to the K&ESR website, it will run to Robertsbridge again 'if there is an economically viable case for doing so' – what an incongruous phrase![49]

Tilmanstone's coal traffic kept the last short section of the East Kent open until 1986. For several years afterwards, the track rusted gently, but in 1993 it too reopened as a preserved railway. The newcomer was a much less slick operation than the Bluebell or the K&ESR have become, but still very obviously a labour of love: the yard at Shepherdswell once again a museum disguised as a scrapyard. In its very early days, a scruffy diesel unit, still in the weather-worn livery of Strathclyde Passenger Transport Executive, would crawl along from Shepherdswell through the half-dug tunnel and stop in a field in the middle of nowhere, wait a few minutes and go back – it felt a very authentic Stephens experience. Transport acts come and go, but the determination of the enthusiast to win lost causes endures.

Chapter 3

A terrible tangle: the Isle of Wight and the end of integration

In the first three years of its existence, the British Transport Commission's operating surpluses were not sufficient to meet its central charges and the resulting accumulated deficit grew to nearly £40 million.[†] In September 1951, the Labour government's Minister of Transport, Alfred Barnes, submitted a paper on the Commission's long-term prospects to the Cabinet which made two recommendations: a speedier process of raising charges to cover any increase in costs and the establishment of a royal commission to examine what role the railways should have in a 'fully integrated system'. 'Until this fundamental issue is cleared,' Barnes's paper warned, 'it is hardly possible for the country to have a coherent transport policy ... and capital investment in transport will be devoid of firm guiding principles.'[50] The paper made three things clear: for Barnes and his officials, 'a fully integrated system' meant a more rapid and extensive closing of branch lines than had taken place so far; aside from the benefits of a more responsive charging structure, it suggested that such a programme would be

---

†   The reader may find it helpful to bear in mind that £1 in 1950 would be worth nearly £28 today. Equivalent figures are (to the nearest 50p): 1955 = £21.50; 1960 = £18; 1965 = £16; and 1970 = £13.

the most likely source of the economies required to balance the books; and it recognised that the BTC's employees, its executives and its customers would resist these proposals. The regions were already coming under pressure from the Commission to accelerate closures and, even as the paper was printed for the Cabinet, opposition to precisely the approach to integration Barnes envisaged was being organised on the Isle of Wight. The year 1951 would have been a good time for a royal commission on transport. It might have brought the question of what kind of railway the nation was prepared to pay for to the forefront of the public mind before the BTC's financial position became irretrievable or plans for modernisation were laid – and before the Isle of Wight experience infused the whole debate with an air of suspicion. It was not to be. When Barnes turned up at the next Cabinet meeting, only one item was on the agenda: the dissolution of Parliament and the forthcoming general election. Labour lost power for thirteen years and Winston Churchill returned to Downing Street at the head of a new Conservative administration.

The Conservatives had accepted nationalisation of the railways, as with most of the post-war Labour government's nationalisation programme, as a *fait accompli* but nationalisation of the iron and steel, sugar and road haulage industries represented the limit of that acceptance. Under the 1947 Transport Act private hauliers were either bought out by the BTC or restricted to operating within 25 miles of their base.[†] The haulage industry was typified by the small operator who had built

---

[†]   Under the licensing system introduced in the 1930s, lorries were either licensed for public traffic (A and B licences) or owned by a trader who only used them to carry their own goods (C licences, which made up 80 per cent of the total). The 25-mile limit, introduced from 1 February 1950, only applied to privately owned A and B licensed vehicles; proposals to limit the range of C licence holders had been dropped after intense opposition.

his own business from nothing. He did not take kindly to the state appropriating it, compensation or not. The Road Haulage Association (RHA) waged an intense campaign against nationalisation, offering opposition MPs much practical help in the debates. Both the campaign and the links the RHA forged with the Conservatives continued after the Act was passed, through the election campaigns of 1950 and 1951 and into the life of the new government. Within a week of the 1951 election, the RHA was successfully lobbying to halt the BTC's acquisition of its members' vehicles. It was this relationship that lay behind a commitment in the Conservative manifesto to reverse the 1947 Transport Act by giving hauliers whose firms had been nationalised an opportunity to return to the business. This aim required a time machine rather than an Act of Parliament and if one were to seek out a case study of how a new government's efforts to change policy can go wrong, the genesis of the Conservatives' 1953 Transport Act would do very nicely. Among its several failings, the Act effectively removed the Commission's coordinating imperative just as its Isle of Wight test case reached fruition, but this drawback was rather obscured at the time because, as we shall see, the experiment did more to demonstrate the difficulties of integration than its possibilities.

It is a testament to Victorian optimism that the Isle of Wight, an area of less than 150 square miles, managed to acquire 55½ miles of railway involving eight companies by 1923 when they were all brought into the Southern Railway, despite its attempts to avoid acquiring the long-bankrupt Freshwater, Yarmouth and Newport Railway. The Isle of Wight Central, which emerged from four of the original companies, had occasionally paid a dividend, while the Isle of Wight Railway, which owned the prime route south from Ryde along the island's east coast to Ventnor, generally offered its ordinary stock holders a regular, but small, return. The key to the island's railway system was Ryde pier. The two mainland companies that served Portsmouth, the London Brighton and South Coast and the London and South Western, opened the short line from the pier head to connect with the island system at Ryde St Johns Road in 1880; they didn't operate it, but they profited handsomely from the traffic it brought to their Portsmouth trains and the ferries they owned. Ryde quickly became the point at which the overwhelming majority of visitors to the island arrived. Tourism was central to the island's economy and on summer peak Saturdays at the end of the 1940s the railway carried 25,000 passengers a day from Ryde. The pier could not carry buses or more than a very few light cars and the railway was only able to cope by diverting those who were not travelling beyond the town onto a diesel-operated pier tramway and by running four trains an hour each way on the, mostly single-track, line to Ventnor, an operational feat much admired by those with an interest in railways.

Apart from the Ryde–Ventnor line, the island network consisted of a second line from Ryde, heading west to Newport and Cowes; a branch from Newport to the more remote western side of the island at Freshwater; and a third line from Newport heading south and then east to Sandown on the Ryde–Ventnor line. Finally there were two tiny branches: from Brading on the east coast route to Bembridge and from Merstone on the Newport–Sandown line to Ventnor West. In theory it was possible to travel between Cowes and Ventnor by three different routes. In a home service broadcast shortly before it closed, John Betjeman described the approach to Ventnor West in almost ecstatic terms, revelling in the 'alder-bordered meadows' and 'chalky downs ... high and golden brown with grass' and, on emerging from a tunnel 'between the ash-tree branches, an unexpected silver shiny sea'.[51] The island's railways were part of many people's memory of childhood holidays. The Southern had invested in the system and traffic had nearly doubled by the end of the 1940s to 3 million journeys a year. But this was set against 17 million bus journeys and, more importantly, disguised a huge disparity between peak summer traffic and the rest of the year when overcrowded buses passed almost empty trains. Betjeman was virtually alone on the train to Ventnor West.

While the railway was a quaint delight for many visitors, it was considered vital by the Isle of Wight County Council and the island's Chamber of Commerce, not because islanders used it, but because it was fundamental to the holiday trade upon which the island economy depended. It is ironic then that it should have been the Chamber of Commerce that planted the idea in the minds of the BTC that the island would be the perfect test-ing ground for transport integration. The Chamber wrote to the Railway Executive in November 1949 complaining of overcrowd-ing on buses and at bus stops on the island, while the trains were lightly loaded except on summer Saturdays. It suggested reduc-ing train fares to the same level as bus fares and introducing a common ticketing system. Shortly afterwards the BTC told the Railway, Road Passenger and Road Haulage executives to look at how the passenger and freight operations on the island might be integrated. An initial study, reporting in April 1950, looked at all aspects of integration – how joint headquarters and maintenance facilities might work, for example – but, as general merchandise was already dealt with entirely by road, there was little to be done on the freight side. On the passenger side, raising bus fares to benefit rail was ruled out as something the licensing authority, to which such increases had to be submitted, would not approve of. The key finding was that Southern Vectis, the BTC-owned island bus company, believed it could carry all rail passengers except the peak summer traffic on the Ryde–Ventnor line. This prompted an immediate call from the Commission for another report, followed by nearly a year of wrangling between the executive and the region, the main outcome of which was that the Ventnor West branch, which had been about to close, was reprieved while the branch line committee went back to square one to look at the entire island. In February 1951 the region concluded that all the island lines were losing money; expenses exceeded receipts by £121,845 a year in total, to which could be added £92,931 under the heading 'interest'.[52] Nevertheless, Ryde–Ventnor had to be retained for holiday traffic and the region felt Ryde–Cowes might as well be too, as most of it would be required for freight to Cowes's Medina Wharf, and that the lines from Newport to Sandown and Freshwater, on the face of it both obvious candidates for closure, should be retained pending an investigation of a common fares and ticketing system for rail and bus (a suggestion Southern Vectis appears to have opposed). This left only the Ventnor West and Bembridge branches to close, although part of the latter would be needed for engineers' supplies. The Railway Executive, which had already raised the possibility of reducing the entire operation to a summer-only service on the Ryde–Ventnor line, took a much less favourable view and asked for another report on the practicalities of closing everything except Ryde–Ventnor. A year later it was still waiting.

The investigation had proved immense and provoked

complaints that the 3,000 hours of work it had generated in the accountant's office by January 1951 diverted the region's already meagre resources from other more straightforward cases. Nevertheless, the region was dragging its heels. Like the Southern Railway before it, the region regarded the Isle of Wight lines as the extremities of the Portsmouth main line. It suspected that the ends of many main lines would appear unprofitable if their finances were considered in isolation from the rest of the network, but that they encouraged enough traffic on the rest of the line to justify their existence. This view needs to be seen in the context of the £715,510 earned by traffic to and from island stations on the mainland network as a whole.[†] The region's attitude was also influenced by concerns about the effect on the island's economy and the difficulty in redeploying the island's railwaymen. This was not usually a problem in the early 1950s, indeed railway managers frequently complained of labour shortages, but being an island, the Isle of Wight was a special case. The region also correctly anticipated that local opposition would be formidable and damaging to the BTC's reputation, a view strengthened by the surprising level of interest in the East Kent closure. In the summer of 1951, rumours of the BTC's plans began circulating the island. The BTC met the council and Chamber of Commerce to discuss them in August and, in November, received a memorandum arguing against closure of all but the Ventnor West line and making numerous suggestions as to how the island railways' deficit could be reduced. These were taken seriously and factored into the investigation, prolonging it, but the region concluded they would make little difference.

---

†   Such earnings are known as contributory revenue, a term explained later in this chapter.

In June 1952, after further pressure from the executive, the region finally confirmed what the bus company had said in the first place, that all rail traffic other than between Ryde and Ventnor could be accommodated by road without any great difficulty. Closure of the Ventnor West line was already underway and took place in September 1952. Chief Regional Officer C. P. Hopkins recommended a staged withdrawal of the Freshwater, Bembridge and Sandown–Newport services by September 1953, but wanted the Cowes line reviewed in three years and retained until at least 1958. He hoped this would mollify opposition, with which he clearly had some sympathy:

> We have done so much in the past to develop the Isle of Wight and no doubt in the process incurred losses in certain directions to be more than recouped in others, that a gradual approach to a policy of closing the railway in the island would be more consistent with past practice and more easily accepted than an abrupt reversal of previous policy.[53]

By the time this report finally emerged, the political atmosphere had changed significantly and the project that had started out as a test case for integration was beginning to look like its last hurrah. This was not because the new government wanted to keep loss-making railways open but because, while ministers wanted to free road haulage from the claws of an acquisitive state, they were far from comfortable with the implications of doing so for the railways and far from confident that they knew what to do about them.

By 1951 the Conservative Party had abandoned plans to sell off the entire BTC Road Haulage Executive (RHE) as impractical and intended to pass a limited Bill abolishing the 25-mile limit on private hauliers' operations quickly, with major reform delayed until the details could be worked out. Although it was pledged to halt the nationalisation of bus companies, the party proposed to leave the majority of nationalised road transport in public ownership, abolish the BTC's various executives and set up regional boards to coordinate publicly owned transport, within a competitive environment in which the BTC was to be given greater freedom to set its charges. Once in office with a majority of only seventeen, however, ministers decided that both road haulage and iron and steel should be denationalised as soon as possible, in order that the process could be completed before the next election returned a Labour government committed to halting it. The task was entrusted to Lord Leathers, the Secretary of State for the Coordination of Transport, Fuel and Power, one of several 'overlords' Churchill appointed to coordinate the work of individual ministries, an innovation not generally considered a success. Leathers lacked the political experience and skill needed to steer what was to prove a very difficult Bill through Parliament and his shortcomings were not significantly ameliorated by the assistance of John Maclay, a Minister of Transport and Civil Aviation whom Churchill bullied into a nervous breakdown in just over six months.

It is fair to say that ministry deputy secretary Sir Cyril Birtchnell found it difficult to adjust to the change of government. Horrified at the prospect of damaging the Commission and abandoning integration 'without having any considered plan for transport as a whole to put in its place', he tried unsuccessfully to revive the idea of a royal commission.[54] Lord Hurcomb, former permanent secretary at the Ministry of Transport, was now chairman of the BTC. Latching on to Hurcomb's reported warning to Leathers that even a modest relaxation of the 25-mile limit on private haulage would inflict major damage on the BTC's haulage operations, Birtchnell recommended that the whole of the RHE would have to be sold off after all. Hurcomb later denied making the comment and events proved this fear unfounded and the sale impossible. As it was felt necessary to arrange the demise of the RHE in a manner that would prevent its employees finding out any sooner than necessary, Hurcomb was not consulted and so the ministry was unaware of his denial until it was too late. Meanwhile, ministers turned their attention to the even greater fear that the BTC would be left with a loss on the sale of the RHE, while deprived of the surplus from its operations, and an increasing loss on rail operations in the face of road competition. Alarm bells rang at the Treasury, and the Cabinet set up a committee to consider the details. After nine meetings, the committee remained divided over Birtchnell's proposed solution: imposing a levy on road transport.

The levy would be paid by hauliers and consisted of two parts. The simple part, part one, would compensate for the loss on the sale of the RHE. The absurd part, part two, would compensate the BTC for the financial effect on the railways of any loss of freight traffic as a result of road competition *minus* any savings that the Commission was able to make as a result, or that it should have made – a reference to closures made possible by a loss of traffic to roads. The levy summed up the dilemma the government faced between wanting competition and not wanting a railway deficit, a dilemma which arose from the fact that fulfilling the pledge to free road haulage was far more important than any ideological imperative. Administratively, part two of the levy required a calculation of impossible complexity. Economically, it made no sense at all to introduce competition and then, as one minister put it, to 'tax road hauliers to the precise extent of their economic superiority over the railways'.[55] Politically, the levy was bound to be opposed by the Road Haulage Association – the one group who might otherwise have been the chief cheerleaders of the government's policy. It was a poll tax on wheels. Under constant pressure from Churchill, backbenchers and Conservative supporters to announce a policy, the committee only reached a decision once Churchill tinkered with its membership. Few liked the levy but no one was able to come up with a better way of allaying the Treasury's fear that it would have to bail out the railways (a move it warned would remove any incentive to efficiency and release the brake both on pay claims and the public's 'desire … for wasteful transport services'[56]). Despite the levy's obvious shortcomings, despite the likelihood that it would prove impossible to sell the entire RHE or to ensure that any part of it was bought by an expropriated haulier and despite the opposition of some ministers, a White Paper proposing both the sale and the levy was published in early May, a few days after Maclay resigned through ill-health, and a Bill followed in July.

The unpopularity of part one of the levy, although significant, was easily overshadowed by that of part two; there were doubts as to whether it could be carried in Parliament. Fortunately, the haste with which this policy had been worked out proved unnecessary, as Churchill's plan to extend the parliamentary session into 1953 was abandoned and the Transport Bill did not proceed. However, the government had to have a new Bill ready in October. Aware he was in the running for Maclay's job and keen to remain at the Colonial Office, Alan Lennox-Boyd fled London for Brighton in the hope that if Churchill couldn't find him he would give the job to someone else. His efforts to avoid becoming Minister of Transport failed, but once in post he diligently sought an alternative policy. By September he was plotting behind his officials' backs to drop part two of the levy in favour of 'drastic' decentralisation and deregulation.[57] The difficulty was that he had no way of proving this would enable the railways to survive the impact of road competition and his assertions that it would were denied by his officials, who put a paper to the Cabinet committee refuting the arguments of their own minister.

Lennox-Boyd advocated a complete rethink on the railways' commercial restrictions. He started from absolute freedom and asked that each restriction justify itself, an admirably radical approach which terrified his officials, who envisaged extortionate charges imposed on traffic such as coal, which was effectively tied to rail (and which could surely have been protected). Unfortunately, Churchill had rather undermined the government's commitment to commercial freedom for the railways when, in order to improve the Conservatives' chances in the London County Council eelctions, he forced Maclay to veto proposed fare increases planned for May. In so doing Churchill had defeated the BTC, the Transport Tribunal, the Central Transport Consultative Committee (CTCC), Maclay (this was a factor in his breakdown), Leathers, the initial advice of ministry officials that the move was unlawful and his own government's nascent policy of increasing the Commission's freedom to raise charges, which was amended as a result. It certainly did not help Lennox-Boyd's case.

In the absence of a commitment to denationalisation across the board, shifting power within the public sector from national to regional bodies – 'decentralisation' – had attracted the Conservatives in opposition as a means by which competitive principles could exist within the state sector; little thought had been given to what this actually meant, however, and Nigel Harris has argued that it involved attributing 'magic qualities to the concept ... designed to wish away problems'.[58] Lennox-Boyd certainly offered little detail on what 'drastic' decentralisation actually meant in practice and the hope that it might stimulate competition through the publication of separate accounts for each railway region eventually fell foul of the complexities of railway accounting and was never implemented. If only Lennox-Boyd could have been transported across the river to the Southern Region's headquarters at Waterloo where the region's commercial superintendent, W. H. F. Mepstead, considering the Isle of Wight council's memorandum late the previous December, had recognised both the power of some of its arguments and the effort the islanders would muster in opposition if the closure proposals went ahead. Correctly, he foresaw the damage such a fight might inflict on the Commission and suggested a coordinating officer be appointed to oversee and integrate the rail, bus and road haulage activities on the island. It was the sort of proposal the Conservatives had advocated in opposition, but there was effectively no channel by which the minister could draw on real railway experience to inform his policy, especially in the face of his officials' opposition.

By October ministers were completely divided over the levy and the Cabinet was unable to agree a definitive line in time for the party conference. Leathers told the Prime Minister that the committee now 'felt forced to think out our policy again from first principles'.[59] Twelve days and two meetings later the

Cabinet reached agreement on what Housing Minister Harold Macmillan called 'a really terrible tangle', primarily to avoid the embarrassment of not having a Bill ready for the new session of Parliament.[60] Part two of the levy was abandoned, leaving the railways reliant on the unknown benefits of decentralisation and the, as yet undecided, extension of their commercial freedom, in response to the denationalisation of road haulage and the abolition of the 25-mile limit from the end of 1954. The Cabinet Secretary's note of the meeting shows that Churchill and Sir Arthur Salter (Minister for Economic Affairs and former chair of the conference that led to the creation of the haulage licensing system in 1933) saw a railway deficit as inevitable anyway; none of their colleagues disagreed. A revolution in transport was coming anyhow, said the Prime Minister; 'is it wise to seek to slow down the change artificially?' Predictably, the attempt to sell off the entire RHE failed and failed in particular to attract the small man back into the business. Another Act was required in 1956 to legitimise the retention of unsold vehicles; the RHE's long-distance haulage survived and prospered as British Road Services. Nor did the Act fulfil Lennox-Boyd's hopes of commercial freedom or radical decentralisation, as we shall see. Its real failing, however, as some Cabinet members recognised, was that while it was clear that integration was not the Conservatives' answer to the implications for the railways of growing road competition, it did not really set out what was, nor did it address the fundamental question of what sort of railway the nation wanted and was willing to pay for. Having rejected Labour and the levy, and watered down Lennox-Boyd, what was left? 'Breathing space for four years before the government has to aid the railways,' was Churchill's view.[61] He was spot on.

Although far less attention had been paid to buses than lorries in framing the Bill, its proposals in that respect ended attempts at integration on the passenger side as effectively as the more controversial proposals on freight.[†] The 1947 Act had not nationalised all bus services, but had given the BTC the power to establish area bus 'schemes', under which it could in effect take control of all bus services in an area, a possibility that had been considered on the Isle of Wight. The first version of the 1952 Bill stripped the Commission of these powers and prevented any further acquisition of bus companies; the second version added powers allowing the minister to direct the BTC to sell its bus assets. Although ministers were not irrevocably committed to denationalising buses and although no 'scheme' had ever been implemented, these proposals put a new perspective on integration. If the Commission lost control of bus and haulage services it would find it difficult to offer an alternative by road when closing branch lines in future, which probably explains the ambivalence evident in the Commission's closure policy by the middle of 1952. On the one hand it was pushing the Railway Executive to press forward with its branch line investigations and then move on to look at lightly used secondary lines; on the other, it asked the Executive to consider cost-cutting measures and improved services before recommending a line for closure. The difficulty in providing alternative services if the Transport Bill became law certainly strengthened the Executive's doubts about rationalising secondary lines, some of which represented 'national, social and economic obligations' which the Executive saw no means of escaping.[62] By December the branch line committee was concerned that closures would either lead to

---

[†]   Except in London, where – like the deregulation of buses by the Conservatives in the mid-1980s – they did not apply.

criticism of the Commission for failing to provide alternative road services, or would hand traffic to and strengthen road competitors. It wanted closures deferred unless the case was 'absolutely clear and no competitive issue is likely to arise in future' and began to consider whether some lightly used railways might be converted to tramways, free of signalling and with reduced staff, in preference to surrendering traffic to road.[63]

By the end of 1952 then, the impetus that had been behind the branch line committee's efforts in 1951 was fading as a result of the Transport Bill. Such doubts encouraged the Commission to consider retaining the Freshwater and Newport–Sandown lines using cheaper operating methods, but it appeared that there was no prospect of eliminating the loss (a significant factor being the unwillingness of local highway authorities to authorise unstaffed level crossings) and, as lightweight diesel railcars would be unable to carry the summer peak traffic, the idea was ruled out. In November, Hopkins informed the Isle of Wight County Council and the Chamber of Commerce of the decision to close the Bembridge, Freshwater and Newport–Sandown lines, expressing his

regret that I have to convey such a decision because the Southern Region, and its predecessor the Southern Railway, have always taken a warm and even sentimental interest in the Isle of Wight services and can fairly claim to have done a great deal for these services.[64]

When he wrote these words it is doubtful whether any group of rural railways in Britain had ever been studied as thoroughly as those in the Isle of Wight and, whatever shortcomings the study suffered from, a predisposition towards closure on the part of those conducting it was not one of them. Yet, implementing these conclusions was to bring accusations of dishonesty, bogus figures and a disregard for the public against not only the Commission, the Executive and the region, but Hopkins personally. His letter sparked outrage on the island and within days local papers were claiming that the 'bombshell' decision to close the Cowes line 'within five years' had been taken behind the back of the council, which had believed negotiations were ongoing.[65] The island representatives' meeting with Hopkins and his colleagues in December was a rather tense affair. The railwaymen had been put out by the islanders' reaction, given that Hopkins's letter had said the Cowes line would be retained for *at least* five years, not closed within that period, and that the conclusion of their investigation was the one they had warned the islanders to expect the previous year (and about which the island delegates' leader had said 'there could not be much serious complaint'[66]). However, the consistency of the region's position raised islanders' suspicions – wrongly – that their views had simply been ignored. The region's refusal to share their report to the Commission reinforced this impression.

The council and the chamber briefed a QC, Melford Stevenson, to act for them at the public hearing the TUCC had agreed to hold and prepared two substantial memoranda setting out the case for retention, suggesting alternative operating methods for *all* the island's lines. They wanted the TUCC to take these memoranda as the basis for the inquiry and a context for the railways' proposals. Aware that the council's primary concern was to ensure the long-term future of the lines from Ryde to Ventnor and Cowes, it was clear to Mepstead and Hopkins that by discussing their plans – and therefore revealing the original possibility that *all* the island lines would be proposed for closure

– they had added significantly to the opposition they now faced in seeing through more limited proposals. Mepstead warned of the council's 'adroit manoeuvring' and Hopkins 'was sorry to have talked at all to these people'; he even suggested that the passing of the Transport Act be used as a reason to withdraw the proposals.[67] The railways felt it was vital to prevent the TUCC hearing turning into a tribunal, a fear strengthened by the fact that the TUCC chairman appeared favourable to such a development, and decided against engaging counsel. Convinced that any delay would be a victory for the opposition, the railways refused to provide details of the calculations supporting the case for closure to opponents they believed would simply use them to prolong the process.

By the time the TUCC public hearing began at the county hall in Newport in May 1953, the closing down of railway lines was ceasing to be the curiosity it had been when Douglas Macdonald Hastings stumbled across Singleton. The Railway Development Association had been established as a focus for opposition. In the same month as it put forward the Isle of Wight proposals, the Commission decided not to restore services over the Brightlingsea branch, which had been severed by flood damage in February. A TUCC hearing that summer was attended by three MPs. Accepting that the line lost money, the committee nevertheless recommended that services be restored because local roads were inadequate, although they were good enough for half of the 1938 traffic to have deserted the line. None of the improvements in traffic forecast by objectors materialised and the line closed in 1964. Even the proposal to close the tiny Woodstock branch (average train loading: five passengers) brought forth letters to *The Times* containing the soon-to-be-familiar allegations that the Railway Executive had deliberately diverted traffic to roads in order to make the line seem uneconomic and that a combination of social need, the scope for cheaper operations and the increased traffic that lower fares and future housing developments would bring meant that the line should not be closed. Objectors' complaints about the opacity of railway figures had led the East Midlands TUCC to raise the issue with the Commission in the autumn of 1952 and in early 1953 the CTCC accepted the BTC's offer to provide estimates of gross savings, traffic loss, additional delivery costs, net savings and any additional savings in all cases. The Commission warned that it would be impossible to treat branch lines as entirely separate businesses for which a profit and loss account could be produced and argued that, as it only put forward cases where the case for closure was obvious (because revenue fell short of even direct costs), the Railway Executive's accountants were instructed not to waste time preparing detailed figures. This was a question of expediency, as the complaints from the Southern Region's accounts department about the burden the Isle of Wight investigation placed on it demonstrate, but it left the railways vulnerable to criticism if they tried to argue the case for closure pound by pound, which was exactly what Hopkins ended up having to do.

It is worth digressing slightly at this point to consider the complexities of calculating railway costs and the savings from closures. These were always at the heart of debates over closure in the 1950s and the Isle of Wight case brought the issue to the fore. The first difficulty in pinning down the finances of a particular service was collecting the data – no small task in 1953. The timing of surveys was always open to criticism; objectors demonstrated that the Isle of Wight survey taken in July 1952 showed much

lower levels of traffic than were found in August, when the
Newport–Sandown line saw an extra 400 journeys each way a
day. Once the data was collected, a series of assumptions had to be
made about shared costs. If different services use the same track
(or staff, or signalling, or stock) how are the costs of providing
them attributed to each? This is a particularly pertinent question
given that calculating the cost of a service is not the same as
calculating the savings from its closure. For example, if the cost
of providing track on a branch line is X, and the reduction in that
cost by withdrawing passenger services is Y, then the withdrawal
of all the remaining freight services and complete closure of the
line will save track costs of X minus Y, which we will call Z.
If, on the other hand, the freight service is withdrawn and the
passenger service continues, this will not produce a saving of Z,
but a much smaller saving we will call A, because it does not in
general cost much more to carry freight on a track already maintained to passenger standards. So in attributing track costs to the
freight service, should we choose Z or A? The answer is either or
neither depending on the purpose of the calculation. The point
is that costs and savings are different and that neither calculation
is necessarily straightforward. In the case of the Isle of Wight,
many of the railways' figures for individual lines had been arrived
at by dividing the island total between the various routes on the
basis of train mileage, which threw up a variety of anomalies and
did not necessarily represent the likely outcome of closure. For
example, the number of locomotives and coaches required and the
consequent maintenance bill would not necessarily fall in exactly
the same proportion as the reduction in train miles produced by
a particular withdrawal. Bearing in mind that, as a whole, the
island system lost money and it was the social and economic

consequences that prevented the whole system being closed, this was not quite as slapdash or dishonest as it could be made to look, but it could be made to look very slapdash and dishonest by a good barrister, and Melford Stevenson was certainly that. Long-term costs posed similar problems. Objectors pointed out that about a third of the anticipated saving in the Isle of Wight case arose from 'interest', which included a notional payment of 4 per cent on a notional fund set up to cover depreciation costs. Not only did this fund and the payment to it not actually exist, but it was based on a 'replacement cost' approach to depreciation, while the Commission's own accounts used 'historic cost' depreciation. Using replacement cost made the case for closure look better, but objectors made much of the apparent absurdity that depreciation was being charged on locomotives that were clearly so ancient as to be 'life expired' – and not incurring depreciation charges – as far as the Commission's accounts were concerned.[†]

As if shared costs and depreciation did not make railway accounts complex enough, the intractable issue of contributory revenue was, in many cases, a bone of contention. Contributory revenue is the income the existence of a particular service generates on other services; for example, the revenue earned on the Waterloo–Portsmouth and Ryde–Newport lines

---

† Depreciation is how accountants ensure that the cost of replacing an asset which will eventually wear out (e.g. a locomotive) is not ignored year after year until suddenly the entire cost of renewal falls in a single year. Allowing for depreciation on a 'historic cost' basis means writing off the cost of the asset over a period of time representing its estimated working life, say twenty years. At the risk of stating the obvious, 'replacement cost' depreciation is based on the cost of replacing the asset. This is significant in the Isle of Wight case because the rolling stock was generally so old that one would not expect it to incur a charge under historic cost accounting, but of course it would eventually need replacing, so it was reasonable to take some account of this when calculating the savings from closure. By 1960 the BTC was being criticised for the shortcomings of its depreciation provision and Gourvish recalculated its results in 1986 using replacement rather than historic costs to show that its position was (even) worse than it had appeared at the time.

and the railway-owned Portsmouth–Ryde ferry by the existence of the Newport–Freshwater branch. The key question here is, if the Freshwater branch closes will those using it who have started their journey in London continue to use the railway to reach Newport (in which case none of the contributory revenue is lost and the case for closure is strengthened), will they make the entire journey by road (in which case all the contributory revenue is lost and the economics of the other two services might be adversely affected to the point where the closure makes no sense) or will they go to Margate by train instead (in which case, the precise balance of lost and new revenue is virtually impossible to gauge)? When one considers that a resort might earn contributory revenue on a wide variety of routes, the complexity of the calculations involved in the pre-computer age becomes clear. The fact that figures for contributory revenue were gross revenue, and therefore took no account of the profitability of the services on which they were earned, adds another complication. The Isle of Wight lines might generate a large amount of additional traffic on the London–Portsmouth main line during the summer; but if that traffic required the provision of extra signalling, coaches, locomotives and staff that were only used on a few summer weekends, it was not necessarily profitable. In 1953 the railways do not appear to have been concerned about this, but it was to prove a key element of Beeching's approach to lines serving holiday resorts. In short, both the amount of contributory revenue and the amount which would be lost on closure were open to almost endless debate. The Isle of Wight was a less complex case than most, as the significant contributory revenue the island lines earned on the mainland was assumed to be retained after closure because passengers had to break their journey at the coast anyway. The region was criticised, however, for ignoring the revenue earned on the Ryde–Cowes and Ryde–Ventnor lines from traffic through to the rest of the network. Finally, there was always room for objectors to argue that more could be done to cut costs. As we have seen, this was considered and ruled out in the case of the Isle of Wight on the grounds that the gulf between costs and earnings was too great to bridge.

It was inevitable then, that Melford Stevenson would have much to work with once the objectors persuaded the CTCC to request more detailed figures from the railways and reveal them to the objectors. He ridiculed the 'interest' portion of the saving on the grounds that if the same methods had been used for the Commission's accounts, its profit for 1952 would have been a loss (the answer to this is that the Commission should have been using replacement cost and should have been showing a loss, so Stevenson had a point, although not the one he imagined). On the basis of expert evidence, he claimed to have shown the real saving would only be £20–30,000 not the £90,000 the railways had claimed and that losses were concentrated on the Newport–Freshwater line. Hopkins put up a credible defence and was able to cite examples of inaccuracies that *underplayed* the case for closure, but the case provided a stark warning of how the difficulties of obtaining irrefutable figures could provide a canvas on which railway officials could be depicted as underhand conspirators against their own services. Towards the end of the final day of the hearing, Hopkins was challenged on evidence he had given that new sleepers were used when track was replaced. Stevenson cited a recent example where second-hand sleepers had been used on the Bembridge branch. Hopkins explained that the railways had intended to close the branch on

8 June to avoid track replacement expenditure, but had postponed closure once the committee began its task and had to operate it safely in the meantime. Using old sleepers to do so was a one-off, short-term exception to normal practice, irrelevant to the argument for closure; but Stevenson fixed on the point as a 'disturbing' example of the unreliability of railway statements, drawing an angry protest from Hopkins. Stevenson summed up in full Perry Mason mode, reminding the committee of 'the terribly important responsibility that rests upon them, and of the great public interests that now lie in their hands': the railway's figures were false, a loss of £20–30,000 was quite a different matter, old sleepers had been used – Hopkins could not be trusted. 'I do not know what confidence you feel in the information you have been given when every test works out that way,' he concluded. 'I can only ask you to say that they have failed, and failed hopelessly to establish this case.'[68] It was a straightforward demonstration of barristerial hyperbole and of how to use peripheral inconsistencies to undermine a witness's credibility, but it has stood the test of time. Stevenson's allegations were repeated in Parliament, and both the Railway Invigoration Society's 1968 pamphlet *The Great Isle of Wight Train Robbery* and David Henshaw's *Great Railway Conspiracy* treated them as if they were the verdict of the judge Stevenson later became, rather than the point-scoring of the advocate he was at the time.

The TUCC approved closure of the Freshwater branch, but was unable to reach agreement on the Bembridge branch and recommended that the Newport–Sandown line be retained and reviewed in two years' time. This was more than the council would have settled for; Stevenson had earned his fee. However, the committee chairman had not been impressed by Stevenson's allegations and his enthusiasm for public hearings waned. Combined with the Eastern TUCC's experience over Brightlingsea, the example led the TUCC chairmen and CTCC members to ensure future hearings were not conducted along the lines of full-scale courts of inquiry. They resolved to rein in barristers, avoid lengthy, formal enquiries and prohibit the introduction of matters other than the proposals themselves. The Railway Development Association, which had assisted the objectors, was barred from participation in hearings unless it could show that it was representing people who actually used the service in question. The motive was not to stifle debate but to make the proceedings manageable and preserve the committees as 'men sitting round a table to hear both sides of a problem, without the frills of advocacy … with the object of producing practical solutions'.[69] Nevertheless to opponents of closure this only served to increase suspicion of the committees, as we shall see in Chapter 5.

The unprecedented nature of the affair left the ministry waiting for the CTCC's views with bated breath. The CTCC endorsed the findings but came down on the railways' side in approving closure of the Bembridge branch. The county council tried to get the minister to direct the Commission to retain the lines, but Lennox-Boyd was advised that to go against the CTCC's recommendations would undermine the procedure and leave him as the final arbiter in closure cases: 'an unfortunate position'.[70] The TUCC and CTCC also recommended that tripartite discussion be established between the council, the Commission and the ministry to examine the council's ideas on operational improvements and the implications for the roads of further closures. Little progress was made as far as the Sandown–Newport line was concerned and by 1955 it was not earning enough to pay the wages of its staff. It closed in February 1956 and is now a cycle path. Beeching proposed closure of the rest of the network, contradicting an assurance from the BTC in 1955 that it had no intention of closing the lines in the next ten years.[†] The Cowes line and the Shanklin–Ventnor section both closed in 1966, following another contentious TUCC process, which, combined with the leaking of the railway's intention to propose closure again in ten years' time, reinforced the impression of skulduggery formed in 1953.

By 1968, opponents of closures were citing the progressive diminution of the island's railways as proof that 'if you cut the branches the tree will die', but the lines had been losing money in 1951.[71] The 1966 closures did not take place because the system was deprived of traffic from Ventnor West, Bembridge or Freshwater, but because the state was not willing to continue to subsidise the lines involved and the island's dependence on rail-borne tourism had declined and appeared likely to reduce still further. As we shall see, 1975 turned out to be slightly different than imagined ten years earlier. Talk of an independent concern taking over parts of the island system and running a commercial railway came to nothing (although the part of the Newport–Ryde route not underneath Newport's bypass is now a very successful steam tourist line). The tourist trade survived; in the year commencing 19 July 2010 just over 2.5 million people visited the island; in the seven-week summer peak roughly two-thirds arrived by car or coach and a third on foot. Of those staying overnight, over 70 per cent travelled around the island by car, 15 per cent used

---

†   There is no reason to suppose this assurance was not given in good faith; the BTC had no intention of going broke in the next ten years either.

coaches or local bus services and 3 per cent the train.[72] Ventnor is still lovely.

While the development of the new government's transport policy in the year after the October 1951 election was somewhat chaotic, its shortcomings should not obscure the fact that integration had made little progress. The Isle of Wight experiment produced little given the volume of work over three-and-a-half years. In 1951 the branch line committee, in the spirit of integration, was seeking examples of lines that, although profitable in themselves, could be replaced by road services at a net benefit to the Commission. The southern part of the K&ESR was touted as an example where this approach could be tried, when the rest of it, which lost money, closed. Here was integration in practice; the trouble was that – thanks to the structure of the BTC and the web of regulation surrounding it – it didn't work. Although carried by the RHE, the traffic remained 'railway' traffic with the RHE acting as agents. As the RHE charged high rates for short distances, it would probably cost the region more to take traffic from the nearest remaining railhead to its destination by lorry than it had previously done by rail and it would not be able to pass these costs on to the customer because of the way freight charges were structured. Moreover, the region intended to leave freight customers to make their own arrangements – and bear the cost – when it closed the northern section of the line, but did not feel it would be able to do this if it transferred traffic from the southern section to BTC road services. Integration could end up increasing costs. In short, there must be real doubts whether the BTC would ever have made a success of the policy, especially given the opposition it encountered on the Isle of Wight. This is only speculation; what actually happened was that the slow development of a 'properly integrated' system was cut short by the ill-considered policy of the Churchill government.

The Titfield Thunderbolt was released in March 1953 and one wonders whether any of the participants in the drama over the island lines saw its depiction of an inquiry and, if so, what they made of it. The film ended in typical Ealing style, with the emphasis on social harmony as, following an inspection of the line by an official, the ministry shrugged its fuddy-duddy shoulders and accepted that their amateur opponents had won a fair fight. The Isle of Wight case could hardly have been more different. Hopkins's efforts to consult local interests ended in lasting bitterness and suspicion. The islanders initially won more than they would have settled for, but in the long term it probably made little difference. The lesson the railways learned was that frank discussion was a route to disaster and their response was caution and secrecy. The sad reality is that it is difficult to see how things could have been different. Once the islanders knew there was a possibility that at some point the Ryde lines might close, it was always likely that they would bring to bear whatever pressure they could to rule out this risk to the island's economy as completely as possible for as long as possible – and this made acquiescence to almost any cut unlikely. The case had a significant impact on attitudes to railway closures for the rest of the decade and, together with the 1953 Transport Act, ensured that anything more than a case-by-case piecemeal approach to rationalisation was off the agenda in the short term and harder to put forward in the long term. If this sounds like a victory for the opponents of closures, it does not appear to have felt like one at the time. The events described in this chapter did much to postpone a full-scale national debate over the future shape of the railway system until Beeching delivered his report a dozen years later. Had a royal commission been established in 1951, that debate might have been informed and even a little dispassionate. Instead, by the time the issue came to a head positions had become entrenched, passions inflamed and suspicions aroused on both sides. In this respect, Titfield was pure Hollywood.

Chapter 4

Chromium dreams: the 1955 *Modernisation Plan*

On 14 July 1951, passengers in the second coach of the 3.48pm *West Riding* express from King's Cross to Leeds noticed smoke coming from under a seat at the London end. They alerted the guard, a Mr Nunn, who, having had no training on what to do in the event of a fire, assumed the cause was a hot axle box and decided to have the train stopped at Peterborough. To this end, he wrote a note to throw out of the window at Huntingdon and went looking for a potato in the restaurant car to wrap the note around. His search was interrupted by a soldier from the second coach, who told him that the smoke was now much worse. The floor of the coach was hot; the rubber underlay was melting; a flame had been seen. It had taken the passengers some time to find the communication cord and when one of them pulled it, the driver had not immediately noticed its application. Realising he was now at Huntingdon Number One signal box and having found nothing to wrap his note around, the guard threw it out of a window anyway and returned to the coach, which he now realised was on fire. At this point both the driver, who now noticed that the communication cord had been pulled, and Nunn applied their brakes. The guard attempted to tackle the fire with an extinguisher, only to find it was broken. The interior of the coach was lined with Rexine – leather cloth treated with nitrocellulose, a substance as flammable as it sounds. Flames shot up the walls of the coach and swarmed along the roof, the smoke became so thick that it was difficult to breathe and almost impossible to see, and sixty-five people tried to get out of a single door at the other end of the coach. Caught between the inevitable crush and the flames, some began trying to smash windows with suitcases.

Signalman Munro in Huntingdon Number Two box had watched the train pass by at about 40mph. He could see the passengers clearly and nothing appeared to be wrong, but a couple of minutes later he noticed the train had stopped about a mile away and smoke was coming from the coaches. He phoned the next box to the north to stop traffic on the up line and then phoned Huntingdon Number One to summon help. Back at the scene, driver Cartwright looked back along the train he had just brought to a halt and saw smoke, suitcases, passengers and then flames come flying from the windows behind him. Soldiers among the passengers helped others down to the track. Some, too frightened to jump, had to be dragged through the broken windows before they burned alive. Nunn's note was found under the platform at Huntingdon the following day; he was lucky it was not his epitaph. He had carried on fighting the fire even without an extinguisher; severely shocked, with burns to hands and face, he escaped through a window and got on with helping his passengers. Twenty-one others suffered cuts and burns, but no one was killed. The fire was probably caused by a piece of burning coal falling from the locomotive (a bar that should have prevented this was missing), hitting a wheel and becoming lodged in a hole in the underside of the coach where the asbestos packing was also missing. It was the third serious fire on a passenger train in two years, during which there had been an average of eighty-seven potentially serious fires a year.

The worst railway accident in English history took place on a foggy October morning at Harrow and Wealdstone the following year. The guard of a packed commuter train had just told some passengers they could ride in his van and turned to shut the doors in the two coaches behind when, to his horror, he saw a 500-ton overnight express about to smash into the rear of his train at 50 or 60mph. He hurled himself to the other side of the platform and sheltered behind the platform edge until the succession of hideous impacts subsided. When he emerged, he found the three coaches he had helped to fill completely destroyed. The express locomotive, having smashed into his train, had deflected to one side and collided head-on with a second express, sending that train's two locomotives scything across another platform. Three trains and part of the station's footbridge had become a 30-foot-high pile of wreckage and people. One hundred and twelve were killed and 157 injured. Many of the passengers were railway employees on their way to the London Midland Region's Euston office; three of whom got out of the fourth coach from the rear of the local train, which was partially destroyed, to play key roles in organising the rescue of the injured. As the driver and fireman of the first express died in the crash, it was impossible to be certain why they had ignored three successive signals, but it is possible that the driver did not see the first one in the four seconds it should have been visible to him and, continuing to look for it, missed the next two which were mounted at a higher angle. Whatever actually happened, the inquiry demonstrated that the safety of hundreds of people on the busiest main line in the biggest city of a relatively wealthy nation should not depend on one man who had spent nearly four hours looking at signals through fog and night not being distracted for four seconds. It also showed how much more resistant post-1950 coaching stock was to the impact of a crash than older vehicles. It implicitly made the case not only for an enhanced warning system but complete conversion of the line to colour-light signalling. There was more to these accidents than underinvestment, but the lack of modern safety measures – the missing bits of kit, the semaphore signals, the steam traction, the construction of the coaches on the nation's premier main lines – helps to explain why by 1954 even a Treasury official could say that 'everybody wanted and expected the railways to spend money', without complaint.[73]

In 1969 Christopher Booker looked back at the preceding two decades and concluded that in the late 1950s and early 1960s Britain had been caught up in a collective 'vitality fantasy', a significant element of which was 'the sense of being carried into a modernistic future'. As this fantasy progressed from dream to nightmare, a struggle took place between 'New England' and 'Old England', culminating in the latter's defeat in the 'terrible year of 1963'. Booker said little about the railways and he probably did not have the Treasury in mind when he wrote that by the mid-1950s 'as prosperity went on increasing, people were beginning to forget the past and turn their imaginations with ever rising expectation to the future'.[74] But it wasn't only the public who had money to spend; while the increasing ownership of cars and televisions transformed Britain, the Treasury authorised huge investment programmes in the nationalised

industries. At a press conference on 24 January 1955, anxious to
stress the newness of what he was proposing and to prevent the
railways appearing anachronistic, General Sir Brian Robertson
(GCB, GBE, KCMG, KCVO, DSO, MC) launched the BTC's
Plan for the Modernisation and Re-equipment of British Railways
(the *Modernisation Plan*). At a cost of £1,240 million over fifteen
years, the plan promised 'a thoroughly modern system', featuring
high-speed track, colour-light signalling, automatic train control,
modern telecommunications, 'several thousand electric or diesel
locomotives', modern coaches and computerised marshalling
yards, which would allow the railways to earn at least £5 million
a year more than was required to meet their central charges by
the early 1970s.[75] By 1962 Robertson's appeal to the mood of the
times had failed. In that summer's bestselling *Anatomy of Britain*,
Anthony Sampson described the railways, with their 'picturesque, feudal and delightful way of life' as 'the most embarrassing
of all Britain's Victorian leftovers... [A] kind of caricature of all
Britain's problems.' Sampson found Beeching 'reassuring'.[76] He
did not interview Robertson. That Old Englander had retired
the year before, with a hereditary baronetcy, to run boys' clubs
in Gloucestershire and take a seat on the board of a sleeping-
car company. The *Modernisation Plan* came to be considered so
disastrous a failure that it poisoned relations between Whitehall
and the railways for two generations. The 2004 White Paper *The
Future of Rail*, which condensed the industry's entire history
into seven paragraphs, still found space to refer to the 'ill-fated
modernisation plan of the 1950s', the failure of which to reverse
the decline of rail traffic led to the 'Beeching closures'.[77] So what
went wrong?

A casual reader of the 1955 *Modernisation Plan* could be

forgiven for thinking that it was related to a specific set of detailed proposals to begin within five years and be completed in fifteen years. In fact, although the plan set out the main principles of modernisation (improving track and signalling, replacing steam, new rolling stock, continuous brakes for goods wagons, marshalling yards), turning these principles into specific projects was the responsibility of the area boards established by the 1953 Transport Act to manage the railway regions (Southern, Western, Eastern, London Midland, North Eastern and Scottish). There is no precise point at which one can say modernisation under the *Modernisation Plan* began; by the end of the 1950s it had emerged that the BTC saw modernisation as an ongoing process with no definite end either. Significantly refined under Beeching and his successors, modernisation delivered the elimination of steam traction by 1968 and the electrification of the west coast main line between London and Manchester/Liverpool, alongside a variety of improvements in safety, efficiency and comfort. Most notably, it laid the groundwork for the undeniable success of the High Speed Train and the success that the Advanced Passenger Train could have been had the country not lost faith in publicly owned industry in general and rail in particular. All this had its roots in the 1955 *Plan*; nevertheless, much of the criticism of the BTC's modernisation programme is justified. Travelling north on the west coast main line out of London's Euston station today, you may notice, as you approach Bletchley, a flyover rising beside the main line on your left, crossing it and descending again on the right. It is not one of those brutally simple ones the railway builds nowadays that seem to have been designed to say 'please note that we have not spent a penny more than necessary on this'; the Bletchley flyover is a slightly more delicate affair with

retaining walls of patterned concrete which offer a little nod
to the ornate balustrades and other ostentations one associates
with the Victorian railway. You have just passed a monument to
the failure of modernisation.

A key element in the perceived failure of the plan was that it
did not concentrate sufficiently on those traffics best suited to rail
(bulk freight, long-distance passengers and commuters). On the
passenger side, this was not really the Commission's fault, as we
shall see in the next chapter, but its freight strategy is harder to
defend. In terms of both freight ton-miles and market share, the
railways' freight business appeared much healthier in 1946 than
in 1938 and passenger mileage (including London Transport)
rose from 21,700 million to 31,700 million in the same period.
This traffic was carried with a significantly reduced maintenance
budget, however, and the railways were left in a poor condition.
By the mid-1950s the railways were faced with a restoration
and intensification of the sort of road competition they had
experienced in the 1930s. The number of commercial vehicles
in 1945 was only slightly below the 1939 figure at 570,000. This
doubled by 1950 and had reached almost 1.5 million in 1960 and
1.64 million by 1969. Although the railways' freight ton-mileage
remained fairly steady until 1954 and only experienced a slow
decline in the following three years, rail's market share declined
continuously from 1946, when it was more than 50 per cent, and
in 1955, at 40 per cent, fell below the 1938 figure. The fall would
have been greater had the Commission not overestimated the
traffic, in particular general merchandise traffic, that could be
retained as a result of technical improvements and changes to its
charges scheme.

While the 1953 Transport Act encouraged a closer relationship between costs and charges, the latter remained subject to an interminable process of approval. The Commission had not finished work on a merchandise charges scheme it had started drawing up under the terms of the 1947 Transport Act, when it was obliged to begin again in response to the 1953 Act. After five months of consultation with customers, the scheme was submitted to the Transport Tribunal, which, having considered objections for sixteen further months, asked the Commission to modify its plan. It was not finally implemented until July 1957. In the interim, the prospect of the scheme's introduction took on something of the status of the rapture or the revolution: an almost magical event that would make everything all right. Similar faith was placed in the effects of modernising freight operations. As a result, while the *Modernisation Plan* talked of concentrating on the bulk carriage of passengers and goods, the railway carried traffic at a loss which it hoped to be able to carry profitably in future. Marvellous computerised marshalling yards were built at great expense, never to be fully used. The Bletchley flyover was built as part of a London freight bypass carrying goods traffic from such a yard at Swanbourne, in the middle of nowhere, on the line to Oxford, over the west coast main line towards Bedford, Cambridge and another vast yard in the middle of nowhere at Whitemoor near March. The London freight bypass scheme was abandoned in the 1960s, by which time it seemed obvious to an experienced and intelligent railwayman like Gerard Fiennes that 'railways must live by concentration and not dispersal'.[78] The through route between Oxford and Cambridge closed at the end of 1967. It is arguably the most regrettable of the 1960s closures. The flyover has a future as part of the proposed east–west route and the whole route would probably be reopened tomorrow if it had been kept intact – but at the time it was quicker to travel between the two university cities via London.

Between 1957 and 1963 the decline of rail freight accelerated significantly (ton-miles fell by nearly a quarter from 20,900 million to 15,400 million) and by the end of the 1960s rail's market share was 18 per cent. This was largely a result of a shift in the balance of the economy from heavy industry (providing the sort of traffic best suited to rail – bulk minerals) to new industries better suited to road because they required door-to-door delivery and careful handling. Pilkington Glass was the example later used by officials when they explained to a Labour government hoping to shift freight from road to rail why there were only limited prospects for such a policy, but any manufacturer of the white goods that characterised the growth of consumerism would have served as well. By the mid-1970s freight was rail's secondary activity, but as late as 1967 railway managers still saw freight as the most important part of the business. The enormity of this change should not be understated: the railways were built for freight and it had been their core business for nearly 150 years.

Strategic shortcomings were compounded by technical failings. The Commission embarked on a programme to equip all wagons with vacuum brakes before deciding air brakes would be better and installing them. Many of the diesel locomotives built under the modernisation programme proved inadequate and the Commission's purchasing procedures were subjected to heavy internal criticism, an inquiry and a White Paper. Government interventions were not helpful. The chief example being that government policy encouraged diesel locomotive orders from British manufacturers, rather than more experienced foreign firms. The Commission intended to test a series of prototypes and pick the best for mass production, but government pressure to accelerate modernisation in order to bring forward its financial benefits cut short the tests and led to a plethora of incompatible types, some of which represented very poor value. In particular, the government's desire to reduce unemployment in Scotland led it to encourage the BTC to give some orders to the Scottish-based North British Locomotive Company, leaving the Commission saddled with an unsatisfactory collection of overpriced, underperforming machines.

At the heart of the problems with railway modernisation lay the 1953 Transport Act. The abolition of the Railway Executive under the Act left the BTC with the dual role of overseeing all nationalised transport and acting as central authority for the railways, an arrangement its Financial Comptroller, Sir Reginald Wilson, called 'a first-class English mess'. [79] For the first fifteen months after the Executive's demise, an interim organisation was in place. This was superseded in January 1955 by a new organisation which Gourvish describes as 'a great semi-military bureaucratic edifice', which lacked a clear chain of command, confusing and demoralising railway managers. [80] The fact that the *Modernisation Plan* was produced during this disruptive double reorganisation of 1953–5 contributed to its shortcomings. The new area boards, staffed with part-time appointees, were too weak to satisfy the Conservatives' hopes for decentralisation but were strong enough to hamper the BTC's attempts to run the railways effectively. The BTC was responsible for making policy in regard to investment and the withdrawal of unremunerative services, but in both cases individual proposals came from the area boards. If the Commission's attempts to adapt the railways to future needs were flawed, then the area boards' tendency to ignore those attempts was as significant a problem. The most obvious example of pointless decentralisation was the decision of the Western board to order diesel locomotives with hydraulic transmission while everyone else favoured diesel-electric (although it did make trainspotting more interesting).

The one single factor that was to mark out the 1955 *Modernisation Plan* as a beacon of public sector misspending was the failure to deliver a solvent railway. The *Modernisation Plan* indicated that at the end of the modernisation period the railways would deliver a net annual surplus of £5 million. † In 1956, a White Paper entitled *Proposals for the Railways*, supposedly the result of more detailed thinking, estimated that the Commission would break even on its operating account by 1961 or 1962. A reappraisal of the plan in 1959 put this estimate back a year. The railways did not just miss these targets, they made a mockery of them. While the plans described a sober journey to solvency, the Commission careered off on a trail of profligacy, laughing and waving out of the window as their promises became less and less credible – or at least that is how it must have looked. In 1954 the railways had operated at a profit, although too small a profit to pay the interest on stock issued to shareholders at the time of nationalisation; by 1962 the operating deficit alone was over £100 million and half that again was incurred in central charges – the real picture was worse. It was this disparity between promised and actual financial performance (the 'angle of unreality' as it later became known in the ministry[81]) that saddled the *Modernisation Plan* with its toxic reputation and did so much to brand the railways as

---

†   The plan indicated that modernisation would deliver net benefits of £45 million – this included benefits from measures such as closures which required no investment, so was in itself a dubious figure. This was set against the official annual deficit of £25 million and a £15 million increase in depreciation provision.

the lamest of lame ducks. Although there were other reasons for modernising the railways, the financial benefits were absolutely central and there is no doubt that the sketchy calculations in the three plans were deeply flawed and hard to relate to any detailed work within the BTC. The Commission certainly made errors in the financial justification for modernisation, for example by calculating a return on 'betterment', the difference between the cost of renewing existing equipment and the cost of modernising, which was not a valid calculation if the original equipment was operating at a loss. The most striking failure of the original plan was that its calculation made no allowance for the cost of paying interest on the investment while it was taking place and before its benefits emerged, which wiped out the apparent surplus. No wonder many in Whitehall looked back to the *Modernisation Plan*'s publication as an almost inexplicable error. Yet, whatever the failings of railway management, the fact that the plan published in 1955 contained thoroughly misleading figures was entirely the fault of government, as the story of the plan's genesis shows.

Although the government wanted the railways modernised, its real purpose in approving publication of the plan in January 1955 was to justify the cost of avoiding a strike by the National Union of Railwaymen, and ministers knew, or ought to have done, that its figures were misleading. For all Lennox-Boyd's talk of commercial freedom during the debates over the Transport Bill in 1952, the greatest restriction on the railways' commercial freedom in the 1950s was the government's tendency to treat the nationalised industries, in the Treasury's words, as the 'hand-maidens of other policies', by constantly involving itself in their pricing decisions and industrial relations.[82] The electoral success of the Conservatives during the 1950s was largely dependent on convincing potential Labour voters that the Conservatives could be trusted to deliver prosperity while maintaining full employment and avoiding confrontation with the unions. This was particularly important in 1951–5, when the Conservatives had only a small parliamentary majority. At the time, railway wages were subject to a complex and almost constant process of annual negotiation, the shortcomings of which were evident in dissatisfaction over pay, poor productivity, difficulty recruiting staff and regular threats of a strike. Railwaymen were not only significant in terms of the massive disruption they could cause through strike action, but as a benchmark for other workers. As a result, Conservative governments in the 1950s were never more than a year away from the potential collapse of their industrial-relations policy (and electoral strategy) over railway pay and this issue dominated the government's relationship with the BTC. It is said that when Churchill appointed Robertson as BTC chairman in September 1953, he told him 'the money doesn't matter, what matters is the chaps'; he certainly told the Cabinet much the same thing.[83] Indeed Robertson's appointment only really makes sense if one sees the railways as a collection of offic-ers and men (the words used to differentiate management and non-management within the industry at the time), rather than a business. A proven administrator, Robertson had very limited business experience. He was almost immediately persuaded by ministers to buy off a strike in late 1953, despite his reluctance to pay more than had been recommended by the extensive negoti-ating process. As a good soldier he could usually be relied upon to accept an impossible position.

The 1947 Transport Act required the BTC to break even 'taking one year with another'. This was all very well if some completely unexpected problem, a severe winter or a strike, meant the Commission lost money in a particular year and spread the cost over the next few; but once ministry officials felt that 'we have come into an era in which the railways are going to be in the red for quite a long time, and perhaps for always', as they did by August 1954, the Commission was arguably in breach of the Act.[84] Taking one year with another, of course, it remained possible to argue that it was not; and the temptation to indulge in that pretence proved too much for ministers to resist when it offered a way out of other difficulties. In the aftermath of the 1953 pay deal, Lennox-Boyd admitted to the Cabinet that the warnings his officials had given about railway finances when the Transport Bill was being drafted had proved correct. He suggested that the BTC might need financial assistance with modernisation. The Treasury was not prepared to offer anything that might be construed as a subsidy, but the Chancellor, Rab Butler, did promise to consider any proposals Lennox-Boyd brought forward. This sort of 'offer' doesn't usually mean anything. Ministers in any government rarely say they will *not* consider a proposal; that can seem unreasonable. It looks much better if one turns down a proposal having given it 'due consideration'; nevertheless it encouraged the Commission to draft a plan for modernisation that would require a government loan of £500 million on special terms, complete with extensive proposals to electrify lines.

There was no chance of this being accepted by Treasury officials, who suspected Robertson was trying to use modernisation as an excuse to get a concealed subsidy to solve the Commission's existing financial difficulties; but throughout 1954 they were increasingly anxious to see the plans. In January that year the

official responsible for day-to-day Treasury work relating to the
Commission, Alexander Grant, had realised that the Commission
was borrowing just to keep itself going (i.e. to fund replacement and renewals rather than investment). A Bill extending its
borrowing powers would have to be brought forward in the 1954-5
parliamentary session or their limit would be reached (an Act
extending them was passed in March 1955). The Treasury began
putting pressure on the Commission to produce even an outline of
its plans by the summer, so that officials could examine the spending that would effectively be approved in this Bill. Not only had
nothing arrived by September 1954, but officials now learned the
borrowing the plan required would be *additional* to that provided
for in the Bill. One consequence of the pressure the Commission
was under to produce its plan quickly was that the *Modernisation
Plan* was essentially 'a lot of mouldering schemes which the
BTC and the Regions had found after a hurried search in their
pigeon holes', hastily brushed up by a committee under Reginald
Wilson.[85] The committee began work on 18 November on a draft
which admitted that it might be impossible to meet interest
payments on the investment in the period before the plan bore
fruit. On 6 December, John Boyd-Carpenter (who had replaced
Lennox-Boyd as minister) sent his officials to the Treasury to pass
on Robertson's suggestion that some form of deferred interest on a
government loan would solve the problem. The Treasury estimated
this would amount to a subsidy and prepared to resist.

As Christmas 1954 approached, the annual wage round had
once again reached the point where the threat of a railway strike
was being discussed almost daily by the Cabinet. Robertson,
again, did not feel the BTC could afford to increase its offer, but a
government-appointed court of inquiry dismissed this resistance

with the phrase, 'having willed the end, the Nation must will the means'.[86] These were dangerous words. Anxious as they were to avoid a strike, ministers were even more anxious to avoid this phrase being interpreted as meaning that if nationalised boards could not afford to pay decent wages they should be subsidised until they could. What the Cabinet needed was a formula allowing the railways to be treated as a special case. Paying the kind of subsidy the Treasury feared, linked to modernisation but in fact reflecting other problems, provided one. On 8 December, as Grant was warning his superiors to expect a further approach for a subsidy, the Cabinet discussed the possibility of 'a government contribution towards capital expenditure on a programme for modernising the railways', as a way of encouraging the BTC to feel justified in temporarily increasing its operating deficit to fund higher wages and avoid a strike.[87] The following day, a senior Treasury official, Sir Bernard Gilbert, discussed the crisis with Sir Reginald Wilson, who agreed that the railwaymen's claim would have to be settled and that there was nothing fundamentally wrong in a temporary deficit redeemed by the effects of modernisation. Yet he mentioned that the Commission might need help before the plan bore fruit in the form of a capital write-off. Some people, perhaps those not preoccupied with the potentially catastrophic consequences of a winter rail strike in a country where most homes were heated and factories powered by rail-carried coal, might have seen this as grounds to question whether the plan would actually improve the Commission's financial position, or instead saddle a loss-making body with even heavier debts. Gilbert took the view that 'all this is for the future, and anyhow a subsidy on any such ground is of course entirely different from a revenue subsidy to meet a wage claim'.[88]

On 10 December a small group of ministers met at Downing Street to discuss the crisis. Henry Brooke, the Financial Secretary, arrived fresh from a briefing on Gilbert's meeting with Wilson, while Boyd-Carpenter, under no illusions that settling the pay claim would leave the BTC in the red for years to come, suggested that Robertson might be persuaded to accept this in return for financial assistance with modernisation. On hearing Boyd-Carpenter's plan, Churchill dismissed the benefits of modernisation and proposed that the Commission be publicly directed to increase its offer, after which his colleagues' chief concern was to dissuade the Prime Minister from doing so. Boyd-Carpenter was despatched to give Robertson 'a hint that "subsidy" might be made respectable as "deficit"' and the government would consider sympathetically any request for financial assistance with modernisation.[89] The note of the their meeting the following day put it more delicately: Boyd Carpenter asked Robertson 'on a purely hypothetical basis what his reaction would be if Her Majesty's government ... were prepared to assure him that in their view he need not trouble himself unduly about the size of his deficit in view of the long-term prospects of the Commission when railway modernisation took effect'.[90] Ten days later the *Modernisation Plan* arrived at the Ministry of Transport complete with the calculations showing an eventual surplus, but omitting the cost of interest on the funds the plan required during the period of its implementation. Officially, it has never been clear on what basis this calculation was inserted by Wilson's committee or why interest was ignored; unofficially it has long been obvious that the figures in the *Modernisation Plan* had more to do with settling the strike than with the finances of modernisation.

By 4 January, the Cabinet's position was that modernisation, the new merchandise charges scheme and improvements to productivity would allow any deficit arising from the pay deal to be recouped at some point in the future. Ministers genuinely intended to push the Commission and the unions into achieving improvements in productivity, but they had no real idea of how to do so, and when Robertson objected to their proposal for an inquiry on the matter they had little option but to give way. Robertson had been reluctant to accept Boyd-Carpenter's assurance unless it was stated publicly; but in order to maintain the fiction that they had not intervened, ministers wanted the General to settle the dispute first and then ask whether the government supported him. Naively, he agreed. On 7 January he made his request in a letter to Boyd-Carpenter, indicating that the accumulated deficit would be £50–60 million by the end of 1955 and there would be further deficits to follow, to which would be added the burden of financing modernisation, which was unlikely to produce substantial increases in net revenue for some years. The letter made it clear that he was expecting to discuss a major reconstruction of the Commission's finances with the minister that would encompass the funding of modernisation. The same week he publicly implied that funding the wage deal was not his responsibility but the government's, a statement which caused discontent on the Tory backbenches. The Treasury stalled a reply while it considered four ways in which the Commission might be offered assistance: public borrowing under Treasury guarantee; a revenue subsidy from the Exchequer; a government loan for investment at an uneconomic rate of interest; and allowing the BTC to fall back on the Treasury guarantee of its existing stock (in effect allowing the railways to go bust). The last of these would 'brand the BTC as the one [nationalised] body which had not met its obligations',[91] thereby deterring the others, and no legislation would be required. It also meant that the government could avoid an immediate decision on a subsidy and simply wait and see. This was the course officials favoured. By the time the pretence that the Commission was paying its way became untenable, the officials centrally involved in the events of December 1954 and January 1955 had all departed the scene. In 1960 a junior official was asked to go back through the files and establish just how it had been claimed that the BTC was covering its accumulated deficits before 1957. No clear answer emerged.

Had Treasury officials been asked to endorse fully the *Modernisation Plan* in January 1955 they would not have done so. Only Grant had had a chance to study it in any detail and he knew full well that while the proposals seemed sensible, the figures were 'made to measure'.[92] He had no information on the thinking behind them, could not divide the benefits derived from closures from those requiring investment and could not estimate the extent to which the plan might be accelerated or what its short-term effects might be. It was not until April 1955 that he discovered that there was no detailed programme of projects behind the plan, the figures were aggregations of estimates, the details were expected to take another year to work out and the real planning had only just begun. Why was the plan accepted with so little study? Because 'acceptance' appeared to involve no real commitment. Boyd-Carpenter told the Cabinet that he merely intended to give a general endorsement of the document, which was all he was required to do by law. When the Cabinet approved publication on 20 January 1955, publication was all it approved. It was generally believed in Whitehall that there would be little spending under the plan for five years and that virtually none of the borrowing involved would be covered by the Bill extending the Commission's borrowing powers, so there would be plenty of time to study, modify and, perhaps, accelerate it.

The omission of interest was not the only flaw that Butler ignored when he told the House of Commons that 'allowing for all the uncertainties of forecasting fifteen years ahead, there is a reasonable prospect of the Commission's plan paying its way'. The *Modernisation Plan*'s calculations also took no account of the £10 million cost of the wages settlement, which wiped out the promised surplus irrespective of interest charges. This may have been a genuine mistake, but his comment that 'I have no reason to think that the Commission counts on any Exchequer subsidy to help it in fulfilling its statutory duty' could only be true in the sense that Robertson did not think what he was asking for counted as a subsidy.[93] The reality of Butler's endorsement of the plan is contained in a passage Grant drafted for, and Butler excised from, the latter's Cabinet paper on it:

> it may be said that [the BTC's] figures are optimistic and that solvency is too much to hope for ... but ... even if hopes are not realised in full, this is still the best way to minimise losses... What is the alternative ... can anyone contemplate that by continuing as we are now there is any prospect of solvency? I cannot see any alternative to the plan ... something on the lines proposed is inevitable, and ... the longer a decision is postponed the greater the danger of an ultimate charge falling upon the Exchequer.[94]

There was a danger that Conservative backbenchers would not tolerate all this. The first achievement of modernisation was to convince a joint meeting of the party's backbench transport and labour committees in January 1955 that modernisation, not subsidy, would fund the settlement. This was just part of a wider political effect, summed up by *The Economist* (which was not fooled itself):

> From the grime and muddle of 1955, from a very recent piece of politicking which everybody would like to forget, the public is invited to lift its eyes towards 1974. Look; there is an electric or diesel (or, just possibly, atomic) train pulling silently, briskly competitive, smog-free, out of the glistening chromium of the new King's Cross.[95]

It was a railway fit for Dan Dare, yet the government was neither committed to a firm programme of specific investment nor sure that the plan would work. The *Modernisation Plan* – the document published in 1955 – did exactly what such documents are supposed to do. The BTC wanted the go-ahead for modernisation, which it got; the government wanted the all clear for the strike settlement, which it got. The plan was, in this sense, a remarkable success. The public were entitled to conclude that the Commission had found a way out of its difficulties and while some details needed to be worked out, the government had agreed to help. In reality the Commission had admitted that it couldn't solve its financial problems, the government had added to them and it was hoped on all sides that at some point in the future investing in modernisation would at worst improve the position and at best resolve it, although no one knew how. The Commission expected financial help and the government had pretended it did not. How easily the railways were bankrupted.

Against this harsh judgement must be weighed the reality that there were no easy solutions to the problems facing Cabinet and Commission in December 1954. Had the government supported the Commission and faced a strike it is impossible to say who would have won and the strike would probably have cost more in the short term than the settlement (ministers decided to resist the Associated Society of Locomotive Engineers and Firemen's claim in the summer of 1955, but the resulting strike did not resolve the railway pay issue in general). Nor were there simple solutions to the problems the Commission faced. Nevertheless, the events of December 1954 meant that when the deficit reached catastrophic proportions it was the Commission rather than the government that appeared to be at fault. The contrast between the false promise of a profitable railway and the reality of a huge deficit helped create the impression that railway modernisation had failed. Finally, the handling of the crisis, and in particular the failure to address the underlying causes, meant that the submission of the *Modernisation Plan*, like the passing of the 1953 Act, was a missed opportunity to ask what sort of railway was required and how much it would cost. Had it not been for the pay crisis, that debate could at least have begun before modernisation appeared to be underway, rather than when it appeared to have failed; and perhaps we would ride through Bletchley today without wondering what that funny-looking bridge is all about. We might even be able to change there for Cambridge.

Chapter 5

The Bluebell and Primrose Line: the 1956 closure plan

Horsted Keynes sits towards the western end of the triangle of Kent and Sussex bordered by the sea, the London to Brighton main line and the South Eastern Railway's original route from Redhill to the channel ports – just beyond the reach of London and dominated by the Downs. Is this the England people think of when they think of England? Artist Frank Newbould and filmmaker Ismail Merchant, respectively seeking a backdrop for the wartime poster *Your Britain – Fight for it Now* and an imagined Edwardian idyll for *A Room with A View*, both chose this part of the world. It is the England of Tibby Clarke and Dr Beeching, East Grinstead neighbours. Other Englands are available, of course; but Horsted Keynes station is in the process of becoming the default image of the rural steam railway, as the local station for *Downton Abbey*, Eel Marsh House, Windy Corner, *The Railway Children* and *Miss* (Beatrix) *Potter*, among others.† The real Horsted Keynes station lies on the former

---

†   'South Downs' is one of three *Your Britain – Fight For it Now* posters designed by Newbould during the Second World War. Windy Corner is the home of the Honeychurches in *A Room with a View*; Eel Marsh House is the setting for *The Woman in Black*. The *Railway Children* referred to here is the 1999 television adaptation.

Lewes and East Grinstead railway, once the least used part of a web of railways belonging to the London Brighton and South Coast Railway (LBSCR) based around a line which, diverging from the Brighton main line at Croydon, ran south-east to Oxted and eventually divided into three routes heading south towards the sea. The Lewes and East Grinstead was the most westerly of the three, running roughly parallel with the Brighton main line from Oxted, through East Grinstead, Kingscote and West Hoathly to Horsted Keynes. Here a short connecting line branched off to rejoin the Brighton route at Haywards Heath, creating a double track relief route for the main line between Croydon and Haywards Heath. South of Horsted Keynes, the Lewes and East Grinstead, now single track, served Sheffield Park, Newick and Chailey, and Barcombe before rejoining the second route south from Oxted, which ran via Uckfield, to reach Lewes (the third route ran via Hailsham to Polegate and Eastbourne). At East Grinstead and Groombridge these north–south lines connected with one running west to east from Three Bridges on the Brighton main line to Tunbridge Wells on the South Eastern Railway's line from London to Hastings.

Most of these lines would never have been so expensively cut through the downs were it not for the LBSCR's determination to prevent the South Eastern Railway using the absence of railways in the area as an excuse to reach Brighton itself by building its own line south-west from Tunbridge Wells. When Henry Bessemer, grandson of the inventor Henry Bessemer, moved to the mansion next to Newick and Chailey station before the Great War, he arranged to have a special gate built to reach the footpath alongside it. His daughter Madge picked bluebells by the line. 'The pleasantly undulating country it serves makes it one of the most attractive branches in the south of England,' wrote the *Railway Magazine* in 1954,[96] but the view from the carriage window came at a price. East Grinstead, Oxted and Uckfield aside, there was little traffic to be had and the lines shared not only their tactical origin but a tendency to feature stations named after stately homes (Sheffield Park), hamlets (Horsted Keynes) or two equally distant villages (Newick and Chailey). In the 1950s only 7,000 people lived in the area served by the Lewes–East Grinstead line, outside the two terminal towns. Even those stations that had a source of traffic (West Hoathly) were usually at the bottom of a steep hill on top of which lay their market. The Horsted Keynes–Haywards Heath section was electrified in 1935 and the Southern Railway hoped to electrify the whole of the diversionary route (and the Uckfield line) in the future. However, even the Southern's faith in the power of the 'sparks effect' to encourage traffic did not extend to the single line south from Horsted Keynes to Lewes. By the 1950s the lines were popular with wealthy commuters who drove to the stations, particularly at the northern end where large villas spread south from London. Goods traffic, never heavy, had become very light after the war, while local passengers used the bus.

The Lewes and East Grinstead railway was precisely the sort of line the Commission had in mind when it responded to the CTCC's request, made in the wake of the Isle of Wight case, for more information on the use of lightweight diesels on branch lines. The Commission was in the process of introducing diesel multiple units in a number of areas in 1954, but while diesels could operate a more intensive service than steam, this was only an advantage if the traffic potential justified it. On lightly used branches the crucial comparison was not with the existing steam service but with road transport. The decisive advantage of the bus was convenience, because it could pick up passengers nearer their home; but it also won on cost, being available for a third of the price of a railcar and not requiring dedicated track and signalling, all of which was nearly as expensive to maintain for one train a day as for twenty. Moreover, on lines where a steam locomotive could operate freight and passenger services, or where seasonal and other peaks might need longer trains, diesel railcars could not cope.

By 1954 the Lewes–East Grinstead line was up for closure; the TUCC was examining the case and Madge Bessemer was leading the opposition. By the end of 1955, the ministry's file was fat with correspondence, chiefly to and from Miss Bessemer and her brother, H. Douglas Bessemer, one of the nation's leading collectors of butterflies and stamps. At some point in the campaign to save it, the line had begun to be referred to as the Bluebell and Primrose line, possibly at Madge's instigation. In accordance with the Railway Executive's policy since 1953, the costs of alternative operation had been considered, but with passenger receipts at around £10,000 a year and a net saving of £59,000 from closure, there was no prospect of closing the gap, assuming the figures were accurate. That assumption was vigorously disputed and the refusal of either the BTC or TUCC to provide objectors with detailed figures was the cause of much complaint, but the line closed anyway in June 1955. And that, it appeared, was the end of the story; when the last trains ran over the Lewes and East Grinstead, there was no sign that the controversy around its closure would help derail attempts to publish a Beeching-style closure programme in 1956.

By 1953 the BTC had established that stopping-train services outside urban areas and short-distance haulage of small freight loads were fundamentally unprofitable, and by the end of 1954 a further traffic survey had found that about 40 per cent of stopping train services earned only a third or less of their movement costs (the cost of running the train itself). In October 1955 the Cabinet had realised that the provisions in the 1953 Act that would have required the BTC to sell its bus assets were a deterrent to closures and had decided not to implement them. The same month, the CTCC received a BTC paper arguing that few rural services would benefit from the use of railcars and by December the ministry had seen a BTC paper anticipating the replacement of many rural services by buses. By March 1956 the Commission had asked the area boards to review uneconomic services and submit comprehensive proposals to replace them with buses. The Commission was planning a campaign of publicity and persuasion designed to expedite the closure process. It prepared a memorandum for area boards to send to TUCCs, warning them to expect a number of major proposals for the complete withdrawal of stopping services, pointing out that 'even if diesel operation were to double the receipts and halve the costs, a substantial proportion of stopping services would not even cover their direct costs' and requesting cooperation 'in carrying out this new and urgent programme of positive improvements with all possible speed'.[97] These developments caused some excitement at the ministry. Convinced that there were large potential savings in a programme of closures, the parliamentary secretary, Hugh Molson, was keen to find some way of bypassing the consultative process. Anticipating that a large-scale closure programme would be ready by the time the BTC's 1955 accounts were published, he suggested they be published simultaneously and accompanied by a ministerial authorisation to bypass the TUCCs.

Ministry assistant secretary, Alison Munro, influenced by the apparent health of the Dutch railway's finances as a result of closing more than two-thirds of the stations open before the war, supported Molson's suggestion. Munro does not quite fit the myth of a ministry packed with pro-road officials. Having lost both her parents at thirteen, she was left a widow by the Battle of Britain when just two months pregnant aged twenty-seven. A single mother, she became a rare woman in a civil service that required female staff to resign when they married. She had all the dynamism and ability required to survive these circumstances and had made an important contribution to the development of post-war civil aviation before arriving at the railways and inland waterways division of the ministry (she went on to become High Mistress at a leading girls' school in the 1960s where she abolished many regulations, including the uniform – motivated, she said, by practicality rather than liberal ideology, but doubt-less typifying 'New England' to some of the more conservative parents). She had backed the *Modernisation Plan* when it arrived at the ministry and, forty years on, was one of the few people who had a good word for it:

> I gave [railway modernisation] that gigantic kick and I'm glad I did. If it had been nowadays it would have got bogged down by nitpickers, the statisticians would have got hold of it ... we'd lived through the war and Churchill won the war because he thought big and I admire him for that reason... I know I've been criticised much since [for lack of economic analysis] ... but ... [the critics]

don't realise the state the country was in, nothing had been spent
on the transport infrastructure in the whole of the war.[98]

By the 1980s she was chair of the CTCC where she was praised
by opponents of the proposal to close the Settle and Carlisle
line as 'a doughty champion of the consumer'.[99] Nevertheless,
in 1956 she felt the savings from closures to date represented
only a 'minute fraction' of what was possible and that the closure
procedure could be speeded up if 'some really startling and
comprehensive statement of Commission policy' were made. She
suggested setting out the new policy in a White Paper accompanied by clear ministerial support.[100] This was fortuitous, as a
White Paper was just what the minister needed.

Harold Watkinson had been appointed Minister of Transport
and Civil Aviation just before Christmas 1955, his experience as
parliamentary secretary at the Ministry of Labour during the
previous winter's pay dispute still fresh in his memory. He was
determined to turn the railways into a sensible business. Eager to
make an immediate impact, he supported a swift pay award in the
hope that this would improve industrial relations and encourage
progress on productivity. When the settlement was followed by
the usual application for increased charges, the Cabinet saw an
opportunity to demonstrate its determination to break out of
the wage-price spiral, using the BTC as an example. Anthony
Eden had succeeded Churchill as Prime Minister in April 1955,
winning an election with a secure majority the following month.
Unwilling to pursue legislative curbs on trade unions, a formal
incomes policy or to abandon the commitment to full employment, Eden's government attempted to create a wage and price
'plateau'. Ministers could only exhort private sector employers

and the trade unions to show restraint and keep wages and prices stable, but they could impose such policies on the nationalised industries (albeit informally through discussion with their chairmen). In March 1956, Brian Robertson was pressured into setting an example by agreeing to a six-month moratorium on some passenger fares and only half of the increase he had wanted in freight charges. In June, before the moratorium was up, the government imposed a general six-month price freeze on all the nationalised industries. The policy failed to stabilise anything, and its destabilising effect on the finances of the nationalised industries was an important stimulus to the Treasury's subsequent search for a different approach. The year 1956 was the first in which the railways officially operated at a loss.

The March moratorium was heavily criticised and by May the opposition was claiming that the government had forced the BTC to breach its statutory duty to break even. Watkinson, who knew that the BTC would probably be left with a deficit for years to come, defended the decision by announcing in April that he and the Commission were undertaking a major review of its prospects. The minister was now effectively committed to producing a document in six months' time that could justify a deficit heading in the direction of a million pounds a week. The ministry's deputy secretary George Stedman dismissed Munro's proposal for a White Paper as 'a little over-dramatised and highly coloured' and issued dire warnings of the political consequences of bypassing the consultative committees.[101] However, Molson was filled with enthusiasm, pointing out that CTCC recommendations meant nothing unless the minister issued a direction as a result – and he would hardly issue one that contradicted his own policy. If the BTC were told to meet 25 per cent of its deficit through savings and cut its coal consumption by half a million tons, Molson told Watkinson 'the burden would be carried on your broad shoulders'.[102] Watkinson liked the sound of this. 'Let us cut off all the heads at once in a White Paper if necessary,' he told Molson; 'I have no objection to drastic action,' he told officials.[103] He told Robertson he wanted a comprehensive programme of closures for a White Paper and warned the chairmen of the TUCCs to expect one.

Officials began writing the report they wanted the Commission to provide, a draft of which was sent to the Commission on 17 May. This set out six strategies used to tackle the problems of rail systems worldwide: modernisation, productivity improvements, charging freedom, subsidy, the restriction of road transport (which it ruled out) and, heading the list, closures. This is what the ministry invited the Commission to say on the subject:

> The conclusion reached by this reassessment is that the railways will always, as far as can be foreseen, have an essential function to perform, but that they can only perform this function efficiently and economically if there is a radical change in the pattern of railway services and if the non-essential and unremunerative services are rapidly eliminated... The target for all railway policy planning must therefore be to adjust, as rapidly as circumstances permit, the railway system to this more limited but essential function and to eliminate the dying wood. This is the basic thinking underlying the ... modernisation programme.[104]

The final document was expected to contain statistics showing the financial and traffic improvements expected, the mileage closed to passenger and/or freight traffic, the numbers of stations closed and of passenger services to be discontinued in 1956 and succeeding years. At a meeting with BTC representatives in May, chaired by the minister, it was agreed that 'there was no time for prolonged discussions if results were to be produced in time for the White Paper ... it was important to show a progression of lessening deficits over a reasonable number of years until a balance was secured. Some five or six years at most should be the aim.'[105]

Unsurprisingly, the figures produced in response were essentially cosmetic alterations to the made-to-measure predictions in the 1955 plan, which in no way justified the predicted surplus of £3 million in 1961 or 1962 and £48 million in 1970, excluding interest on the accumulated deficit (or a deficit of £17 million and a surplus of £38 million respectively if interest payments on the accumulated deficit continued). Within days of the meeting at which the need to show the BTC breaking even in five years had been discussed, ministry deputy secretary George Stedman had been warned by Sir Reginald Wilson that 1961 or 1962 was 'the very earliest date at which the Commission can hope to break even in the most favourable circumstances', and had concluded that it was important to avoid giving the Cabinet the impression that 1961 or 1962 was 'in any way a firm date'.[106] Wilson's warning was made before the government imposed its second price freeze, a development which clearly did not fall within the compass of 'the most favourable circumstances'. On 12 June, Watkinson told the Cabinet that the full extent of the Commission's financial woe would soon be public knowledge. The BTC's accumulated deficit would probably top £100 million at the end of 1956 and the operating account would probably be in the red for many years to come. Hard decisions would be necessary, he warned, including closures.

The realism of Watkinson's plan was always open to question. Success rested on a willingness to ride out any storm and the signs were not encouraging. Watkinson expected the BTC's emphasis to be on withdrawing stopping trains on lines that would remain open for through traffic, which he felt could be treated as time-table changes that – unlike closures – need not be referred to the TUCCs before they were implemented. It was never clear that this would actually make closures easier, because there was no way of preventing passengers affected by timetable changes from referring them to the committees anyway. By early April the TUCC chairmen had baulked at the widespread opposition any attempt to prevent objections would provoke, the unmanageable increase in their workload if the 'timetable changes' were referred to the committees (as experience suggested they would be) and the impossible task of judging proposals already endorsed by the government. They wanted the detailed proposals to be published before they were implemented so that public reaction could be assessed and perhaps dealt with at an inquiry into the propos-als as a whole. Meanwhile, officials queried whether Watkinson should endorse the closure programme himself, thereby compro-mising his position as the final arbiter of individual proposals. Did the advantages, they wondered, of having 'one big row' over a programme of closures outweigh the prospect of stirring up 'a hornet's nest of opposition all over the country' – in Scotland in particular?[107]

Even as the ministry and Commission laid their plans, some-thing was stirring in Sussex: the Bluebell and Primrose line was rising from its grave. Miss Bessemer obviously suspected that if she dug around in the technicalities of the law long enough she would find a chink in the ministry's armour. She wrote several letters in an apparent attempt to demonstrate that the minister had, technically, not received a recommendation to close the line from the CTCC, which she presumably thought invalidated the closure, before she hit the jackpot. Either she or her solicitors uncovered a clause in the Act of Parliament under which the Lewes and East Grinstead company had been absorbed into the London Brighton and South Coast Railway, requiring the LBSCR to run four trains a day for passengers. In February 1956 her solicitors wrote to Waterloo arguing that the clause now applied to the BTC. Such clauses were not unheard of and checking that there were no legal barriers to closure was standard procedure, but it was unusual for them to be contained in an Act transferring a line to a second owner. One can only imagine Hopkins's reaction on receiving a letter from the BTC's chief solicitor in early April stating 'it was most unfortunate that when my department was asked to advise whether there was any legal objection to closing the line, attention was not drawn to the statutory provisions'; all we know is that he put a line in pencil next to this statement, possibly with some force.[108]

Given that the BTC's argument for closing the Bluebell line had been accepted, Hopkins was prepared to leave it closed until the troublesome clause could be repealed. Munro encouraged him to 'play for time by such well-known methods as discussions with the parties, investigations of costs of restorations etc.'. He was defeated by the Commission's legal department, which did not want to ask Parliament to repeal an Act it was disregarding, especially as it had been successfully sued in a similar case involving the Kennet and Avon canal only the previous year. Munro and her superior J. R. Willis were tearing their hair out at the region's decision to reopen the line – 'lamentable', she wrote – but the ministry could hardly tell the Commission to disregard a law.[109] The news provoked a clearly fuming Willis to the only direct expression of anger I have ever seen in a civil service minute:

> this is a sorry tale which hits us at an unpleasantly inconvenient time when we want to streamline the procedure... Also, it makes me very angry that the Bessemers, who – I suspect from motives of pride rather than disinterested regard for the public good – have inflicted a lot of wearisome correspondence on us and wasted hours of official and ministerial time, should get away with it like this.[110]

This reaction needs to be seen in context – there was more at stake than whether a railway closed.

The Crichel Down affair, with which two correspondents had compared the case, had arisen from the poor handling of a small parcel of land requisitioned for wartime use and not properly returned.[†] In the panorama of government activity it was an even smaller speck than the closure of the Bluebell line. Yet in the summer of 1954 it had led to the resignation of a government minister, had damaged or wrecked the careers of several officials and provided the catalyst for the appointment in November 1955 of Sir Oliver Franks to inquire into the conduct of the myriad of tribunals now involved in British life. Franks's report was still a year away, but the fact that it stressed the importance of impartiality and openness reflected the concerns behind its

---

†   One correspondent was Mr Bessemer, the other was a Colonel Temple, friend of Miss Bessemer and old school friend of the Home Secretary, to whom he had written a not-even-thinly veiled threat to go to the press if something was not done.

establishment and shows what dangerous ground the ministry and Commission were now on. Although the TUCCs were not tribunals, there were many for whom the distinction was unclear and many others who thought they should be (including Miss Bessemer, who later devoted a great deal of effort to providing the ministry with a lengthy memorandum on the subject). Bessemer's MP, Major Tufton Beamish, was far more concerned by the secrecy surrounding the process and the inability of opponents to challenge, or even see, the evidence than the fact of closure itself and this view was widely shared. Nor was the Bluebell an isolated example of dissatisfaction. The Railway Development Association, which had supported objectors to the Isle of Wight closures, had now been joined by the Society for the Reinvigoration of Unremunerative Branch Lines in the United Kingdom (1954) in organising opposition. The Isle of Wight hearing inspired a private member's Bill in December 1955, supported by thirty-three MPs, which sought to replace the consultative procedure with a public inquiry under the Transport Tribunal at which the BTC representatives could be cross-examined on the detailed figures they would be obliged to publish. For good measure, it would also reopen all cases heard in the previous five years. A week later branch line closures were debated again and in March 1956 the House returned to the topic of rural transport. This was not a good time to mishandle a closure, nor to reopen a case in which the TUCC had been criticised for precisely the shortcomings Franks was examining. It was an even worse time to try to bypass the consultative process altogether.

Any chance of a radical programme of closures was already fading by the time the ministry learned in June of the Commission's decision to reopen the Bluebell line. The doubts

raised by the TUCC chairmen in March had encouraged a
rethink at the BTC, by the time it received the ministry's draft
White Paper in May. The Commission began downplaying
closures in favour of attempts to make savings of £20–25 million
through replacing steam with diesel railcars. This change was
certainly a response to the difficulties of the consultative procedure, which the calamity in Sussex emphasised. It was probably
also encouraged by the success of the early diesel multiple unit
schemes, particularly in the West Riding, in not only cutting
costs but attracting new traffic. However, there had always been
a range of opinion within the railways and although it was Sir
Reginald Wilson, the Commission's Financial Comptroller,
who had established the Commission's costings division, he was
not entirely convinced by its output. Wilson suspected that the
losses attributed to stopping services had been exaggerated in
separating 'the cost of the "wool" from the cost of the "mutton"'
(i.e. dividing shared costs between services), which required
'abstractions based on all kinds of apportionments which in real
life could not take place'.[III]

When the Commission submitted its draft contribution to the
White Paper on 29 June, closures had been demoted to second
place in the list of approaches to the railways' problems and the
emphasis placed on modernisation. The new draft argued that as
branch lines already existed, as new technology promised great
economies, and allowing for the importance of such services in
feeding traffic to main lines, 'on balance it seems probable that
a considerable proportion of the rural railway services will be
retained', and 'for a long time ahead ... the fundamental pattern
of routes will change only slowly'. There were no detailed proposals, just an eventual annual saving from closures of £3 million

(in addition to the, still unspecified, savings from closures in the *Modernisation Plan*), to be achieved over six years 'by which time the process will be more or less complete as far as the present pattern of things is concerned'.[112] Watkinson fumed. There was nothing in the document to justify a six-month review, but he had to have a White Paper and, despite attempts to get the Commission to accept a redraft, he could not force the BTC to give him the one he wanted. He could not even delay it long enough to challenge the new approach. Any implication that he lacked faith in the Commission's plan risked provoking Robertson into responding that the BTC's finances were in a mess because it had done what the government had asked of it. A couple of weeks before the Bluebell reopened in early August, the minister recommended the Commission's new plan to his colleagues. His argument echoed the hopelessness evident in Alexander Grant's paper on the original *Modernisation Plan* the previous year:

> unless the plan was put into effect, the government would be open to the damaging criticism that it had, by the 1953 Transport Act, destroyed the Commission's prospects of solvency... The government could not avoid incurring very substantial expenditure on the railways for many years to come. It would be better that this should be applied constructively, rather than in financing a continuing deficit.[113]

The reality behind this statement was that the effect of the price freezes on the Commission's revenue meant that Robertson would have to be given something like the financial reconstruction he had been lobbying for since 1955.

As Grant was on leave, the task of working out the details fell to Treasury principal Leo Pliatzky – in fairly chaotic circumstances, as he later recalled. Pliatzky had no contact with the Treasury minister on the Cabinet committee set up to oversee the review, Financial Secretary Henry Brooke, but

> the minutes of one meeting said that at the next meeting the Financial Secretary would present his own proposals, which I found rather astonishing. I had no idea what his proposals were, but nor had he! It turned out ... that I was supposed to produce his proposals for him... I was absolutely flabbergasted. So I came up with the proposal that the BTC ... should have power to capitalise interest on their borrowing. I knew such an arrangement existed for it was provided for in the legislation for the North of Scotland Hydro-Electricity Board which is where I came across it... I had no experience of it ... but I was in a spot.[114]

Pliatzky's task and achievement was to draw up something which could be defended on the basis that it was 'not a subsidy but corresponded on a massive scale to an ordinary commercial operation in which an undertaking with good prospects has to be specially financed during the period before new investments bear fruit'.[115] The result was the Transport (Railway Finances) Act 1957. This placed the BTC's accumulated deficit, the deficits it expected to make in the years to 1962 and interest payments on deficits and modernisation spending in a separate account which was not covered by the Commission's obligation to break even. It was a licence to lose money, but not in perpetuity. Interest would gradually become payable after 1962, by which time the Commission – according to the figures in the White

Paper – would be earning enough money to cover the payments. If, however, the Commission fell short of this target, a further reconstruction of its finances would become legally necessary. Politically, the legitimacy of the entire operation rested on the assumption that the Commission's estimates of its results over the next five years were not just numbers that had been made up to fit a predetermined timetable at the request of the ministry.

How did this get past the Treasury? Officials had every intention of getting to grips with the Commission's investment proposals in the wake of the *Modernisation Plan*'s publication, just as they had had every intention of studying the investment related to the 1955 Borrowing Powers Bill before its publication. And just as they had failed in the latter task, they had learned very little indeed about the 1955 plan before the 1956 version came along. The chief problem was one of organisation. In the mid-1950s, the Treasury was in the process of transition from a system under which the investment programmes committee controlled all investment in order to manage the allocation of scarce resources, to one in which controls over private investment were abandoned and the Treasury was concerned with the revenue-earning potential of nationalised industry investment. That was the theory, but Treasury officials had no experience in judging investment on this basis, let alone a fifteen-year programme of railway modernisation. 'Who was I,' Pliatzky asked several decades later, 'to challenge the railways plans?'[116] The most obvious manifestation of this inexperience was that the whole system revolved around a discussion between the Treasury, the ministry and the BTC lasting one-and-a-half hours once a year. The Treasury had no direct contacts with the Commission and relied on the ministry to act as a go-between, but its relationship with the ministry tended to come down to contacts between Grant and Ira Wild, the ministry's director of finance. Contacts between Wild and the Commission, usually through the ministry's 'Trains and Drains' (railways and inland waterways) division, were hampered by the BTC's resistance to any attempt by Whitehall to interfere in its planning. When one considers that the Commission itself had a less than perfect knowledge or control of the railways' regional organisations, the difficulty the Treasury faced is obvious. The inadequacies of this approach were plain enough; what to do about it was less obvious. If total investment appeared neither too large nor too small there was little the Treasury could do in individual cases, unless it felt that the board in question was not up to the job; as a result, it was very difficult to get sufficient information to judge whether the BTC was investing sensibly until one could show that it was not. Nevertheless, before going on leave that summer, Grant had advised that ministers refuse legislation or financial help pending an outside inquiry, a view echoed by his superiors but overruled by ministers' need to justify the price freeze. Watkinson's expectations are fairly clear from his comment to ministry officials that 'the Commission would have to do as well or better than forecast in their plan or face the consequences. This would be the time for an outside inquiry.'[117] Publishing the White Paper and passing the Railway Finances Act were not a recipe for disaster; they were a disaster that was in the oven on a timer.

This time there was to be no fanfare for modernisation, just a written answer in the House of Commons announcing publication of the White Paper, *Proposals for the Railways*; very much a defensive stroke, but enough to deflect criticism of the price freeze. In contrast, the Bluebell line was reopened on 7 August

1956. Press interest ranged from the *Daily Telegraph* to *Meccano Magazine*. Microphones and cameras recorded the event and cheering crowds greeted the first train at some of the reopened stations (and at Barcombe, which remained shut). A BBC radio reporter travelled with about 200 people on the first train, interviewing Miss Bessemer and the vicar of Barcombe, who was, inevitably, a leading opponent of closure. Reverend Webb criticised the service, which was inconveniently timed and did not serve Barcombe, the line's busiest station. The Act only required four trains a day, did not require them to stop at Barcombe and did not say when they should run. The railways were determined to do no more than the law required and had no incentive to attract traffic which would only make it harder to close a line that had no chance of paying its way. Although the inconvenient timings were the result of running the service within the shift of a single crew, they can only have strengthened the general suspicion among opponents of closures that British Railways used timetable alterations to drive passengers away from lines it wished to close. The Commission was accused of sulking; Watkinson probably knew how it felt.

The Bluebell line closed for a second time in March 1958; nine coaches were required to accommodate all those who turned up to ride the final train. During its brief reopening 'any unusual event on the line ... even the excess blowing off of steam by engines, was being closely observed by a critical and interested public', determined to show that the line could be run more economically.[118] In the face of such opposition, the BTC was only able to persuade Parliament to repeal the obligation to run a service by agreeing to a public inquiry into the whole closure proposal. In effect this overturned the South Eastern TUCC's endorsement of the original case for closure. The committee's members, already furious at MPs' criticism of their proceedings, went on strike when Watkinson overlooked them and asked the CTCC to hear the case instead. The new inquiry was held at the assize court in Lewes over three days in October. Advocates of a tribunal-style approach had got what they wanted. Detailed figures were available to all, and both sides had QCs, although this turned out to be a less confrontational affair than the Isle of Wight hearing. For reasons that are easy to imagine, Hopkins left it to his deputy to give evidence. The committee was impressed by witnesses who

> had little or no experience in public speaking and must have found it an ordeal... The majority ... were obviously moved by a deep sense of injustice – by the feeling that their convenience, or in some cases their livelihood, was being jeopardised by policy decisions made in London by a railway management of whose capacity and sympathy they had genuine doubts and by a sense too of duty and public spirit. We were left under no illusions about the depth of feeling which had been stirred by the decision to close the line, or about the very real measure of disturbance, inconvenience and sometimes even hardship which is caused in a rural community by such a decision.

Once again, the 'interest' portion of the Commission's figures came in for criticism. The committee found it 'unreal' and 'not a proper figure to put in support of a case for closing a branch line unless it is an appropriation from actual profits of the system as a whole', concluding that 'it would be far better from the point of view of the public good if Consultative Committees are asked to consider factual savings only'. The committee's objection seems in part to have been that it just did not understand the figures. It was on firmer ground, however, in arguing that assets such as stations should not attract a charge because they would never need replacing and others – tunnels being the most obvious example – would continue to represent a financial burden long after closure. The committee also criticised the use of regional averages for fuel consumption and locomotive repairs and its recommendation led to improved figures being provided in future cases, despite the Commission's reluctance. The BTC was warned that, in future, closure cases that relied on 'interest' savings were unlikely to be approved. If opponents of railway closures welcomed this rap across the Commission's knuckles and felt they had kicked away a major prop of the case for closures, they must also have been aware that the committee had found that closure of the Bluebell line would save £33,000, that a full analysis of a diesel-operated interval service had undermined arguments that better, more efficient services could save such lines and that the committee had concluded that much of the objectors' evidence 'was based on a misunderstanding of the operational needs of a railway'.[119]

The BTC's decision not to proceed with the closure programme it had planned in early 1956 and to seek savings through modernising rural lines instead, resulted in an order for twenty rail buses for use on lightly loaded lines and the introduction of an experimental service on the Buckingham–Banbury line in August 1956, a week after the Bluebell reopened. This produced impressive results. Operating costs were cut by over a quarter; an improved service and new unstaffed passenger halts increased custom and helped more than double receipts within two months. By 1958 they had more than quadrupled. But even then receipts were still only a third of operating costs and if passenger numbers had tripled to bridge the gap it is unlikely the railcar could have coped. By 1960 railcar operations had generally demonstrated that the Commission had been right in arguing against their use in 1954–5.

The annual receipts of the Lewes–East Grinstead passenger service withdrawn in 1955 (approximately £11,500) were not even half-way to covering the £25,000 or so needed just to staff and fuel the trains. These costs came down to around £6,500 if a diesel railcar operated the same service; but the service would need to generate almost a fourfold increase in receipts to cover its total costs while an improved hourly-interval diesel service would require earnings of almost five times those of the steam service. Nevertheless, if one ignored interest altogether, dismissed station expenses on the basis that the guard could issue tickets, assumed the Commission had overstated all the other costs and that an improved diesel service would quadruple receipts as it had at Banbury, it was just about possible to argue that the line didn't lose very much and that the Commission had a duty to provide the service. In reality it was unlikely that the potential traffic existed in the area and if new equipment were provided it would be more difficult to argue that interest (depreciation) should be ignored. Just as it was entirely understandable that secret figures bred suspicion, so one can see why the Commission was so reluctant to provide figures and why, as the BTC's losses mounted, the temptation grew stronger to step back from such detail and simply ask how the Commission could be losing money if it was not on lines like this. If the Isle of Wight case had left Hopkins regretting his decision to sit down with local opponents of closure, the Bluebell case had a similar effect on ministry officials.

The objectors would have done well too, to heed the concluding paragraph of the CTCC's report, which called for their future submissions to avoid 'attacks upon the capacity and probity of the ... Commission, who are only trying in the national interest to save expense', and instead to 'assist the committees to assess how far their convenience and livelihood will be affected by such closure or withdrawal'.[120] If the outcome of the Bluebell case was to make more work for railway officers, it also foreshadowed the limits that would eventually be imposed on dissent, when the 1962 Transport Act restricted the committees to a consideration of 'hardship'. By the summer of 1958, Tufton Beamish was trying 'very hard indeed to stop a number of my constituents going on flogging the dead horse of the Bluebell line' but Miss Bessemer refused to listen.[121] She miscalculated a loss of only £3,000, using the figures supplied to the CTCC. The committee's secretary, Chambers, tried to explain the figures to her, but concluded that she did not understand figures. When a Mr Bostel of the Lewes and East Grinstead Railway and Transport Facilities Committee sent him four letters in little more than a month on the point, he finally snapped. The line, he told Bostel, 'is now closed and will not be re-opened. Neither, so far as I am concerned, will this correspondence.' Miss Bessemer wrote to the minister to complain.[122]

Of the network of lines between the Brighton and Hastings main lines, only those to East Grinstead and Uckfield survive today. Closure of the Uckfield–Lewes section involved a bizarre procedure when the condition of a viaduct required a replacement bus to operate for the final months of the service. It could not get up the approach road to Barcombe Mills station so the BRB had to provide a taxi to take passengers from the station to the bus, but, farcically, they had to walk up the same road to buy a ticket at the station first. Closure marked the start of a long-running campaign to reopen this line on the grounds that it is silly to remove such a short link, so far without success. A tiny part of it is preserved as the Lavender Line. The Eridge–Tunbridge Wells section has been preserved as the Spa Valley Railway, having closed in 1985 despite the TUCC's recommendation, enabling the extensive site at Tunbridge Wells to be used for a supermarket. The Bluebell, of course, is the most famous of the area's survivors, saved primarily by a bunch of teenage students, inspired by Miss Bessemer. Inching towards East Grinstead as I write, it reopened between Horsted Keynes and Sheffield Park in 1960 as the first standard-gauge passenger line to be preserved in Britain, initial hopes of restoring a commercial service using a former GWR railcar having been abandoned. Among the visitors in its first season was Prime Minister Harold Macmillan. Madge Bessemer is commemorated in the name of the tea room at Sheffield Park station and rightly so; without her it is unlikely that it would have survived to be preserved. Those seeking a simple symbol for the supposed decline of the industrial spirit in 1960s Britain need only to compare her quixotic defence of this unnecessary but delightful relic with her great-grandfather's invention of the Bessemer Converter, from which she must have derived much of the wealth and social standing she used so effectively against the BTC. Miss Bessemer did not single-handedly derail the attempt to 'cut off all the heads at once', but the Bluebell case highlighted just why that attempt got nowhere. As the Commission's representative Lord Rusholme put it when explaining the change of direction to the CTCC, the BTC 'were under an obligation to pay their way, but no one allowed them to run the business as if this was their object'.[123] Watkinson arrived at the ministry thinking that he could turn the railways into 'an organisation that functions on normal and sensible business lines'.[124] Older and wiser, he later reflected that 'three years in charge of the Transport ministry provided … a useful corrective to any illusions that politics is about doing things in a businesslike fashion'.[125]

Chapter 6

White elephants: the M&GN and the collapse of faith in the railways

The 200-odd miles of the Midland and Great Northern Joint Railway (M&GN) were created when a variety of small local companies coalesced under the joint ownership of the Great Northern and Midland companies in 1893. Although the point of the M&GN was to break the monopoly of the Great Eastern Railway (GER) on traffic to the resorts of Norfolk, peace very soon broke out and the final parts of the system were constructed jointly with it. The M&GN route started in the middle of nowhere as a continuation of a branch of the Midland Railway from Saxby on the line from Leicester to Stamford. This was joined at Bourne – the original starting point – by a branch from the Great Northern main line, which predated the M&GN and had taken over the elegant seventeenth-century Red Hall as its booking office. Attempts to demolish the hall at both the inception and demise of the M&GN were thwarted by public protest and it still stands, having seen off the passing industrial irritation. From Bourne the line headed out across one of the most daunting of English landscapes: the Fens. Maybe it is because I was brought up in inner London, but there is something eerie about somewhere so utterly flat and deserted. Between Bourne and Spalding the former marsh was so sparsely populated that the stations were named after drains: Twenty, Counter Drain and North Drove (disappointingly, the railway ignored the names of local hamlets and spared the timetable 'Counter Drain for Tongue End'). Having bypassed the relative civilisation of Spalding, to which it threw out a couple of spur lines, the main route was joined by a branch from Peterborough at Sutton Bridge where the Nene was crossed on a swing bridge. The few passengers changing here for Wisbech could enjoy possibly the most highly polished waiting room in the land and check their hair for smuts in its table's mirror finish. From here, the M&GN meandered the length of Norfolk; at first through fruit farms around King's Lynn and then fields of wheat or beet or cattle before a sumptuous concluding section through the Broads to sun, sea and sand dunes, down the coast to Yarmouth and the joint GER line to Lowestoft. Beyond King's Lynn, which it did its best to avoid, the only places it served of any size at all were Fakenham and Aylsham, each of which was at least as well served by the Great Eastern and neither of which can boast 10,000 souls even today.

The M&GN delighted in an array of enticingly named destinations: Eye Green, Bluestone, Corpusty, Hindolveston, Potter Heigham, California Halt and Clenchwarton; but the most important was Melton Constable, from which a branch headed south to Norwich (*much* better served by the Great Eastern) and another north to Sheringham and Cromer. From Cromer another joint GER line looped back around the coast to rejoin the 'main' line at North Walsham. Busy as Melton was when summer was in full swing, one could hear cows in the milking shed when standing on the platform. The entire network was single track and on busy summer weekends between the wars it would be chock full of specials to and from the Midlands and the north, with harvest peaks of freight that could be almost as extreme. Absorption of its parent companies into the LMS and the LNER initially made little difference and, although Melton lost its works in the 1930s and the line was absorbed by the LNER, little had been done to divert traffic to the roughly parallel Great Eastern route from Peterborough to Norwich and on to the same coastal destinations before the war.

In a single nationalised system the M&GN's straggling duplicate route was an easy target for anyone seeking expensive burdens to shrug off and by 1958 throwing off expensive burdens was very much on government minds. The national humiliation of Suez saw petrol rationing return and Eden resign in January 1957 a broken man – his replacement Harold Macmillan, former director of the GWR, was initially unsure if his government would survive more than a few weeks. Most importantly, however, Suez brought home the reality of Britain's diminished status in a world dominated by superpowers and by the growing fear that conflict between them could unleash the Third World War. Whatever people's feelings on international politics, the shock of Suez created a context in which concerns about the nation's economic performance gave rise to the widespread suspicion that something was fundamentally wrong with Britain and required change, even if it was not always clear what that something was. Macmillan is remembered today for the apparent complacency of his comment – made in a speech some six months after he became Prime Minister – that 'most of our people have never had it so good', but the theme of his speech was the danger to that prosperity posed by inflation and the uncertainty over whether it was possible for Britain to combine full employment, stable prices and economic growth.[126] Divisions in his government over how to address this problem cost Macmillan his Chancellor and two Treasury ministers at the start of 1958. Even as he appeared to epitomise 'Old England' to the satirists who rose in response to the mood of dissatisfaction that typified the turn of the decade, Macmillan was as aware as anyone of the need to modernise and it was the question of how to do this that kept him awake at night.

In both symbolic and economic terms rural railways were out of step with this new mood. In June 1958 the BTC announced its intention to close 174 miles of this 'railway relic of the last century' from Saxby and Peterborough to Yarmouth and Norwich.[127] This was by far the greatest closure to date and the operation had been well planned. The region provided a confidential book for the two area TUCCs that would hear objections (the public got a less detailed one). This made a strong case for the railways' expectations that most of the freight worth carrying would be retained – about 100 miles would remain open for freight and there had been discussions with most customers about alternatives. The Commission's figures were presented on the basis agreed after the Bluebell inquiry and supported by detailed calculations. They pointed to net savings of £640,000 a year, which were defended as a conservative estimate because they ignored renewals on stock rendered surplus and savings on other parts of the network that depended on closing the M&GN. The usual uncertainty over line renewals was reduced by the need to replace Clenchwarton Bridge at a cost of over a quarter of a million pounds. BTC-owned bus companies would provide more than half-a-million additional bus miles of alternative services a year; none of the stations was more than about 13 miles from an alternative rail facility; the average load per train was forty passengers.

These preparations paid off when the East Anglian and East Midlands TUCCs approved the proposals and the CTCC praised the BTC's handling of the case. Closure was implemented in March 1959; but if this was a strong case – and it was – its strength simply reiterated the impossibility of closing any railways without causing hardship and the widespread dissatisfaction with the idea that loss-making railways should be closed in the national interest. While many holiday expresses were quicker after closure than before it, there was no avoiding the fact that sending traffic from the Midlands to Cromer via Norwich instead of Melton appeared to be, as one local critic put it, like 'going round the candlestick to find the handle', adding over 40 miles to the route; and Yarmouth was never going to welcome the possibility of losing roughly a quarter of the holiday business that had formerly arrived via the M&GN.[128] The most obvious difficulty arising from closure was that of Melton Constable. As discussed in Chapter 1, Melton owed its existence to the railway that a third of its entire population now worked on. As John Marshall, a fifty-year-old signalman and vice chair of the parish council pointed out, while they were likely to be offered jobs elsewhere on the system, this would be of little comfort to those like him who owned homes they feared they would be unable to sell – 'nobody will want to live in Melton'.[129] Wary of criticising the railways publicly, other Melton men helped brief opponents of closure among the public.

There was protest enough elsewhere in any case. Complaints that the consultative committees had prejudged the case and rushed their hearings reached the minister, a deputation of parish and district councils reached the parliamentary secretary, a petition from the 'humble subjects and parishioners of Hindolveston' (who were losing a pretty good diesel service straight to Norwich) reached the 'Gracious Person' of the Queen, asking her to intervene on the grounds that the 'high-handed, arbitrary manner in which the decision to close the line was announced and the absence of factual proof of losses makes nonsense of our claim to be a democracy'.[130] Elsewhere, it was suggested that the line should be retained in case of another petrol shortage (the Suez crisis had led to petrol rationing between November 1956 and May 1957). L. J. Roll, who had represented one of the councils at the East Midlands hearing and delivered a thirteen-page treatise to the ministry opposing closure, was one of many who complained that the line had been deliberately run down. Here was an argument the BTC could not win. There was no sensible case for running through traffic between the Midlands and the coast on both the former M&GN and GER routes when it could all be accommodated on one with investment in faster services concentrated there. However, when concentrating through traffic on the GER line left the M&GN with insufficient traffic to justify its retention, efficiency began to look like conspiracy. The M&GN was a duplicate interloper, built to challenge a monopoly, and was now transferred by the BTC into the control of a regional management that had previously run that monopoly. Obviously they were running it down with malice aforethought. Similar complaints were heard around the closures of the Somerset and Dorset and Great Central. It was nonsense, but damagingly believable nonsense.

The warning in the BTC's press release announcing the M&GN closure that 'a new point of balance must be found between the obligations of public service on the one hand, and the requirements of the railway budget on the other', combined with the unprecedented size of the closure and the TUCCs' acquiescence, were indications of a shift in attitudes to closure at the BTC as its losses mounted.[131] The M&GN contributed to a massive increase in the estimated savings from closures authorised in 1958 (£1,069,000 compared to £179,000 the previous year and a similar figure in 1956). The year 1959 saw the closure of another white elephant duplicate route, the Hull and Barnsley, and the first nail in the coffin of the biggest of the lot, the Great Central, when its express services were removed. By the time the M&GN closure was proposed in mid-1958, the trade and industry representatives on the CTCC were pushing for a more extensive closure programme. The same week, R. G. M. Street, chair of the Wales and Monmouth committee, shocked at how few people actually used some services, suggested that the BTC submit lists of cases that it felt required no further investigation to the TUCCs who could then agree to the immediate suspension of services for six months, pending further study.

Perhaps encouraged by the post-Suez mood of national self-criticism, Minister of Transport and Civil Aviation, Harold Watkinson, and his officials also wanted to see more done to increase the 'almost pitiful' savings closures had produced in 1957.[132] An opportunity to do so presented itself when they found themselves obliged to justify the Cabinet's claim that a wage rise paid to avoid a strike in May 1958 had been funded by new savings. Watkinson met the CTCC and TUCC chairmen in June to urge swifter progress and for his part agreed to publicly state that the BTC was under no obligation to ensure that alternative services were available following closure. He did so twice in July, telling the House of Commons that 'the railways are no longer a monopolistic organisation with an obligation to provide all sections of the community with a railway service … [and] the Commission is under no obligation to provide an alternative service'.[133]

Change was slow, however, and limited by the BTC's fear of the public's reaction in the wake of the Bluebell controversy. It rejected Street's suggestion of closures in advance of inquiries and an attempt to resurrect the use of timetable alterations that reduced services to the legal minimum. Similar fears undermined the effect of Watkinson's statement when, in attempting to reassure opposition members that passengers' needs would not be totally ignored, he mistakenly implied that the TUCCs had a statutory duty to take alternative services into account when judging closure proposals. The list of closures the Commission produced in response to the ministry's request for savings to fund the wage deal confirmed official suspicions that the proposals were half-baked and deflated expectations of an increase in the committees' workload. Of the thirty-two lines on the list, only eight or nine would close completely and seven of these had lost their passenger services some years previously. The M&GN proposal may have benefited from the use of the financial data agreed in the wake of the Bluebell case, but that agreement had only been reached after months of haggling motivated by the BTC's fear that more detailed figures would be too onerous to prepare and would expose it to increased criticism from objectors. The tension between the pressure for savings and the fear of public reaction was encapsulated when the BTC representatives used their votes at the North-Western TUCC to secure a majority in favour of closing the Coniston branch only for the BTC, in the face of the subsequent controversy, to instruct its representatives to refrain from voting in future.

By the end of 1958 such vacillations were beginning to look irrelevant as the railways faced what today would be routinely described as 'a perfect storm', but in the more inventive mind of Sir David Serpell, recalling the circumstances that brought him to the ministry as deputy secretary, appeared 'like one of those old films in which a girl is tied to the track and there are *two* trains approaching'.[134] The two trains were the deficit and the Guillebaud inquiry into railway pay. The May 1958 pay deal had been reached in a desperate hurry by a government that did not want to fight the railwaymen and the London bus drivers at the same time. In order to persuade the railwaymen to accept less than they wanted, the Cabinet agreed to establish an inquiry into railway pay under the academic Claude Guillebaud. Guillebaud did not report until 1960, but his inquiry quickly developed such political momentum that a major pay award was certain.

In the autumn of 1958, as the TUCCs prepared to hear the Midland and Great Northern case, Treasury officials realised that even without the effect of Guillebaud's report, the Commission was unlikely to meet the financial targets set out in the 1956 White Paper. Not only had Watkinson expressed a determination to have a proper inquiry into the Commission's position if it failed to meet these targets, but Treasury officials would not allow a third plan for the railways to slip through their grasp – a major investigation of the Commission's prospects was inevitable. The bad news for the railways was the context in which that investigation would be conducted. By 1959 the government's policy

towards the nationalised industries and the Treasury's view of
the nation's future transport needs had both altered significantly
since the 1955 *Modernisation Plan* had been framed. It was this
change, rather than a simple reaction to the BTC's losses, that
explains the *Beeching Report*.

Having failed to get to grips with the investment programmes
of the nationalised industries when they were launched in the
mid-1950s, the Treasury was keen to rectify this in the second
half of the decade. Officials recognised that the existing machinery of investment control, under which a public spending total
emerged from an annual series of individual discussions with
departments (such as those which had failed to shed much light
on the *Modernisation Plan* in 1955), did not provide an effective
mechanism for controlling public expenditure as a whole or allocating cuts in times of crisis. The key, but by no means only, shaper
of Treasury thought on what to do about this was Otto Clarke,
the man who had invented the FTSE index and who, by 1958,
was the head of the Treasury's Home and Overseas Planning
Staff where he oversaw the move to a rolling five-year spending
programme from 1961. Clarke believed that if the Treasury was
to allocate limited funds effectively between spending departments it would need to understand the investment programmes
it was funding and therefore the likely shape of future demand
in various sectors of the economy.

Ministers' desire for a distinctive policy on nationalisation for
the 1959 general election provided officials with an opportunity to
get a firmer grip on nationalised industry investment. Watkinson
flirted with thoughts of denationalisation, his colleagues would
probably have settled for something to do with decentralisation,
but the Treasury took a more sophisticated line. In January 1959

the Padmore committee (a group of civil servants including
Clarke, led by a senior Treasury official, Sir Thomas Padmore),
was asked to produce a report, which reached the Cabinet in June
1959 and eventually led to the 1961 White Paper *The Financial and
Economic Obligations of the Nationalised Industries*. Officials were
worried about the position of several of the nationalised boards
by 1959, but it was already clear that the BTC was in a league
of its own in terms of financial disaster, as had been anticipated
at the Treasury in the wake of the 1955 wages settlement. The
White Paper argued that while the nationalised industries' social
role meant they should not be expected to yield the same rate of
return as private investment, if their prices were too low demand
for their services would be artificially stimulated, thereby increasing their investment requirements. As the industries were failing
to fund their own investments, such demand would restrict the
finance available for profitable private investment and damage
the economy. The implication of all this was greater Treasury
control of nationalised investment and the setting of clear financial targets for the nationalised boards.

It was not so much the extension of the Treasury's power that
boded ill for the railways as the consequences of its attempts
to understand the future demand for transport. The rush to
publish *Proposals for the Railways* in 1956 had prevented Clarke
from examining it beforehand. It was not until June 1957 that he
arranged a survey of long-term transport requirements, covering
the period to 1970. This was just one of several long-term studies Clarke initiated, but as the first transport study of its kind
within Whitehall, it had difficulty in making predictions even
for 1960. The statistics were inadequate: the post-war years were
abnormal and officials were as unsure how to estimate the impact

of different investments as they were unsuccessful in seeking a common unit for the measurement of commuting, pleasure motoring and flying. In charting the growth of road freight, for example, the report relied on one survey carried out over a week in 1952 and multiplied the average ton-mileage carried by each class of vehicle by the number of vehicles licensed in that class in each year between 1948 and 1956; there was no information on what the lorries were carrying. The BTC lobbied successfully to have a representative added to the group and to ensure the report backed up its own estimates. Nevertheless, the erosion of Treasury confidence in railway investment had begun. Clarke's deputy, Matthew Stevenson, expressed his dissatisfaction that the vast investment in modernisation would only increase rail freight traffic by 11 per cent and passenger traffic by 7; this, in his view, typified a tendency to treat capital expenditure as the solution to national problems and to ignore cheaper alternatives. The ministry's estimates of demand for road space – exposed as the products of inadequate machinery – were judged to be too low. Most importantly, a tendency developed to see total transport demand as something which could be met 'by any number of combinations of road and rail investment plans': the growth of road transport could be slowed to encourage more traffic onto the railways and maximise the return on their investment – or the rate of investment in rail could be slowed.[135] This spelled trouble for the railways because restricting road transport was always likely to run into political difficulties; the justification for investing in rail depended increasingly on the hope that it would reduce the railways' deficit. Unfortunately faith in this prospect was also fading.

In the early summer of 1958, Clarke, influenced by the financial difficulties of American railways, told Stevenson that 'the evidence points increasingly to the need for cutting down the whole system to what is commercially viable on a basis to charge what the traffic will bear'.[136] This was not government policy, it may not even have been a definite conclusion in Clarke's mind, but it is significant. It illustrates how, quite independently of debates around the viability of individual lines, the consultative procedure and the BTC balance sheet, the Treasury's efforts to manage public investment were heading in the direction of a large-scale closure programme. This process was accelerated by the annual discussion on investment during the summer of 1958. Until this point the Treasury had expected 1964 to be the peak year of spending on railway modernisation, with a significant decline thereafter freeing resources for other ends. Now it turned out that not only had the cost of the plan increased but that this was just the latest estimate of what the BTC thought was desirable to spend by 1970; it did not cover *everything*. The prospect of substantial modernisation spending continuing throughout the 1960s put the Treasury's doubts about its value into a new context. If the BTC's representatives had given the impression that it knew what it was doing, officials might have been less concerned. However, while the Commission said it wanted to spend £210 million in 1960, it could not say what that expenditure would be on until the area boards told it at the end of the year. The BTC's grasp of the revenue position in the regions was no better. The fact that the Commission turned up at the Treasury to discuss investment not only so ill-prepared but so willing to admit to it, says much about the way things had been done in the mid-1950s and how great a change was now underway. There was immediate talk of cutting the Commission's investment programme.

This, then, was the context in which Whitehall received the news in the autumn of 1958 that the Commission's performance was making a nonsense of the path to solvency set out in 1956. Publicly, this was blamed on a temporary slump in coal and minerals traffic, and a *Reappraisal* of the modernisation plan, published in July 1959, simply wrote off 1958 as an aberration and moved the break-even date back a year to 1963, while the 1957 Railway Finances Act was amended to increase the amount of debt the BTC could run up. Watkinson made his usual call for short-term savings, the Commission made its usual attempt to bypass the consultative procedure on the grounds that only closures could achieve them (this time the proposal was to close small stations without consultation) and there was the usual lack of progress as this was rejected by the consultative committees, many of whose members seem by this point to have been demoralised by the increasing workload and by pressure from the public on one side and the government on the other.

The *Reappraisal* referred to a possible reduction of another 1,800 route miles and 1,000 passenger and goods stations by 1963. If this was the writing on the wall for many lines, much larger writing was on the wall at the Treasury. Keen observers would have noticed that the *Reappraisal* was published without government endorsement. The truth was that it had destroyed any credibility the BTC had left in Whitehall. Remembering 1956, the Treasury made a determined effort to investigate the BTC's position itself, and Watkinson was only able to assert his department's independence because of a series of personnel changes, in particular the arrival of James Dunnett as deputy secretary in preparation for his replacing Gilmour Jenkins as permanent secretary in April 1959. Dunnett's arrival signalled a change in the ministry's attitude which, in the words of one of the officials he brought in, had been 'pretty fuddy-duddy' under Gilmour Jenkins, when the ministry had tended to make

> a basic assumption that the railways were the railways were the railways ... the whole attitude of the ministry was to back up the railways ... no one had really appreciated the vast expansion of road traffic ... it's easy to think now 'they must have been blind', but it wasn't quite like that at the time... [One] should not underestimate the difficulty of turning a government department round ... the inherited attitudes just go on and [are] passed on from the seniors down to the juniors.[137]

Dunnett ordered a study of future transport needs to see just how large a railway system was actually needed. The new mood at the ministry meant that senior officials were more receptive to the doubts its statistician, Kenneth Glover, had been voicing about the railways' prospects for years (including during the 1957 study). By the end of January 1959, Glover had produced a paper based on three different sets of assumptions about the economy and the railways' performance, which concluded that 'there is no prospect of profitable employment for a railway system of the size the *Modernisation Plan* is creating', and estimated an overall loss in 1970 of between £247 million and £432 million.[138]

By the time the *Reappraisal* was published, efforts to rectify the lack of knowledge about freight trends revealed by the 1957 study had undermined the assumptions about rail freight prospects that study had made. Road freight was growing in an almost inverse proportion to rail's decline; the economy was becoming more transport efficient than had been thought (in other words

the growth in demand for transport generated by a 1 per cent
rise in GDP was smaller); coal output would be lower. Now it
appeared that the deterioration in the BTC's position during 1958
was generally in line with traffic trends that had been disguised
in 1956 and 1957 by the effects of the Suez crisis, in particular
through petrol rationing. Investment aimed at maintaining the
railways' share of general freight was beginning to look like 'large
expenditure on a task which may be hopeless and indeed pointless'.[139] Glover's recommendation could have been cut and pasted
into Beeching's report:

> there are wide ranges of activity carried on by the railways which
> do not pay and these activities can now be fairly well identified
> ... cutting out these activities would seem to be a much more
> promising line of approach to railway solvency than further heavy
> investment. It is certainly difficult to see why the Commission
> should make any effort to increase merchandise and stopping
> passenger traffic in the way that the plan contemplates.[140]

By the end of the year these dire warnings had been reinforced
by the results of further Treasury work on the economic case for
road building. This argued that as car ownership would inevitably grow and as the trend of traffic appeared to be from rail to
road, demands for spending on motorways could not be ignored
and, if met, would call into question the competitiveness of the
railways. Although officials still wanted a viable system of
comparing road and rail investment and were unconvinced by
the Road Research Laboratory's methods for justifying road
schemes, Whitehall opinion was now increasingly moving
towards the view that investment in the railways should enable

them to do 'as economically as possible what only they can do and no more', and that 'no railway line outside the main network should be kept open where public road transport can do the job'.[141]

Having published the *Reappraisal* as quietly as it could, the Cabinet asked officials to study it in detail. The ministry's estimate that the BTC would earn a working surplus of £35–50 million in 1963, produced two days before the 1959 general election, seems optimistic today, given the BRB's operating loss of over £80 million in 1963, but the important point was that future surpluses would be too low to meet the increase in the BTC's expenses as the interest-free period under the 1957 Railway Finances Act began to expire. This was a crucial point because the government had no legal power to subsidise the BTC, only to lend it money. If Dunnett, as the person responsible to the House of Commons Public Accounts Committee, could not say he believed the loans would be replayed, he was left in a 'most unsatisfactory' position.[142] In early 1960 the Treasury, further discouraged by its questioning of the Commission on its investment programme the previous autumn, endorsed the ministry's findings and added a warning that the financial implications of Guillebaud's report on pay alone would probably be enough to render the Commission's forecast invalid.

The suspicion that the railways had overestimated the amount of traffic they could win back from the roads and that investment proposals were based on technical, operational or social, rather than financial considerations, was no longer a suspicion, it was a fact. Even the flagship electrification of the Euston to Manchester main line was of questionable value and fears that the Commission was simply spending as much as it could (and the government could be persuaded to part with) were not allayed

Former South Eastern Railway 31065 at Headcorn, preparing to haul the 08.50 to Robertsbridge on the last day of the Kent and East Sussex Railway's passenger service, 2 January 1954. © Ben Brooksbank

The 31065 at Tenterden on the final day. Built in 1896, it worked until 1961 and has since been preserved on the Bluebell Railway. © Ben Brooksbank

Photographer Ben Brooksbank braved a cold and damp morning to attend this early closure. At Tenterden, one of the small band of enthusiasts who accompanied him talks to the driver, while others seek vantage points to record the occasion.

© Ben Brooksbank

In a 'traditional' railway scene that could still be found at rural junctions across Britain in 1954, the branch train waits in the bay platform at Robertsbridge as a Hastings to London train passes.

© Ben Brooksbank

Sixteen years later, and nearly a decade after the final freight service, Northiam station illustrates the typically basic nature of the facilities Colonel Stephens provided.

© Crown, National Archives MT 124/629

Platform 3 at Newport station before and after the arrival of the 16.02 from Freshwater,
Wednesday 12 August 1953. The passengers in the second photograph are waiting
for the 16.10 connection to Sandown. These pictures were part of the council's evidence to
the TUCC inquiry, demonstrating the use by tourists of two of the threatened lines.

Saturday 14 July 1951, the start of the high-summer season: an express from Derby via Melton Constable and the M&GN enters Yarmouth Beach station. © Ben Brooksbank

Bourne station and the Red Hall two years after the closure of the M&GN to passengers. Today the Hall appears unchanged, but there is little to suggest the grass beyond it was ever a station, except the name of a new housing development, Great Northern Gardens. © Ben Brooksbank

Chevening Halt in its final days (1960) and the view today from the bridge that has replaced the one in the earlier picture. The site of the halt is behind and to the right of the modern photographer; the higher of the roads continues under the bridge to obliterate the vantage point of his predecessor. Bottom image © Author collection

Brasted station on the Westerham branch, 1977. In the foreground the M25 takes shape, in the background the English downland it defiles. © Nick Catford

Beeching and Marples – could that be the Wells-next-the-Sea file the minister is holding? © Getty Images

'Like some eleventh commandment' – Dr Beeching presents *Reshaping* to the world, 27 March 1963. © Getty Images

'Their footsteps echoed off tiled walls', Leicester Central in 1967. The lift and one of the passageways are closed. Such disparities of scale between patronage and grand facility could be found on several parts of the network in the post-Beeching era. © Nigel Tout

The abandoned restaurant of Leicester Central station, intended for passengers contemplating Paris, now a ghost of the great age of rail travel, 1967. © Nigel Tout

LEFT Smaller than now but bigger than Beeching: Barbara Castle, Sir Stanley Raymond and the *Network for Development* map.
© Getty Images

BELOW Closed to passengers in 1930 and to freight in 1962, Bridport West Bay station was used as a boatyard and then left to rot. Purchased by the local council, restoration began in 1995. Beyond the coach, the trackbed footpath leads to a bypass.
© Author collection

by the news that it wanted to invest £1,000 million on top of the existing £1,660 million cost of modernisation by 1970. Far from offering a route to solvency, the modernisation programme was producing such a poor return that it seemed more likely to add to the Commission's debts than expunge them. On 4 January 1960 Dunnett signed a memorandum entitled 'The Railway Problem', informing ministers of the urgent need for a new policy on the railways and recommending that 'we will have to approve in detail their capital investment programmes for the future. This will give us control over the parts of the railway system that are to be modernised.'[143] This was a logical response to what the ministry had learned in the preceding twelve months, but it also drew on the desire of the Padmore committee on the national-ised industries to increase ministerial supervision of nationalised industry borrowing in order to ensure a clear distinction between those investments that were socially desirable but unremu-nerative and those that were simply commercial failures. It is impossible to pinpoint the extent to which this was an example of the reform of the BTC being conducted within a new policy framework established for the nationalised sector, rather than that framework being born out of experience of addressing the railways' problems. The two processes informed each other.

Officials recognised that questions were now being raised about what purpose the railways served that could not be answered purely in financial terms. Ministers would have to decide 'whether the railway system ... is to be regarded as a social service, a commercial undertaking or a mixture of both'.[144] The principle of applying cost–benefit techniques to the railways' role in reducing road congestion had been raised in the Treasury and the Padmore committee had recognised that the BTC might require 'a special subsidy related to its uneconomic services which were kept in operation for social needs'; as had ministers.[145] The Padmore committee had also considered whether the lines north of Perth and Dundee should be treated as a separate accounting unit as they were socially necessary but would always lose money. It had reached no conclusion, because the whole question of reorganising railway accounts on a regional basis was being looked at as part of the ongoing debate over the nationalised industries. But the idea had not been ruled out. In August, Dunnett tried unsuccessfully to get an idea of how far the Commission would rationalise the railway system if it did so on a purely commercial basis, the question Beeching was eventually brought in to answer. Dunnett also asked whether there were any particular areas in which railway services could be subsidised and, if so, what amounts might be involved? The Commission agreed to consider studying three areas: Scotland north of Perth; central Wales; and the former Southern Railway lines west of Exeter.

The Commission's response to Dunnett's request was a memorandum, 'Fringe Areas', which reached the ministry in December. Unfortunately, as its treatment of the former Southern Railway lines west of Exeter illustrates, 'Fringe Areas' was a wasted opportunity to make the case for socially necessary railways. The former Southern route headed north-west from Exeter, skirting Dartmoor to run via Okehampton and Tavistock to Plymouth. It threw off various branches on the way to serve Barnstaple and the coastal towns of Ilfracombe, Bideford, Bude and (via Launceston and Wadebridge) Padstow. From Bideford a line ran back inland to Torrington, which was also served by a line from Halwill Junction on the Bude branch. From Wadebridge a short branch served Bodmin (this section, originally opened in 1834, had been acquired by the London and South Western Railway in 1846 but remained isolated from its parent company until the line from Okehampton arrived almost fifty years later). The Atlantic Coast Express, which left Waterloo for Padstow with portions detached en route for most of the above-named destinations, was a favourite of Betjeman's.

Because 'Fringe Areas' attributed losses to areas rather than to services, the existence of (probably profitable) bulk freight traffic on parts of this network was submerged within the overall operating loss (several quarries and clay-pits in the area kept their rail connections long after the passenger services had gone). Equally, the case for providing rail connections to the otherwise remote resorts and towns of reasonable size was surely weakened by the inclusion of the little-used services between Launceston and Wadebridge and Halwill and Torrington. On the latter line – engineered by Colonel Stephens and one of the last railways to open in England – 'a single empty coach ... passed through Hatherleigh each way twice daily, the driver, fireman, guard and signalman being amazed if a passenger was seen'.[146] Most significantly the memorandum ignored the fact that the area was also served by former GWR lines. If there had ever been a need for two railways to Barnstaple or Launceston, the existence of parallel lines between Tavistock and Plymouth more than a decade after nationalisation illustrated the limited extent to which rationalisation had taken place. Rival routes between Exeter and Wadebridge and between Wadebridge and Bodmin merely served as a memorial to the occasional bouts of insanity that afflicted Victorian railway promoters (and the failure of the Western and Southern regions to notice nationalisation!). A schoolboy with a map and a pen could have saved the taxpayer a good deal at any time after nationalisation.

The memorandum's figures took account of impending economies for which 'substantial capital expenditure would of course be required'; but, as central charges were not included in the calculations, the interest on this investment appears to have been ignored. Receipts were broken down by traffic type but expenses were not, so it was impossible to gauge the effect of, say, transferring merchandise traffic to road. The document also admitted that its figures 'do not represent the financial effect which would result from the closure of the lines', which hardly encouraged the ministry to consider seriously whether a grant should be paid for such services.[147] An independent 1963 study of some of the lines in north Devon argued that by continuing to serve small hamlets, the railways were running slow and inconvenient services, thereby losing the long- and medium-distance traffic between the main towns, but there was nothing in 'Fringe Areas' to suggest the Commission had considered how the area might be better served. As a whole the memorandum can only have helped reinforce the suspicion that the Commission's belief in its social obligations concealed waste and complacency.

The Commission's shortcomings were not the only factor at work here. The real bone of contention was not how its debts were to be paid, but its independence. Dunnett wanted a subsidy to be called a subsidy, so that the Ministry of Transport (MoT) could impose greater financial discipline on the Commission. The Commission wanted to avoid a subsidy to preserve its independence, and a grant covering the loss on these lines would make little difference to its overall financial position. In this political battle the issue of social service subsidies fell by the wayside, at least for the time being. Instead, the Commission sought a capital write-off and suggested that the government take over the ownership of track and signalling and rent them back to the Commission. Officials were not interested in the details of the scheme, which they ruled out as a disguised subsidy in January 1960. When, in the same month, ministers raised the question of a general separation of the commercial and social activities of the nationalised industries, they were told the Padmore committee on nationalised industries had examined this and considered it impractical. The Commission had missed an opportunity to provoke a different conclusion, but it had had little incentive to take it.

Even if the Commission had been interested in pursuing social subsidies, would it have made any difference to Melton Constable? Unsurprisingly, the line there from Sheringham did not survive the Beeching Axe, inflicting the limited, if intensely felt, hardship discussed in Chapter 1. Given the small numbers involved it is hard to imagine that any kind of social analysis would have justified keeping it open. By the 1980s only the Sheringham to Cromer line remained, the population of Melton had roughly halved and the heart of the M&GN was reduced to some relics in an industrial estate and a couple of iron brackets from the station incorporated into a bus shelter. Yet … when the main route closed in 1959 a society was formed with the intention of preserving the entire route as a working railway, not a heritage line. Despite the patronage of Major Cadbury, the former CTCC chair, it got nowhere and parts of the route began to be used for road schemes, notably the King's Lynn bypass, for which the route was ideally suited. When the Melton–Sheringham section lost its service the preservationists were ready and today the

Poppy Line between Sheringham and a new station at Holt (the original is under a bypass) is a successful steam-fuelled seaside attraction. In 2010 the level crossing linking the Poppy Line to Network Rail at Sheringham was restored and there is talk of extending at the other end to Melton and Fakenham to join another heritage line, the Mid-Norfolk, and create the Norfolk Orbital Railway (Norwich–Cromer–Melton–Fakenham–Wymondham–Norwich). Some might say this sounds like a bit of a white elephant, but time will tell.

Events at the Treasury in 1957–9 represent a tipping point in the course of transport policy in Great Britain and it was public expenditure policy rather than transport that provided the context. In 1956 and again in 1958, closures had been seen as a way of making economies in response to immediate financial problems. Watkinson had wanted a more rigorous approach, but this was still a response to the deficit. By the end of 1959, however, the argument had begun to shift. The issue was no longer how many lines would have to close to eradicate the deficit, but what the railways were there for and was railway modernisation a sensible use of scarce resources? It wasn't simply that closing lines could save money, but that there seemed no point in a railway system providing stopping-train services or pick-up freight in 1970. The logical implication was a shift away from making the case for individual closures to making the case for individual reprieves; and this change in emphasis can be discerned in the subsequent course of policy. To anyone even vaguely familiar with the economics of transport policy-making today, this chapter probably reads like an account of the stone age and the treatment of demand for transport is hideously over-simplistic. Starting virtually from scratch, Whitehall had little choice but to try to apply logic to a set of unclear circumstances. As one Treasury official complained to Otto Clarke in 1961, the rapid growth of road transport had left Whitehall 'collectively fumbling after a new policy to meet new conditions which threaten to overwhelm existing outlooks'. 'Indeed,' he continued, 'they may already have done so.'[148] Amid the uncertainties, the need for a smaller railway must have appeared reassuringly obvious. In early 1960 senior Whitehall figures were left uncertain, in Sir Thomas Padmore's words, as to 'what size or kind of railway system we ought to be aiming at. But everyone concerned is pretty well convinced that it ought to be smaller, perhaps much smaller, and that a great many unnecessary and uneconomic services ought to be cut out'.[149] Now they needed someone to do it: enter Ernest Marples.

Chapter 7

Westerham, Marples and the M25

'I like my estate as a man might like his garden,' complained one landowner at the prospect of a railway along the Westerham valley in 1876. The line would cut his land in two and he would have to 'see the smoke of the engine from the time it starts from Dunton Green till it gets to Westerham'. What would the poor man say if he could see what the branch's historian, David Gould, calls 'the concrete monstrosity of road interchanges which now befoul the area'?[150] Whatever the merits of the M25 and M26, which meet in the vicinity of the former trackbed, few who are familiar with this part of London's green belt would dispute Gould's judgement. The Westerham Valley Railway, on the other hand, typified the way such lines seemed almost a permanent part of the countryside by the 1950s and the objections to their construction bizarre, outdated nonsense. The nearest steam-operated line to London south of the river, this simple, single-line branch left the former South Eastern main line at Dunton Green just north of Sevenoaks and ran for four miles through what was, even in 1960, the fairly rural downland valley of the Darent River, past the tiny Chevening Halt, near nowhere in particular, and one equally secluded intermediate station – its name, Brasted, picked out in white stone on the ground opposite the single platform. Over streams and through coppices, it continued to a charming, slightly ramshackle terminus not too far from the centre of Westerham. Church spires, oast houses and the grounds of Combe Bank house, with its lines of Lebanon cedars, could be glimpsed through the trees along the track. With its fifty-year-old rolling stock and chatty guard who knew all the regulars, it could have been the model for Titfield.

The guard would undoubtedly have been aware of John Francis Archibald Browne, the sixth Baron Kilmaine, although he probably talked *about* his lordship – a formal type who expected deference – more than he did *to* him. An infrequent user of the line, Lord Kilmaine, resident of Brasted, was nothing if not public spirited. A 'recognised doyen of trust administrators', he played a significant role in preserving the nation's historic churches and mediaeval wall paintings and was a pioneering supporter of industrial archaeology.[151] When, in November 1951, he heard that the branch might close, he felt he ought to do something for those of his neighbours who depended on it daily, and wrote to an old Oxford contact in the Railway Executive in an attempt to verify the rumour 'before making the usual kind of public fuss and mobilising one's MP etc'.[152] Reassured that no such decision had been taken, Kilmaine expressed the hope that in considering the branch the Executive would not simply look at its economics. He warned that there was

a growing feeling abroad that these large nationalised undertakings no longer consider the idea of service to the public as of great importance, but tend more and more to be influenced only by the question of whether a particular activity is remunerative.[153]

He compared the Commission unfavourably to lawyers and doctors, who he believed did not abandon clients or patients simply because they were 'unremunerative' but cross-subsidised them from earnings elsewhere for 'the goodwill'.

Westerham was on the branch line committee's list for investigation in 1951 and maintenance was reduced to a minimum in anticipation of the result; but rather than close it, the Southern Region decided in early 1955 to cut weekday trains outside the peaks and reduce the weekend service. Similar steps had been taken in the early 1930s in response to bus competition; a familiar tale of road services running through the centre of the villages and taking passengers directly to Sevenoaks, where most of them wanted to go. However, electrification of the main line had improved traffic, or at least expectations of it, sufficiently for the cuts to be reversed before the war. A second investigation of the branch's performance was already underway towards the end of 1956, when the civil engineering department warned that the £16,000 backlog of maintenance would have to be addressed in 1957 or the service might cease abruptly. Typifying the railways' mid-decade reluctance to close lines, the money was spent despite expectations that the case for closure would be a strong one. By the end of the decade, Westerham typified the BTC's treatment of branch lines. Losses had been reduced but not eradicated, nothing had been done to modernise it and there was no prospect that if it were modernised there would be any significant upturn in its fortunes.

When the BTC proposed complete closure in April 1960, it was because the times had changed, as discussed in the previous chapter, not the circumstances of the line. The 1955 investigation compared gross passenger receipts of £13,254 against a saving of

£20,622 if the line was closed. It concluded that, as around £8,000 a year could be saved by the service reductions described above with little effect on gross receipts, the branch would just about pay for itself. However, the line's gross receipts included the full fares paid by passengers travelling on to London, which the overwhelming majority did. The branch was only paying for itself if one assumed these passengers would abandon rail travel entirely were it to close and all of the income from each journey was entirely lost to the railway. If, however, they simply got the bus to Sevenoaks and caught the London train there, only a small proportion of gross receipts would be lost on closure and on this assumption the line was nowhere near to paying for itself. It was this argument that prevailed in 1960, when the region calculated that complete closure would produce a £9,000 annual saving (plus £2,740 a year on renewals) even after a subsidy of £6,500 to London Transport for an improved bus service. The line was being used by fewer than 150 people a day during the week and 100 a day on summer weekends; even the busiest trains averaged fewer than forty passengers. Yet it was immediately clear that this would be a difficult case and its glacial progress through the consultative machinery was a source of great frustration at Waterloo. A Westerham Branch Railway Passengers Association was formed to coordinate opposition, with support from the county council, Sevenoaks council and the relevant parishes. The initial TUCC hearing was postponed so that the railways could provide more detailed figures requested by the association and when the hearing did take place, in July 1960, all it produced was a request for more figures and a further postponement until October. As the objectors generally (and understandably) accepted the argument that commuters would still use rail for the major part of their journey, debate revolved around the adequacy of the alternative bus service, congestion on the A25 and whether the 30 to 55 minutes added to daily travelling times represented unacceptable hardship given the savings involved. Using the figures the railways supplied, the objectors put forward an apparently credible case for saving almost as much by getting rid of station staff and signalling and operating a diesel railcar service.

By the time the TUCC met again in October, the Southern Region had produced detailed responses to a list of questions posed by the objectors. The committee, convinced by these answers, approved closure by nine votes to one. However, the CTCC sent the case back the following month on a technicality. The objectors had not been given a chance to challenge the region's answers, contrary – so Sevenoaks council argued – to the practice of 'any normal Court or Tribunal'.[154] The TUCC set up a working party which went over the ground yet again and endorsed the railways' case for savings of nearly £9,000 a year from closure against a loss on a rail-bus service of £15–17,000 a year and capital costs of about £32,000. However, when the committee received this view in February 1961, a significantly different set of members attended and, although only one of them actually changed their vote, it rejected the proposal on the grounds that it would cause undue hardship. Despite lobbying from the Commission and a certain amount of wavering, the CTCC endorsed the finding in May, perhaps influenced by the fact that one of its number, Sir Charles Pym, was a user of the line and testified to the inadequacies of the A25.

Behind the scenes, the region had begun making preparations for defeat even before the first TUCC hearing by investigating the finances of operating diesel or electric services on the branch. But attitudes were hardening at Waterloo. At the end of 1960, having established electrification as the most practical option if the branch could not be closed, Hopkins resolved that his request for BTC authorisation of the necessary expenditure would be 'calculated to bring to a head at the highest level the BTC, and possibly the ministry, attitude towards a planned branch line closing that is clearly justified on grounds of economics but that may go against us on social grounds'.[155] At least one senior railwayman thought nothing should be done to prepare for electrification and 'if we find the decision goes against us and after withdrawing steam in June 1962 we cannot maintain the service, it is just too bad'.[156] The frustration of men who had spent their lives running railways only to find that they were not allowed to do so because everyone from the minister to the man on the 18.07 from Dunton Green thought they could make a better job of it was growing. When the CTCC's recommendation reached the ministry, attitudes to closure did indeed come to a head. The protestors must have felt satisfied with their efforts – it had been a model campaign. But the Commission, at the region's prompting, was lobbying the ministry to overrule the CTCC and authorise closure. The objectors had reckoned without what Anthony Sampson called 'the disturbing phenomenon of Ernest Marples'.[157]

Appointed as Watkinson's successor as Minister of Transport after the Conservatives' victory in the 1959 general election,[†] Marples has been seen as 'opposed to railways' more or less from the moment he took office and is still subject to accusations that he was part of 'a conspiracy between ministers, civil

---

†   Civil aviation was transferred to a new Ministry of Aviation.

servants and the road lobby to shift investment from rail to road and disinvest in a substantial proportion of the rail network'.[158] David Henshaw's *Great Railway Conspiracy* describes Marples as 'a Minister of Transport who was not only road-biased, but a successful road-engineering contractor into the bargain', who used the railways' financial plight as 'an opportunity to humble' them.[159] Marples's announcement – on 2 August, just before Parliament rose for the summer – that he had approved closure of the Westerham branch has long provided grist to these mills. The minister's unprecedented rejection of a CTCC recommendation was greeted with such outrage that he was obliged to justify it in detail to Parliament when it resumed in October; not that there was any danger of the debate changing his mind. His speech emphasised the cost of the line to the taxpayer (who met 88 per cent of the costs versus the 12 per cent covered by fares) and dismissed his critics with a backhanded compliment:

> They have marshalled their forces with great tenacity. In fact they presented a petition signed by 2,400 people – an impressive number. Alas, only 167 people use the line regularly. I should like to get a petition signed by 167 people with 2,400 travelling on the railway.[160]

What could better illustrate Marples's central role in the conspiracy to destroy Britain's railways at the behest of the road lobby than his overturning of the established procedure to close a line that stood in the way of the M25?

The suggestion that Marples had acted unconstitutionally in rejecting the consultative committees' recommendation, although technically wrong, both typified and fuelled perceptions of

Marples as a man who had the ability 'to locate a single objective and to get there, never mind how', a doer rather than a talker or a thinker.[161] To Sampson, Marples, with his air-conditioned home full of 'gadgets', was:

an unusual British minister, much more typical of North America or Germany, and almost unique in the upper reaches of Conservatives ... a self-made tycoon with no political connections and a passionate interest in business which distinguishes him from the rest of the Cabinet. He sees himself less as a politician than a technician, devoted to efficiency ... first and last a businessman ... he doesn't even pretend to be an amateur. [162]

This was a vision of himself that Marples appears to have thoroughly bought into; he liked to tell Macmillan that 'a time of crisis is a time of opportunity' or 'the crucial point is that on all fronts we must retain the initiative and keep moving all the time'.[163] The son of a socialist foreman, since leaving school at fifteen, Marples had risen through accountancy and property development to run his own company. During the war, he went from private to captain; after it, he began climbing the political ladder. Conservative MP by 1945 and parliamentary secretary to Macmillan at the Ministry of Housing by 1951, he played an essential role in the mission that was the making of the future Prime Minister's career: fulfilling the party's ambitious pledge on house building. Ernie wasn't Eden's type, but in 1957 Macmillan made him Postmaster General – Marples launched premium bonds, reorganised telephone exchanges and introduced the postcode. It was no coincidence that when the cartoonist Vicky caricatured Macmillan's Cabinet as a football team, Marples was

the centre-forward.[164] He was the very model of a modern Tory
minister, except… Except that what appeared to some as refresh-
ingly modern and dynamic struck others as cheap and corrupt, a
problem Harold Wilson would also encounter.

Marples gave the impression of running the MoT with little
concern for Parliament. He offended Brian Robertson with a
dinner party performance the General found disgusting, was
unable to conceal their subsequent antipathy and upset the
rail industry by the tone of an anecdote he told at the 1960
Conservative conference about a crane he had once had moved
by train, some part of which the railways had lost. His relationship with the road lobby was hardly perfect either, provoking a
split in the Roads Campaign Council in 1963. He demonstrated
a consistent carelessness towards rules that impinged on his
personal convenience, which appears to have stemmed from a
reckless enjoyment of flirting with political danger almost for the
hell of it. Rumours of an exotic private life abounded among his
colleagues and nearly brought him down when, in the summer
of 1963, Lord Denning was asked to report into any possible
security implications arising out of the Profumo affair, which
had seen the Secretary of State for War resign after sharing a
girlfriend with a Russian diplomat. Denning warned Macmillan
that his investigations had identified an important minister
whose liaison with a prostitute involved practices that put him at
risk of blackmail. Thanks to Richard Lamb's *The Macmillan Years*,
we can be certain he was referring to Marples; but a combination
of Denning's old-England discretion and Marples's new-English
cunning kept his name out of the report. Marples later claimed
that he arrived at a meeting with Denning to find a prostitute
he knew present. Aware that Denning was not allowed to delve

too far into the past, he greeted her warmly, saying 'it must be nearly ten years since we last met'. Pointedly, Denning's report stated that he would 'normally regard ... perverted practices with a prostitute as creating a security risk, at any rate if it was of recent date'. After Macmillan's departure, Marples fell foul of the Cabinet Secretary over an attempt to import wine from his French vineyard, to which he fled suddenly in 1974 to avoid a crippling tax bill and a couple of lawsuits, one of which related to his thoroughly unedifying activities as a landlord. When tracked down by the *Daily Mirror*'s Richard Stott he was driving while disqualified and waving a resident's permit which he pretended was a Monaco licence. Questioned about his departure from Britain, he told Stott that the man from the Inland Revenue 'was a socialist ... there was nothing I could do, so I said "Fuck 'em, if that's their attitude, I'm off"'.[165]

While these stories emerged after his career as a minister, it was well known at the time that Marples owned some 80 per cent of a company, Marples Ridgway, which built roads, among other things. He had resigned as managing director in November 1951, shortly after he became a junior minister, and claimed to have received no payment from the firm since then other than expenses; by 1960, however, his share of the firm had come to be worth something in the region of £350–£400,000. Matters came to a head in January 1960 when the *Evening Standard* reported that Marples Ridgway had won the contract for the Hammersmith Flyover. The potential embarrassment was increased by the fact that a lower tender from another firm had been rejected (for the entirely proper reason that it had not matched the specifications for the job). The tender was in fact handled by the London County Council, not the ministry, although MoT engineers endorsed the council's decision. Marples had begun arranging to sell his share of the firm in October 1959, but he initially arranged to do so in a way that left him open to the charge that Ridgway was acting as an agent to ensure Marples could buy back the shares when he left office (giving Marples an incentive to see the firm do well). This was prevented by the Attorney General and, having sold his shares, Marples was careful to ensure that any contracts awarded by the ministry to his old firm were approved by other ministers. Given that Marples had no inherited wealth to fall back on if he lost office, it was perhaps an understandable error of judgement. It was a significant one, however. Once he became Minister of Transport, the firm's involvement in road building was clearly in breach of the rule that ministers must not allow a conflict of interest to arise or *appear to arise* between their official and private work, and whether or not he actually got away with this (he allegedly sold his shares to a company owned by his wife) he certainly tried to.

Marples combined a flair for publicity, a desire to be seen – and to see himself – as a dynamic man of action and an apparent desire to flirt with political disaster so effectively that it was all too easy to believe not only that he was the driving force behind an anti-rail policy, but that his motive might be personal enrichment, either via the benefit to Marples Ridgway of a pro-road transport policy, or as the road lobby's man on the inside. Quite apart from the fact that this involves a massive overestimation of the power of ministers of transport, the problem in attributing changes in policy to Marples's personal influence is that policy did not change but developed along lines that had already been set in train under Watkinson. In contrast to Sampson's description of him as a doer rather than a thinker, Dunnett recalled

Marples as being 'a great publicist, and he was interested in new ideas, but he had not much effect as far as the railways were concerned ... he wasn't awfully good at following through ... it's difficult to put your finger on what he actually achieved'.[166]

It is difficult to attribute a decisive influence on policy in the Marples era to the road lobby because the arguments for motorway-building tended to be backed up by the available evidence. There is no question that Marples was an enthusiastic road-builder, but so were his two predecessors. Late in 1954 the ministry had sought approval for an annual road programme of £60 million per annum but had been left with one of £40 million. Throughout 1957, Watkinson, whose 'first priority was obviously that of getting a national road programme moving at any cost', pressed for more road spending.[167] A long-term road-planning group was established that year and by the time Marples arrived its studies had provided considerable support for expanding the programme, which now stood at £60 million a year; the ministry was pressing for £90 million. Preparing a list of topics for consideration by the new government prior to the 1959 general election, Treasury officials expected an expansion of the road programme to be 'the first priority of the next Minister of Transport', whoever it was.[168] When, in December 1959, Marples began pressing the Prime Minister for more roads spending, he was acting on the basis of the ministry's work rather than his own whim. In March 1960 his request for a five-year road programme was referred to a committee of officials under Padmore, which reported in July 1960 that the five-year motorway programme, while desirable in principle, should not be settled until a clearer picture of railway investment had emerged. However, the Cabinet's economic policy committee concluded that expanding the road programme would bring quick economic benefits through reducing congestion and accidents, so the Cabinet gave Marples most of the funds he wanted for 1961–2 and 1962–3. Although the economic case for providing better roads for motorists was weak, the congestion those motorists caused was damaging the economically significant road freight industry, which carried more than half the nation's goods. Even a 10 per cent increase in railway passenger and freight traffic (which seemed unlikely) would reduce road traffic by only 5 per cent on 1959 levels. The case for road building was a combination of the political (responding to motorists' complaints about congestion) and economic (speeding up road freight); the alternative appeared to be watching the roads grind to an unpopular halt. Further support for this policy was provided by the pioneering cost–benefit study of the first section of the M1 published in 1960 and the positive public reaction to this first long stretch of British motorway. It was only when the Greater London Council attempted to carve a swathe through urban London in the late 1960s that opposition to motorways took off.

Pressure from the roads lobby undoubtedly encouraged these developments. Mick Hamer has shown that organisations such as the British Roads Federation made great efforts during the 1950s to encourage motorway building and the BRF's individual components certainly carried weight with officials. The Road Haulage Association had a good relationship with the road transport division of the ministry, which ensured that when Marples established a Special Advisory Group to investigate the BTC in 1960 the RHA had an opportunity to give evidence to it. The RHA feared that the group would recommend restrictions on road transport to benefit the railways, which it felt enjoyed widespread public sympathy. It complained that taxes paid by hauliers were being used to subsidise their chief competitor, which was also cross-subsidising freight services to undercut them by carrying traffic at less than cost price, an allegation it was able to support with examples. At a meeting with Marples in March 1960, RHA representatives called for a study of 'true comparative costs as between road and rail' in the clear belief that such a study would support the case for allowing road haulage to grow and reducing rail investment.[169] Rather than conspiring to undermine the railways through some clandestine deal, the RHA was confident of its members' ability to win traffic from them through fair competition.

Similarly, the Society of Motor Manufacturers and Traders (SMMT) and representatives of motor industry unions successfully lobbied the Treasury to set up a study on the potential growth of the motor car industry and its economic implications in 1959, which the SMMT hoped would lead to a greater appreciation of the motor industry's importance and consequently to more account being taken in Whitehall and Westminster of its needs. The committee fulfilled the SMMT's hopes in as much as it recognised that:

> the progress of the motor industry is clearly a matter of very great interest to the government both because of its economic importance and its physical and social effects. Through the investment which it has recently agreed to undertake in areas of local unemployment it has now become an important instrument of the government's employment policy. It forms a valuable source of revenue.[170]

Should we take this conclusion as indicative of the pernicious influence of the road lobby on transport policy? Clearly the

SMMT had its own agenda, but so too did the Treasury, which
had hoped to use the study to consider whether or not the industry's growth should be slowed in response to the social costs of
increasing car traffic. That this was not the outcome was partly
a result of the ministry's inability to calculate what the social
costs were. The overwhelming factor, however, was the political
impossibility of restricting road traffic in the early 1960s. Any
party committed to such a policy risked losing the votes of the
750,000 working in the industry, existing motorists and those
affluent workers saving for their first car, the purchase of which
fuelled 'a feeling of modernity and adventure that would never
be won so easily again' in Booker's view.[171]

While the railway industry's decline seemed fairly obvious in
1960, the systemic difficulties the UK motor-car industry was in
fact suffering did not become apparent until the 1970s. Hamer
makes a reasonable case for the view that the lobby influenced the
pattern of motorways and the order of priorities within the roads
programme, but he does not show that it achieved an unwar-
ranted diversion of funds away from rail towards road building
and his suggestion that 'there is scant evidence of any public
concern' over the inadequacies of Britain's roads is unconvincing.[172]
By 1959 there was a cross-party consensus on the need for new
roads and the 'pathetic inadequacy' of the road system was clear
enough for Michael Robbins to comment on it in his 1962 history
of *The Railway Age*.[173] Even the left-of-centre think tank, Political
and Economic Planning, while critical of aspects of government
transport policy, accepted that investment in road transport was
long overdue and should include motorways at some point. Less
thoughtful critics attacked Marples's perceived failure to improve
road conditions with a campaign of car stickers that read 'Marples

Must Go', while official attempts to tackle urban congestion by introducing parking meters led one motorist to saw a meter off its stand in north London and hurl it through the front window of the minister's west London home. While it is true that the road lobby called for increased road building – and road building did increase – one has to ask whether, had people not wanted cars, wanted to use them and then complained about the state of the road network, the lobby would have got anywhere? Indeed, given that the Attlee government had announced a ten-year plan to build 800 miles of motorway in 1946, that Britain's first motorway did not open until December 1958, that by the time *Reshaping* was published only 194 miles were open and that before 1960 the ministry consistently underestimated future traffic levels, the lobby's efforts do not seem to have been an unqualified success.

The decision to apply the brake to the Commission's investment programme just as it got going also owed little to Marples or the road lobby. The decision was prompted by the 'Railway Problem' memorandum Dunnett sent Marples at the start of 1960. Dunnett's paper reflected five developments: the impending report of the Guillebaud inquiry into railway wages and its effect on the deficit; the collapse of official confidence in the Commission's ability to spend wisely; the implications of the Treasury's investigation into the likely future demand for transport; the need to find a legal way of subsidising the BTC; and the Padmore committee's recommendations on the nationalised industries. When Macmillan returned from his 'wind of change' tour of Africa to 'a great log-jam of problems', he saw the solution to this one in terms of a reorganisation of the BTC, bringing in new men to oversee a new plan and persuading the unions to accept these measures, and a smaller railway industry, in return for the government's acceptance in principle of the Guillebaud Report.[174] In a statement to Parliament on 10 March 1960 he stressed the need for the unions and the public to accept the remodelling of the industry and of the modernisation programme to 'a size and pattern suited to modern conditions and prospects'.[175] This statement is the fulcrum of the public face of railway policy, the point at which the dream of the *Modernisation Plan* began to become the nightmare, or at least the reality, embodied in the *Beeching Report*, but it owed little if anything to Marples. The following month the appointment was announced of a Special Advisory Group (SAG) to examine the Commission and advise how to put Macmillan's statement into practice.[†] The idea of getting outside experts to advise on how to apply the new policy on nationalised industries to the railways had been raised by the Padmore committee in June 1959 and Watkinson had considered asking an industrialist, a chartered accountant and the head of Canadian Pacific Railways to consider the reappraisal. The SAG's chairman, Sir Ivan Stedeford, also the chairman of Tube Investments, suggested Frank Kearton of Courtaulds and Sir Frank Ewart Smith of ICI as other members. The Treasury recruited Henry Benson, an accountant from Cooper Brothers who Dunnett believed was interested in replacing Robertson. Two civil servants, Sir David Serpell and Matthew Stevenson of the Treasury, were also appointed to the group. The introduction

---

† At the same time the House of Commons Select Committee on Nationalised Industries cross-examined the ministry and the Commission for its own report on the railways. This increased the pressure on both and its recommendations required a White Paper containing the government's response, but it had little if any direct impact on policy-making. A railway strike was averted in February by an interim award and Guillebaud's recommendations were largely implemented under an agreement reached in June, the ultimate cost of which was over £40 million. The problem of how to continue funding the BTC was eventually solved by including the sums as spending rather than lending in the 1960 Budget.

to the railway industry of its most controversial figure was an afterthought – Ewart Smith was unavailable, but recommended ICI's Technical Director, Dr Richard Beeching. A physicist by training, Beeching had worked for Ewart Smith at the wartime Ministry of Supply. Impressed by Beeching's analytical mind, his former boss recruited him to ICI where he gained hands-on experience in how to manage and improve business efficiency. He was successful, but had not yet risen to prominence. Unlike most of the upper echelons of the BTC since nationalisation, he was just coming into his prime. Between June and October 1960, the SAG produced a series of recommendations which formed the basis of a White Paper entitled *Reorganisation of the Nationalised Transport Undertakings*, published in December 1960 (these are discussed in more detail in the following chapter). This was followed by the Transport Act 1962 which wrote off much of the railways' debt and created a strong central British Railways Board (BRB) to run the industry, hiving off the other parts of the BTC to separate boards. The contributions of Beeching and Benson had convinced officials that solving the railways' problems required 'someone of the stature and width of mind of Dr Beeching relying on the accountancy expertise possessed by Mr Benson'.[176] They had to do without Benson, but Beeching joined the BTC in March 1961, becoming chairman in June with a salary of £24,000 (Robertson had received £10,000). This figure caused a storm Marples and Macmillan were willing to weather, but it fuelled suspicions that Beeching had been paid to implement Marples's anti-rail agenda.

While the SAG made important recommendations on the abolition of many of the commercial restrictions hampering the railways and on achieving a closer relationship between costs and charges in setting freight rates, its proposals on productivity amounted, to a large extent, to a call for further studies and greater effort. A programme of closures therefore represented the most tangible way of reducing losses in the short term. An updated BTC modernisation plan covering 1961–4, produced in December 1960, indicated an increase in both the number of proposals and their complexity.[†] The ministry appreciated that the pace of the process 'was limited not by lack of knowledge as to how far the railway system should in the long run contract, but by the political difficulties involved in any contraction'.[177] Therefore, by the time the Commission, now under Beeching's leadership, sought ministerial support in its fight with the Westerham Branch Railway Passengers Association in June 1961, officials were already working to ensure that the Transport Bill would reduce the role of the consultative committees in order to speed things up and quieten them down. While officials realised that it would be politically impossible to free the railways entirely from the consultative process as far as passenger services were concerned, the 1962 Transport Act left the BRB free to withdraw freight services without consulting anyone, downgraded the CTCC to a supervisory body monitoring the work of the TUCCs and reduced the latter's role to an assessment of the hardship a closure would cause and the means by which it might be alleviated. This would then be reported to the minister, who would consider all the relevant factors before consenting to or refusing closure. He could also attach conditions to his

---

[†]   It referred to a possible 2,554 route miles of passenger closures to be *considered* by the commission. This was a significant increase on the 1959 *Reappraisal*'s reference to the *possible* closure of 1,800 route miles (including some freight-only closures), but still only half of the *Beeching Report*'s concrete proposals

consent; for example, that an alternative bus service must be provided and subsidised by the BRB. As it would now be for the minister to weigh hardship against savings, there would be no need for the committees or objectors to be given any figures, nor would there be any need for the committees to take evidence on anything other than hardship and its remedies. The most controversial aspects of the whole process could simply be bypassed. That, at least, was the intention behind the Act.

This was not simply a question of political expediency. During the SAG's discussions Beeching had argued that the government rather than the BTC should be responsible for deciding whether or not to retain loss-making lines for social reasons. The Select Committee on Nationalised Industries made a similar point in its report on the railways in 1960. The White Paper, *The Financial and Economic Obligations of the Nationalised Industries*, published in April 1961, established the principle that nationalised boards should be given clear financial targets and ministers should take responsibility for interventions which interfered with the boards' ability to meet those targets. The single most important element of the 1962 Transport Act was the division of responsibility between the BRB and the minister. The railways were now legally obliged to break even 'at the earliest possible date' before 1 January 1969 and relieved of any social obligations that might cloud their judgement. It was now the minister's job to temper the drive to solvency should the social cost prove too great. This marked the shift from the concept of nationalised transport as a coordinated comprehensive service to a publicly owned business (although neither the BTC nor the BRB represented an absolute fulfilment of these concepts). It was ministerial interventions over pay and charges that Padmore and his colleagues had in mind when devising policy, rather than the social obligations represented by unremunerative rail services. However, as far as it applied to closure decisions, this change absolves Beeching from the suggestion that he ignored the social consequences of closures out of callousness; it was his job to take a narrower view and if social costs *were* ignored then it was the government that was to blame.

This division of responsibility – the very one Watkinson had shied away from in 1956 – was to prove rather more attractive to the Cabinet in theory than in practice. For Marples, however, it was precisely the challenge he loved and it was in exercising this responsibility that he made his name. His perverse combination of dynamic self-image, desire for attention and attraction to the risk of disapproval meant presenting the closure programme as an exercise in dramatic modernisation was a role he was born to play. In this respect Westerham served as a template for his handling of the recommendations in the *Beeching Report*. Closing the line 'was my personal decision', he told the House of Commons. 'I take full responsibility for it and [objectors to the closure] must not blame anybody else.' Claiming to have visited the line incognito to see how few people used it, Marples justified his decision in typically modernising terms:

I know that certain people will be inconvenienced. I know that there is a sentimental attachment to these two coaches which chug along on a Sunday with a little steam engine drawing them, with more people in the engine than in the train. I know that it is a nice sight to see this train coming along a track with grass sprouting up between the lines, but I think that it does not play a part in this third quarter of the twentieth century.[178]

This must have seemed a typically dynamic personal intervention given that both announcement and debate preceded
publication of the Transport Bill with its new closure procedure.
The more prosaic reality was that to have accepted the CTCC
recommendation and reprieved the service irrespective of its
financial implications would have been at odds with the new
policy. It would also have meant rejecting a request from a body
chaired by Marples's own appointee and setting an awkward
precedent by defining the consequences of this closure as hardship rather than mere inconvenience. Explaining the decision to
the CTCC, Dunnett argued that while the operating loss on a
diesel service might be little different from the cost of subsidising additional bus services, the investment involved would be far
greater. If Westerham had been the only branch line in Britain
this might not have mattered, but the ministry was not about to
set a precedent that could derail the whole closure programme
and which would be at odds with its conclusions about
rail investment.

Not everyone shared Marples's view of what did and did
not belong in the third quarter of the twentieth century. In
Westerham, a plan was formed to run the line using two former
GWR railcars for commuters and steam trains at the weekend
under the auspices of the Westerham Valley Railway Association.
The Association combined a practical appreciation of the wider
economic benefits of maintaining an area's rail links with an
echo of Squire Chesterford's branch line ideology. In an appeal
for members headed 'Growth and not decay', it argued that 'a
railway line acts as a magnet and the reverse is a truism … a railway line creates roots and traditions, whereas a road – especially
a bypass, has the opposite effect'.[179] The report of a railway official

who attended a meeting at Westerham in April 1962 provides a snapshot of those involved:

> officers of the Association [and] the chairmen of the Westerham and Chipstead parish councils were on the platform, together with certain other persons representing various Preservation Organisations... The local press were represented together with the *Sunday Express*. The hall was well-filled – about 150 people all told – mostly teenage railway enthusiasts, together with a smattering of older men and what were obviously housewives. So far as I could ascertain only one commuter was actually present.[180]

If there was a chance of the plan succeeding, it rested on the Association being able to get the new service up and running quickly, before commuters made alternative arrangements – but this proved impossible. The BTC and the ministry entered into discussions with the WVRA, but the prospect of 'serious services [operated by] bands of enthusiastic amateurs' were the stuff of officials' nightmares; not because they were afraid the amateurs might succeed, but because they feared being left with the consequences of failure: an unmaintained railway; an unprovided service; and – disaster – no statutory procedure for dealing with it.[181] The Association was almost certainly being unduly optimistic in anticipating a small profit and was certainly optimistic in hoping to pay a sliding-scale rent linked to the number of passengers transferring to the national network at Dunton Green. It also had a habit of rounding up commuter numbers to 200 and hoped to more than double its membership while increasing fees from 2s 6d to a pound. A copy of the proposal in the region's files has a number of scribbled criticisms and queries, including over the estimate of maintenance costs and discrepancies between wage levels and union rates. The Commission decided in April 1962 that in future it would only transfer lines to preservation societies through outright sale, possibly in response to events in Westerham. The Association continued to lobby for a lease and began looking for the £60–70,000 it would need to buy the railway. In the meantime it leased Westerham and Brasted stations, restoring them and connecting them by telephone for the first time; occasionally a car mounted on a railway truck was driven along the abandoned track. Meanwhile officials had drawn up a set of questions to establish both the safety and the financial stability of the WVRA's proposed operation. Its answers were only partially satisfactory and, before the remaining queries could be dealt with, the Association abandoned its plan to run a commuter service, precipitating the collapse of the whole effort under a wave of tarmac.

Marples was fascinated by the prospect of rebuilding urban Britain to accommodate the motor car and was heavily influenced by Professor Colin Buchanan's 1958 book *Mixed Blessing: The Motor in Britain*. He appointed Buchanan to produce a report, *Traffic in Towns*, published in November 1963, which put forward expensive proposals for reconstructing cities to cope with traffic. That such an approach appealed to Marples the construction magnate is unsurprising, but if he saw profits for his kind in such an approach, he was also genuinely inspired – like so many others – by dreams of a new, concrete Britain. In 1962, as Macmillan tried to develop his ideas on modernising Britain into a theme for the next election, Marples proposed retraining tens of thousands of redundant railwaymen and shipbuilders for two massive construction projects: government acquisition of urban areas (between 100 and 200 acres) for redevelopment and 'the high-quality design and production of living units, such as kitchens and bathrooms'. [182] In October that year, he sent Macmillan a proposal infused with what appears now as an almost tragic enthusiasm for modernity:

> We are on the brink of a new motor age. Traffic will double by the 1970s, treble by the 1980s. Present plans will cope with traffic between towns. But in the towns congestion and stagnation will soon become intolerable – unless we radically step up the scale of our attack... [The *Buchanan Report*] will inevitably show that the problem goes far wider than traffic. The people must come first. They must have environments fit to live in. They need to be saved from accidents, noise and fumes... Most of our old city buildings are ripe for renewal... Whole towns need redevelopment... We need to provide housing for 6 million more people by the end of the century. This is equivalent to six new Birminghams or sixty large new towns... We must arrest the drift of people to the South; the North must be made live and attractive ... What does all this amount to? No less than the rebuilding of most of our urban fabric. There is, of course, a lot going on... But much of it is piecemeal and fortuitous. It requires coordination. And it is on far too small a scale... I am sure we could produce something really worth having by mid-1963... The results could be launched on the public in a major campaign. Buchanan's report would come out as part of the operation. [183]

This was Marples speaking, not his officials, and he hoped to be placed in charge of the project, but nothing came of it as Macmillan's modernisation project focused on short-term goals. Buchanan's appointment and report helped fuel a conflict in transport policy advice between physical planners and economists which was to fester over the following decade. In hindsight, this diverted attention from the need to develop an effective pricing mechanism for road use by raising the false prospect that the car could be physically accommodated. It might appear that this was the real legacy of Marples's predilection for road building, but the Treasury's interest in road pricing had not even begun to address the practical and political difficulties of such a measure in 1959 and the idea received no more encouragement from Barbara Castle than it had from Marples.

It was the physical approach to the car problem that finally finished off the Westerham branch. The fact that the M25 has subsequently been built over most of the route has raised suspicions that it was closed in order to facilitate road building, but in fact the railways division of the ministry had no idea 'there was a line on a plan somewhere' indicating the route of the road, until it began discussing the sale of the trackbed after closure.[184] The South Orbital Road, as the M25 was then called, was originally planned to run along the northern side of the branch and Kent County Council initially argued that closure should be postponed until the road could be opened, in order to minimise the traffic on the A25. Once the line closed, however, the council soon expressed an interest in using its route for the road and, although it agreed to stand aside until the outcome of the WVRA's efforts was clear, it no longer felt bound by this agreement once plans for a commuter service were dropped in 1963. The cost of providing a bridge over the line for the Sevenoaks bypass was the catalyst for the Association's capitulation, but this was only part of the eventual savings. By 1964 the dream of reopening was dead and by the end of the decade the lovingly restored stations had been razed to the ground. Legend has it that the platform of Chevening Halt lies buried in the vicinity of the M25/M26 interchange, waiting for the oil to run out.

The Westerham case illustrates the gulf between objectors and ministry officials by 1960. Objectors started from the view that the existence of a railway line was a good thing and closure was something to be avoided if possible. Therefore, they attached significance to the argument that a loss could be reduced to a negligible level with a bit of effort and investment. However, following on from the developments discussed in the previous chapter, the basic objective behind railway policy was now to reduce investment that did not earn a return. Showing that losses could be reduced – even to zero – was largely a waste of time. Officials were only really likely to be influenced by arguments demonstrating the very assumption objectors made to start with, that closure was a bad thing. This required strong evidence of significant hardship, which was virtually impossible to produce in the case of a line as lightly used as Westerham. The objectors' argument on costs was not accepted by either the ministry or Commission in any case; but even if had been, it was unlikely to make much difference, which helps to explain why the ministry appeared to objectors to want to close lines almost for the sake of it.

There is a certain irony in the fact that while green belt regulations were a factor in closing the line, because they ruled out significant future traffic growth, they did not stop it being submerged beneath a couple of motorways. Perhaps the enthusiasts should have questioned whether a steam railway would attract visitors once the South Orbital ran alongside it, but if their efforts were doomed from the start, the lasting bitterness the case engendered can be heard in the closing paragraphs of the line's history:

> If the story of this small railway seems to have been told in great detail...the refusal by authority to allow the preservation of this line for some slight advantage [in building the motorway] ... must represent one of the worst environmental follies of recent years, and many people must feel that some slight comfort can be taken from an adequate preservation at least in print.[185]

There can be few places where rural England has died more horribly – at least in recent years – than the Darent valley. At one point the future of the very river itself seemed in doubt, so low had its water fallen. Now the tranquillity of Brasted Station in the afterglow of a woodland stroll on a summer's afternoon has been replaced by the incessant roar of the motorway; the wild flower cuttings and silent platform obliterated by concrete and tarmac, strewn with shreds of old tyres – *The Titfield Thunderbolt* remade as a video nasty.

Chapter 8

The nitty gritty: shaping *Reshaping*

On 27 March 1963, Dr Beeching presented the world with the report that would make his name, holding it up for the cameras like some eleventh commandment he had brought down from a technocratic mountain-top. Here was the truth. *The Reshaping of British Railways* was accompanied by a series of maps. Map nine, the one that everyone looked at, showed the lines it proposed to close, while maps one to four showed how little traffic they carried. Others showed the network of bus services that could take the traffic forced off the railways (rather misleadingly, as it gave no indication of their frequency) and the flows of freight that rail could win back. The report itself offered an easy progression from 'The Nature of the Problem' (two pages) through 'Analysis of the Problem' (seven pages) and 'More Detailed Consideration of the Main Groups of Traffic' (thirty-seven pages) to 'Operating and Administrative Economies' (two) 'Reduction in Manpower' (four) and 'Financial Consequences of the Plan' (two). A couple of pages on 'Other Factors' assured the reader that social cost–benefit studies and future development would not make any difference except to suburban services. Sandwiched between over thirty pages detailing the traffic studies Beeching had based the report on and two brief appendices on liner trains and rolling stock reduction, came the section everyone turned to, Appendix Two: thirty-four pages listing the services to be withdrawn and the stations to close. It would have been easy to miss the introductory paragraphs to this section, which warned of a continuing process of reshaping during which additions to the lists would be made.

The Beeching press conference was the culmination of a significant presentational effort, discussed at two Cabinet meetings and overseen by a committee of ministers. It was considered vital to present the report as an exercise in modernisation and to 'avoid giving the impression that the government were concerned primarily with making the railways pay'. Instead, the message must be that 'losses arose from the fact that the system was not related to present needs and the principal objective should be to reshape it'.[186] The press conference was part of a plan that included a statement in the House from Marples, the recruitment of the comedian Tony Hancock to be the acceptable face of Beeching and a specially made film explaining the plan broadcast by Granada Television. The 'surgical' nature of the operation was emphasised. All this came on top of months of statements which made it pretty clear what to expect, at least in terms of rationalisation, stretching back to the publication of two maps showing the density of passenger and freight traffic the previous summer; back, in fact, to Macmillan's statement in March 1960. On the evening after the press conference to launch *Reshaping*, Beeching and Marples dined with their wives at the Café Royal in Piccadilly and posed for pictures to scotch rumours of a rift between them.

Beeching himself was vital to the effort. Writing to *The Times* from Castle Leod in Rothshire, Lord Cromartie compared Beeching to 'a very efficient, very expensive computer, brilliant but completely soulless' (before suggesting that closing the railway north of Inverness would lead to 'the extermination of a people and their way of life').[187] Such criticisms merely served to reinforce Beeching's image of cool, ruthless detachment and the idea that, however unpalatable the harsh facts he presented might be, they appeared equally unarguable. Although endowed with an aura of calm, the antithesis of Marples's tense dynamism, Beeching was, like the minister, of 'New England'. He was a grammar school boy with a first in physics, whose managerial abilities had allowed him to rise 'with apparent effortlessness' through the ranks of ICI. Sampson described him as having a reputation for efficiency, generating confidence, being 'visibly astonished' at the railways' lack of information about their activities and giving the impression 'above all of a striking intellectual honesty'. His doctorate replaced his Christian name and preceded his surname like the man with a red flag who walked in front of early motor cars, proclaiming his modernity and inviting images of 'the dispassionate expertise of a surgeon'. He was 'the antithesis of the old English ideal of the amateur', a point reinforced by the storm over his salary.[188]

The perfect combination of *Reshaping*'s logical progression from problem to solution and Beeching's expert status undoubtedly succeeded in conveying the size of the problem and the reasons for railway closures to the public, as well as establishing the government's modernising credentials. A generally (although by no means universally) positive reception included praise from Labour MP and Transport Salaried Staffs' Association General Secretary Ray Gunter and the ASLEF General Secretary;

Reshaping's presentation was seen as a template for the handling of the *Buchanan Report* later that year. Yet, the effect of this presentational success was undermined by the fact that even when lines had been listed for closure in the report, specific closure proposals still had to be published, considered and reported on by the relevant TUCC and that report and other factors had to be considered by the ministry. The preparation of closure proposals by the BRB took longer than anticipated – as did every aspect of their consideration. As a result, the positive reception the report received had worn off to an extent by the time individual decisions began to be announced in significant numbers from January 1964 – and its reputation has subsequently tarnished further. The case against *Reshaping* is that it ignored the social consequences of closures, examined the railways in isolation from transport as a whole and got the figures wrong. Some have suggested that these were deliberate shortcomings, cooked up as part of the secret agenda developed by the Special Advisory Group (SAG) which led to Beeching's appointment. How valid are these criticisms?

The SAG has achieved a mythical status among the critics of Beeching and Marples, primarily because the recommendations it made to the government remained secret until the publication of the official history of British Railways in 1986 and because Beeching was one of its members. Given these two facts, it does not take a great deal of imagination to conjure up a picture of a secret version of the *Beeching Report*'s closure programme emerging from conspiratorial meetings in some Whitehall bunker. Ironically it was Alf Robens, the Labour MP who was shortly to become chairman of the National Coal Board (NCB), who claimed that the SAG members were appointed to be 'the handmaidens of government policy', but the suspicion that it was a 'Marples Gestapo' set up by the minister 'for the sole purpose of facilitating railway closures' was common and has endured.[189]

Whitehall would probably have kept the recommendations of the SAG secret out of instinct, but the overriding reason for doing so was that the group quickly divided and these divisions quickly became personal. The government did not need outside experts to convince it of the need for a railway closure programme in 1960. What it did need was advice on how best to reorganise the Commission along more effective lines. The SAG was given secret terms of reference designed to steer it towards proposals which would fulfil ministers' desire for greater decentralisation. This was a steer Stedeford and Kearton were happy to take; however, Beeching and Benson felt a strong central board was a necessary step in getting a grip on the railways' finances and cutting the system down. This disagreement was paralleled by a fundamental division over how best to approach the group's task. Beeching and Benson wanted, through a series of studies, to begin by establishing what the railways should be doing. Stedeford, aware that ministers wanted organisational proposals sooner than Beeching's approach would allow, resisted. Robertson and his colleagues learned of these divisions through sympathetic officials at the ministry and saw advantages in good relations with Stedeford. They pursued this objective with such success that Stedeford appeared willing to allow the BTC to review the modernisation programme itself, to the dismay of Beeching, Benson and the two officials. Following a particularly fractious meeting on 13 June 1960, Stedeford threatened to resign. Enlisting Benson's help, Serpell spent most of the following two days persuading him to stay.

The conflict over methodology was solved by creating a new group to examine the future size and shape of the railway system, the Ministerial Group on Modernisation (MGM), but while the SAG made recommendations on finances and commercialisation which influenced the 1962 Transport Act, it was unable to agree on organisation. To the surprise of Serpell and Stevenson, who agreed with Beeching and Benson, ministers proved willing to abandon decentralisation in order to achieve a pragmatic solution to the railway problem. The Regional Railway Boards created under the 1962 Act were subordinate to the BRB, which was directly responsible to Marples. The advantage of this approach (from the government's point of view) was exemplified by Beeching's ability to compel the Scottish Region to put forward major closure cases such as Inverness–Wick–Thurso and Edinburgh–Hawick–Carlisle, which it would not have done on its own initiative (and which it privately invited the Scottish Secretary to direct it to retain in 1963). As far as direct advice on closures was concerned, however, the group offered no surprises. It recommended only that a dated programme of further proposals should be drawn up, repeating what it had been told by some TUCC chairmen 'that the majority of the cases now coming before them for the withdrawal of uneconomic railway services could have been put forward several years earlier ... and that, from their experience there must be a considerable number of similar cases not yet prepared'. It concluded that 'action may have been retarded by a sense of public obligation'.[190]

The SAG's internal divisions have contributed to an impression of Beeching and Benson as hawks to Stedeford and Kearton's doves. In fact, the group quickly and unanimously concluded that the modernisation programme should be fundamentally reviewed and, particularly unimpressed by Sir Reginald Wilson, wanted a senior official appointed to the Commission to take responsibility for finance. Stedeford expressed this view to the Treasury in strong terms:

> Sir Ivan ... felt that if in a private firm shareholders' money had been committed with the recklessness which characterised the inception of some of the projects making up the modernisation scheme those responsible would have been indictable... [I]t almost seemed ... as if the judgement whether or not to start a scheme had depended on the degree of support which it received from the particular technicians or other people in authority in, say, a particular region rather than on any economic justification.[191]

In June the group recommended that modernisation projects that were at an early stage should be halted and no new works begun until a review of the whole programme had been undertaken. The merits of the flagship project of the modernisation programme, electrification of the Euston–Manchester/Liverpool main line, were unclear and it was only restarted in January 1961 to avoid damaging railway morale and the export efforts of the electrical industry and wasting the sums already spent. The financial benefits the Commission expected never materialised. There had been no disagreement over the need for such a review, only the form it should take. The SAG's verdict on the BTC's investment programme was as damning as Whitehall's the year before and the cutting back of modernisation by Marples needs to be seen in this context.

Beeching's desire to begin with a study of transport was in tune with Whitehall's thinking on the need to set clear objectives and to base investment on a picture of transport trends, but it was easier to wish for than accomplish. The position was not helped by the poor relations between the Road Research Laboratory of the Department of Scientific and Industrial Research (DSIR) – generally seen at the time as the centre of official research on transport economics – and the ministry and Treasury. In 1960, when the RRL's economics committee wanted to begin its own study of transport requirements for the next twenty to thirty years, the ministry and Treasury successfully lobbied to keep it off the territory they now wished to occupy. This was unfortunate as the RRL had better links with academics and local authorities than the ministry. Dunnett was well aware of the need for expert advice and of the inadequacy of the ministry's economic, statistical and scientific resources, but recruiting staff to rectify this was not easy and these problems continued to frustrate official attempts to get to grips with issues such as the costs of the growth in road traffic. In the circumstances, Stedeford's reluctance to wait for Beeching's studies was understandable, for these were every bit as methodical as one might expect – and proved completely impossible to conduct.

Beeching had argued that the Transport Acts of 1947 and 1953 had set the railways potentially conflicting objectives, which could only be reconciled through precisely the kind of detailed study of transport as a whole which he was later castigated for failing to conduct as a basis for the *Beeching Report*. He proposed a study of total traffic flows and the railways' share over recent years. This data would then be sub-divided into types of passenger journey (commuting, inter-urban business, inter-urban pleasure, local business, local private, holiday, excursion) and freight classes that took account of distance, size and loadability. In each category of traffic Beeching proposed a study of the merits of rail relative to other forms of transport, previous trends, the likely effect of changes in charges or quality of service, handling costs and the effect of various improvements on costs or quality. These figures would then be applied to estimates of future traffic flows in the country to assess the railways' probable share, given various possible improvements and taking account of likely developments in other forms of transport, to arrive at an indication of what investments would be most likely to bring worthwhile results. In addition, he drew up a list of nineteen points to be answered in relation to each specific project. The MGM attempted to boil all this down to two studies: one of current costs (to show which rail traffics were currently profitable); and one of likely future traffic trends for rail and other transport modes. This was expected to take a year to complete. However, as the preparations began for the detailed work, attention increasingly focused on rail. In particular, the estimates of future traffic were to be based upon a study of existing levels of rail traffic in various categories and estimates of future demand derived from a study of the past relationship between the development of the industries concerned and the levels of the rail traffic they generated. A market research study would then estimate how much of this potential traffic would go by rail given various assumptions on fares and charges.

This approach was almost entirely dictated by the absence of information on non-rail transport, in particular on road costs and future traffic estimates; but it was hampered by the Commission's inability to produce the requisite figures and the impossibility of finding anyone who could undertake a market research study on the factors influencing industry's choice of transport mode (officials ruled out asking the DSIR). There seems also to have been a degree of misunderstanding between Beeching, who was interested in establishing what traffic the railways could and should carry in the future given the right kind of investment, and the ministry, which was still trying to ascertain where the railways were currently losing money and whose officials had reservations about Beeching's cost-based approach, as cost was not necessarily the chief determinant in industry's choice between transport modes. Beeching hoped to proceed using estimates and research but this would have involved an even longer and more complex exercise. The MGM petered out, overtaken by what Sir David Serpell described later as 'the nitty gritty of actually doing things' and Beeching's appointment to the BTC.[192] Beeching introduced a new emphasis on the utilisation of the network, traffic flows and the possibility of winning new profitable traffic at the Commission; but the studies he pursued there, dependent on the data provided by existing work within the BTC and reflecting current conditions rather than predicted trends, were a pale shadow of his original intentions.

In October 1962, the BTC produced a map showing freight flows not travelling by rail that were considered suitable for rail. However, in December, ministry officials were disconcerted to learn that the total of some 90 million tons of such freight was based on 'subjective estimates made by district commercial officers on the basis of their personal experience of the economics of handling traffic by rail and the known characteristics of each group of traffic' and that 'the plans for attracting freight traffic at present passing by other means of transport were a longer-term and more hazardous task than that of cutting down the system to a realistic size and reducing operating costs'.[193] It appeared that no assessment had been made of the capital investment necessary to win this traffic or how charges should be altered to attract it. There were also fundamental problems with some of the new technology upon which the plan relied. Several months after *Reshaping*'s publication the BRB's studies of new handling methods and other factors were still incomplete and the Board could not relate the total savings and earnings under the various headings in *Reshaping* to any specific timescale. The case for closures seemed sound in principle; the case for investment more speculative. *Reshaping*'s estimate of a £20–27 million financial improvement from winning back freight and introducing freightliners were its least convincing aspects.

In the summer of 1961, with Beeching now ensconced at the Commission, Dunnett tried to address the shortcomings that had derailed the MGM by recruiting Sir Robert Hall, the former Chief Economic Adviser to the government, to chair a group supervising the ministry's own study of transport requirements over the next twenty years. Hall was asked 'to consider the questions which this study should be designed to answer, the assumptions on which it should be based and the methods by which the necessary data should be sought'. If this indicates that the ministry was merely at the starting gate, Hall's report a year later represented very limited progress.[194] It identified the problem of allocating investment among rail, urban roads and inter-urban roads as one of two fundamental problems facing the ministry but was unable to find a common yardstick for assessing road and rail investment, which the ministry concluded would have to continue to be assessed separately. As the extent to which rail could attract freight from road would have only a marginal effect on the road programme, rail investment would continue to be judged on its likely rate of return.

The second key issue Hall identified was urban traffic. Although it was the publication of Buchanan's report on *Traffic in Towns*, in November 1963, that highlighted this problem publicly, the Transport and Housing ministries had begun laying the foundations of a joint group on traffic and urban planning in the spring of 1961. Hall's report warned that 'rail transport in the cities which have it is an asset which should not be lightly eroded'.[195] The ministry had already taken this issue up with Beeching and suggested that it might wish to have advance consultation before urban services were proposed for closure. Traffic surveys were being conducted in a number of towns by the time *Reshaping* was published and Beeching was persuaded to omit urban services losing some £25 million a year from the report, over half as much again as the total direct saving from closures. This was a significant acceptance that rail services had a social benefit (although not necessarily a permanent one, as the report indicated further study would take place here). The report acknowledged that suburban services were important in Glasgow, Edinburgh, Newcastle, Manchester, Liverpool, Cardiff, Leeds and Birmingham, and were vital in London, and that social benefit studies and a coordinated approach to urban transport would have a role to play in deciding their future. The Hall and Beeching reports stimulated Treasury officials to begin considering the idea of creating conurbation transport authorities. Nevertheless, Beeching was not prepared to hold back urban proposals indefinitely. He had included a surprisingly large number of services affecting the cities listed above in his closure programme on the grounds that social benefit studies would not show them to be worth keeping, a claim which officials found unconvincing. Beeching also underestimated the railways' potential role in reducing urban congestion in smaller cities, such as Nottingham, where lines have since reopened, Bristol, Exeter and Hull. As far as urban transport was concerned, Beeching's terms of reference had been overtaken by the development of Whitehall thinking by March 1963 and urban closures were to prove one of the major issues of contention between Beeching and the government in 1963–4.

Officials warned ministers that careful consideration would need to be given in these cases, for example by considering all proposals in a given area together. In March 1963 Marples was advised against taking the coordination of urban transport as the theme for a speech in Manchester because his officials had not yet worked out what advice to give him about either the policy or tactics on suburban closures included in *Reshaping*; and by the end of the year ministers were concerned over criticism that the *Buchanan Report* had thrown its policy on urban transport into disarray. Government sensitivity on the issue was reflected in Marples's reluctance to overrule the London TUCC a second time by closing the Woodside–Sanderstead line in south London in December 1963, even though he felt the TUCC's findings on hardship were insubstantial (the line is now part of the Croydon tram system). The concerns which had influenced the preparation of the report continued to affect decisions on urban closures and few had been dealt with by the time of the 1964 general election, although three closures in Bristol had been approved.

The widespread view that the social consequences of railway closures were being ignored is easy to understand, but wrong. As the previous chapter discussed, assessing the wider social and economic case for maintaining a service was the government's problem, not Beeching's. Combined with the limited remit of TUCCs under the 1962 Act and the absence of any provision for subsidising specific services on social grounds, this created the lasting impression that social need was being ignored. Yet, whether or not Beeching really believed that all the closures put forward in *Reshaping* would be approved, it was always anticipated in Whitehall that some lines would survive on social grounds and a number of public statements to this effect had been made prior to the publication of *Reshaping*. In September 1962, Macmillan set out the policy as he understood it in a letter to Marples:

> If the government decides that on social grounds a railway from Inverness to Wick is necessary then ... Dr Beeching will quote a price ... for keeping the line open ... the government will pay this, if it decides to do so, as a social service, but the management of the railway will not be accused of inefficiency or an increase in their deficit made a subject of attack on them on this account.[196]

The Prime Minister made this sound rather simpler than it proved to be but, as the principle was clear enough, why was nothing done to legislate for the payment of subsidies for specific rail services until 1968? The practical difficulties of legislating for and calculating individual subsidies, exacerbated by the BTC's objections, were certainly a factor here. There were concerns, too, that the availability of subsidies would encourage demand for them in every case and make the closure programme harder to implement. Once a subsidy was paid, officials feared, there would be no prospect of ending it or incentive to reduce it through efficiency. Moreover, there was little incentive to legislate for subsidies reflecting the social value of specific services, given that the Treasury would obviously have to cover the railways' general deficit for years to come.

The 1962 Act was not expected to be a final settlement of the railways' finances. The SAG had revealed a horror story of inadequate depreciation provisions, unfunded pension liabilities, dire productivity (the railways earned less than £900 per year per employee) and miserable prospects. Of the railways' supposed value (£1,600 million), it deemed £400 million irretrievably lost, recommended that another £400 million continue as interest-bearing debt and that £800 million be placed in a suspense account (and probably written off eventually). It is a mark of the severity of the railways' problems that their total debt had risen by £450 million by the time the BRB was established. As a result it carried £900 million of interest-bearing debt when it was given the target of breaking even by the end of 1968. Stevenson had been eager to err on the side of caution in writing off railway debts chiefly because he was wary of encouraging other nationalised industries to seek similar relief, but he recognised that the railways had been set 'a Herculean task' and neither he, Macmillan nor the committee of officials from across Whitehall set up to examine *Reshaping* in the summer of 1963 expected the Board to get to 1969 without another review of its finances.[197] The technical and political difficulties of subsidising individual services could wait until then.

The absence of specific subsidies from the 1962 Act did not mean that the social benefits of rail services were simply being ignored. In fact, behind the closed doors of the ministry, the wider implications of closures *were* considered. A division ('Railways B') was created in the ministry under an assistant secretary and two principals devoted entirely to handling closures. The assistant secretary chaired a working party that considered individual closures. This included representatives of various MoT divisions

and other departments, such as the Board of Trade. It received
TUCC reports on hardship, financial information on services
and reports from the ministry's divisional road engineers on what
road improvements might be required if a line closed.[†] Once a
case had been considered here, it passed to another committee
chaired by the parliamentary secretary, which in turn advised the
minister. This was certainly not the equivalent of a rigorous cost–
benefit analysis – for the same reasons that Beeching's report
was not. Sir Christopher Foster has credited the cries for help
emanating from the ministry from the late 1950s with a crucial
role in stimulating interest in the application of cost–benefit
analysis to transport, but there was little experience or expertise
available for the ministry to recruit in what was very much still
a developing science in the early 1960s. The retrospective study
of the M1 conducted by Michael Beesley and others in 1960 was
the first of its kind in Britain; Foster and Beesley's 1963 study of
a proposed new tube line in London (which became the Victoria
Line) was the second; and in 1963 the ministry asked Foster to
carry out a similar study of proposals to electrify the commuter
lines out of King's Cross.

By 1971, when British Rail asked Foster to carry out a cost–
benefit study of two suburban lines in Manchester which had
been listed for closure in the *Beeching Report*, the technique
had only been applied to a handful of lines. Foster concluded
that by reducing road congestion the services provided benefits

---

†   The financial information covered the direct earnings (exclusive of contributory revenue) and
direct expenses (movement costs – the cost of running trains themselves; terminal expenses –
the cost of providing stations – and the track and signalling costs attributed to the service); a
figure representing expenditure on maintenance and renewals over five years (at historic, not
replacement, cost); and estimates of: gross contributory revenue; the revenue lost following
closure; the net financial effect of passenger closure; and the additional saving if freight traffic
was withdrawn.

to those not using them, which outweighed the financial loss incurred by their operation, and that the services should be retained and improved. It would be a mistake, however, to assume that this conclusion could be applied in blanket form to all rail services. In their 1975 work *The Rail Problem*, the economists Richard Pryke and John Dodgson reviewed the six cost–benefit analyses of individual lines carried out in the previous decade and updated them. Both the original studies and their recalculations indicated that the social benefits of rural services tended not to justify the cost of retaining them while those of urban services did. By extrapolating an average social benefit of approximately 2.2p/passenger mile (at 1971 prices), Pryke and Dodgson argued that eighty-nine services and 2,137 miles of passenger routes then open should be closed.[198] This suggests that few lines closed before 1971 would have justified a subsidy on a cost–benefit basis, in particular because many of the urban closures proposed in the *Beeching Report* – those most likely to have been saved by cost–benefit analysis – did not proceed. Whether this judgement is correct or not, the absence of cost–benefit analysis from the consideration of closures within the ministry was a question of practicalities rather than a deliberate omission. In its absence it was left to civil servants to weigh up in each case the figures that the railways offered against the factors that made almost every case a special case – the holiday traffic, the hardship, the bad road, the particular likely investment or development put at risk, the undesirability of leaving a really large area devoid of any railway. This was the minefield Beeching had entered. Whether this process took *sufficient* account of social factors is discussed in more detail in the following two chapters, but it certainly did not ignore it.

The difficulty in establishing the exact costs of rail services and the saving that might be achieved by closing them has been a theme of this book and Beeching did not provide any comprehensive solution to the problem. Painting the big picture proved the easy part. Beeching's studies showed that as a whole, general merchandise freight services' operating costs were nearly double and stopping-train passenger services nearly three times their revenue. In July 1962 Beeching produced his two maps showing that half the rail network carried only 5 per cent of freight traffic and half the network carried 4 per cent of passenger traffic. The passenger and freight halves were not exactly the same, but there was sufficient correlation to mean that 92.5 per cent of all rail traffic travelled on half the network. A third of stations produced 1 per cent of passenger revenue. Translating this simple and effective demonstration of the problem – which was not news to railway managers – into a series of clear cases for individual closures remained a difficult and time-consuming task, which continued to produce disputable figures.

Originally, the BTC had hoped to be able to justify closures through a general demonstration that below a certain density of traffic a line could not break even. This was reflected in the text of *Reshaping*, which set the bar at 10,000 passengers a week (more if there was no freight traffic), a figure widely regarded as too high and too dependent on the assumption that track and signalling costs could not be reduced. The figures used in individual cases were generally worked up in the months following the report's publication. The ministry was told that annual earnings figures for individual lines were calculated by multiplying the results of surveys carried out over one or two weeks, a process hardly beyond question. In fact a variety of methods was used, none without its failings, and often the work was slipshod (as we shall see in the following chapter). Both Richard Hardy and Gerard Fiennes, senior managers at the time, agree that these figures were in some cases vague calculations in support of a general principle that rural railways did not pay. The pressure under which the figures were compiled can be glimpsed in a letter from David McKenna, who had replaced Hopkins as the Southern Region's chief officer, to his senior managers in April 1963:

> Short cut methods must be adopted. There is no need at this stage to go into fine detail because the figures on which we assessed our portion of the plan are evidence in themselves of [its] necessity... I do not therefore want any request for more detailed financial information to hold up submissions to me. ... If and when the Minister wishes to challenge us on financial background there will be adequate time to carry out further inquiries.[199]

Life might have been easier had freight and passenger closures been taken together, as the inclusion of the balance of track and signalling costs could have a dramatic effect on the financial case (for example in the Aberdeen to Fraserburgh and Peterhead case, an annual saving of nearly £60,000 from passenger closures would be increased by £150,000 if freight was withdrawn). However, discussion of the figures of individual cases rather misses the point. *Reshaping* was produced precisely to avoid such discussions, by having a plan.

There had been some uncertainty in Whitehall as how best to launch the closure programme Beeching would inevitably produce, but no one doubted its potential for trouble. Reforming the consultative process was one way of reducing the controversy;

another was to revive the idea of having one big row over national or regional closure plans, a view influenced by 'French experience, where the mere existence of an economic plan had a powerful psychological effect'.[200] The Commission resisted this, even after Beeching became chairman, on the grounds that it would be quicker to publish proposals as soon as they were ready, but to no avail. In June 1962 Serpell had hoped that the overall presentation of the need to reshape the railway system could be provided in the BTC's annual report for 1961, due to be published that month. This would be followed by a press conference at some point the following winter presaging regional plans soon afterwards. But, despite pressure from Beeching, the regions were not ready by October. Just as the positive aspects of Beeching's plans had not been fully worked out when *Reshaping* was published, so the façade of logical analysis disguised the incomplete nature of the closure programme. Like the *Modernisation Plan* before it, *Reshaping* was a statement of intent, the practicalities of which had only partially been established.

The *Beeching Report* was in effect a snapshot, not only of the stage that Beeching's work had reached, but also Whitehall's, a picture created when the slow development of transport planning and railway costing was frozen in time by the need to act before the deficit got any worse. This is evident from the fact that a similar mileage was closed between Beeching's appointment and *Reshaping*'s publication as was closed in the subsequent two years, and several lines which were listed for closure in the report had in fact already been closed by the time it appeared. Its list of closures was only the first of a three-part programme and can be seen as the conclusion of the work begun by the branch line committee in the early 1950s of cutting out the railways' dead wood.

The second stage involved identifying a core network of trunk routes, on which it was hoped investment would be concentrated in the following twenty years. The task of collating information and building predictions took until late 1964 and even then the routes chosen in the report published as *The Development of the Major Railway Trunk Routes* the following January were not a definitive selection. The report identified a core network of 3,000 miles of trunk routes and by August 1965 the final stage of the process, an investigation of the remaining lines outside the trunk network, had identified an 8,000-mile railway network, much of which would carry freight only. Although a network of roughly this size was implied by *Reshaping*, it is *Trunk Routes* which really deserves the title 'Beeching Report'. *Reshaping* may have read convincingly as a technocratic argument, but *Trunk Routes* was much more obviously based on detailed studies and provided convincing justification for its selection of certain routes over others based on estimates of future traffic and the economics of carrying it.

Beeching's approach was criticised on various fronts. His assumptions about bus costs – soon challenged in a long-forgotten piece in *Modern Railways* – his treatment of track and signalling costs, assumptions over the extent of contributory revenue that could be retained, were all debateable. However, while the overarching policy context may have been the Treasury's desire to get public spending under greater control and reduce public investment, both *Trunk Routes* and *Reshaping* grew out of a genuine attempt to address the rail aspects of that problem by considering transport as a whole. The calculations supporting some individual closures may have been slapdash, but the determination to cut out lightly used parts of the network was based on knowledge that they *were* lightly used and ten years' experience of the impossibility of achieving change quickly under the pre-1962 closure procedure. The extent to which Beeching focused on rail in isolation was dictated by the limits of what was possible if the deficit was to be addressed reasonably quickly. Similarly the judgement of social factors was hampered by a lack of expertise, although it is unclear how much difference this actually made. For all the experience and ability that qualified him to lead a nationalised industry, Beeching neither possessed nor had access to the expertise and knowledge necessary to put together the unanswerable analysis which *Reshaping* was presented as being; nor did he have the time. The need for an orchestrated demonstration of the inevitable logic behind the closure programme – indeed the need to publish a 'plan' – arose, at least in part, from the difficulty of presenting an unarguable case for his proposals. In retrospect, this most brutal of modernisations exposes just how in need of modernisation the British state was.

Chapter 9

Wells-next-the-Sea and the general election

It is a funny place, North Norfolk. I once travelled by road from London to Cromer through the blistering heat, blue skies and green verges of a proper English summer's day to find the town completely enveloped in freezing sea fog, every sound muffled, the people huddled in tea rooms, and the end of the pier hidden or possibly not even there. Cromer, like Hunstanton at the other end of the coast, is a typical English resort; love them or not, you can never quite escape the feeling that they are not what they were and they won't be again; perhaps Cromer was always a little grander or perhaps Hunstanton has fallen a little further, having lost its railway. With the exception of Sheringham, a bustling seaside town where the Bittern Line (the Norwich–Cromer–Sheringham service) meets the Poppy Line (the preserved North Norfolk Railway), the small brick and flint villages between Cromer and Hunstanton seem to have forgotten they are by the sea, probably because of the marshes or dunes that lie between them and the largely undeveloped coast. 'Unspoiled' and 'delightful' are the sort of words you find yourself forced to say, unless you consider the influx of second home owners and rat race refugees has spoilt it all. Burnham Market, a 'bijou village' with a stream through its middle, is lovely; lovely like the set of a film about England that hopes to do well in the US, a 21st-century Titfield.[201] Obviously all the cars will have to be moved before shooting actually starts, the boutiques will have to be disguised as a chandler's, a post office and a bank and the inevitable shot of a steam train arriving at the station will have to be filmed up the road at the Poppy Line. The station at Burnham is now an inn offering 'trendy yet stylish' accommodation (it has 'statement wallpaper'), including the chance to sleep in a refurbished Victorian carriage; a step up, one imagines, from the camping coaches available at many seaside stations into the 1960s. Its goods shed is now a five-bedroom house, on the market in the summer of 2012 for £1.6 million.[202]

Wells-next–the-Sea, where the line from Burnham terminated, has a less polished feel. Although the granary that dominates its small harbour is no longer used as a granary, the quay looks as though people might actually use it for landing fish. It has proper old-fashioned seaside holiday shops and there's a campsite. On the outskirts of town is a ramshackle bookshop where you will not be disturbed by unwanted offers of help; the sort of shop in which, just when you feel you have looked at every book in the place, you spot a doorway you had not noticed before and another room full of books just beyond it. You may suddenly be disturbed by a very loud banging you will have to investigate, cautiously. Seeking an explanation (it is a kiln, as the place is also a pottery) you wander out through the back door and it may be only now that you realise you are in an old railway station. Wells-next-the-Sea is my favourite old railway station, the perfect antidote when it seems England has become a sanitised, stylised production of itself; it may well be the perfect bookshop. Wells is also my favourite old station because its closure exemplifies how a policy that is rational, sensible and probably necessary at a general level can be harsh, unreasonable and dishonest in its specifics. Wells also raises the possibility that Dr Beeching helped put Harold Wilson in Downing Street as the first Labour Prime Minister since 1951. It is only a very small possibility, but it is significant because a great deal of effort went into ensuring that railway closures did not put Harold there and the inability of that effort to guarantee success helps to explain why we do not have a very much smaller railway today than we do.

At the time of *Reshaping*'s publication in March 1963, Prime Minister Harold Macmillan hoped to make 'Modernising Britain' or 'Britain in top gear' the main theme of the general election which would probably take place in the spring of 1964 (and which had to be held no later than October).[203] The *Beeching Report* offered an opportunity to show the public that modernisation was not simply a slogan, while modernisation provided a positive context for the report's controversial programme of railway closures. Macmillan's modernisation theme caught the mood of the times, but it was a contrary mood, as the contemporary journalist Samuel Brittan recognised:

> [T]he fashionable belief among Left and Right alike is that if a country is to get moving, it needs not a new financial policy but more fundamental changes in its industrial and business structure... Yet whenever any such structural change is proposed all hell is immediately let loose.[204]

Backing Beeching was central to Macmillan's attempts to present the government as 'full of life and vigour with some new plans'; but it was also a gamble that doing so would win enough electoral support to outweigh the damage the Labour Party – led by the young, dynamic Harold Wilson – could inflict by playing on opposition to closures.[205]

The chances of this gamble paying off were not enhanced when, in October 1963, Macmillan fell ill and resigned the premiership. He was replaced by his Foreign Secretary, the sixty-year-old fourteenth Earl of Home, who immediately renounced his various titles and was elected MP for the vacant (and safe Conservative) seat of Kinross and Western Perthshire as Sir Alec Douglas-Home. If Macmillan had struggled to present himself as a moderniser when compared to Wilson, Douglas-Home did not even struggle. It was 'dull Alec versus smart-alec', as the then young, dynamic satirist David Frost put it on the groundbreaking television show *That Was The Week That Was*. In his survey of post-war British Prime Ministers, Peter Hennessy describes Douglas-Home as virtually 'the final flowering of an admirable breed... Like the last of the steam locomotives which were on their twilight journeys at exactly this time... He was *Mallard*, pulling one last express from King's Cross.'[206] In contrast, Wilson inspired supporters with his promise, in October 1963, to harness the white heat of the technological revolution and, following his subsequent victory, to deliver a hundred days of dynamic action. In opposition, Wilson argued that Beeching's terms of reference should have covered the whole of inland transport, not just the railways, and that 'transport is not a single problem capable of being looked at in isolation. It is part of the wider planning problem – economic planning, social planning, town planning.'[207] Labour's manifesto stressed the new thinking that would make a new Britain, attacked the Victorian nostalgia of Conservative economic policy, offered virility in place of sterility, planning (both national and regional) in place of chaos and, in a section the Treasury described as 'more of an incantation than a set of proposals', it promised a plan for transport and that while regional plans were being worked out major rail closures would be halted.[208] With the Conservatives predicted to lose office at the forthcoming election throughout 1963 and 1964, it was not for nothing that a series of Cabinet committees oversaw the *Beeching Report*'s publication and Marples's handling of closures; nor was it coincidence that once the initial presentation of the report was out of the way, these committees were led by successive party chairmen (Iain Macleod until October 1963, then Lord Blakenham). When ministers first laid eyes on *Reshaping* in February 1963, some, deputy Prime Minister Rab Butler in particular, were tempted to 'reduce the size of the bang by removing some of the explosive', cutting out those proposals which were bound to be rejected on social grounds before the whole plan was made public.[209] A significant factor in the decision not to do so was the fear of being caught and looking weak.

The first and most obvious hurdle to clear was union opposition. This proved much easier than might have been expected. Macmillan had already identified the need to use redundancy payments to mitigate the effects of industrial change and here the railways set an example followed in both public and private sectors and which met the main aim of the National Union of Railwaymen. The NUR's opposition was hampered by the unwillingness of the wider union movement to support action which might jeopardise the election of a Labour government, to which the unions looked for a change of policy. Its general secretary, Sid Greene, was not well suited to leading the type of campaign effective opposition to *Reshaping* would have required. Both sides were helped by the fact that the plan for rationalising railway workshops, launched in 1962, offered a dry run for the closure programme and produced agreements on redundancy that provided a basis for those relating to *Reshaping*. Union anger at the way the workshop proposals had been published without prior consultation brought home to the government the dangers of treating closures in the same way and, dissatisfied with Marples's handling of the issue, Macmillan told him:

> We must not hesitate from the slogan 'Growth means change – innovation and change are all the time necessary', yet we must not let it be thought that so far as men and women are concerned that they are to be treated in the Victorian happy-go-lucky way when they thought of humans almost less than they thought of machines.[210]

Marples and Beeching managed to follow this advice well enough to allow the government to use the contraction of the railway industry as a positive example of modernisation: freeing the resources tied up in decaying industries for redeployment in growing ones without abandoning full employment.

Some of the backbench 'opposition' was even easier to deal with. When Nicholas Ridley saw Marples over the closure of lines to Cirencester and Tetbury in his constituency, he expressed support for the policy but concern at his constituents' reaction (in the event, they burnt Marples in effigy). He left with a promise that the minister's office would draft a letter of complaint for him to send to the minister and provide a draft reply from the minister with it. Nevertheless, the government's majority was cut by about twenty in a debate on *Reshaping* in April, with Scottish and West Country MPs prominent among the rebels. By May 1963 backbench unrest had reached a level which prompted the Chief Whip, Martin Redmayne, to convey his concern to Macmillan 'as to whether the Minister of Transport is going to handle the political implications of the Beeching proposals in a way which will necessarily be acceptable to ministers generally and to the party'.[211] It was Redmayne's idea to have Marples's decisions in individual cases overseen by a Cabinet committee, a suggestion the minister does not appear to have welcomed.

Criticism of the consultative procedure, in particular the limited nature of the financial information given to the TUCCs, built up as the committees began to hear cases in the wake of *Reshaping*. In 1962 the ministry had given in to pressure from the committees and abandoned its argument that there was no need for them to receive financial information now their role was restricted to the consideration of hardship. Instead, they could have figures showing the direct earnings (exclusive of contributory revenue) and direct expenses of the service in question, plus a figure representing expenditure on maintenance and renewals over five years. A year later, amid allegations of excessive secrecy, the government announced that MPs, councils and other 'responsible bodies' could get the same information direct from the railways.[212] However, this concession merely encouraged complaints of inaccuracy, forcing Marples to ask Sir William Carrington, a former president of the Institute of Chartered Accountants, to consider what financial information should be supplied to the TUCCs. Carrington's hurried endorsement of the figures was condemned a few years later by experts in the ministry's economic section; however, they had no doubt that the lines affected would have been losing money.

Carrington's report, completed in October, did little to defuse concerns about the process. In a furious private letter to Marples in October, in which he called the BRB's figures 'a damned lie', Lord Stonham of the National Council on Inland Transport warned the minister that he was receiving 200–300 letters of support a week and enclosed one from a female correspondent typifying, he claimed, the rural Conservative Party.[213] Stonham's campaigning was receiving favourable attention in the press and worrying the ministry. However, Marples told his colleagues that fuller calculations would be open to criticism because they inevitably involved a certain amount of estimation. In December he called the waverers' bluff by offering to set up an independent body to assess the economic case for closure, while warning his colleagues that this would probably mean spreading implementation of the proposals over 'ten years instead of two or three'.[214] The matter was dropped. In the wake of all this, what the Railways B division of the ministry probably wanted least for Christmas 1963 was a case which rolled all the criticisms of the Board's figures and the consultative procedure into one handy file and justified them, but that is what it got. The file was marked 'Wells-next-the-Sea'.

The line from Heacham, on the King's Lynn–Hunstanton branch, through Burnham Market to Wells had closed to passengers back in 1952, when Burnham was just a village and even Carnaby Street did not have boutiques. On the night of 31 January 1953 devastating floods killed over 300 people on the east coast of England, nearly 2,000 in the Netherlands and a few hundred more at sea. Wells station was flooded and a train on the Hunstanton branch collided with a floating bungalow. Between Burnham and Wells the line was so badly breached the Commission decided to close it to freight and abandon it (a decision which stood, unlike the attempt to close the Brightlingsea line after similar damage in the same storm). This left Wells with just one rail connection, which ran south through Walsingham and Fakenham, where it crossed the Midland and Great Northern and the river Wensum to run along its southerly bank for a mile with the M&GN opposite, through County School (junction with the 'round the world' line to Wroxham) to Dereham, where it joined the line between King's Lynn and Norwich via Wymondham. The railway reached Wells in 1857, but it brought prosperity neither to the port nor to investors in the Wells and Fakenham Railway and, unlike the lines to Cromer and Hunstanton, was not linked to the development of holiday trade. Wells was too far from London and a marshy mile away from the sea. In 1950 the train from Wells still took about two hours just to get to Norwich.

In 1956 a new diesel service was introduced on both routes through Dereham, offering a quicker and more frequent service from Wells: Dereham in forty minutes and Norwich in ninety. This improvement undoubtedly made the proposed closure of the line to Dereham, published in September 1963, and its replacement with buses that would take twice as long, all the harder to accept. In winter, 500 people a day used the line, nearly 700 a day in summer, well below Beeching's much-criticised estimate that 10,000 passengers a week was the minimum requirement, but about three times as many as the Westerham line (and Wells would be a lot further from anywhere without its trains than Westerham was from Sevenoaks). Mr A. R. Bull of Church Farm,

Cranworth, probably spoke for many when he wrote to Marples in November claiming the TUCC process was a pre-judged waste of time and dismissing the idea that buses were an adequate replacement. 'Five hundred people per day do not pay good money for the fun of travelling by train,' he added, 'not Norfolk people anyway.'[215] Petitions were signed by 2,400 local residents and 570 pilgrims (who used the line to reach Walsingham). The TUCC hearing in November heard the usual disputes about numbers. The summer census had missed the extra traffic in the school holidays; but the Board pointed out that a census in the holidays would have missed schoolchildren. The figures also ignored a regular football special and, much more significantly, pilgrim trains to Walsingham. The discrepancy between the council's claim that as many as 3,000 arrived on some days by train (a figure the roads would struggle to cope with) and the region's less daunting figure of 750 was never resolved, because the TUCC was told that special trains would continue to run for pilgrims as the line would stay open for freight. In any case the saving, even with freight maintained, was a pretty clear-cut £27,000 a year. The TUCC drew attention to the shortcomings of the proposed replacement bus service and suggested some improvements, but there was nothing in its report to suggest that this would be a particularly complicated case. What the TUCC did not know was that the figures showing costs of £54,000 against earnings of £27,000 were out of date. The Eastern Region regularly made a mess of its figures at this time and the saving was a tenth of the size it had claimed; small enough, in fact, to be outweighed by the cost of providing replacement buses. On the face of it closure would cost more than retention.

By the time the TUCC sent its report to the ministry in late

November 1963, the rate of closures had slowed to a trickle as the new machinery took time to get underway and the threat of the whole process grinding to a halt was growing. Such was the fraught atmosphere and pressure to clear the backlog that ministry under secretary Peter Scott-Malden actually collared the chairman of the South-Eastern TUCC alongside a ship he was about to board with two friends in December 1963 in order to get his agreement to the committee meeting in his absence. The chairman agreed but was suspicious of this 'unhealthy interference' with the committee's independence, which he blamed on 'some other quarter' than the ministry or BRB. He warned his committee to be on its guard.[216]

Whatever the precise source of Scott-Malden's mission, there was a significant risk that the whole policy would collapse by the end of 1963. There is no evidence that government concern at the effect of closures on its popularity affected the outcome of any individual case and the Cabinet committee only dealt with a small percentage of cases; but it devoted much effort to managing the programme as a whole in order to minimise the electoral damage.[†] Bearing in mind that the BRB was required by law to publish individual proposals covering each of the closures proposed in the *Reshaping* report and that the overwhelming majority of these had not been published in the summer of 1963, ministers sought to influence the order in which these proposals appeared. Their initial aim was to complete work on two types of proposal before the general election: relatively uncontroversial closures offering large savings; and controversial proposals that

[†]   Files on the decision to reprieve the riverside loop in Tyneside immediately before the 1964 general election in which the Conservatives defended a majority of ninety-eight at Newcastle East have not survived, although this decision did affect the sort of urban line which stood a good chance of being reprieved in any event.

would be refused. This, they hoped, would postpone the most unpopular decisions, while demonstrating a balance between support for the Board and due concern for hardship. This strategy was fraught with problems. Macleod, charged with overcoming them, pursued what he saw as an impossible task, mainly to prevent accusations of ineptitude if he was not seen to try.

It was virtually impossible to know what the decision would be in any particular case or how long it would take to emerge. There were practical difficulties in altering the plans of the BRB and the TUCCs and political dangers in being seen to do so. Marples and his officials were generally reluctant to interfere with Beeching's timetable and were enthusiastically backed by the Treasury, which took the view that 'our job is to facilitate the closure of the lines: there will be no shortage of advocates for the defence'.[217] Beeching was not generally prepared to delay proposals simply because they might prove unpopular. However, the chief flaw in this attempt to manage the programme was that it was based on the false assumption that the more money a closure saved the less controversial it would prove. Generally, the opposite was true. Lines which cost more to operate tended to have more trains (and passengers) on them than lightly used branches. To take an example from the cases set out in detail in *Reshaping*, the York–Hull service earned £90,400 a year in fares, while Banff–Tillynaught earned a mere £600, indicating that far fewer people would be affected by its closure. Yet the former offered savings of £81,110, the latter £10,900. More obviously, long lines offered greater savings than short ones, but tended to leave communities more isolated and harder to serve by bus when they closed. While the twenty-one closures Marples approved in March 1964 saved an average of less than £40,000 a year each, the two he vetoed at the same time (Shrewsbury–Llanelli and Ayr–Kilmarnock) would have saved a total of £215,000.

As the ministry had anticipated in 1956, Scotland was the focus of opposition to closures. A visit by Beeching in the autumn of 1962 had inflamed opposition and by May 1963 the Scottish Secretary Michael Noble was pressing for the government to announce that five major proposals in Scotland would be deferred for three to five years.[†] He was unhappy at Beeching's reluctance to supply him with information on them (it did not arrive until November, despite significant pressure from Macmillan). Over the summer of 1963 Macleod compiled a list of controversial cases in England based on the huge number of replies he received to a request for information from the party. Although he limited it to those in which the relevant MP had complained, it still affected thirty-three. By October the list had expanded to include the five Scottish cases and six in Wales. No sooner had this list been compiled, however, than the whole question of timing was thrown into confusion when Macmillan fell ill and resigned unexpectedly in October 1963, putting the anticipated election date back from the spring of 1964 to the autumn. This left ministers uncertain whether to accelerate unpopular proposals to get the decisions on them out of the way before the election or to postpone them. No decision had been taken by December, when it became clear that the whole process was taking longer than anticipated and so accelerating publication of any further proposals would be of little use (it was too late to reach decisions on them before polling day). On 2 December Marples was instructed to halt publication of proposals on the list until a

---

[†]   Inverness–Wick/Thurso, Dingwall–Kyle of Lochalsh, Ayr–Stranraer, Dumfries–Stranraer, and Edinburgh–Carlisle via Hawick, known as the Waverley Route.

decision on how to proceed was taken (in fact this made no difference as none of them was due for publication before the next meeting of the Cabinet committee on closures). Sufficient areas of potential delay had now emerged to threaten the credibility of the whole programme: Lord Stonham had called for 131 urban closures in *Reshaping* to be postponed (rather optimistically, as one proposal had attracted no objections); Marples was being pressed to defer the publication of some thirty proposals relating to holiday resorts until the autumn; and on top of the 'sensitive' list, there was now a second list of proposals officials wanted deferred on the grounds they might conflict with another plank of modernisation, regional planning.

The closure of lines to holiday resorts was at the heart of the transformation of the railways in the 1950s and 1960s. The railways had created many holiday towns; however, holiday traffic was concentrated over a very short period. In the West Country some resorts saw a third of their holiday trade in a single peak fortnight, a far from lucrative arrangement for both the railways and the trade. In 1959, out of 18,500 coaches allocated to fast and semi-fast services, 6,000 were used on no more than eighteen occasions, and a third of these on no more than ten. Beeching estimated these coaches cost £3.4 million, but earned only £500,000. *Reshaping* proposed the closure of lines to 127 holiday resorts, including inland destinations such as Richmond (Yorkshire) and Ballater, and promised the complete elimination of high peak stock by 1965 (a proposal with implications for plans to mobilise the army and disperse the urban population in the event of war).

The issue came to the attention of the Cabinet committee on rail closures when it considered proposals to keep the short line to Porthcawl open on a summer-only basis in December 1963. It called for a report on holiday lines. Marples attempted to overcome the obvious problems of conveying luggage on buses by suggesting they be permitted to haul luggage trailers. Officials estimated that closures would only affect 2 or 3 per cent of non day-trip holidaymakers, who could always transfer their custom to other resorts and were already shifting to road. Similar closures had not had a serious impact in the past (the Isle of Wight and Coniston were cited as examples) and this kind of traffic, although still large, was in decline. In 1955 roughly a third of holidaymakers travelled to their destination by rail, a third by car and a third by coach or bus. By 1962 rail was carrying only 26 per cent, while a further 18 per cent travelled by bus or coach, leaving over half travelling by car. In the same period the number of cars on the road had almost doubled from 3.6 million to 6.6. million. The trend was clear. Although closures might mean hardship for resorts that lost business, it was argued that they should be adapting themselves 'more vigorously' to car-borne visitors and 'modernising their promotion to this end'.[218] The committee was persuaded that holiday lines should be judged on their individual merits, which was curtains for Porthcawl. The one concession the Cabinet committee made to worried boarding-house land-ladies, hoteliers and deckchair attendants throughout the country was the announcement on 12 February 1964 that if any closure proposals affecting holiday resorts were published from then on, the line would not close until 1 October. Two of the ten busiest resort stations listed for closure in *Reshaping* came to the ministry before the 1964 election. Whitby was reprieved, but lost two of its three routes; hardship was an additional factor in the decision to reprieve the third. Withernsea, only slightly less busy, was closed.

Regional planning concerns proved harder to dismiss. Before his resignation through ill-health, Macmillan had incorporated into his modernisation theme measures designed to address the perceived decline of the industrial areas of Scotland and the north-east of England and the contrasting growth of the south-east. The difficulty the government faced was that resisting this economic trend might damage national economic growth, a story which has become familiar in the ensuing half a century. Macmillan wanted government to stimulate growth in the areas threatened by unemployment, leading the Conservatives to a new emphasis on regional planning, which was maintained under Douglas-Home. Macmillan had given Lord Hailsham special responsibility for drawing up a development plan for the north-east in January 1963 and by mid-1963 a series of Regional Study Groups (RSGs) covering the south-east, north-east, north-west, West Midlands and central Scotland had been established as part of the government's attempt to get to grips with the future distribution of population and employment. *Reshaping* contained potential conflicts with attempts to assist declining areas and with regional policy in general, most obviously because government had no say over the withdrawal of freight facilities. In August 1963 the Ministry of Housing and Local Government (MHLG) drew up a list of fifteen cases it wanted postponed so that regional studies could be carried out first. By December, the Board of Trade and the Scottish Development Department had between them added another twenty-three cases.

Together, the 'planning' and 'sensitive' lists accounted for about 20 per cent of the programme. Marples resisted any deferment through three meetings of the Cabinet committee and one of the Cabinet, before agreeing to a compromise in January 1964.

This consisted of the announcement about holiday lines referred to above and a request to Beeching to defer publication of nine cases: the Waverley line, St Pancras–Barking and seven in the north-west. Beeching agreed to eight, although the Barrow–Whitehaven and Broad Street–Richmond proposals appear to have been abandoned as well. Although there seems to have been genuine concern in the Cabinet over the implications of closures for development and urban traffic, the Cabinet Secretary's notes suggest that the discussion was as much about finding a 'respectable' reason to delay controversial cases.[219] Nevertheless, faced with the obvious truth of Marples's warnings that too many exceptions would undermine the whole policy, his colleagues were persuaded not to court political disaster.

Between the publication of *Reshaping* and the general election in October 1964, Marples consented to the closure of 127 services affecting 701 stations and closing 1,341 route miles in all; he refused consent in eleven cases affecting seventy-six stations.[†] The ministry certainly attempted a thorough investigation of individual cases. Treasury officials complained of the detail the 'marathon' meetings of the interdepartmental working party went into.[220] The Hon. Henrietta Brewer was not entirely correct when she told the *Catholic Herald* on behalf of Walsingham's pilgrims that no consideration was being given to the cost to the taxpayer of widening roads and getting children to school, or the wider economic effects. In the Wells case, for example, concerns about the effect on the holiday trade and on the shellfish and lugworm traffic carried by passenger trains were considered, but not felt to be particularly significant. Nevertheless, the effort

---

†   These figures exclude cases published before *Reshaping* even where decisions emerged after October 1963.

did not amount to the 'full investigation ... into the effects on the area as a whole' that Wells council, among thousands of other objectors to closures across the country, wanted.[221]

When ministers were wondering how best to handle *Reshaping* in February, Marples had assured Macmillan that 'our procedures are designed to ensure there is no real hardship', by which he meant that where the 'essential needs' of rail users could not be met more cheaply by a bus service, the rail service would continue, although the intention was to postpone closures until roads could be made adequate, rather than retain lines permanently. [222] Defining the 'essential needs' of users was an inexact process and it is difficult retrospectively to extract hardship as an issue from other concerns that influenced refusals. However, the definition that emerged over the following eighteen months can be summed up as being able to get to work or school without an absurdly long journey and not being completely cut off otherwise. In considering the provision of alternative bus services, officials would take account of journeys made for reasons other than to get to work, but disruption to these journeys was not generally considered hardship. A key point in the evolution of this definition was ministers' consideration of the Romsey–Andover line in the early summer of 1964, the first to come before them in which it was clear that hardship could not be satisfactorily relieved by a bus service. In recommending closure they argued that a balance had to be struck between the degree of hardship, the numbers involved and the cost to the public. In this case an increase in journey times of up to of thirty-seven minutes and a ninety-minute maximum journey was considered acceptable to remove a subsidy per regular passenger of £100–200 a year.

A few weeks later officials recommended that Hull–Hornsea

should close on the grounds that the times and subsidies were roughly the same as the Andover–Romsey case. In doing so they refined the definition of hardship by calculating the subsidy using only the 3,400 commuters on the grounds that extended journey times for 2–3,000 day-trippers from Hull on fine summer days, 200 shoppers and various other users was inconvenience, not hardship (for good measure, officials argued that refusing consent to Hornsea would cause bitterness and jealousy in Withernsea, which was due to lose its service to Hull at the same time, therefore both should close). These were very rough calculations and the Hornsea decision led members of the TUCC to consider resigning en masse or appearing before the traffic commissioners to oppose the granting of licences to replacement buses. A certain amount of cynicism about claims of hardship was understandable; even in Wick a local claimed that 'most of the people who are making all the fuss have not used the railways for years'.[223] Marples was more cynical about it than most and in one case (Cambridge–March) he had to be restrained by his colleagues from withdrawing a service in advance of complex arrangements for a replacement bus service being completed (the service eventually closed when these arrangements were established in the 1970s). Hardship was not ignored, but it was defined in a manner that maximised the number of consents, and in the cases Marples rejected it tended to be combined with concerns about urban congestion, regional development or the holiday trade.

In the Wells case, the TUCC had found that unless the proposed bus service was improved, hardship would be caused to a number of commuters, shoppers and day-trippers (schoolchildren were the education authority's problem). However, officials felt they could not insist that the BRB subsidise better bus services if their cost wiped out the savings. When the ministry wrote to the Board, pointing out that the line would cost more closed than open, it got a stark reply. Even if the service were able to break even, the Board argued, 'it would not be the sort of service which we ought to be engaged in. It is against the whole conception of the Reshaping Report that we should', because, as *Reshaping* put it, the 'proposals in the plan are interdependent ... realisation of many of the savings depends upon the adoption of the plan as a whole'.[224] This argument reflected the extent to which costs were shared between services – which was not covered by the figures that went to the ministry. It was what the government had signed up for and the only good news for officials was that the Board had now decided it would be closing the line to freight after all, at which point the savings would increase by £34,400 and justify the necessary improvements to the bus service. The easiest course was to withhold consent to passenger closure until this took place; the working party recommended this course. But attaching such a condition to a formal consent would mean admitting that the board had got the figures wrong and had misled the TUCC over the provision for pilgrims. However innocently made, these errors would have provoked calls for the case to go back to the TUCC and would have undermined both Carrington's assurances and the credibility – already weak – of the consultative process.

Marples's parliamentary secretary, Tom Galbraith, rejected officials' advice and recommended refusing consent to the Wells closure and requiring the BRB to make a new proposal if freight was subsequently withdrawn. He did so in part to balance consenting to closure of the Brightlingsea branch, in which the bus subsidy also outweighed the saving, but chiefly to avoid the political difficulties of closure. However, there had clearly been some tension in the office and Scott-Malden intercepted Galbraith's minute before it reached Marples, to suggest an alternative. Wells was not Cromer or Hunstanton, let alone Skegness. Objectors had raised the issue of day-trip traffic on the line but this was one of a range of issues rather than a life-or-death matter for the town. Nevertheless, Scott-Malden pointed out to Marples that Wells was a holiday resort, however minor. While any announcement that the line would be kept open until October in order to maintain facilities for summer visitors would raise awkward questions about why others had not been treated similarly (it had been published too early to fall into the group of holiday lines the government had just promised would not close until then), if the Board was persuaded informally to keep it open until freight was withdrawn, the mess it had made of the case could be kept quiet and the 'holiday case' explanation would serve as a fall-back if the delay was questioned. On 2 March Marples formally consented to closure, while in a separate letter the ministry privately agreed with the BRB that this would not take place until freight was withdrawn, at which point the balance of costs would make the case clear-cut. All very neat, except that this pushed the closure date closer to the general election.

Beeching's agreement in February 1964 to postpone publication of the Waverley proposal reflected the continuing intensity of opposition in Scotland. An organisation known as MacPuff had been formed to oppose closures north of Inverness and was attracting Conservative support. In December 1963 the Conservatives' majority at Dumfries was cut from over 7,000 to 971, its lowest for thirty years, in a by-election at which the proposed closure of the line to Stranraer had encouraged opposition hopes.

The following month the chairman of the party in Scotland, Sir John George, warned the Prime Minister that

> feelings are red hot among the executive committees and Divisional Councils throughout Scotland on the ... subject. No one believes that the [Inverness–Wick and Dumfries–Stranraer] lines in fact will be closed but all are distressed and dismayed that we are giving our opponents such a long run to flay us mercilessly.[225]

Pressure from Number Ten succeeded in squeezing a refusal of consent to the closures north of Inverness out of Marples as soon as was decent after the TUCC reports arrived, despite his hopes that the Inverness–Kyle line could be closed once major road improvements were carried out. The Stranraer lines proved more problematic and it was not until July that Marples was able to announce his refusal to Ayr–Stranraer and the reopening of a short connecting line that would allow trains from the south to reach the port once the line from Dumfries closed (opposition to these two proposals being as much about connections to Northern Ireland as rail services in south-west Scotland). Meanwhile, Douglas-Home had to be persuaded that it would not look good if the Gleneagles–Crieff section of the Comrie branch (which lay in his constituency) was reprieved when other more deserving cases had not been. In September 1964 Noble successfully lobbied for a decision on Aviemore–Forres to be deferred on purely political grounds.

Controlling the order in which decisions were announced offered a less problematic way of defusing opposition than manipulating the order in which proposals were published, but even this was not trouble-free. Closures were generally announced in batches so that consents were accompanied by refusals. The first such group was announced on 14 January 1964, when five Welsh consents were balanced by the refusal of Cardiff–Coryton. By February Noble was insisting that the next batch must contain a Scottish refusal. Marples was able to offer Kilmarnock–Ayr and announced around twenty decisions at a press conference in March including this and a second refusal, Shrewsbury–Llanelli.

Every letter written to the minister about rail closures received a reply written by officials. Although standard texts were used for all letters about a given line, unique paragraphs were usually provided in response to specific points. A good example is the reply offered to a twelve-year-old schoolboy who wrote to the ministry in 1967 with a lengthy account of his reasons for hoping that the Hull–Scarborough line would not close, during the course of which he asked whether two unrelated stations had been closed and whether the ministry could send him some maps of railways. The ministry's reply updated him on the progress of the Hull case, informed him that he could send an objection to the Yorkshire TUCC, answered his questions on the two stations and suggested he ask the BRB for maps, enclosing their address. His letter may even have come as a welcome relief from the angry rants and, more often, heart-rending appeals – 'we do not own cars and if the trains were stopped my children and I would not be able to meet and they are all the family I have being a war widow' – all to be answered in the same calm, rational language.[226] It must have been a depressing task to draft these letters; all those years of education and experience devoted to the crafting of a perfectly logical explanation and defence of policy that the author must have known would be in no sense satisfactory to its recipient. The provision of even partially tailored replies made letter-writing an effective form of protest in as much as it delayed the whole process. The preparation of – and correspondence resulting from – the March press conference slowed the pace at which the ministry could process cases and by May the press was claiming that this was deliberate; by July the Board was complaining. In fact, Marples was being pressed by colleagues to speed up his decisions as early as April, in the belief that delays increased controversy.

In the early summer, concern about the electoral consequences of closures was mounting and ministers sought to persuade Beeching not to publish new proposals in the run-up to the election. Although he appears to have agreed not to publish controversial proposals, he refused to stop publication entirely. Marples's rash of decisions in September, consenting to a further thirty-eight closures, was prompted partly by his colleagues' desire to end uncertainty, but he was admonished for overdoing it by Lord Blakenham in the middle of the month. Over 200 *Reshaping* proposals had yet to be dealt with (of which about half had been published). Some thirty decisions were implemented between the start of September and the general election, the Wells branch among them. Had the ministry required passenger services to be retained until freight was withdrawn, rather than trying to conceal the railways' error in providing the wrong figures by reaching a private understanding with the BRB, Wells (or Fakenham at least) might still have a railway today. In August the BRB told the ministry freight would continue as far as Fakenham into 1965; in fact it did so until 1980. In June 1964, Lord Stonham had claimed that Labour would keep the line open if it won the general election. However, the

BRB had already told the ministry that it would close the line to passengers on 5 October, a month before it intended to withdraw freight. A scrawled note on a scrap of paper in the file attributes this to 'political reasons' but does not reveal what these were.[227] The obvious inference is that the Board brought closure forward to get it out of the way before the election. However, 5 October was a common date for several closures and the BRB wrote to the ministry in May, before the precise date of the election was known and before Stonham's speech had raised the prospect of a new Labour government intervening to prevent the closure. In any case if the BRB was acting to thwart such a move, it need not have worried, as we shall see.

Fulminations against Beeching on the part of candidates of all parties were common during the 1964 election, but are not generally considered to have affected the result. At Buckingham, where closure of the line to Bletchley in September was followed by Robert Maxwell's victory for Labour in October, the local paper reported that only forty people turned up for the last train, none of whom were local, while the reprieve granted to the Newcastle riverside loop in September was not enough to save the Conservatives' majority of ninety-eight at Newcastle East. However, Maxwell certainly felt there were votes in the issue – in September 1964 he led a deputation from Castlethorpe to Marples's doorstep to petition against closure of the station. Voters in some constituencies were given greater cause to believe they should vote Labour if they wanted to save their railway. Marples's consent to the closure of the lines from Malton and Scarborough to Whitby in September had been greeted with outrage in Whitby and the local Conservative MP had quickly found himself obliged to disown the decision. In a fine display of campaigning local journalism the *Whitby Gazette* gave front-page prominence to the case on an almost weekly basis for the rest of the year. Wilson's letter to the local Labour Party in September assuring them that 'an obviously major decision such as the Scarborough–Malton–Whitby rail closure would be covered by the statement in the Labour Party manifesto "major rail closures will be halted"', was interpreted by the paper as meaning that if Labour won the election the closure would not go ahead.[228] At Silloth the party went further, organising the demonstration described at the start of this book, reports of which gave much prominence to the promise that trains would run again if Labour got in.

Silloth and Whitby both lay in safe Tory seats, but on the penultimate day of the campaign the *Hull Daily Mail* reported an election meeting at Hornsea, which along with the neighbouring Withernsea branch was due to lose its service the following week, at which a Labour councillor claimed that if Labour won 'the closures which had not already taken place would be stopped until every line had been examined, not purely on the basis of whether they paid or not, but whether they provided a service to the community'.[229] Many of the voters in marginal Hull North (where Labour overturned a Conservative majority of 702 to win by 1,181 votes) used the lines for summer day-trips and would have read reports of the campaign to save them if Labour won on the front page of the local paper on polling day. The closure of the Northampton–Peterborough line through Wellingborough in May 1964 probably came too early to influence the election result, but even a minuscule protest vote could have cost the Conservatives dearly as Labour won by forty-seven votes. In both the Scottish Highlands and Cornwall it is possible that the extent of Beeching's proposals fuelled a sense of regional disaffection reflected in the Liberals' capture of Inverness, Ross & Cromarty, Caithness & Sutherland and Bodmin.

Darlington, Doncaster and Bury were among the seats Labour took at the election. At Darlington the threat to the railway workshops and to the industry in general in a town put on the map by its association with the Stephensons was a key factor in the campaign, as the Central Office agent for the north had predicted it would be the previous autumn. The local Labour Party went to the trouble of tracing railwaymen who had moved to other works and ensured that they had postal ballots. The swing to Labour here was a strong 6.4 per cent. Similar concerns may have helped Labour in the railway town of Doncaster, which also changed hands, but where the pro-Labour swing was only 4.8 per cent. At Bury, which had featured on the list of sensitive closures the previous year, David Ensor turned a Conservative majority of nearly 4,000 into a Labour one of over 1,000, helped by the first Liberal candidate since 1950. The electric service to Manchester, used by 7,000 people a day including 4,000 commuters, had been proposed for closure in February. In an election speech reported locally a week before polling, Ensor pointed out that under the proposals listed in the *Beeching Report* the town would lose all its rail links and implied that Bury would benefit from Labour's manifesto pledge. Although the local Conservative MP was a prominent oppo-nent of closure, both Liberal and Labour candidates pointed out that he had voted in support of *Reshaping* itself and a *Times* feature on the constituency identified rail closures as one of two significant local issues. Ironically, the other was the unpopu-lar plan to use Bury as an overspill town for Manchester, the very measure which had ensured two other Bury–Manchester services were among those postponed in February.

Finally there was North Norfolk. This is an odd case to cite, in that Labour held it against a Conservative swing. Yet the majority of just fifty-three, reduced from 658, is so small that the closure of the Wells and Mundesley lines ten days before polling and the fear that Sheringham–Cromer would follow may well have done enough to prevent the Conservatives repeating their success at Norfolk South West. The possibility that seats in Norfolk would swing towards the Conservatives and the significance of local issues was appreciated during the campaign (although the Conservatives themselves focused resources on seats they were trying to hold). As the Conservative vote in the area tended to come from the towns (with Labour's support based on agricultural workers) it is surely possible that a handful of Conservative voters were persuaded either to stay at home or vote Labour in the hope of saving or restoring their local rail link, or simply in protest. The local Labour candidate failed to utilise the campaigning opportunities provided by the two closures in the way that his counterpart at Silloth did, but closures did feature in the campaign and fears for the Sheringham line's future were expressed in the local press in the weeks leading up to the vote.

It is impossible to make a watertight case for closures costing the Conservatives a single seat in 1964, and even where closures were an issue they did not dominate campaigns to the exclusion of all else. Transport did not even feature in a *Sunday Telegraph* poll of election issues. The *Carlisle Journal*'s supplement on transport on 9 October concentrated entirely on the possible impact of a Labour government on the local road haulage industry and Ensor's final speech of the Bury campaign ignored the railway issue altogether while criticising the Conservatives for not building enough roads. Given that implementation of the closure programme coincided with a Conservative recovery in the polls, it seems likely that the strategy of backing Beeching in order to present the party as a modernising force, rather than risking the appearance of weakness by not doing so, was right. Marples's belief in being frank about the need for closures seems to be supported by his personal ratings; in December 1963, 55 per cent of those surveyed by Gallup thought he was doing a good job, with only 24 per cent disagreeing. Nevertheless, the scale of the potential impact of closure on Bury, the tiny Labour majority in North Norfolk, and the centrality of the industry to Darlington raise the possibility that Labour owed its victories in these three seats – and with them Wilson's outright majority – to the government's inability to manage the programme with a combination of absolute cynicism and perfect foresight.

There was more to the work of the various Cabinet committees and the ministry-led meetings of officials than simply trying to manage the electoral consequences of the *Beeching Report*. In their consideration of urban closures and the effect on the holiday industry civil servants conducted detailed analyses and gave serious thought to the wider implications of the closure programme, as did ministers. The consideration of hardship also contradicts the idea that the suffering caused by railway closures was simply ignored, although it is obvious that all concerned were determined not to allow concerns over hardship to undermine the basic policy of a significant contraction of the network. This is particularly evident in a case such as Wells. It is probably true that closing the line to passengers saved the railways money but it is pretty obvious that the saving cannot have been great, that the consequences for users were harsh and that there was significant usage of the line.

Stuffed in the same fifty-year-old file as letters pleading for the line's retention, the BRB's declaration that, loss or no loss, this was not 'the sort of service which we ought to be engaged in' makes unpleasant reading. When the line closed, the timetable on the remaining section through Dereham was recast, leaving the new buses with no connection to the surviving rail services to Norwich and King's Lynn. Officials discovered this purely by chance some three months later. As the bus journey time was double that of the railway, it would be surprising if Stanley Jenkins's history of the line is wrong to say that most people heading to Norwich went straight there by road after closure. In any case, when the other line through East Dereham closed in 1968 (to King's Lynn, completely) and 1969 (to Wymondham to passengers) the assumptions on which the TUCC had assessed hardship were undermined. Given that so much of the route survived as a freight line for so long, given the fulfilment of local suspicions that the line onwards from Dereham would be next to go and given the difficulty in accommodating the 100,000 pilgrims to Walsingham each year on the local roads today, it is difficult not to feel that if the line had been given a chance, the benefits would have outweighed the loss. It is difficult not to see the closure as slapdash and unreasonable and to ask why anyone's journey to work should be doubled to over an hour, for the sake of a drop in the ocean. But the Board's letter needs to be read in the context of every previous chapter in this book. For a decade or more lines that had long since served their purpose had proceeded through the interminable closure process at a snail's pace while taxpayers' money leaked out of the system. So dynamic action was taken – debate was restricted, procedure was simplified, progress was made. And this is what that looks like. It would hardly be surprising if the closure of the Wells-next-the-Sea branch inspired a handful of local Conservative voters to stay at home or register a protest. But whether or not Beeching actually made any difference to the election, the significant effort Conservative ministers devoted to managing the programme offered a warning to future governments. The potential impact of the closure programme on the election was clearly appreciated by Wilson; although if Labour won any votes through its pledge to halt major closures until a plan for transport was worked out, it did so on a false prospectus, as we shall see in the following chapter.

Chapter 10

Unmitigated England: Tom Fraser
and the Great Central

S ir Edward Watkin, chairman of the South Eastern,
Metropolitan and Great Central railways in the late nine-
teenth century, shared Ernest Marples's dynamism and ability
to generate ideas, although his dreams of a high-speed railway
from Paris to Manchester got a lot further than Marples's plans
to prefabricate the cities of the future. Like Marples, Watkin was
not everyone's cup of tea; his intense rivalry with James Forbes,
chairman of the London, Chatham and Dover and Metropolitan
District railways brought misery to passengers and penury to
shareholders, although it did help to ensure that anywhere that
is anywhere in Kent has at least two railways to London. 'The
Feud', as relations between the South Eastern and the Chatham
became known, brought forth one of the most absurd railway
lines in England, the South Eastern's branch from Strood to
Chatham Central, expensively built across the Medway right
alongside its rival's line, to a station so far from the centre of
Chatham that it was actually in Rochester High Street. The
extension from just north of Nottingham to Marylebone station
in London, with which Watkin turned the Manchester Sheffield

and Lincolnshire Railway into the Great Central, turned out to be an even more expensive folly; but while Chatham Central was clearly the work of a lunatic, the Great Central was a beautiful dream that has continued to capture imaginations from the day Watkin persuaded the first unlucky investor to back it.

The sheer scale of Watkin's ambition, its foresight and the fact he got so much closer to fulfilling it than most of us do is surely part of the attraction. In addition the Great Central was marvellously executed: relatively flat and straight, with elegant bridges and viaducts and neatly arranged stations, it demonstrated all the lessons of three quarters of a century of railway-building. The romance attached to this fabulous railway is elevated to national angst when the English compare all those high-speed lines on the other side of the Channel Tunnel to the ruin of the nearest thing they had to one before HS1. The Great Central's downfall was that, like one of Colonel Stephens's lines, it connected places with little potential for traffic via countryside with none. Nottingham, Loughborough, Leicester and Rugby had already been well served by the Midland (and in Rugby's case the London and North Western) for decades by the time the London Extension opened in 1899 and, although the country between Rugby and Nottingham did yield a little local traffic, between Rugby and Aylesbury there were already more railways than the sparse population would prove able to support. And therein lies the final element in the appeal of this railway romance: the Great Central ran through what even today is as close to unspoiled countryside as England has got. A high-light was the viaduct over Swithland Reservoir with its wooded backdrop of silver birch and bracken, 'especially very early on a cold morning when mist hung above the placid water and the trail of smoke from a speeding express drifted idly away through the winter trees'.[230] 'Unmitigated England', Betjeman called it in his *Great Central Railway – Sheffield Victoria to Banbury*; hunting country, with 'ridge and furrow shadows' and church steeples shining silver 'above the barren boughs'.[231]

Nationalisation completed the Great Central's transition, initiated when it was absorbed into the LNER, from challenging competitor to spare part – one main line more than was really needed between London, the East Midlands and south Yorkshire. By the 1950s the line's chief value was as a useful north-east to south-west link via a spur from Woodford Halse, a junction in the middle of nowhere, to Banbury on the GWR. By 1959 a plan had been drawn up to concentrate freight and parcels traffic on the Great Central in order to free capacity on the former Midland main line from St Pancras to the East Midlands. This would allow passenger services on the Midland line to be accelerated, while the Great Central's expresses would be replaced by three semi-fast trains a day between London and Nottingham and three between Sheffield and Manchester. The first stage, announced in 1959, saw the end of express services from Marylebone to Manchester, Bradford and Sheffield, saving an estimated £140,000. Although they offered a slower journey from the East Midlands to London by the late 1950s, the Great Central's expresses were more comfortable and reliable than those on the Midland route (which was particularly unreliable at the time of their withdrawal) and as they left Marylebone with an average seventy-two passengers, you could always get a seat in first class. Their withdrawal provoked strong opposition and led to the formation of the Great Central Association, an organisation distinguished from other anti-closure groups by its focus on restoring long-distance services, but similar to them in its aim of 'protecting the public against the whims of the large and ponderous organisations which run the public services of the country … for their own administrative convenience'.[232]

Anticipating a similar reaction to stage two of the plan to rationalise the Great Central, which involved withdrawing the stopping trains, closing twenty-five stations and withdrawing the Sunday service, the East Midlands division produced a pamphlet explaining the plan. This sought to associate opposition with a privileged minority of 'influential people in Nottingham and Leicester particularly, [who] have grown up to hold the GC line in almost sentimental regard as their own particular way of getting to and from London in comfort and reasonable speed' and others who were motivated by an outdated loyalty to their favoured line (an interesting reversal of the criticism aimed by objectors at ex-LMS managers supposedly taking revenge on the rival LNER-owned Great Central). Whatever truth this may have contained, the argument that local opinion in Nottingham had been coloured in favour of the Great Central because its Victoria station 'happens' to be better sited than its Midland rival and then enjoyed 'advantages …[that] are simply the embodiment of several decades' additional experience of what a station should be and the facilities it should provide', was an odd way to promote its closure.[233]

When the East Midlands TUCC met to hear objections to the stage two proposals at Leicester in February 1962, the Divisional Traffic Manager, a Mr Gray, set out his case with regret:

No railway officer worth his salt likes to see even the smallest facility reduced, but he is under statutory obligation to make ends meet and it is therefore my unenviable task to have to put before the committee proposals which I believe are eminently sound, but which must make a few people think that railway officers are hard hearted.[234]

His task did not become any more enviable as the area committee criticised the apparent carelessness of the traffic survey and found the Commission's proposals would cause unacceptable hardship between Leicester and Rugby. An attempt by the region to recast the semi-fast timetable to meet these concerns merely earned a rebuke from the chair of the central committee, who expressed a lack of confidence in BTC figures. The former Midland route between Leicester and Rugby had closed since the census had been taken and objectors argued that this had improved use of the Great Central. As the region had promoted the merits of the GC line as an alternative when it closed the Midland route, this was a difficult point to dispute. At the TUCC's recommendation, the Rugby–Nottingham local service and two of its stations (Ashby Magna and East Leake) were retained in addition to those served by the semi-fast trains. The rest of the local services were withdrawn in 1963.

By the time stage two was considered by the East Midlands TUCC in early 1962 the plan to concentrate parcels traffic on the line had been abandoned and there was already talk of withdrawing the semi-fast trains. At the end of the year the Commission decided to examine north-east/south-west routes with the aim of closing the Great Central completely. By the end of 1963 this study had identified potential savings of £3.3 million (£1.24 million more than could be saved by simply switching to diesel operation) and work began on a proposal to close all of the Great Central, except the Rugby–Nottingham local trains recently reprieved, which was anticipated to be complete by June 1965. However, by the time the report was ready for publication a Labour government had been elected, pledged to halt major rail closures while regional transport plans were prepared by new regional bodies.

There was no sophisticated planning system ready and waiting for Wilson's arrival, from which the Conservatives had averted their eyes when implementing Beeching. Indeed, if the Conservatives could have conjured one up in 1962 they almost certainly would have done so. If Labour's plans were to be based on a serious analysis, it would take a long time to close the Great Central. Yet almost immediately the new government was under great pressure to save money and the Chancellor, Jim Callaghan, was very much taken with the promise of £20 million just waiting to be saved by pushing ahead with the closures programme. The Transport and General Workers Union (TGWU), implacably opposed to any assistance to rail that could not be justified on economic grounds, had its own ears and voice within the Cabinet in the shape of Frank Cousins, Labour's new Minister of Technology, TGWU General Secretary, former head of its road haulage section and rail-sceptic. Meanwhile, much of the rest of the Labour Party, the rail unions in particular, was chiefly attracted to planning, coordination and integration in transport as shorthand for a quick change of policy that would reduce the number of railway closures, protect jobs in the railway workshops and recreate the BTC, which had become 'the ark of Labour's transport covenant'.[235] If Tom Fraser, the pleasant fifty-something Scottish ex-miner Wilson appointed as Minister of Transport, was unlucky to be caught between these competing desires, he was foolish in thinking that devising a transport policy based on the principles of sound economic planning offered a way out.

Wilson's promises of change meant that Fraser was in difficulty from the off. Aside from those affected by closure decisions, his problem was not public opinion – he told Wilson that the favourable reception *Trunk Routes* received indicated public support for modernisation – but Labour Party opinion. One of the first things Commander Harry Pursey did following his October 1964 re-election to one of the safest Labour seats in the country, Hull East, was to tell the *Hull Daily Mail* that he would immediately urge the new Labour government to reopen the branch lines from Hull to Hornsea and Withernsea which were due to close that weekend. Pursey was by no means the only Labour MP who would be calling for a halt to rail closures in the ensuing weeks. The new government's tiny majority meant an early general election was inevitable and the embarrassment of Wilson's abandoned pledge to stop Beeching was a sensitive issue.

The possibility that Labour would at least halt and possibly reverse closures had caused officials at the ministry and Treasury a great deal of anxiety. In the fortnight before the election, the ministry prepared for a change of government by obtaining advice from the Treasury Solicitor on a Minister of Transport's powers to undo the work of his predecessor. The advice officials passed on to Fraser in the early weeks of the government's life was that while he could issue directions of a general nature to the BRB, a direction to halt closures approved by Marples but not yet implemented would not be of a general nature as it would only affect about twenty-five lines. Therefore, no power existed to direct Beeching to reopen lines. Nobody wants to go back over their past two years' work and undo some of it. Quite apart from tension between what civil servants are supposed to do and what human beings are actually like, however, Treasury officials were concerned that the closure programme was the only way in which they could exercise a direct influence in reducing the railway deficit. They were eager to know what was happening at the ministry in the election's aftermath and to impress upon the new regime the belief that there were £20 million of savings to be made through closures (although the BRB had confirmed this figure, it was merely a rough estimate – a caveat that was not passed on to ministers).

The pressure on Fraser intensified when, a week after the election, British Railways announced its plans for the Great Central, provoking demands from all three rail unions for ministerial action to protect the 1,700 staff affected. Yet Fraser's officials were surprised at the ease with which they convinced him to continue the programme. A week after the election, briefed by his officials 'entirely in accordance with the Department's earlier thinking', Fraser warned the Cabinet that the party's manifesto 'appeared likely to be misconstrued' as a promise not only to halt all rail closures but to reverse those of Marples's consents that had yet to come into effect.[236] The clearly disputable advice that Fraser had no power to intervene was quickly accepted not only by him, but by the Cabinet.

This apparent retreat was covered by a statement in Parliament reiterating Fraser's commitment to halt major closures while regional transport plans were drawn up. The impression of change was reinforced by announcing Beeching's agreement to leave the track in place where lines did close and a new 'early sift' procedure, under which proposals were sent to the minister before publication so that any obviously unacceptable ones could be vetoed.[237] For good measure Fraser also announced his refusal to close a number of stations on the Settle–Carlisle line. However, neither 'early sift' nor the retention of track amounted to a significant change, nor were they expected to. There is every likelihood that Marples would have reached a similar decision on the stations Fraser reprieved, as the BRB's inability to meet the ministry's requirements for alternative services had been the subject of discussions since the spring. Crucially Fraser had done nothing to alter the criteria his officials considered when advising him on individual closures. By ensuring the £20 million figure had made an appearance in the statement while defining 'major closures' as those likely to conflict with plans that would not exist for some time, officials laid good ground for continuity. The gradual erosion of the *Whitby Gazette's* post-election optimism, leading to its profession of bewilderment at Fraser's statement, makes sad reading.

Almost the first question Fraser was asked in the wake of his statement was whether the Great Central would be classed as a major closure and by the start of 1965 he may well have regretted the policy of 'early sift'. Instead of being able to rebuff queries about the proposed closure of the Great Central until it had made its way through the TUCC machinery, he was under pressure to veto it before it was published. With savings of over £800,000 at stake from the passenger closure, this was almost out of the question. At the start of February ministry officials recommended allowing publication of the Great Central closure on the grounds that the 'publicity and pressure have got out of all proportion' given that only a handful of passenger trains were affected and the minister had no say on the freight side anyway.[238] Fraser and most of his colleagues accepted this, but

Wilson was increasingly concerned. The publication of *Trunk Routes*, although generally well received, in January had brought the issue of rail closures back into the spotlight (despite Fraser's success in getting Beeching to tone down the maps to make it look less like a closure programme[†]). Shortly afterwards the insincerity of Labour's pre-election talk of halting closures was exposed when it refused to make time to pass a ten-minute rule Bill introduced by the Conservative MP for Scarborough and Whitby, Sir Alexander Spearman, which would have amended the Transport Act to allow Fraser to reverse Marples's decisions. This was all the more embarrassing as Spearman reminded the House of Commons that Wilson had 'clearly ... precisely and unconditionally' pledged to halt the Whitby closures and had subsequently confirmed that this would have been done were it not for the 1962 Act.[239] To be told by Fraser, on top of this, that the Great Central case was 'very far from being "major" in any sense of the word' was too much.[240] Wilson brought the whole issue back to the Cabinet, telling Fraser,

> I am very worried about this. Our election pledge was clear – to halt major closures. We qualified this in November ... Now we seem to be going much further. The Aylesbury (G.C.) line really is a major closure and we do not appear to be halting it.[241]

His concern increased two days later when he saw that the Cabinet committee had approved the closure of the Guildford–Horsham line despite the TUCC's finding of hardship.

---

†   Officials tried fruitlessly to persuade Beeching to change the date in the report from 1984 to 1985 to avoid jokes about the former's Orwellian implications – 'he is notoriously insensitive to public reaction' sighed the under secretary (NAPRO, MT 124/1103; Scott Malden, note, 1 December 1965).

Wilson seems to have genuinely wanted a change, and Fraser would not have stood in his way for long. However, while the Treasury was willing to accept a strong social or economic case for retaining services (for example, Manchester–Bury and Huddersfield–Penistone), once the initial post-election controversy was over its officials began trying to get the programme back up to speed, especially when it became clear that the railway deficit would be as much as £130 million in 1966. Officials presented the issue to ministers as a test of their ability to govern, and in particular to take the difficult decisions necessary to modernise Britain, and hoped to help them convince Labour supporters by calculating that the railway deficit represented five-and-a-half pence on a packet of cigarettes and three-and-a-half pence on a pint of beer. The Treasury was able to count on support from the Minister of Power, Fred Lee, who feared that if the rail closures stopped the NCB's pit closure programme would be next. The Department of Economic Affairs (DEA), which Wilson had set up as a rival source of economic advice to the Treasury, presented no counter argument to justify a halt. Douglas Houghton, Chancellor of the Duchy of Lancaster and chairman of a Cabinet committee on transport policy, appears to have been the only minister to seriously resist these pressures. If Fraser had 'fallen into the hands' of his officials he was not alone.[242] Wilson ensured that Fraser did not welcome *Trunk Routes* in a way that might imply the government was contemplating closures beyond the existing programme, and Fraser announced greater consultation with the Regional Economic Planning Councils (REPCs) that Labour had established, but once again this was little more than a cosmetic change and by the end of the year Treasury ministers and officials were united in calling for action on the implications of *Trunk Routes*.

Formal regional consultation was a development of the Conservatives' informal practice of referring proposals to the Regional Study Groups they had established and it made little difference outside the north-west, where the REPC rejected any proposal affecting Liverpool or Manchester until it had finished its plan. Attempts to draw up regional transport plans were bedevilled by the same lack of data and expertise that Whitehall faced – regional bodies were given no information on freight until well into 1966. These difficulties were compounded by a lack of direction and overshadowed by the difficulty of drawing up wider economic plans. Regional opinion was not necessarily unfavourable to closures in any case. For example, the South West REPC saw the closure of ten intermediate stations between Salisbury and Exeter as a good thing, because it would speed up services to London. As far as the Great Central was concerned the introduction of a further largely irrelevant consultation simply delayed the inevitable. Fraser's officials drafted a letter consenting to publication, which both Fraser and the BRB hoped would provide an opportunity to publicise the railways' case and emphasise the massive financial benefits. But it was left on the file unsent while the proposal went through the new procedure. In June the East Midlands council dealt with the case 'in about thirty seconds flat'; and the thirty seconds were devoted to Nottingham City Council's view on the importance of redeveloping Victoria station.[243] The proposal was finally published in August 1965, two months after the BRB had been ready to close the line. As this suggests, the changes to procedure introduced under Fraser did little except delay decisions. He presided over some particularly controversial cases including consenting to closure of the Somerset and Dorset (Bath–Bournemouth), probably the closure most regretted by railway romantics, and Oxford–Cambridge, probably the closure most regretted by modern rail planners.

The inability of 'early sift', track retention and formal regional consultation to satisfy demands for a fresh approach within the Labour Party increased pressure on Fraser to deliver a new plan for transport. Probably the best chance of doing so quickly was lost when the Cabinet derailed the appointment of Beeching to draw up Labour's plan. Given that Wilson's critique of *Reshaping* had been the supposedly narrow remit given to its author, giving Beeching a wider one was a logical move and Fraser had persuaded Beeching to take the job. However, the Cabinet, with Cousins prominent, saddled Beeching with a team of 'assessors'. As those behind this move probably hoped, Beeching decided to go and was replaced as chairman at the end of May 1965 by experienced railwayman Stanley Raymond. Cousins may well have been motivated by Beeching's view that heavy lorries were not covering the costs they imposed on the road network, but there were few tears in the Labour Party at the departure of someone so closely associated with an unpopular Tory policy. This reaction was not universal. Michael Shanks, leading contributor to the 'What's Wrong With Britain?' debate, bemoaned Beeching's departure and lauded his achievement: 'It is hard to think of any man in Britain who could have done more to overcome the obstacles facing him in the time he had available.'[244] One senior railwayman, Gerard Fiennes, reflected that Beeching 'opened a lot more things, including minds to ideas, than he closed'; another, Richard Hardy, wrote a biography of Beeching subtitled *Champion of the Railway?* – its author certainly thought so.[245] There is little doubt that Beeching had a galvanising effect on a railway management that had appeared confused and outdated under his predecessor, but whatever their reaction to his departure, few contemporaries would have disagreed with the *Sunday Telegraph*'s view that 'the impact he has made will last long after the word "Beechingisation" has disappeared'.[246]

The man appointed to conduct the study in Beeching's place, Lord Hinton, felt that the railways only existed because modern road transport had not been available when they were built. Unsurprisingly, his views were not what Labour was looking for and by the summer Wilson was seeking ways to bury the whole exercise. Meanwhile, Fraser was at loggerheads with Houghton, over the latter's plan for the creation of a British Transport Authority. Based on proposals from Raymond, and supported by the NUR and TUC, this would have had significant powers to force freight traffic onto rail. Fraser won the battle, but had no alternative ready to put in a Bill. His continued insistence that Labour's transport policy should be based on thorough studies of the problem created mounting frustration among his colleagues, the rail unions, Labour backbenchers and other Whitehall departments. The ministry began constructing a transport costs model covering the next thirty years, a study of future demand and an examination of how road pricing could be used to increase the cost of using congested roads. There was little prospect of results before 1967 and these studies, like the ones Beeching had proposed to Stedeford, were overtaken by the need for action. With an election obviously approaching, Wilson sacked Fraser in December and brought in Barbara Castle to heal Labour's divisions on transport. Transport planning, it turned out, was at odds with the maintenance of an aura of dynamic change.

Raymond wrote to Castle just before the March 1966 general election begging for a decision on the Great Central, which had now become a ghost line: all freight traffic diverted; the few remaining services sometimes leaving Marylebone with no passengers at all; a demoralised skeleton staff awaiting the inevitable end. Raymond used the line himself and was appalled at the waste. A recommendation on closure had been sitting in Castle's in-tray since the middle of February. The assistant secretary dealing with the case, admitting it was 'not for officials to advise on the electoral aspects', but clearly frustrated, tried to give Castle a push. He suggested that a consent to closure that mentioned the enormous savings would surely be as likely to achieve 'a favourable effect' as a refusal and if she wasn't convinced could she 'at least' take the decision now for official release after the election to 'avoid the necessity for these papers to take their place in the long queue that will inevitably have built up … with the money still ticking up at £2,400 per day'.[247] He was clearly getting used to the new minister's ways and she took up the latter suggestion. Castle was not afraid of tough decisions but she fully appreciated the electoral significance of transport. This was most obvious in her promise to authorise a bridge over the Humber during Labour's successful campaign in the vital by-election in January 1966 at Hull North. In the subsequent general election she made a point of visiting North Norfolk to reassure voters over the future of the line to Sheringham.

Once Labour was re-elected with a workable majority, Castle's decision was announced and the Great Central closed in September 1966. But there was a sting in the tail for the ministry. In the early years of the twentieth century, the GWR and the Great Central had constructed a joint line which allowed

Great Western trains from London to Birmingham to avoid Oxford by running direct from Paddington to Banbury via High Wycombe. Great Central trains used the route to avoid the congested line into London it shared with the Metropolitan, by running from Marylebone to West Ruislip, over the joint GWR line to a junction at Ashendon and then on a new Great Central line to Grendon Underwood junction on the original London Extension. By the time the Great Central faced closure the Ashendon–Grendon Underwood link was used by just one through train from the main line a week. Unfortunately, this train had been forgotten and the link line had not been mentioned in the formal closure proposal. It had been unlawfully closed. Needless to say, the Great Central Association spotted this and the whole rigmarole of formal closure had to be gone through. The association objected to the new proposal, but this was no Bluebell; the only stations on the line had been closed for years, no one else noticed and no grudging service was temporarily restored.

In October 1967 Castle gave her consent to the disposal of the Great Central route south of Rugby. There do not seem to have been many takers and the route is still largely untouched, except at Brackley where a bypass has severed the viaduct. The Great Central Association had talked to the ministry about taking over the Nottingham–Rugby section to run a public service even before it closed. This came to nothing, although parts of the London Extension have been preserved as a steam railway, reopened as a commuter line and reused by Nottingham's trams. From the 1960s onwards opponents – and would-be reversers – of the line's closure have pointed to its potential as a high-speed route connected to the Channel Tunnel, often citing its large loading gauge as an advantage in this respect. However, it was not actually built to the standard later adopted on the continent. HS2 – according to the planned route at the end of 2012 – follows the line of the Great Central south of Brackley but uses relatively little of the trackbed. What side, one wonders, would Betjeman have taken in the contemporary struggles over this latest scar on the Chilterns?

Although the most strenuous complaints at the closure came from those who saw the Great Central as a lost main line, it was Woodford Halse that suffered most. Like Melton Constable, Woodford was a railway village where the large engine shed and goods sidings had been the mainstay of local employment. As well as the main line, it lost its trains to Banbury. Not many people used the station (about sixty on weekdays and 120 on Saturdays) but those who depended on it to reach Banbury's shops (and one woman who used the main line to visit her elderly mother in Loughborough) were now marooned in the middle of nowhere and the 6.40am bus for those employed at Rugby was not much help for anyone else. The TUCC had recognised their plight but was unable to suggest a solution, given the tiny numbers involved. One ex-driver resident had been in the army with Fraser during the war and wrote to him after publication of the closure proposal asking the minister to receive a deputation from the village and reminding him that 'in those days no matter was too small for your personal attention'.[248] The feeling of betrayal among men who had worked for the railway all their lives was palpable. Today Woodford Halse is a sleepy little village, still in the middle of nowhere, but more comfortable with it. One imagines the residents are pretty relived HS2 goes nowhere nearby.

Closure of the Great Central as a main line left the stopping train trundling between the ill-named Rugby Central and the cavernous and otherwise deserted Nottingham Victoria as the last remnant of Watkin's dream – until BR cut the service back to a reopened Nottingham Arkwright Street to make way for a shopping centre on the site of Victoria. Connecting with nothing at either end, half of the intermediate stations closed, the rest more abandoned than unstaffed, it was a very sorry farce that limped on into 1969. Every weekday evening, a few people would leave behind the bustle of Leicester's rush hour and head down a back street to the grandiloquent Leicester Central station,

> along a gloomy subway where their footsteps echoed off the tiled walls. At the top of a stairway stood the bleak platforms… where twenty or thirty people sat on shabby benches under the decaying iron canopy … the only sounds were distant ones.[249]

By the time it closed, Leicester Central was typical of the urban remnants scattered around the post-Beeching network in the sixties and seventies, when the term 'inner-city' began to emerge to describe a landscape of dysfunctional modern estates, derelict or half-abandoned Victorian industrial structures and the run-down homes of those who had worked in them. Unmitigated England indeed.

Chapter 11

A tiger in the tank? Barbara Castle and the stable network

When he begged Barbara Castle to take the job of transport minister in late 1965, Harold Wilson told her, 'For God's sake, say yes. I must have a tiger in my transport policy and you're the only tiger we've got.'[250] (At the time, Esso petrol was promoted using the slogan 'put a tiger in your tank'.) Castle said she'd sleep on it. When she arrived at the ministry the studies Beeching set up had arrived at their conclusion, implying an 8,000-mile network of which under 5,000 miles would be open to passengers. Yet the cuts this implied were never made and in March 1967 Castle published a new map, *British Railways Network for Development*, based on the idea that the system should be stabilised at 11,000 miles, with approximately 8,000 miles open to passengers. In the retrospective notes that accompany her diaries, Castle claimed to have built a transport policy virtually from scratch, updating the Labour Party's commitment to the coordination of transport to take account of the massive increase in road transport since the war, trying to transfer traffic from road onto rail and bringing more economists to bear on the transport problem. Her reputation as one of the few politicians who can claim to have played 'a distinct leadership role in transport over the course of the last century' rests primarily on *Network for Development* and a series of measures contained in the 1968 Transport Act: introducing subsidies for socially necessary rail services; urban and freight transport coordination; and attempting to transfer freight from road to rail through a 'quantity licensing' system for road haulage.[251] These measures created the impression that she successfully challenged the supposedly pro-road bias of the ministry and its Permanent Secretary Sir Thomas Padmore and turned 'the tide against railway closures'.[252] Just as Marples's willingness to sell the closure programme made a difference, so Castle's attempt to present her policy as stabilisation of the rail network had an impact; but, as with Marples, Castle's significance is not as great as has sometimes appeared.

Wilson's overriding transport policy objective was to make sure transport policy was not a problem and it was Castle's job to deliver that objective. Thanks to the narrow majority he had won in the 1964 general election, the Prime Minister needed to go to the polls again in 1966 and did not want to do so with no policy on a contentious issue that was already proving divisive in the party. Without an integrated transport policy, he told Castle, 'I can't hold the Party ... And the Party is the key to everything.'[253] Virtually her first act as minister was to avert a potentially damaging strike by the NUR in early 1966 by promising a new deal for the railways, a promise supported by her commitment to creating a new body to coordinate nationalised freight transport, which was intended to benefit the railways. She reinforced the pledge after the election with a presentation at which she and Raymond showed union representatives maps of the closures implied by Beeching's studies and what they proposed to do instead.

For Wilson, the need to defuse party divisions over transport policy appears to have far outweighed any interest in what the policy actually was. Once the threat was removed – and in the face of declining popularity and threats to his leadership – he whisked Castle off in April 1968 to deal with a similar but larger problem at the Department of Employment. If the content of her massive Transport Bill had really mattered to him, he would probably not have moved her when it was in committee stage in Parliament facing over 2,000 amendments – Castle was presenting its clauses while waiting for the call confirming her new appointment. He certainly would not have replaced her with a minister – Richard Marsh – who did not support key elements of quantity licensing. Castle believed in her policy enough to criticise Marsh for not following it through, but not enough to resist a promotion into 'the thick of it'.[254]

If Barbara Castle was one thing, she was a party politician. Her achievement as minister was to produce a policy that kept both the rail unions and the TGWU, and both the party and her officials, if not happy then at least quiet. To this end she built on the attempts to strengthen the ministry's planning that had been underway since the start of the decade, restructured railway finances, produced coordination without further nationalisation (the National Freight Authority and urban Passenger Transport Authorities) and – in quantity licensing – promised a transfer of freight from road to rail (at some point in the future, to an extent that would implicitly make economic sense – and therefore be limited). This was no simple reversal of Beeching and Marples, but a mixture of continuity dressed up as change and change that looked more radical than it was. As we have seen, the lack of subsidies for individual services had never meant that all loss-making lines would close. Likewise the introduction of subsidies now did not necessarily mean a larger network. The writing-off of more of railways' accumulated debts was the logical and likely (if not inevitable) development of Conservative policy, while Passenger Transport Authorities was an idea the Treasury had been attracted to before the 1964 election. The initial pro-rail aim of the National Freight Authority was soon abandoned and the body itself fell short of the recreation of the BTC that was the party's ideal, while quantity licensing was largely a device to secure the support of the rail unions for a policy that was not all they had wanted. Castle accepted a compromise that delayed the introduction of quantity licensing until the Freightliner network had proved itself. Although she later blamed her successor for failing to implement the scheme, she would have found it difficult to justify doing so, given this restraint. Castle was also well aware that any measure designed to produce a shift of freight from road to rail which could not be justified on economic grounds would never have been accepted by the TGWU and the MPs it sponsored. At the same time she strongly defended the roads programme against cuts. She understood the political dangers of antagonising motorists (she received death threats over introducing the breathalyser), particularly as increasing numbers of Labour supporters would be acquiring cars in the future. The development of road pricing, which officials saw as a vital component of the modernisation of transport policy, but which Castle realised would be controversial, received no ministerial encouragement. Meanwhile, total gross investment in the railways in 1969 was over a third lower in current prices than in 1964 and lower in real terms than at any time since nationalisation.

Nevertheless, Castle's attempt to identify and fund a social railway was genuine. The outcome fell short of her ambition, due to the familiar shortcomings of state machinery – or the unrealistic nature of the aim, if you prefer. Castle had hoped to apply cost–benefit analysis to every unremunerative line, but this proved impossible, not least because the BRB could not produce the data required. A test-case analysis of Machynlleth–Pwllheli produced in 1969 took two years to complete and recommended closure, although there was a great deal of argument over its findings and the line remains open. An attempt to analyse rail services using a computerised survey announced in March 1970 proved so complex that it was abandoned two years later when officials realised the survey would be out of date by the time it was completed. In the absence of cost–benefit analysis the ministry sought a simpler means of arriving at similar results using an estimate of the value of time lost to passengers, hardship and social and economic factors. However, this was too time-consuming to be applied to every case and so the ministry used a simple test of deficit (i.e. grant) per passenger mile to select services that would be proposed for closure and then subjected to the fuller analysis. Those with a deficit of less than sixpence per passenger mile were generally given a grant and those with a deficit of more than eight pence per passenger mile were likely to be put forward for closure (the deficit per passenger for whom no alternative service was available was also calculated). Officials recognised the limitations of this crude approach and in 1970 it was replaced by a calculation of earnings as a percentage of short-term and long-term costs, but this was not much more sophisticated. The grant-aid procedure involved officials in decisions over the level of service, fares and the relationship between services. Even without a full cost–benefit analysis, it proved impossible to process much more than two-thirds of the grant applications before the 1968 Act came into force. By 1970 it was clear that the level of grant bore little relation to the marginal cost of retaining a service and that, without more staff, the ministry could not hope to fulfil the objectives of the 1968 Act in terms of assessing the value of services. If this was some distance from the ideal of a railway funded on the basis of cost–benefit analysis, did Castle identify a socially necessary railway in a way that was a departure from previous practice?

The proposal to stabilise the railways at 11,000 miles came from the BRB and while Castle appears to have been glad to accept it, it would have been very difficult for her – or anyone else – to have closed more lines more quickly than she in fact did. Had the proposals Beeching's studies implied been implemented, there would be no passenger railway today north of Glasgow–Aberdeen; most of Carlisle–Kilmarnock and the Stranraer, Oban, Fort William and Mallaig lines would have closed. The sum total of lines in Wales would have been the main lines to Holyhead/Caernarfon and to Swansea plus a few branches in the Cardiff area and Shrewsbury–Wrexham–Chester. The Shrewsbury–Hereford–Newport route would have closed almost entirely. In the south-west only the main lines from Bristol to Plymouth/Torquay and Basingstoke to Weymouth, a branch to Westbury and another to Salisbury would have been left. Skipton, Whitby, Scarborough, Skegness, Cromer, Newbury, Yarmouth and Lowestoft would have had no railways. Huddersfield to Manchester and Oxford to Worcester would also have closed. While some railway managers had enthusiastically backed Beeching's approach to rationalisation as a way forward for an industry in trouble, there had always been sceptics, even among those who, like Gerard Fiennes, thought highly of him as a chairman. From late 1963, the view that the emphasis of attempts to improve the railways' finances should be on reducing total operating costs on all services, rather than simply cutting out unremunerative ones, gained ground within the BRB. In early 1966 this bore fruit in the proposed 11,000-mile network.

The ministry had already begun to receive detailed proposals arising out of the *Trunk Routes* study, by the time the BRB suggested a different approach. Officials realised that these proposals ran counter to their recommendations in existing cases involving east Lincolnshire, Settle–Carlisle and Huddersfield–Manchester. Even the larger network Raymond favoured implied a couple of dozen closures officials identified as doubtful. Some had been rejected by Marples (Middlesbrough–Whitby, for example), others were commuter services (North Berwick, Ashford–Ramsgate and the Tyne electric services), served major holiday routes (York–Scarborough) or were lines whose retention had been integral to other closure consents (Peterborough–Oakham). In June 1966 Skegness was reprieved as the result of a rethink Fraser had imposed on the basis of concern expressed by the Board of Trade, the MHLG, the Ministry of Agriculture, the area TUCC and the Central Electricity Generating Board. In September 1966 Castle announced a batch of decisions on twenty-six closure proposals, some of which involved refusing consent to lines that would have closed under Raymond's proposals. Despite attempts in the accompanying press release to identify the decisions with Castle personally, these refusals were broadly in line with the policy Marples had followed,

in particular the general concern of his officials over holiday
lines and commuter services. For example, Castle's reprieve of
St Erth–St Ives and Liskeard–Looe reflected official advice that
both carried substantial numbers of holidaymakers and 'present
an intractable road traffic problem for alternative bus services';
but her 'determination' to preserve rail links to holiday resorts
did not extend to the Bodmin–Wadebridge–Padstow line, where
the ministry felt the roads and buses could cope.[255] Other refusals
on the list had been foreshadowed by the MHLG's concerns in
August 1963. The continuity of the official machine is evident
in a draft letter to Philip Noel-Baker, the Labour MP for
Swindon and a long-standing opponent of closures, presented to
Barbara Castle when she replaced Fraser in December, containing a repetition of an assurance Marples had given Macmillan
that 'our experience is that in fact opposition to closures nearly
always peters out once the decision has been made, and the forecast hardship hardly ever materialises'.[256]

If Castle's map was largely a reflection of existing policy, both
its content and presentation took account of the political difficulties of rail closures, which were brought home to her during the
1966 election campaign. The map portrayed a smaller network
than the one existing at the time but the key presentational
point was that it was larger than the one Beeching would have
put in place. Indeed, under the headline 'Burying the Beeching
Plan', the *Financial Times* published a version of the map showing some 3,000 miles of 'Reprieved Lines' as thick broken
lines. Only 672 miles of these had been proposed for closure in
Reshaping, the rest being cuts Beeching's further studies implied.
Visually the effect was a marvellous distraction of the eye from
the thin dotted lines representing 'Possible Closures'. 'Basically

what Mrs Castle has done', the paper reported, 'has been to "save" some 3,000 miles of passenger-carrying line.'[257] The ministry decided not to publish a list of closure proposals with the map, because it 'would echo the Beeching method of presentation and impair the different impression of handling railway matters which the minister is trying to create'.[258] Crucially the Treasury was willing to allow the map to be published and presented in a positive light because officials believed that it represented the practical limit of what the closure programme could achieve by 1970, irrespective of any ultimate target. This was a reasonable estimate given that in 1967 the network stood at about 13,000 miles in total, of which about 10,000 miles was open to passengers (indeed *Network for Development* implied a number of closures which did not take place by 1970 – or subsequently. For example, Ashford–Hastings, Leeds–Carnforth, Barrow–Whitehaven and the lines to Uckfield, Sheringham and Pwhelli). Pressure from the Treasury and the DEA obliged Castle to accept privately the possibility of a further contraction after 1970. The two departments also watered down references to halting drastic reductions in the network contained in Castle's *Railway Policy* White Paper published some eight months after the map in November 1967. They were anxious to stress that a larger network should not mean a larger investment programme to develop the core network in the intensive way Raymond had envisaged and to this end wanted the original title of 'Lines for Development' altered to 'Lines for Retention'. Replacing 'Lines' with 'Network' kept both sides content.[259]

Castle's sudden departure left her bemused successor Richard Marsh with three particularly tough decisions: Edinburgh–Hawick–Carlisle (the Waverley line), Shrewsbury–Llanelli and the east Lincolnshire lines (Peterborough–Grimsby and the branches to Skegness and Mablethorpe). These cases indicate the difficulty any minister would have faced in going beyond the closures *Network for Development* implied. The common factor in all three was the extent to which closure would leave large areas with poor roads far from any rail service. The Waverley line was considered by ministers in spring 1968. Reminding the Prime Minister of recent nationalist electoral successes, the Scottish Secretary put up a very strong, but unsuccessful, fight in favour of at least retaining the northern half (Hawick–Edinburgh) for three years, as it served an area to which the government was attempting to attract industry. However, while the population had decreased by 9.5 per cent during 1964–7, the number of passengers north of Hawick had dropped by 30 per cent and the number of cars had risen by 120 per cent. There was a strong element of symbolism on both sides. Marsh argued that it was more important than ever to reduce the burden of the railway deficit and that rejecting this closure would make it harder to justify others, while the Scottish Secretary pointed to the damage the closure would do to economic confidence in the area. Given that there were only thirty season ticket holders between Hawick and Edinburgh and the subsidy of over £390,000 a year for that section compared with an anticipated annual subsidy of £150 million to the railways, both could be accused of inflating the significance of the case, although the reaction to closure suggests that they were not alone. On the penultimate day of operation two trains were delayed by bomb scares and passengers on an excursion train were jeered by a crowd at Hawick. The final train was stopped by a crowd on the level crossing at Newcastleton and in the ensuing confrontation the minister of the local kirk was arrested. Following mediation involving the local MP, David Steel, an exchange of prisoners was agreed, the minister was released and so was the train. Negotiations for private acquisition failed and the line was eventually dismantled. In 2006 the Scottish Parliament passed an Act paving the way for the reopening of the northern section as far south as Tweedbank.

The Waverley line closure seems particularly hard to defend given the outcome of the proposal to close Shrewsbury–Llanelli, which ministers discussed in the summer of 1969. This too would leave a substantial area without a rail service, but usage had declined significantly since 1964 (when Marples had refused his consent to closure) and the line had only six regular daily passengers. It served no intermediate place of comparable significance to the border towns and required a subsidy of 21d per passenger mile, against the 16.8d which would have made Edinburgh–Carlisle one of the most expensive lines to keep. Nevertheless, the Welsh Secretary, George Thomas, defended it as strongly as his Scottish counterpart had defended the Waverley line the year before. Thomas had warned Wilson of the dangers of being seen to 'out-Beeching Beeching' as a result of the treatment of Wales in *Network for Development* the previous summer.[260] The decisive difference between the two cases was that three marginal seats bordered the line, there was a strong nationalist challenge posed in Llanelli and the case had taken on a national significance in Wales. Thomas was strongly supported by Eirene White, the party chairman, who warned Wilson that 'closure would at once give the Nationalists exactly the rallying cry they need. We should lose Brecon and Radnor and Cardigan and forfeit any hope of defeating Gwynfor Evans in Carmarthen. It could make things more difficult in several other seats.'[261]

Armed with this warning, the Prime Minister chaired a discussion of the case at which – surprisingly, given their view the previous year that the Waverley line mattered little to the economy of the border towns, but unsurprisingly given White's warning – ministers decided that the development of Mid-Wales might increase traffic on the line and deferred the decision for review in 1970. The railways grant budget does not appear to have been increased to cover the cost of saving the line, thereby causing other more useful services to close.

The east Lincolnshire proposal, although it had aroused considerable opposition, posed fewer political problems; but its complexity illustrates the difficult territory surrounding really large savings. Essentially the problem was how to maintain services for holidaymakers to Skegness and Mablethorpe, given that they were on the end of separate branches from a duplicate through route between Peterborough and Grimsby, connected to Lincoln by another line, none of which seemed worthy of retention other than as conduits for holidaymakers. Marples had deferred his decision on the Lincoln line in 1963 so that the whole network could be considered together, and Fraser had rejected the proposal to close it all; but it was not until 1969, after detailed consideration of various permutations, that a decision was taken to maintain only the Boston–Skegness service (although closed, the Peterborough–Spalding section was almost immediately restored with a local authority grant). Closure of the line north to Grimsby, Lincoln–Firsby and the Mablethorpe branch has left a significant area, much of which suffers deprivation, cut off from the rail network. Taken together these three cases indicate the political and administrative difficulties that would have faced any attempt to pursue the 8,000-mile objective.

Publication of the Waverley line proposal had been deferred in 1964, Shrewsbury–Llanelli was rejected that year and resubmitted, and the east Lincolnshire closure was the outcome of a continuous process dating back to 1963. How long, then, might it have taken to implement the closures implied by the 8,000-mile network?

Castle was a reluctant closer of railway lines,[†] but she closed quite a lot of them, accepting ninety-one proposals in full or part, affecting just over 600 miles. She had initially hoped to cut out the TUCC procedure to speed up the closure process and accepted the ministry's hope that Dingwall–Kyle of Lochalsh would close once road improvements were carried out, which had been Marples's intention when he reprieved the line in 1964. In addition the 1968 Transport Act encouraged the BRB to cut out much apparently surplus capacity – reducing some four-track routes to two and singling some double-tracked routes – which has resulted in capacity constraints today that are arguably as regrettable in hindsight as any closures. The gap between Marples's enthusiasm and Castle's reluctance can be seen in his willingness to close Cambridge–St Ives–March in 1964 despite difficulties in providing alternative bus services between Cambridge and St Ives. He was restrained by the committee imposed on him for that very purpose. Castle retained the Cambridge–St Ives section on the advice of officials, although this proved to be only a temporary reprieve. The difference in their attitude was evident but less significant than the consistency of official machinery and advice. However, to dismiss *Network for Development* as

---

†   Her adviser Christopher Hall had led the campaign against closure of the North London Line while working for Castle at Overseas Development so successfully that in June 1965 it had been the beneficiary of an unprecedented announcement of reprieve without a proposal being published; although Hall does not appear to have been involved in devising rail policy following his transfer, and closure of the North London Line was never likely.

purely a presentational trick with no real impact on the closure programme would be to ignore its symbolic significance. Castle may have been forced to accept the possibility of a new closure programme after 1970 but her legacy was that such a programme would be seen as a departure from existing policy, thus raising the political temperature. It also meant that after 1967 few new closure proposals were being published, so any future government would have to produce major proposals quickly if it wanted to implement them before the next election. Whether or not Castle was thinking this far ahead, this was the position that greeted the Conservatives when they unexpectedly returned to power under Edward Heath in June 1970, apparently with their appetite for rail closures undiminished.

Although some have seen the 1970 Conservative manifesto as a sort of proto-Thatcherite declaration of intent, Edward Heath, who had become Conservative leader in 1965, always rejected such judgements and claimed his aim was a modernisation which would preserve the mixed economy, full employment and the welfare state – as far as possible through consensus. Heath wanted lower taxes, lower spending and a stimulus to economic growth. The railway deficit was an obvious target for cuts, in particular given the Conservatives' apparent determination not to support 'lame-duck' industries. Indeed for Heath the survival of rural railways symbolised the need to modernise. Warning his party of the dangers of failing to do so in 1973, he argued that 'the alternative to expansion is not, as some occasionally seem to suppose, an England of quiet market towns linked only by trains puffing slowly and peacefully through green meadows', but poverty and decline.[262] By the time Heath's transport minister, John Peyton, took office within the newly created Department of the Environment, under Secretary of State Peter Walker, his officials had already established a working party to look at a selection of railway scenarios for 1985 or 1990. One involved closing them entirely, although this was probably for comparative purposes rather than a serious suggestion. These studies were given added momentum in September 1970 when the Cabinet examined ways of reducing public spending by £1,000 million by 1974–5. However, in the face of opposition from the Scottish and Welsh secretaries it seemed that the 'battle will be bloody and the gains small'. Twenty closures a year would be required simply to keep the grant at its existing level and even this would cause 'very real political trouble'.[263] The minister was advised to offer no reduction in the grant beyond agreeing to make the London commuter network self-supporting through fare rises over the next three years (a policy undermined by subsequent price restraint). By early 1971 the Department had a list of 110 lines failing to cover even their short-term marginal costs. Fearing that another Beeching-style list would unite opposition, Peyton and his officials decided to announce only the seventy to eighty cases needed to hold the grant at a consistent level and to do so in batches of twelve, a few months apart. Even this proved impossible as the Scottish Secretary refused point blank to accept closure of the Wick line, proposing commuter services as alternatives. The Welsh Secretary was equally intransigent over the Whitland–Pembroke Dock and Shrewsbury–Llanelli services and Peyton and the Chancellor accepted the political case for postponing any announcement. Although Peyton hoped to take up the case for Scottish and Welsh closures again, the Welsh Secretary warned that the closure programme 'has now gone as far as it can go without prejudicing the economic and social life of many parts of Wales' and that he would oppose any further contraction in the next two years, while rumours of a 200-service closure programme had mobilised opposition across Britain.[264] As one official remarked, 'the irrational and sentimental attraction to the retention of particular rail services at a time when so many of the development areas [as the areas of economic decline were now known] are experiencing serious unemployment' was a significant factor.[265] Many people appeared to believe that rail services had a greater transport significance than their traffic suggested. Clearly, maintenance of the Inverness–Wick and Shrewsbury–Llanelli services, at a cost 'almost absurdly expensive in comparison to the standards we use in England', had taken on a symbolic significance that far outweighed the impact which closure would have on the average 525 people who used the former and 360 who used the latter each day, or the £600,000 it was believed their closure would save.[266] The problem for the government was that if bankruptcies and redundancies were blamed on closures, it was difficult to prove otherwise. Less contentious alternatives could be found, but the case for closing them was more marginal. By the time Peyton had compiled a list of twelve cases acceptable to the Scottish and Welsh Offices, the Treasury Chief Secretary expressed concern that the government would look stupid if it proposed closures that would cost jobs while announcing government spending elsewhere to create jobs, and all but four of the cases on the list were reprieved. By early 1972 ministers had effectively placed a political moratorium on closures; its length remained open to question, but the eventual rundown of rural bus and rail services was still seen as inevitable.

Meanwhile, in late 1971, the BRB and the Department had

completed studies designed to test the viability of various sizes of railway, one of which was as small as 3,800 miles. Nearly two years of wrangling followed over how a network consisting only of profitable passenger services, profitable freight services and grant-aided services (which were inherently profitable as far as the BRB's accounts were concerned) could still be predicted to lose large sums of money. The only outcome of this discussion was an agreement that no viable railway had been identified and that the search for the right-size railway should continue. A network of 5,450 miles, from which all grant-aided services had been removed except commuter services, was cheaper than the Board's favoured approach but less cost-effective in terms of the traffic it carried. When a copy of the Department's report on the BRB's further studies was leaked to the *Sunday Times* in October 1972 and the public saw a map on which not only Inverness, Stranraer, Penzance, Aberystwyth and King's Lynn, but Ayr, Middlesbrough, Canterbury, Stratford-upon-Avon, Hereford, Blackburn, Burnley, Aylesbury, Salisbury and Chichester were removed from the rail network, Peyton faced exactly the problem he had hoped to avoid by publishing closures in small batches. All hell broke loose. As the chairman of the Broad Street Line (Richmond) Committee warned, 'Beeching caught the country unprepared [but] there is now scarcely one threatened line that is not forearmed with a defence committee' and many politicians had made promises of support which would now have to be honoured.[267] The NUR promised to fight the plan 'tooth and nail'. In Aberystwyth, which would be left with Shrewsbury as a rail-head, the local council unanimously resolved to organise protest meetings to prevent 'the death knell of Mid-Wales' and the mayor was quoted as saying '[w]e must fight, and fight to the death, even if it means going outside the conventional means at our disposal'.[268] According to Richard Marsh, who was now the BRB chairman, the prospect of a closure programme was killed when he showed Peyton a map indicating its impact on Conservative constituencies in rural areas. Walker told officials that he would not accept any significant cuts in the network; Peyton and Marsh fell over themselves to reassure the public that the leaked map was just one of a series of options being studied (as indeed it was). By the start of 1973, the Department saw little point in continuing studies of the viable railway; it was politically impossible. At the Treasury, officials who wanted a closure programme found themselves impotent in the face of what one of them called 'the overwhelmingly most unsatisfactory part of the whole railway saga ... the fundamental refusal of politicians to countenance the <u>possibility</u> of a significant rundown in rail services'.[269] That reluctance is not hard to fathom when one considers that in 1974 BR identified eighty-two services on which each train carried an average maximum of twenty passengers and revenue was less than half of operating costs; withdrawing thirty-eight of them would allow 1,000 miles of railway to close and save £3.2 million, but provoke howls of protest. The saving was equivalent to 1 per cent of the public subsidy received by the BRB in 1975.[270] A few months later a cross-party consensus had emerged on the need to maintain the network at roughly 11,500 miles, Peyton was claiming credit for the fact that only 135 miles of railway had closed in the last three years compared to 3,430 under Labour and had ruled out large-scale closures to cheers from all sides of the House of Commons. By early 1974 he had announced that even piecemeal closures would generally fail to reduce system costs and several lines whose closure had already been approved were reprieved.

The year 1974 was one of fierce party politics. An inconclusive general election in February was followed in October by a narrow win for Wilson (who had taken office without a majority in March). But the narrow electoral margin made closures harder to propose or implement. In broad terms, the Conservatives did not want rural closures because they tended to be in Conservative seats and Labour did not want them because the rail unions – now vigorously opposing closures – sponsored some of Labour's MPs. The Railways Act 1974, which enshrined rail subsidies as a block grant known as the Public Service Obligation, although passed by a Labour government was essentially the same as legislation the Conservatives had planned before they lost office. It was accompanied by an instruction to the BRB to provide a service from 1 January 1975 that was generally comparable to existing levels.

The inability of the Heath government to get a closure programme up and running or to cut the railway deficit arguably typified the wider failure of that government in the face of opposition to its attempts at modernisation, in particular from the trade union movement. By the end of the century, Heath's name had become 'almost synonymous with the U-turn', but there was more to the rejection of closures in 1970–74 than a lack of nerve.[271] British Rail argued that closures did little to reduce central costs and would in some cases leave it worse off. Whitehall was sceptical but there was no disguising the fact that even a significant reduction in the network was going to make little impact on the deficit. Politically, cutting investment was much easier. The Treasury saw the 1974 Act as a formal recognition 'that British Rail is no longer a viable commercial enterprise, and that there is no foreseeable prospect of restoring viability'.[272]

Tinged with cynicism as it was, Castle's symbolic halting of railway closures had paved the way for a real halt. A few lines closed in the ensuing years, but despite repeated efforts on the part of some officials a closure programme was never resurrected. The Beeching era was over.

Chapter 12

Aftermath: the management of decline

In the years since 1974, although attempts have been made to revive the idea of a programme of railway closures, they have never looked likely to succeed. Maintaining the size of the network has became a commitment no politician dare renounce. But this trend did not reflect a restoration of faith in the industry. The vagueness of the relationship between the wider social and economic benefits of rail services and the subsidies paid to the BRB left it saddled with an air of failure and did little to encourage investment. By the end of the twentieth century the railways were once again a metaphor for all of Britain's problems. Meanwhile the railway Beeching and Marples had supposedly destroyed grew as an ideal in the national imagination, emphasising the inadequacies of the industry that had emerged from the 'destructive' period of modernisation.

The impossibility of another closure programme was most dramatically illustrated when in 1982 Sir David Serpell, veteran of the Stedeford Committee, and former Permanent Secretary at Transport and part-time member of the BRB, was asked to lead an inquiry into the railways' finances and recommend ways of producing better results over the next twenty years. Part of the report sought to discuss long-term policy options. This contained a series of maps illustrating networks of different sizes and estimates of the financial results such networks would achieve in 1992. Only option A, a network of 1,630 miles (essentially the west coast main line plus the main lines from London to Newcastle/Leeds, Norwich, Cardiff/Bristol, Bournemouth, Portsmouth, Brighton/Newhaven, Folkestone, Dover and Southend) showed a profit. Even a 40 per cent cut in the network would leave a subsidy of over £500 million and this would involve closing all the railways in north and central Wales and west of Exeter, in Scotland north of the Glasgow–Edinburgh belt (except the Aberdeen route) and in East Anglia except the main line to Norwich. According to Serpell, the point was to illustrate the impossibility of cutting the network down to a profitable core; but maps do attract attention and these were taken seriously enough by contemporary observers. Their reaction, which helped the BRB sideline the report, indicates how politically difficult further closures would be. 'As cures go,' wrote one journalist, 'it's a killer.' [273]

Even the Thatcher government, so willing to slaughter sacred cows elsewhere, was not about to take on opponents of closures en masse. Nevertheless, the possibility that a significant proportion of loss-making services could be replaced by buses remained on the agenda until 1989 when it was finally accepted that the benefits would probably not be as great as initially hoped, especially if introduced on individual lines rather than as a specific programme. There was no political appetite for the controversy and it appeared that investing in rail services was as good an option. Suggestions that railways might be converted into roads, although investigated, also got nowhere in the 1970s and 1980s. The repeated attempts to revive a programme of rail closures or to replace trains with buses are seen by some as evidence of the inherent bias against rail within Whitehall. This ignores the fact that there are parts of the British railway system whose survival into the 1980s was entirely due to electoral considerations and for which it would be very difficult indeed to present a convincing economic case even today (just as there are other parts whose closure now seems rash). When one considers the dire position of the British economy and the UK government's finances in the late 1970s and the devastating cuts that were made in other areas of government activity as a result, it is hard to support the claim that the railways were the victim of some underhand conspiracy.

There was, however, one great closure battle left. The 1981 closure of the freight-only former Great Central route between Penistone and Hadfield, amid allegations that it was to be used for the route of a motorway or the site of a government bunker, was undoubtedly controversial, but the Settle and Carlisle became a cause célèbre. By December 1983, when the proposal to close it was published, this duplicate main line, traversing thinly populated moorland, stood out as an apparently obvious candidate for easily achieved savings. The local service Tom Fraser reprieved having been withdrawn in 1970, it had only two stations, Settle and Appleby, two trains a day and a massive viaduct at Ribblehead in need of costly repair. But when it attempted to close the line the BRB walked into its most traumatic individual battle since the Bluebell case a quarter of a century earlier. Accusations of false figures and running down services abounded; legal challenges delayed hearings and expanded the scope for objection. BR restored the local service and found it attracted significant numbers of passengers. The Ribblehead viaduct turned out to be cheaper than originally estimated to repair. Initial ministerial approval was suspended while attempts were made to sell the line and then refused when these failed. Every aspect of the closure battles which had deterred rail managers from a more vigorous approach in the 1950s seemed to be combined and writ large in this one case which reinforced the image of railway management as men whose animosity towards the traveller was only mitigated by the incompetence which prevented them from doing their worst.

Even when ministers decided to privatise the railways, they remained aware of the political need to maintain the size of the network. An attempt to use the franchising process to withdraw the sleeper service to Fort William, whose handful of passengers were allegedly subsidised to the tune of £450 a head, was lost to what the franchising director called 'the Scottish lobby'.[274] By the time reform of the closure procedure was proposed by the 2004 Railways Bill, the Strategic Rail Authority had 'been trying for four years to remove one return service from Wales to London Waterloo, which was carrying an average of eight people a day and cost £500,000 a year'.[275] Over 500 of the network's 2,531 stations were used on average by fewer than 100 people a day in 2010/11. Although rail usage as a whole has grown hugely since privatisation, it is probably only the political impossibility of closing them that keeps some of the lesser-used lines open. A closure programme would face opposition strengthened by the tendency to see the rail network as a part of the nation's fixtures and fittings and any contraction of it as inherently contravening a consensus on the need to reduce car traffic, irrespective of the use made of the station or line to be cut. It would also have to negotiate a procedure that has deterred the formal closure even of services that have ceased to operate in any meaningful sense.

In the summer of 2012, the Department for Transport consulted on proposals to withdraw a passenger train service. It posted notices at the relevant stations and published a 32-page consultation document on its website demonstrating that the alternative to closure would be costs of £2.3 million over the next nineteen years, vastly outweighing the benefits of £3,500. The service in question used to run between Wandsworth Road and Ealing Broadway stations as part of a cross-country service removed in 2007. As this was the only passenger service over a few short connecting lines in central London, it proved simpler (until a new franchise needed to be agreed) to run a daily train between Wandsworth Road and Kensington Olympia and a weekly replacement bus to cover the rest, than go through the closure procedure. None of the stations involved will close, the tracks will remain in use for freight and empty stock and there are plenty of alternative services. The consultation ran for twelve weeks and attracted several responses criticising its costings. The department was obliged to admit that it had inadvertently listed for closure a section of line due to be used by the new London Overground service to Clapham Junction. In December 2012 the closure was awaiting ratification by the Office of Rail Regulation. This service is just one of several 'parliamentary trains' operated to avoid formal closure procedures, the best known of which is the weekly Stockport–Stalybridge service which for the best part of two decades has been all that stands between the stations of Denton and Reddish South and oblivion. Reading this consultation one cannot help feeling the Department of Transport has published it as an act of penance for its haste at Wells and other places.

One legacy of the Beeching era is that maintaining the size

of the network has become synonymous with a positive transport policy to such an extent that the BTC's treatment of that
horse tramway in the forest of Dean looks positively draconian.
However, the policy of maintaining and subsidising the railway
from 1974 was more an admission of defeat than a declaration
of confidence. Ideally rail subsidies should be a payment to the
industry for a service provided to those who do not actually use
the railway directly and pay to do so through fares or freight
charges. This service might be the reduction of congestion, pollu-
tion in general and carbon emissions in particular, the economic
benefits of having a rail connection, such as tourism, or the simple
pleasure of knowing it is possible to travel to Thurso by train
even if one does not actually do so. However esoteric the inputs,
a value can be attached to them, a calculation made and the costs
and benefits of a service weighed. In the absence of this idea
subsidies were simply linked to the loss made by a line which it
had been decided should remain open, rather than an arrangement whereby the social value of specific rail services could be
overtly recognised. Whether or not this made any difference to
the size of the network, subsidy became a badge of failure rather
than an income earned. As a consequence, the level of subsidy
tended to equate to the level of government dissatisfaction with
railway management and this in turn consistently influenced the
political willingness to invest in the rail network, even though the
case for investing in, for example, high-speed rail services might
have nothing to do with the reasons for increases in subsidy.

While investment levels picked up from 1969, they stabilised
in the mid-1970s at an unsustainably low level. This owed much
to the enduring Whitehall folk memory of the *Modernisation
Plan*, but official scepticism had been reinforced by the failure

of every subsequent plan to deliver the promised results and continued to be reinforced by failings on the railways' part. By the early 1970s officials had learned that

> [t]he experience of the past quarter of a century suggests that the only safe rule is that if the figures show the future prospects of the railways in a favourable light they are probably wrong.[276]

If this seems to back up the idea of an anti-rail ministry, it is worth emphasising that this was a view based on experience and backed up by examples. Asked to evaluate the Advanced Passenger Train (APT) on the basis of reduced traffic levels, BR showed that the rate of return improved. While officials attempted to understand how this could happen, the project was approved; it later emerged that the Board had simply reduced capital assets and expenditure in line with the reduced level of traffic. The embarrassing story of the APT's abandonment in 1986 after more than a decade of development sums up the failure to invest in railways post-Beeching. Whitehall's investment scepticism was encouraged by technical and project-management failings on the railways' part. However, with hindsight there are elements of self-fulfilling prophecy here in that had the project been more enthusiastically supported its difficulties might have been overcome. Peter Parker bemoaned it as exemplifying a British habit of 'wishing for the moon and not willing the resources', which in this case represented a fraction of the sum lost on Concorde.[277] Parker's attempts to get government endorsement for a major electrification programme were rejected by the Conservatives in 1981, despite a favourable joint BRB/ministry study. Mrs Thatcher's famed dislike of publicly owned railways and the scepticism regarding their prospects attributed to her trusted adviser Alan Walters cannot have helped matters, but the railways' inability to achieve planned reductions in the subsidy or obtain union cooperation on productivity deals were major handicaps to the Board's case. Although results did improve in the late 1970s, published surpluses were revealed to be losses once inflation was taken into account. When the economy went into recession from 1979, the railways' losses seemed once again to be spiralling out of control at a time when the BRB and the government had agreed a reduction in subsidy.

By the late 1970s the railways' investment position was becoming desperate. BR was refurbishing multiple units built under the *Modernisation Plan* in order to extend their lives rather than purchasing new stock. The future of lines such as Inverness–Kyle and Shrewsbury–Aberystwyth was called into question by the postponement of 3,000 miles of track renewal in 1977. Most disappointing was that, following the completion of electrification to Glasgow in 1974, no main line electrification, and little suburban, took place during the decade. The great investment success of the 1970s, the High Speed Train, the world's fastest diesel, was nevertheless a reflection of Britain's failure to electrify much of its main line network. A 1979 study showed that British Rail received less investment per train/km than any other EU railway; this was still true in 1989, only more so. The consequences were thrown into the spotlight by the appalling disaster at Clapham Junction in 1989. Here thirty-five people died and over 500 were injured when one packed morning commuter train – that should have been stopped by a signal – ran into the back of another whose driver had stopped to report a faulty signal; a third train hit the wreckage – fortunately it was empty. The signal which caused the accident had been improperly rewired, but the crash revealed unacceptably dangerous working practices on a project that should in any case have been carried out several years earlier (the technician involved had worked every day for over ninety days with completely inadequate supervision and this was not an isolated problem). This – and the poor crashworthiness of the ageing stock – raised concerns over the safety implications of BR's financial constraints.

From 1988 investment rose steadily until in 1993 it reached a level higher in real terms than in 1960. However, if the Channel Tunnel was excluded, investment in the existing railway was not that much higher than the inadequate plateau of the 1970s, and making up for the chronic underinvestment that had typified the intervening period would not be a quick process. In 1990 investment again paid the price of the railways' failure to meet financial targets as the economy entered a recession. It is difficult to prove, but reasonable to suggest, that an over-emphasis on the size of the network as a measure of government policy encouraged the development of this chronic underinvestment. For example, had the 1,000-odd miles of closures identified as saving £3.2 million in 1974 been implemented, they would surely have provoked a public outcry far greater than a cut of ten times that amount in an annual rail investment budget.

At the same time as the railway appeared to be locked in a process of inexorable decline, two associated trends emerged: nostalgia for the lost pre-Beeching railway, which went beyond the memories of those directly affected, and concern at the effect of the motor car on the environment. When Neil Cooper-Key MP questioned whether the BTC should be allowed to close services in outlying districts just because they lost money in

1953, he specifically drew comparison between rural railways and rural post offices. By the mid-1970s resentment over rail closures had been strengthened by the tendency for public facilities to be concentrated in towns. Today the decline of the rural post office and the village shop is a familiar concern, as they give way to the mini-supermarket at the garage on the dual carriageway or the lure of distant superstores. While many closed railway lines have simply merged back into the fields from which they seemed to grow, others are submerged just beneath the surface of this modern landscape. Take the A361 North Devon relief road, which performs the function of the old Taunton–Barnstaple line as a branch from the main network towards the resorts of north Devon. When the main railway line from Taunton to Exeter was first opened, a station called Tiverton Road was provided, which later became Tiverton Junction when a branch was built to Tiverton itself. The town was also served by trains on the Exe Valley line. Both lines closed in 1963–4, leaving Tiverton Junction once again as the town's railhead. In 1986 it was replaced by Tiverton Parkway station where the railway passes the junction of the M5 and North Devon relief road. The very name of the station illustrates its modern origin, 'parkway' being an epithet applied since the 1970s to stations to which one is expected to drive and park. The relief road bypasses Tiverton but throws off a spur to it, the Great Western Way, under which lies the former Tiverton station. One of the locomotives that frequented it – known as 'the Tivvy Bumper' – has pride of place in the town museum. Heading north-west, the A361 eventually takes over the route of the Taunton–Barnstaple line from South Molton on to Barnstaple, where the A39 takes over, passing a business park, a superstore and a McDonald's to arrive at the industrial estate that used to be Victoria station. Barnstaple Junction survives as the terminus of the 'Tarka Line' from Exeter. The intermediate stations on to Ilfracombe survive as a private house, part of a holiday-home development, a restaurant and a shop; the terminus has been demolished to make way for a factory. Much of the route is a cycle path or footpath. For a few years Mortehoe station was a children's amusement park, four coaches having been placed between the platforms to house the attractions. A heritage railway is busy trying to rebuild as much as possible of the narrow-gauge line from Barnstaple to Lynton. Disused railways have provided the foundations for familiar elements of modern England: ring roads and relief roads, car parks, business parks, retail parks, industrial estates, housing estates, B&Bs, tea rooms, restaurants and heritage attractions. One, Wadebridge, is the John Betjeman centre – a road runs along the old trackbed. Oh dear.

At the same time as such terms as 'parkway' and 'drive-thru' were entering the description of a road-based rural landscape, the branch-line railway became an imagined place, symbolic of a lost and better England. Until rural railways began to close in appreciable numbers, rail enthusiasts were not terribly interested in them, but tended instead to compare the performance of main-line locomotives. As the branch lines disappeared they took on a more romantic aura. I can still recall the moment my mother lifted me up as a small child to look over the bridge in Havant at a derelict track and told me that this was where the 'Hayling Billy' used to run. My youthful fascination with these mysterious pathways, dripping tunnels and crumbling viaducts, recognised and encouraged by Elisabeth Beresford's *The Secret Railway* (1973) must have been widely shared, as witnessed by the plethora of guides to railway walks that have emerged since the 1970s. A further series, 'Forgotten Railways', provides potted histories of all the closed railways in an area with a brief guide to their remains; the Railway Ramblers organisation has been active since 1978. In 1952 H. C. Casserley indicated the growing interest in branch lines with the publication of a slim illustrated list of previous closures, *Service Suspended*. Now virtually every line that has ever existed has a small volume devoted to its history and, like the railway walks literature, they are laced with regret over closures.

In his 1990 guide to walks along former Southern and GWR routes Jeff Vinter, chairman of the Railway Ramblers, admited that he saw Beeching as 'a sort of state executioner', appointed in 'the sixties [which], after all, were a self-consciously modern and destructive age'.[278] In *Forgotten Railways* (1986), H. P. White recounted his 1958 journey over the 110 miles of the former Midland and Great Northern Line from Peterborough to Great Yarmouth at an average speed of less than 25mph. Reading his account it is easy to appreciate that for 'the connoisseur of rail travel' this is a journey to be 'savoured in the memory', but as he acknowledges it is not one that would appeal to the normal passenger.[279] There were few greater connoisseurs of rail travel than Professor White, who took comfort in planning complex English railway journeys during four years as a prisoner of the Japanese during the Second World War. As first-hand memories of the rural steam-hauled railway receded, it was, naturally enough, the connoisseurs who produced accounts that fuelled nostalgia for the M&GN, the Somerset and Dorset and the rest, and introduced them to a new generation. None of this is a bad thing, but such accounts could all too easily be taken as illustrations of a beauty that Beeching destroyed, by readers who forgot – or had never known – the poor service, the decrepit stock, the slowness and inconvenience of it all. Indeed, White's description of the M&GN perfectly illustrates why those who could had generally bought cars before their local railway closed.

Within a year of its preservation, the Bluebell Railway was being used as a film location. The starring role of the preserved Keighley and Worth Valley Railway in Lionel Jeffries's successful 1970 film adaptation of E. Nesbit's *The Railway Children* cemented a relationship which has seen the polished locomotive steaming into the well-kept rural station become a handy symbol of time and place for the filmmaker, taking us to an England which we already recognise in our imaginations and which is in turn secured there by its repeated depiction. By the end of the century, Britain's heritage railways were carrying about eight million passengers a year. In the flesh, as on film, they recreated all that was attractive about the past. In 1993 the pop group Blur sought to reinvent themselves as the harbingers of a new self-consciously English music that would challenge the dominant American sound of contemporary rock. The search for an image for the cover of the album that would launch what eventually became a brief renaissance of English popular culture ended with a painting of the *Mallard* 'chugging through the English countryside', which their biographer describes as 'a 50s *Boys Own* comic conceptualisation of an ideal England'.[280] In the 1950s boys looking for an ideal England in their comics were as likely to look to the future and Dan Dare as to the past and the *Mallard*, but that image would not have said 'England' in the way the cover of *Modern Life is Rubbish* did.

In the post-Beeching era the state of the railways seemed to

symbolise the failure of modernisation, a network characterised by dereliction and decay even where it was still open. Jeff
Vinter's view of the 1960s as destructive reflects a wider feeling
that 'modernisation seemed to produce dereliction' which Robert
Hewison has identified in relation to a variety of post-1945
environmental changes.[281] When one's local station resembled a
vandalised, unstaffed bus shelter placed in a ruin, there was not
much the High Speed Train could do to counter this image. BR's
adoption of the slogan 'this is the age of the train', espoused by an
ageing remnant of the 'swinging' 1960s, merely emphasised that
it was not. By the 1990s, the combined effect of underinvestment
in a 'lame duck' railway, nostalgia and growing environmental
concern helped to create the idea that there had existed in the
past a better railway which, like the nation, had declined since
the 1950s, when it should somehow have been transformed into
a network of high-speed main lines, efficient commuter services
and socially useful rural lines, all justified on a thorough analysis
of costs and benefits. The attraction of this perfect railway was
made all the greater by the privatisation of the railways – a policy
which seemed to sum up all the inadequacies of a government
headed for electoral disaster on a rare scale.

Although decades of underspend meant they did not look it,
by the early 1990s the railways were well run, well organised and
cost-effective. They had developed, in total route modernisation,
an effective approach to investment (under which all elements
of a route were modernised at the same time), an approach
applied to the commuter services out of Marylebone with excellent results. If only the nation had at this point resolved that it
wanted a modern, efficient railway and was prepared to pay for
it. Instead the industry was privatised in the hope that this would

somehow reduce or even eliminate subsidies and solve the problem of underinvestment. The first of these hopes was probably always a delusion and has obviously not been fulfilled. The privatised railways carry almost twice as much passenger traffic (in terms of passenger/km) today as they did before privatisation, but unit costs have not fallen. Meanwhile, the post-privatisation investment in improving infrastructure has increased the Regulatory Asset Base (i.e. the debt which must be serviced) from under £5 billion to £42 billion, incurring an additional £1.5 billion annual charge. In other words the railways carry more people on newer trains and cost around half as much again as they did before privatisation.[282] British Rail could have done this. It is tempting to conclude that the only real benefit of privatisation is the greater willingness of government to give taxpayers' money to private railways than to ones they actually own. However, as much of this money has been given to Network Rail, which *is* publicly owned, even this advantage is questionable. It is probably fairer to say that government has been more willing to give money to the railways since it was able to pretend that their spending is not public spending, because of the ingenious creation that is Network Rail (the structure of which means its borrowing does not count towards public expenditure liabilities).

With the benefit of hindsight, privatisation offers two lessons: if we want a better railway we need to pay for it; and if anyone thinks that reorganising the railways will make them better they should probably think again. If all the energy and money and time that has gone into working out how to deliver railway services since 1990 had gone into actually delivering railway services, we would all be better off. Certainly, the BTC's management of its investment programme seems rather less profligate when

set against the farce into which Railtrack's modernisation of the
west coast main line descended as it became clear that it would
cost more to get a train from London to Manchester at 140mph
than it would cost NASA to put a man on Mars. If there was
ever a hope that privatisation might solve the fundamental difficulties that stem from the dependence of the railway on public
subsidy, it was misplaced. The government continues to be held
responsible for the quality of railway services to an extent that is
not true of the privatised utilities, for example. Closures, subsidies, fares and investment are still subject to a political contest
between ministers, officials, rail managers and the public – and
will remain so for the foreseeable future.

The chaos into which the privatised railway appeared to have
collapsed by the turn of the century significantly enhanced the
industry's status as a metaphor for Britain's perceived decline. On
17 October 2000 a rail disintegrated under a passing express on
the east coast main line at Hatfield killing four passengers and
injuring many more. In the ensuing panic a host of speed restrictions were imposed by the private rail infrastructure company,
Railtrack, which was unable to guarantee that a similar incident
might not occur anywhere else on the railway. The consequences
were horrendous for the country. Hatfield was still causing delays
a year later as Railtrack went into administration and was one
of a series of accidents that tore at the railways' reputation in
practically the only area – safety – where rail had not been seen as
failing in the thirty years before privatisation. Nor did this disaster come out of the blue; rightly or wrongly Hatfield appeared
to be the fulfilment of persistent criticisms that privatisation had
imposed chaos on the rail industry and benefited no one but the
shareholders of the companies involved.

Given that Railtrack was paying dividends to shareholders with one hand and taking subsidies from the taxpayer with another after Hatfield, it is hardly surprising that the railways came to symbolise 'fat cat' Britain for critics such as playwright David Hare (*The Permanent Way*, 2003) or filmmaker Ken Loach (*The Navigators*, 2001). In 2003 Ian Marchant wrote that:

> the railway that you sit on every morning on your way to another shitty fucking pointless day in a drab office in the company of drab work-related acquaintances, is the fruit of political corruption, institutional indifference and short-term profiteering. No one loves it because it is unlovable.

He was obviously not writing just about the railways.[283] Marchant's anger may have been directed first and foremost at contemporary Britain and its privatised railway but he knew where to look for the defining example of the failure of politicians to sort out 'Britain's ageing transport infrastructure' – the failure of the *Modernisation Plan* and its reversal by Marples and Beeching, who 'decimated Britain's railway system, only five years after the investment of the Modernisation Plan. So what hope for [any modern transport minister]?'[284] If the industry symbolised the need to modernise in 1960, by the early years of the twenty-first century it had become a metaphor for the failure of modern Britain itself. At the heart of this view was the popular memory of Beeching the axeman, Marples the road-builder and their heartless, dishonest assault on the railways of a better England.

Chapter 13

Conclusion: ultra-modern horror

The significant memory Harold Macmillan took home from 24 October 1961 was the bizarre juxtaposition of debating a Russian H-bomb test of unprecedented 'ultra-modern horror' ('the "bomb" statement went off quite well'), and the meeting he went into immediately afterwards.[285] This consisted of a 45-minute plea from a deputation including Betjeman, demanding that Macmillan and Marples save the Doric arch at Euston station from the BTC's modernisation of the west coast main line. Macmillan appeared ill-informed and disinterested; perhaps his mind was elsewhere. Alan Jackson's history of London's termini described Euston in 1959 'as a place to get away from as quickly as possible' for most passengers and the Doric arch (or portico) as 'filthy and sad'. 'When we heard,' he continues, 'that at long last a new Euston was to be built, no one was much troubled. The old place would go without many tears, and everyone assumed without a second thought that some way of saving the Great Hall and the portico would be found.'[286] It was not. The cost was too great, although the Commission's figures were, of course, strongly contested (this was the first major campaign of the Victorian Society, formed in 1958). The portico was torn down and dumped in a river on Hackney Marsh. In recent years bits of it have been dredged up. There is talk of a resurrection when a new station is built following the demolition of the 1968 Euston, which, though a functional improvement on the previous station, has never lived down its association with the demise of the arch. That was the modernisation of Britain, that was.

The demolition of Euston's portico encapsulated the clash between enthusiasm for the dream of a new modern England and the increasing hostility that accompanied the emerging reality of modernisation during the 1960s. Ironically, the negative reputation of Ernest Marples as a dishonest, anti-rail minister owes much to his willingness to be honest about the choices facing the nation as far as the railways were concerned. For advocates of modernisation the railways had become symbolic of the nation's problems by 1960 and opposition to rail closures was associated in *their* minds with a refusal to accept reality. Defending the *Beeching Report* in the House of Commons, Marples warned that 'if we funk reshaping the railways, we funk everything, because this is the most patent case for change and change reasonably quickly'.[287] The image of the railways as encapsulating Britain's need to modernise in the late 1950s was an accurate one. Initially, modernisation was conceived primarily as a technological process, but by 1960 the railways, and transport policy in general, were being modernised in a more genuine sense, as part of a wider process that saw the Treasury try to master the complex environment in which it operated. As the nationalised industry with the greatest problems, the railways influenced this wider process of reform. Marples was a dubious character, but there is no evidence that there was anything corrupt in his handling of railway closures, which while hawkish was in line with official advice. The policy of cutting the rail network and investment in it while spending more on roads was not one he conjured up to enrich himself or as part of a conspiracy with the road lobby – indeed *he* did not conjure it up. Nor is it right to characterise the closure programme as a ruthless cost-cutting exercise in which the wider transport picture or the social and economic consequences of closures were ignored. The *Beeching Report*, although aimed at reducing the railway deficit, had its origins in studies of future transport requirements, the belief that responsibility for providing social services should lie with accountable ministers rather than rail managers and, above all, the need to control public investment. The *need* for the report rested on the failure to address either the railway industry's problems or the difficulties of closing lines in the preceding decade.

Although the significant increase in railway deficits during the 1950s was precipitated by government intervention in railway pricing and wage negotiations, it reflected fundamental problems that any organisation – centralised or decentralised, publicly or privately owned – would have struggled to overcome. The most obvious of these were the inability of stopping-train passenger and merchandise freight services to compete with road transport and the implications of a changing freight market; but the legacy of over-capitalisation, outdated equipment and working methods and the effect of intensive wartime use were all factors. Furthermore, for an entire decade after the end of the Second World War, the industry was either waiting for reorganisation to be imposed upon it or coming to terms with reorganisation; and, at times, both. While the 1947 Act arguably gave the Commission a challenging task – to provide an integrated public service while breaking even – and an ineffective structure; the

1953 Act gave it an impossible task and a chaotic structure. The organisation which emerged in the mid-1950s was ill-suited to its role, ill-led and ill-served by governments. By the end of the 1950s the BTC was entitled to wonder whether its chief purpose was to run a public transport service or to provide the government with an extremely ineffective means of regulating the economy and managing industrial relations. One consequence of this combination of failings was an inability to translate the emerging realities of the transport revolution into a consistent policy on investment and network size.

Whether the presentation of the 1955 and 1956 plans as solutions to the railway deficit were acts of incompetence, deception or self-deception on the part of ministers, the mitigation on all three charges is that the government was struggling to get to grips with problems that seemed more important than whether investment in the railways, which was not actually going to take place immediately, would eventually eradicate their deficit. Nevertheless, while the BTC can be criticised for failing to produce better plans and for mismanaging the ones it had, the government had little grounds for surprise when the Commission could not pay off debts that were largely inflicted by government policy and were actually part of the 1955 plan. The one moment in the history of nationalised railways when they were offered a major investment opportunity was in fact the absolute nadir of their treatment by government, because it eventually saddled the industry with an undeserved image of failure. This perception provided an unfortunate context when the nation finally got to grips with the question of the role of the railways in a road-dominated transport sector, some ten years after the first opportunity to do so had been missed.

Although the growth of the deficit made some reform of the BTC inevitable and encouraged the government to make significant efforts to overcome resistance to closures, the key factor in changing policy at the turn of the decade was the evolution of public expenditure control. For the Treasury the loss of large sums in a particular year was less significant than the prospect of an open-ended investment programme earning no return and the implications of this for public expenditure. Addressing this issue led to the setting of clearer targets for nationalised industries and to attempts to estimate future transport trends as a basis for investment decisions. Once it appeared that investing in railways would not reduce demand for road space, the case for investing in rail rested increasingly on the effect of modernisation on the railways' finances. Cuts in the investment programme began in the honest and reasonable belief that much of it would do no more than reduce losses on parts of the network that were no longer essential. It appeared that these losses could be reduced more effectively by simply ceasing to provide services that did not represent value for money. Officials were aware that their understanding of the changing transport landscape was less than perfect, but they faced a choice between doing what seemed sensible in the circumstances – cutting the railways and investing less in them – or approving investment spending that would increase the railways' deficit and do nothing to reduce demands for funds elsewhere. Adopting the first course in turn encouraged the view that detailed figures justifying individual closures were more an issue of presentation than policy-making. It is the Treasury's attempts to control public investment, not the road lobby, that is the key to understanding why Beeching happened.

Whether intended to integrate road and rail transport, eradicate duplicate routes or simply save money, closures tended to take a long time to implement during the 1950s. The problem opponents of closure faced, although maybe not apparent at the time, was that while they were able to make the authorities look silly, untrustworthy or incompetent, they were not able to persuade them that they were wrong. Cheaper means of operation could cut costs and boost traffic but not by enough to turn losses into profits; figures could be picked apart but unravelling them did not reveal hidden treasure; and the consequences of closures were not as dire as objectors warned. The Isle of Wight's roads did not come to a halt and the Sussex countryside was not noticeably worse off without the Bluebell and Primrose line. Consequently, the more successful the opponents of closure appeared to be, the less favourably the state regarded them. The problem that the state, generally in the form of railway managers, faced was that the more detailed its arguments for closures were, the more it opened itself up to attack. The less detail it revealed the more suspicion it aroused. This was not a healthy debate and in the absence of one, the extent to which the problems of the railways revolved around rural branch and secondary lines may well have appeared larger to both sides than was really the case. If so, this can only have been exacerbated by the drift of government policy after 1951 and the missed opportunities to examine the railways' problems in framing the 1953 Transport Act or the 1955 *Modernisation Plan*. The government's determination to grasp the nettle of railway reform – strong enough to overturn the Conservatives' taste for decentralisation – led it to reform the closure procedure under the 1962 Transport Act to hamper opposition to closures. This took place just as objectors' criticism of the procedure reached a crescendo, and just at the point when the closure programme began to deal with services and encounter issues that really did deserve the sort of in-depth analysis objectors called for. The sad irony of the Beeching years is that having struggled with a closure procedure that made mountains out of molehills, the government abandoned it just as it got to the mountains.

In relation to both transport as a whole and the railways in particular, the gradual development of government policy during 1958–74 was more significant than the apparent changes wrought by new governments or new ministers. Although the election of a Labour government in 1964 and the subsequent appointment of Barbara Castle as minister made it harder for Castle's successors to pursue a draconian approach to closures, the search for a profitable core network was never likely to result in every line outside that network being closed, because Whitehall consistently appreciated that loss-making lines might be socially necessary. The pattern of official advice and refusals before October 1964 suggests that even a Conservative government with an overwhelming majority and led by Ernest Marples could not have implemented the final conclusions of Beeching's studies without legislating to abolish the consultative procedure altogether, completely altering the way in which closure proposals were considered within Whitehall, quelling considerable internal dissent and either completely ignoring the wider social and economic impact of closures or spending large sums on road improvements, not to mention resigning itself to a spell in opposition. While it would be a mistake to see the stabilisation of the network by 1974 as an inevitable outcome, *Network for Development* was not very different from the network Marples would probably have arrived at, had he continued to follow advice from officials given on a basis consistent with that given during 1963–4. A minister other than Castle might have tried to establish different criteria and drive the closures forward, but the political difficulties such a course would have encountered are pretty clear (indeed they defeated those who tried to renew the drive for a profitable railway after 1970). However, if Castle was to achieve the party unity over transport that she was appointed to produce, it was essential to portray her policy as a significant change of course.

Following the publication of the *Modernisation Plan*, Enoch Powell argued that 'there must be concealed … in our present railway system, as a sculpture is concealed in a block of marble, the railway system of the future which does pay and does correspond to the economic needs of the country'.[288] This idea remained a feature of debates over railway policy for the following twenty years. The search for a slimmer, financially solvent railway eventually revealed that if Powell's sculpture existed it was a tiny ornament, not a statue. The quest was abandoned because the prize no longer seemed worth its political price. This reflects not only the determination of the rail lobby and users of individual lines, but the political significance of rail services in Scotland and Wales, where their maintenance had become symbolic of a supposed political commitment that far outweighed the real value of the services involved, by the 1970s. The existence of separate government departments for Scotland and Wales and the rise of nationalism made it harder to close lines there; but this in turn made it more difficult to close lines in England where losses were smaller, and so helped bring the entire process to a halt. The closure programme has been characterised as an act of ruthless

disregard for the consequences inflicted on individuals. In fact, it
is evidence of the limitations on the state's ability to act ruthlessly.
Had Whitehall been able to close the lines officials felt served
no useful social or economic purpose, the rail network would be
smaller today. But had financial criteria overwhelmed *any* wider
social and economic considerations it would be far, far smaller.

Explaining why the closure programme in the *Beeching Report*
was produced is easier than judging the policy's merits. Because
the report reflected the railways' side of the new relationship
between government and the nationalised industries, it emphasised financial questions rather than social factors, encouraging
the erroneous impression that the latter were being ignored.
While it is true to say that the reform of the nationalised
industries involved a tendency to treat them as if they were
'commercial undertakings, not social services', setting financial targets was not an attempt to end their role in providing
social services.[289] If politics was the overriding barrier to further
closures by the mid-1970s, the shape of the remaining network
was influenced by official advice as well as by politicians' nerves.
The consequences of the closure programme for the holiday
trade, regional development and urban congestion, and the
extent to which closures left hardship were all considered, but
were the judgements made correct? This is largely a matter of
opinion and it would be foolish to try to retrospectively second
guess contemporary views, but let us try anyway. On urban
closures Beeching was wrong to dismiss the cost–benefit case
for the urban lines listed for closure in *Reshaping*. Although
the government had the right policy in recognising the value
of these lines and rejected many of his proposals, it did not
apply it widely enough. Croydon, Nottingham, Manchester and

Sheffield have demonstrated that heavy rail can be rejuvenated as light rail in urban areas. The failure of officials in the 1960s to anticipate fully the potential for rail to relieve congestion in the smaller conurbations is regrettable, albeit easier to see in hindsight. In dealing with lines to holiday resorts, however, Whitehall correctly identified a trend rather than created one, although in the short term the loss of rail connections probably accelerated the move away from holiday travel by rail in specific cases. If Bude, Hunstanton or Ilfracombe could still be reached by rail would holidaymakers flock there by train today? I suggest not. Mablethorpe may not have prospered in the absence of a railway, but Margate has hardly prospered in the presence of one. The dismissal of day-trip traffic, for example at Hornsea, Withernsea and Porthcawl, may have been more damaging. In depriving itself of any say in railway freight closures the government obviously hampered its own efforts to influence regional economies. While this appeared insignificant because rail was not considered a key factor in regional development, that judgement compounded the error rather than negated it. Some local authorities today see improving links to London as significant transport aspirations because of the economic advantage this brings. The value of a railway is not simply in the traffic that uses it but in the potential it brings to a place. When an area of significant size has no railway its attempts to attract investors are likely to be hampered by that fact; not because there is no other way of getting there, but because the absence of a railway suggests that 'this is a backwater'.

Rail services were maintained if their closure would cause hardship, but hardship was defined in such a way as to enable a service to be withdrawn where it was possible to replace it with a bus service for those whose journeys were economically necessary and whose numbers were economically significant. Is it fair then to conclude that former passengers suffered 'a degree of hardship and inconvenience that does not appear to be widely appreciated by people involved in making decisions affecting rural transport'?[290] There can be no doubt that for many people the closure of their local railway represented a significant deterioration in the quality of their life. The problem officials faced was how to balance the very real hardship caused by rail closures against the notional reduction in other forms of hardship that the savings from a closure produced. Every penny spent on a loss-making rail service was a penny not available to the health service, education, defence or for tax cuts which might generate greater benefits in the long run. My point is not to argue that the balance struck was correct, but to recognise that it had to be struck somewhere – somewhere short of keeping the Great Central main line open for the benefit of a woman in Woodford Halse who needed it to visit her mother. Deciding where to strike that balance was not only difficult, but impossible to do without turning one's back on the consequent misery someone suffered.

The criticism of the programme that seems to carry most weight today, albeit with fifty years' hindsight, is that put forward by David St John Thomas in a postscript to his *Rural Transport Problem*, published in the same year as *Reshaping*. Thomas argued that the procedure under the 1962 Act would make it easy to show that closing little-used stations with inadequate alternative facilities would cause hardship, even though it made no sense for the railways to serve them. It would be much harder, however, to demonstrate the economic damage done to towns with ample bus services by withdrawing busier long-distance trains.

This reflected something of a failure to appreciate the potential value of fast rail services between reasonably large towns. Closure of the Oxford–Cambridge line was delayed – and halted permanently as far as the central section between Bedford and Bletchley was concerned – due to the difficulty of providing buses to the relatively small places between the main towns, yet the potential of the route as a link between the main lines north out of London, with accelerated services connecting the university towns to Bedford, Milton Keynes and Bicester was dismissed on the basis that few people used its slow existing services for this purpose. An even stronger example was the outcome of the proposal to close the Okehampton–Plymouth line and its branch from Bere Alston to Callington. The local geography meant that it was impossible to provide adequate replacement bus services, so the main line was retained between Plymouth and the junction at Bere Alston and the branch kept open as far as Gunnislake, for the benefit of a couple of villages. Meanwhile the link between Exeter and Plymouth via three reasonably sized towns (Crediton, Okehampton and Tavistock) was severed and Tavistock lost its railway completely. It is difficult to describe this decision as anything other than stupid, but it might be fairer to say that such reprieves were intended to be only temporary transitional measures, such was the faith that, as car ownership spread, the retained lines would no longer be required.

Did Beeching place too much faith in the financial benefits of rationalisation? The recommendations in the report were not pursued in total or with the vigour Beeching envisaged, but even if they had been the railways would almost certainly have remained in serious financial difficulty. In 1972, Whitehall estimated that £115 million had been cut from railway operating costs in the four years to 1967 but that this had been largely consumed by increases in wages and other costs, despite improvements in productivity (the workforce was cut by nearly half in 1960–73). Direct savings from closures and withdrawals, including freight, were expected to account for £34–41 million of the £115–147 million total financial improvement envisaged in *Reshaping*. However, much of the rest of that improvement depended on indirect savings which would emerge as the cumulative effect of groups of closures (an expectation that needs to be seen in the context of the problem of 'shared costs' discussed in Chapter 3). The figures published in relation to individual closures from 1963 onwards were not therefore a summary of the entire financial effect of withdrawing a particular service. This helps to explain the apparently blanket condemnation of rural railways and the approach taken in the Wells case.

While it is obvious that there were flaws in the figures used to justify individual closures this should not distract from the reality that, as a whole, passenger and freight trains serving all stations on rural lines lost money. Where they were the only traffic on a line, that line lost money. The idea that cutting the branches damaged the viability of main lines was undermined by studies in the 1970s; the main lines tended to have been built first because they linked major centres of traffic. Closing the Wells–East Dereham line did not help the economics of the other routes from Dereham, which subsequently closed. However, while these were not listed for closure in *Reshaping*, the accompanying maps revealed low traffic levels and they were not part of the system Beeching's further studies identified (i.e. the implication of *Reshaping* was that they would close). Their closure did not fundamentally affect the economics of the main lines to Norwich or King's Lynn. More could have been done to invest in efficient operation for rural railways, but should it have taken priority over spending on parts of the network that were either profitable or had an obvious social value? Gerard Fiennes's account of how he drew up a plan for operating the East Suffolk line as a 'basic railway' in the 1960s has encouraged the view that this should have been done more widely; but it is worth remembering that Fiennes did so only after the political battle to close the line was lost and that he rejected the view that such measures could have saved the neighbouring Cambridge–Marks Tey route.[291] When we consider the limited extent of main line electrification and the abysmal state of some commuter services in the north of England today, for example, it seems perverse to argue that the great failure of railway policy in the last fifty years was not to modernise significant numbers of lightly used lines in order that they would lose less money.

To focus on the fact that Beeching failed to lead the railways to solvency is largely to miss the point of *Reshaping*, which was to travel rather than to arrive, in other words to reduce the deficit as much as was politically and socially acceptable. The fact that closures alone were not the solution to the railway problem does not mean they were wrong. *Reshaping* was only the first stage of a programme that would have left a railway so small that arguments over its viability are hypothetical – it was politically unachievable. The positive legacy of the Beeching era was this realisation and it resulted from a willingness boldly to attempt to tackle a problem that had festered for over a decade. The history of the railways since 1945 is littered with cries that what is needed is for the government and/or the nation to decide what sort of railway it wants and how much it is prepared to pay for it, or words to that effect.[292] When Otto Clarke and Matthew Stevenson decided that they really ought to have a look at the implications of *Proposals for the Railways* in late 1956 those questions began to be asked seriously for the first time since 1945 (and probably since the creation of the big four in 1921) and they continued to be asked more thoroughly in the ensuing eight years than they have been since. There was no more difficult time for Whitehall to begin asking these questions than the late 1950s, just as car ownership took off. The modernisation of the machinery of government in the late 1950s may have resembled 'a rather piecemeal set of running repairs to the post-war settlement',[293] but in transport it was more akin to installing a diesel engine in *Mallard* while it thundered down Stoke Bank.

It suited the government to present the *Beeching Report* as the outcome of sophisticated analysis but in reality it was a snapshot of a work in progress. That work suffered from a shortage of expertise and data in the face of a complex and developing picture. In 1960 'the future' ended in about 1984. Had Britain been frozen in time in 1984 Beeching's analysis might look rather better today. Instead, the railways have experienced a significant growth in demand since the early 1990s that was not foreseen even as it began and the number of private cars on the roads has almost doubled since 1980. Higher rail passenger numbers, increasing congestion, concern over the environmental consequences of the car and the realisation that we cannot simply build our way out of congestion have heightened the impact of those closures which probably should never have been made and increased the number which look wrong in hindsight. Nevertheless, rail policy in the late 1950s and early 1960s represented a significant advance on 1951–6, because genuine attempts to understand and tackle the problem were made. The most obvious omission in the development of transport policy during this period was the absence of an effective pricing mechanism for road use. One problem with the car is that its costs are not sufficiently related to its use and in particular to the kind of use one makes of it; but if this was a flaw in the Treasury's response to the transport revolution, it was one determined by political realities.

In an ideal railway world the taxpayer would pay the rail operator a fee for the benefit provided by every rail service (not just those that lose money) to those who do not pay directly in fares and freight charges. Where the total of fares and non-user payments (or the rationally estimated future total) justified investment, investment would take place; where it did not justify maintenance and offered no prospect that it would, the service would close. In making this statement three points should be obvious from a reading of this book: that the closure of those services which could not survive under this system would be opposed; that the setting of non-user payments would involve complex calculations and debatable assumptions; and that the levels of these charges would be argued over by those seeking to prevent closures and by those seeking to lower taxes and fares. Modernisation failed to produce this ideal system, not because the wider value of rail services was simply lost on or ignored by officials, but because it proved unattainable in a political reality of competing demands for investment, a lack of expertise and resources and the pressure of electoral timetables. It is probably unattainable per se, but Whitehall was certainly closer to it by 1970 than it had been in 1957. Impossible it may be, but such ideals can be useful touchstones when dealing with the nitty gritty of getting things done. Critics of the Beeching/Marples era give too little credit to those involved for at least attempting to relate transport provision to estimates of future needs.

The allegation that this was a policy that failed, was dishonest, callous and too narrowly focused on financial outcomes is too simplistic and to a large extent wrong. How, then, do we account for the passionate conviction with which Beeching is attacked – not simply criticised but 'reviled' and resented – fifty years on?[294] It is important to draw a distinction between the way Beeching is remembered and the nature of contemporary reaction. While there are elements of a romantic Luddism in the opposition to rail closures, Beeching's status as a symbol of the modern approach and the association of rail closures with modernisation were assets in the presentation of a policy which was generally only unpopular with those who stood to lose a tangible service. Even when opposition was based on an arguably outdated attachment to the railway as a symbol of an area's continued significance, this itself reflected a fear of being left behind while the rest of Britain modernised. Even the preservation movement, which might be seen as manifesting a purely romantic attachment to railways, in many cases grew out of a desire to restore a 'real' service. The withdrawal of a local facility, whether rail, hospital or post office, is almost always opposed. It is usually only possible to remove some of that opposition by arguments about the national interest, however well founded they may be. This is partly because once a public service exists people tend to feel they have a right to it; but also because those who suffer hardship will rarely accept that this is justified by some wider averaging of losses and gains, even though it is impossible for governments not to take such an approach. The battle over rail closures was first and foremost a political struggle between those who saw the threatened lines as worthwhile social services and those who felt the nation could not afford them. In order to win that battle the government adopted tactics which were effective in the short term but which fuelled suspicion and resentment over time – limiting debate, withholding information, erring on the side of closure. This conflict took place at a time when romantic nostalgia for the disappearing rural railway co-existed with enthusiasm for modernisation, but on balance the latter was stronger in contemporary reaction to the closure programme. To present opposition to rail closures in the Beeching era as indicating a national rejection of modernisation would be too simplistic; nevertheless it illustrates the contrast between a seductive dream and its problematic reality.

The hardship some suffered as a result of rail closures provides the foundation for the subsequent development of Beeching's reputation, but the popular memory of Beeching today reflects both the 'declinism' Jim Tomlinson sees in economic history and a sense of social decline founded firmly in nostalgia for an England recreated by heritage railways and on screen. The level of infamy attached to Beeching's reputation today reflects the place of the branch line in English culture. The version of the rural railway conjured up in modern popular culture is a myth – part based in fact, but with key elements missing and others imaginatively enhanced – just as the wider vision of England's rural past we entertain ourselves with is rather more attractive than, say, Thomas Hardy's version. In the years after Beeching, regret at the loss of rural railways and an imagined way of life they came to symbolise became entwined with a growing recognition that road traffic and road building do not make the countryside a more agreeable place. In the last twenty years, this effect has been enhanced by the gradual realisation that, like smokers fearing the onset of cancer, we really are going to have to give up emitting carbon one of these days, even if we don't think today is the right day.

Rail closures were part of a transformation of rural England in the second half of the twentieth century. The rural England we imagine as 'traditional' is dead, whether or not it ever existed. That transformation is regretted – at least some of the time – by those who brought it about through their desire to live in the country while enjoying the benefits of a job in a town or city; to drive on dual carriageways and use out-of-town supermarkets; to pay less for goods delivered more cheaply by road; or to drive to the coast. As Marples understood, 'our own car is precious, the rest are a traffic problem'.[295] There is a Squire Chesterford ranting against the lorries and cars and houses with numbers instead of names in most of us. That part of us also regrets rail closures because they symbolise this change and because the branch-line railway is an integral part of the 'real' England depicted in so much of our culture, which the new England appears to have destroyed. Yet this change was caused not by the *Beeching Report*, or by the closing of the railways, but by the motor car and the lorry. It was a consequence of popular choice. As Kenneth Glover put it, to predict and provide a response to road traffic growth 'has become politically incorrect, but at the time it seemed democratic', because it gave people what they showed they wanted.[296] That downland car park, that train puffing slowly and peacefully through green meadows no more, the lane that is now a road, the houses that have numbers instead of names, that cloud of diesel dirt that hangs over every city, those melting ice caps – that was not Beeching and Marples, it was us; we did it. We liked trains, but we used buses and then we bought cars. Why? For the same reason we built railway lines across the hitherto unsullied estates of the aristocracy. We do not want to spend our lives within five miles of the village we were born in. We want to move, we want convenience, we want speed. We want new things. We want to get where we're going. It is almost as if we can't help it.

Glossary

ASLEF	The Associated Society of Locomotive Engineers and Firemen
BR	British Rail
BRB	British Railways Board
BRF	British Road Federation
BTC	British Transport Commission
CTCC	Central Transport Consultative Committee
DSIR	Department of Scientific and Industrial Research
GCR	Great Central Railway
GER	Great Eastern Railway
GWR	Great Western Railway
K&ESR	Kent and East Sussex Railway
LBSCR	London Brighton and South Coast Railway
LMS	London Midland and Scottish Railway
LNER	London and North Eastern Railway
M&GN	Midland and Great Northern Joint Railway
MGM	Ministerial Group on Modernisation
MHLG	Ministry of Housing and Local Government
MoT	Ministry of Transport
MTCA	Ministry of Transport and Civil Aviation

NAPRO	National Archives, Public Record Office
NCB	National Coal Board
NFU	National Farmers Union
NUR	National Union of Railwaymen
Pick-up goods	freight train serving all the stations on a line
REPC	Regional Economic Planning Council
RHA	Road Haulage Association
RHE	Road Haulage Executive (part of the BTC)
RRL	Road Research Laboratory
SAG	Special Advisory Group (AKA Stedeford Committee)
SER	South Eastern Railway
SMMT	Society of Motor Manufacturers and Traders
Stopping train	local passenger train serving every station
TGWU	Transport and General Workers Union
TUCC	Transport Users' Consultative Committee
TSSA	Transport Salaried Staffs' Association
WBRPA	Westerham Branch Railway Passengers Association
WVRA	Westerham Valley Railway Association

Acknowledgements

This book draws heavily on my earlier academic mono-
graph, *Government, the Railways and the Modernisation of
Britain – Beeching's Last Trains* (Routledge, 2006). I am grateful
to Routledge for permission to use this material.

I am also grateful to the trustees of the Harold Macmillan
Book Trust, Copyright and Archives Fund for permission to
quote from the diaries of Lord Macmillan, and to the British
Railways Board (Residuary) Ltd for permission to quote BRB
copyright material (AN and RAIL class records from the
National Archive). I am grateful to Ashridge Management
College for access to the private papers of Lord Watkinson.
I have benefited from, and enjoyed, the willingness of several
participants in the events discussed here, most of whom are
unfortunately no longer alive, to cast their minds back over them:
Lord Boyd-Carpenter; Sir James Dunnett; Sir Christopher
Foster; Kenneth Glover; Richard Hardy; Lady Marples; Dame
Alison Munro; Lord Peyton; Sir Leo Pliatzky; Sir David
Serpell; William Sharp; Sir Geoffrey Wardale; Ivor Warburton;
and Lord Whitelaw. I have also benefited from the exist-
ence of three excellent online resources: the Railways Archive

(http://www.railwaysarchive.co.uk); the *Disused Stations* website (http://www.disused-stations.org.uk); and the website provided by the Colonel Stephens Railway Museum at Tenterden (http://www.hfstephens-museum.org.uk).

I am exremely grateful to Ben Brooksbank, Nick Catford, Nigel Tout and Moon at m24instudio for their very kind assistance in providing illustrations. I am also grateful to the National Archives Image Library for permission to reproduce the image of Northiam station and to the Library and the Isle of Wight Council for permission to reproduce the images of Newport station.

Many colleagues have kept me entertained and encouraged over the years and put up with my ranting about railways, both in academia and at the LGA, but Peter Hennessy's encouragement and guidance in completing the PhD which began my research on Beeching – and his subsequent interest in my work – have been invaluable. My father read an early draft of the book and provided helpful comments and Hollie Teague at Biteback Publishing has helped improve it tremendously. Needless to say, any mistakes and failings herein are entirely mine.

Most importantly I am extremely grateful to my wife and eldest son. Preparation of this book coincided with the arrival of my second child and would have been completely impossible without their forbearance.

Select bibliography

Adley, Robert, *Out of Steam: The Beeching Years in Hindsight* (Wellingborough: Patrick Stephens, 1990)

Allen, Cecil, *The Great Eastern Railway* (Shepperton: Ian Allan, 1955; fifth edition, paperback, 1975)

Anderson, P. Howard, *Forgotten Railways: Volume Two, The East Midlands* (Newton Abbott: David and Charles, 1973; 1985 edition)

Bagwell, Philip and Peter Lyth, *Transport in Britain: From Canal Lock to Gridlock 1750–2000* (London: Hambledon and London, 2002)

Booker, Christopher, *The Neophiliacs: A Study of the Revolution in English Life in the Fifties and Sixties* (London: Collins, 1969)

Burroughs, Robert, *The Great Isle of Wight Train Robbery* (London: Railway Invigoration Society, 1968)

Butler, David and Anthony King, *The British General Election of 1964* (London: Macmillan, 1965)

Butterfield, Peter, 'Branch lines, wayside stations and road competition', *Journal of Transport History*, 16 (2), September 1995, pp. 179–95.

Catt, Andrew, *The East Kent Railway* (Tarrant Hinton: Oakwood, 1975)

Catterall, Peter (ed.) *Macmillan Diaries – Prime Minister and After, 1957–66* (London: Macmillan, 2011)

Carter, Ian, *Railways and Culture in Britain – The Epitome of Modernity* (Manchester: Manchester University Press, 2001)

Castle, Barbara, *The Castle Diaries 1964–76* (London: Papermac, 1990)

Castle, Barbara, *Fighting All the Way* (London: Macmillan, 1993)

Faulkner, Richard and Chris Austin, *Holding the Line – How Britain's Railways were Saved* (Hersham: Ian Allan, 2012)

Fiennes, Gerard, *I Tried to Run a Railway* (London: Ian Allan, 1967)

Garrett, Stephen, *The Kent and East Sussex Railway* (Tarrant Hinton: Oakwood, 1972)

Gould, David, *Westerham Valley Railway* (Tarrant Hinton: Oakwood, 1974; 1981 reprint)

Gourvish, Terence, *British Railways 1948–73: A Business History* (Cambridge: Cambridge University Press, 1986)

Gourvish, Terence, *British Railways 1974–97: From Integration to Privatisation* (Oxford: Oxford University Press, 2002)

Hamer, Mick, *Wheels Within Wheels – A Study of the Road Lobby* (London: Routledge and Kegan Paul, 1987)

Hardy, Richard, *Beeching – Champion of the Railway* (London: Ian Allan, 1989)

Healy, John, *Great Central Memories* (London: Baton Transport, 1987)

Hennessy, Peter, *Having It So Good – Britain in the Fifties* (Penguin: London, 2006)

Hennessy, Peter, *The Prime Minister – The Office and its Holders since 1945* (London: Penguin, 2000)

Henshaw, David, *The Great Railway Conspiracy: The Fall and Rise of Britain's Railways since the 1950s* (Hawes: Leading Edge, 1991)

Hewison, Robert, *The Heritage Industry: Britain in a Climate of Decline* (London: Methuen, 1987)

Hillman, Mayer and Whalley, Anne, *The Social Consequences of Railway Closures* (London: Policy Studies Institute, 1980)

House of Commons Transport Committee, *Rail 2020*, Seventh Report of Session 2012–13, December 2012.

Jenkins, Stanley, *The Wells-next-the-Sea Branch via Wymondham and Dereham* (Usk: Oakwood, 2011)

Joby, Richard, *Forgotten Railways: Volume Seven, East Anglia* (Newton Abbott: David St John Thomas, 1985; first published Newton Abbott: David and Charles, 1977)

Jones, Robin and Brian Sharpe, 'The sixties teenage revolution – railway heritage 1960–64', *Heritage Railway* (online edition), 1 September 2011, http://www.heritagerailway.co.uk/news/the-sixties-teenage-revolution-railway-heritage-1960–64, accessed 21 January 2013.

Lamb, Richard, *The Macmillan Years – The Emerging Truth* (London: John Murray, 1995)

Lapsley, Irving, 'The influence of financial measures on UK railway policy', *Journal of Public Policy*, vol. 3, part 3, 1983, pp. 285–300.

Loft, Charles, *Government the Railways and the Modernisation of Britain – Beeching's Last Trains* (London: Routledge, 2006)

Marchant, Ian, *Parallel Lines or Journeys on the Railway of Dreams* (London: Bloomsbury, 2003; paperback edition, 2004)

Marsh, Richard, *Off the Rails: An Autobiography* (London: Weidenfeld and Nicholson, 1978)

Middlemas, Keith, *Power, Competition and the State. Volume Two: Threats to the Post-War Settlement 1961–74* (London: Macmillan, 1990)

Morgan, John, *The Colonel Stephens' Railways – A View from the Past* (Shepperton: Ian Allan, 1999)

MoT, Report on the fire which occurred in an express passenger train on 14th July 1951 near Huntingdon in the Eastern Region, British Railways, 1952

MoT, Report on the double collision which occurred on 8th October 1952 at Harrow and Wealdstone station in the London Midland Region, British Railways, 1953

Paxman, Jeremy, *The English – A Portrait of a People* (London: Michael Joseph, 1998)

Pryke, Richard and John Dodgson, *The Rail Problem* (London: Martin Robertson, 1975)

Ramsden, John, *A History of the Conservative Party: The Age of Churchill and Eden 1940–57* (London: Longman, 1995)

Riley, R. C., 'The Bluebell Line', *Railway Magazine*, April 1962, pp. 223–30.

Riley, R. C., 'The Lewes and East Grinstead Railway', *Railway Magazine*, October 1954, pp. 665–73.

Salveson, Paul, *Beeching in Reverse: The Case for a Programme of Line and Station Reopenings* (Huddersfield: Transport Research and Information Network, 2002)

Sampson, Anthony, *Anatomy of Britain* (London: Hodder and Stoughton, 1962)

Starkie, David, *The Motorway Age – Road and Traffic Policies in Post-War Britain* (Oxford: Pergamon, 1982)

Stott, Richard, *Dogs and Lampposts* (London: Metro, 2002)

Sykes, Richard *et al*, 'Steam attraction: railways in Britain's national heritage', *Journal of Transport History*, 18 (2), 1997, pp. 156–75.

Theakston, Kevin, *Leadership in Whitehall* (London: Palgrave Macmillan, 1999)

Thomas, David St John, *The Rural Transport Problem* (London: Routledge, 1963)

Thomas, David St John, *West Country Railway History* (Newton Abbot: David and Charles, 1960; sixth edition, 1988)

Thomas, David St John, *The Country Railway* (Newton Abbott: David and Charles, 1976; Penguin edition, 1979)

Thomas, David St John and Simon Rocksborough Smith, *Summer Saturdays in the West* (Newton Abbot: David and Charles, 1973, 1983 edition)

Tolson, J., 'Too little too late – a survey of British Railways diesel railbuses', *Railway Magazine*, January 1968, pp. 4–9.

Tomlinson, Jim, 'Conservative modernisation, 1960–64: too little too late?', *Contemporary British History*, 11 (3), 1997, pp. 18–38.

Tomlinson, Jim, *The Politics of Decline: Understanding Post-war Britain* (Harlow: Longman, 2000, 2001 edition)

Treasury, *Economic and Financial Obligations of the Nationalised Industries* (London: HMSO, 1961)

Watkinson, Harold, *Turning Points – A Record of Our Times* (Salisbury: Michael Russell, 1986)

Weiner, Martin, *English Culture and the Decline of the Industrial Spirit, 1850 – 1980* (Cambridge: Cambridge University Press, 1981)

White, Henry, *A Regional History of the Railways of Great Britain Volume Two: Southern England* (Newton Abbot: David and Charles, 1969)

White, Henry, *Forgotten Railways* (Newton Abbot: David and Charles, 1986)

White, Henry, *Forgotten Railways: Volume Six – South-east England* (Newton Abbot: David and Charles, 1976; second edition, 1986)

Williamson, David, *A Most Diplomatic General – The Life of General Lord Robertson of Oakridge Bt GCB GBE KCMG KCVO DSO MC 1896–1974* (London: Brassey's, 1996)

Winkworth, D.K., 'The Westerham Valley Branch', *Railway Magazine*, September 1952, pp. 624–6.

Wolmar, Christian, *Broken Rails – How Privitisation Wrecked Britain's Railways* (London: Aurum, 2001)

Notes

1   *Carlisle Journal*, 11 September 1964, p. 4.
2   *Railway Magazine*, October 1964, p. 798.
3   *The Guardian*, 28 March 1963, http://www.guardiancentury.co.uk/1960-1969/Story/0,6051,105642,00.html, accessed 4 August 2004.
4   National Archives, Public Record Office (hereafter NAPRO), MT 124/719, Price–Marples, 27 April 1963.
5   Richard Lamb, *The Macmillan Years – The Emerging Truth* (London: John Murray, 1995), pp. 434, 442.
6   Robert Adley, *Out of Steam: The Beeching Years in Hindsight* (Wellingborough: Patrick Stephens, 1990), p. 39.
7   Ian Marchant, *Parallel Lines or Journeys on the Railway of Dreams* (London: Bloomsbury, 2003; paperback edition, 2004), p. 301.
8   Richard Faulkner and Chris Austin, *Holding the Line – How Britain's Railways were Saved* (Hersham: Ian Allan 2012), p. 129.
9   David Henshaw, *The Great Railway Conspiracy: The Fall and Rise of Britain's Railways Since the 1950s* (Hawes: Leading Edge, 1991), p. 7.
10 Hansard, HC Deb, 12 February 1996, vol. 271, cols 641–2; Stewart Francis, preface to Paul Salveson, *Beeching in Reverse: The Case for a Programme of Line and Station Reopenings* (Huddersfield: Transport Research and Information Network), 2002, p. 3.
11 NAPRO, MT 124/726, Gray–Marples, 1 October 1963.
12 BRB, *The Reshaping of British Railways* (London: HMSO, 1963), p. 60.
13 Terence Gourvish, *British Railways 1948–73: A Business History* (Cambridge: Cambridge University Press, 1986), pp. 456–60.
14 Ian Carter, *Railways and Culture in Britain – The Epitome of Modernity* (Manchester: Manchester University Press, 2001), pp. 240–56.
15 David St John Thomas, *The Country Railway* (Newton Abbott: David and Charles, 1976, Penguin edition, 1970), p. 12, Henshaw, *Great Railway Conspiracy*, p. 181.

16   NAPRO, MT 124/1211, Rennison–Castle, 11 February 1967.

17   'Farewell to Adlestrop', *The Times*, 5 April 1963, p. 16.

18   Edward Thomas, 'Adlestrop' and Richard Medrington, 'Still Not Much Going On – Edward Thomas and Adlestrop' in John Simmons, Rob Williams and Tim Rich (Eds), *Common Ground – Around Britain in 30 Writers* (London: Marshall Cavendish, 2006), pp. 13–21.

19   Interviewed in *Ian Hislop goes off the rails*, BBC4, 2 October 2008.

20   John Betjeman, 'Inexpensive Progress', in CPRE, *Where Motor-Car is Master – How the Department of Transport became bewitched by roads*, London: CPRE, 1992; Barbara Castle, *Fighting All the Way*, (London: Macmillan, 1993), p. 388.

21   John Betjeman, *Great Central Railway – Sheffield Victoria to Banbury*, reproduced in John Healy *Great Central Memories*, (London: Baton Transport, 1987), p. 148.

22   John Betjeman, 'Dilton Marsh Halt', *A Nip in the Air* (London: John Murray 1974), pp. 38–9.

23   Leslie Halliwell, *Halliwell's Film and Video Guide 2000* (Harper Collins: London, 2000), p. 843.

24   *The Titfield Thunderbolt*, GB, Ealing, 1952, Dir. Charles Crichton, Script, T. Clarke.

25   'A Branch Line Railway', *Let's Imagine*, BBC, 29 March 1963.

26   Jim Tomlinson, *The Politics of Decline: Understanding Post-war Britain* (Harlow: Longman, 2000, 2001 edition), pp. 21–2.

27   David Butler and Anthony King, *The British General Election of 1964* (London: Macmillan, 1965), pp. 33–6, 78–9, 87–8; Mark Donnelly, *Sixties Britain* (Harlow: Pearson, 2005), pp. 48–51, 74–5.

28   Christopher Booker, *The Neophiliacs: A Study of the Revolution in English Life in the Fifties and Sixties* (London: Collins, 1969). Although contemporary commentators asked 'what's wrong with Britain?', Booker wrote about 'Old England', 'New England' and an 'English revolution' (e.g. p. 219).

29   *Ibid.*, p. 191.

30   Roger Kidner, *Southern Railway Branch Lines in the Thirties* (Tarrant Hinton: Oakwood Press, 1976), p. 72.

31   John Williamson, *Railways To-Day* (London: Oxford University Press, 1938), p. 11.

32   *Evening News*, 16 March 1938, quoted in P. Clark, *The Chichester and Midhurst Railway* (Sheffield: Turntable, 1979), pp. 52–5.

33   C. Dalby of the LNER, quoted in David Smith, *The Railway and its Passengers, A Social History* (Newton Abbot: David and Charles, 1988), p. 88.

34   NAPRO, Rail 390/964, LNER memo, 'Closing of branch lines', 25 January 1934.

35   Thomas, *Country Railway*, p. 133.

36   A Pathé film of the vehicle can be seen here: http://www.britishpathe.com/video/the-motor-railway.

37   Stephen Garrett, *The Kent and East Sussex Railway* (Tarrant Hinton: Oakwood, 1972), p. 17.

38   Andrew Catt, *The East Kent Railway* (Tarrant Hinton: Oakwood, 1975), p. 16.

39   NAPRO, AN 97/19, Branch Line Committee minutes, 1949–50.

40   NAPRO, AN 177/2, note attached to letter from Sir John Elliot, 17 September 1948.

41   NAPRO, AN 97/19, note of meeting, 21 March 1950.

42   NAPRO, AN 13/2415, Cole Deacon–Beevor, 27 October 1950.

43   NAPRO, AN 13/1649, CTCC meeting notes, 9 January 1951.

44   Henry White, *A Regional History of the Railways of Great Britain Volume Two: Southern England* (Newton Abbot: David and Charles, 1969), p.65.

45   'Sentinel S4', post on Kentish History Forum 'Re: Railway stations on Sheppey', 19 March 2012, 02:12:43, http://www.kenthistoryforum.co.uk/index.php?topic=12716.0;prev_next=prev#new, accessed 18 January 2013.

46   NAPRO, AN 13/1675, public relations department memo, 1950.

47   NAPRO, AN 177/2, Harrington–Train, 31 March 1949.

48   NAPRO, AN 177/2, Mepstead–Hopkins, 13 June 1951.

49   http://www.kesr.org.uk/visitor-information/returning-to-robertsbridge, accessed 19 December 2012.

50   NAPRO, CAB 129/47, Barnes, 'Long-term financial prospects of the British Transport Commission', 10 September 1951.

51   John Betjeman, *Trains and Buttered Toast – Selected Radio Talks* (Ed. Stephen Games, London: John Murray, 2006), pp. 276–7.

52   NAPRO, AN 157/520, Southern Region, 'Closing of branch lines: integration of road and rail services on the Isle of Wight', 9 February 1951.

53   NAPRO, AN 177/106, Hopkins–Blee, 23 June 1952.

54   NAPRO, MT 97/66, Birtchnell, 'Transport policy', 27 November 1951.

55   NAPRO, CAB 134/1180, Cabinet committee on road and rail transport minutes, 21 January 1952.

56   NAPRO, T 228/403, Figgures–Mitchell, 3 March 1952.

57   NAPRO, CAB 134/1186, Lennox-Boyd Transport Bill, 18 September 1952.

58   Nigel Harris, *Competition and the Corporate Society – British Conservatives, the State and Industry, 1945–64* (London: Methuen, 1964), p. 88.

59   NAPRO, PREM 11/559, Leathers–Churchill, 17 October 1952.

60   Bodleian Library, Macmillan diaries, C.14/1, 23 October 1952.

61   NAPRO, CAB 195/10, Cabinet Secretary's notebook, 29 October 1952.

62   NAPRO, AN 97/22, 'RE reply of September 24th 1952 to BTC letter of July 14th'.

63   NAPRO, AN 97/22, branch line committee minutes, 4 December 1952.

64   NAPRO, AN 157/521, Hopkins–Baines, 17 November 1952.

65   NAPRO, AN 157/521, cutting, *Isle of Wight County Press*, 22 November 1952.

66   NAPRO, AN 157/520, 'Notes of meeting held at Charing Cross Hotel on Tuesday 21 August 1951'.

67   NAPRO, AN 157/522, Mepstead–Hopkins, 30 January 1953; Hopkins–Coleby, 7 February 1953.

68   NAPRO, MT 115/5, transcript of SE area TUCC proceedings, 18 June 1953.

69   NAPRO, NR 1/1, CTCC minutes, 14 July 1953.

70   NAPRO, MT 115/5, brief, 'The Isle of Wight railways', 18 August 1953.

71   Robert Burroughs, *The Great Isle of Wight Train Robbery* (London: Railway Invigoration Society, 1968), p. 11.

72   http://www.islandbreaks.co.uk/media-and-trade/isle-of-wight-tourism-research-reports, accessed 18 June 2012.

73   NAPRO, MT 124/46, meeting of MTCA and Treasury officials, 6 August 1954.

74   Booker, *The Neophiliacs*, pp. 13, 39, 79, 219, 333–5.

75   BTC, *A Plan for the Modernisation and Re-equipment of British Railways* (London: BTC, 1955).

76   Anthony Sampson, *Anatomy of Britain* (London: Hodder and Stoughton, 1962), pp. 542–4.

77   Department for Transport, *The Future of Rail* (London: HMSO, 2004), p. 9.

78   Gerard Fiennes, *I Tried to Run a Railway* (London: Ian Allan, 1967, revised edition, 1973), p. 78.

79   David Williamson, *A Most Diplomatic General – The Life of General Lord Robertson of Oakridge Bt GCB GBE KCMG KCVO DSO MC 1896–1974* (London: Brassey's, 1996), p. 184.

80   Gourvish, *British Railways 1948–73*, p. 171.

81   MoT paper, 'Examining railway figures: some useful concepts', September 1974 (author's collection). The angle of unreality is that formed on a graph between the railways' projected results over a number of years and their actual results over the same period.

82   NAPRO, T 267/15, Peter Vinter, foreword to 'Treasury historical memorandum eleven – the economic and financial obligations of the nationalised industries, White Paper of April 1961', May 1966 [hereafter T 267/15].

83   Sir Geoffrey Wardale, interview with the author, 24 April 1998; NAPRO, CAB 130/104, *Ad hoc* committee on industrial disputes – railways minutes, 10 December 1954

84   NAPRO, MT 115/14, Lintern–Proctor, 28 August 1954.

85   Fiennes, *I Tried to Run a Railway*, p. 77.

86   Ministry of Labour, *The Interim Report of a Court of Inquiry into a Dispute between the British Transport Commission and the National Union of Railwaymen* (London: HMSO, 1955), p. 7.

87   NAPRO, CAB 128/27, Cabinet conclusions, 8 December 1954.

88   NAPRO, T 234/559, Gilbert–Bridges, 10 December 1954.

89   Bodleian Library, Macmillan diaries, C.16/1, 13 December 1954.

90   NAPRO, T 234/559, Boyd-Carpenter–Churchill, 11 December 1954.

91   NAPRO, T 234/559, Brittain–Grant/Crombie, 10 January 1955.

92   NAPRO, T 234/550, Grant, 'The finance of the railways', 21 January 1955.

93   Hansard, HC Deb, 3 February 1955, vol. 536, col. 1308.

94   NAPRO, T 234/549, Grant, draft Cabinet paper, 'The finances of the railway modernisation plan', 18 January 1955, with Butler's corrections.

95   NAPRO, MT 47/405, cutting, 'Millions for Cinderella', *The Economist*, 29 January 1955.

96   R. C. Riley, 'The Lewes and East Grinstead Railway', *Railway Magazine*, October 1954, pp. 665–73.

97   NAPRO, MT 115/3, BTC draft memorandum, 'passenger services', March 1956.

98   Dame Alison Munro, interview with the author, 15 October 1996.

99   James Towler, *The Battle for the Settle and Carlisle* (Sheffield: Platform Five, 1990), p. 176.

100 NAPRO, MT 115/3, Munro–Willis, 17 February 1956.

101 NAPRO, MT 115/3, Stedman–Molson, 3 March 1956.

102 NAPRO, MT 115/3, Molson–Watkinson, 5 March 1956.

103 NAPRO, MT 115/3, Watkinson–Molson, 6 March 1956; Watkinson–Stedman, 23 March 1956.

104 NAPRO, CAB 130/116, 'The BTC: draft outline note', 20 January 1956.

105 NAPRO, MT 132/32, note of meeting, 11 May 1956.

106 NAPRO, MT 115/82, Stedman–Jenkins, 30 May 1956.

107 NAPRO, MT 115/3, Willis–Stedman, 17 April 1956; Stedman–Watkinson, 18 April 1956.

108 NAPRO, AN 177/194, BTC chief solicitor–Hopkins, 4 April 1956.

109 NAPRO, MT 115/9, Munro–Willis, 1 and 21 June 1956.

110 NAPRO, MT 115/9, Willis–Steele, 2 May 1956.

111 NAPRO, MT 115/3, Wilson–Molson, 18 July 1956.

112 NAPRO, MT 115/82, BTC, 'Further draft of a note by the minister of transport and civil aviation', 29 June 1956.

113 NAPRO, CAB 130/116, GEN 532 minutes, 23 July 1956.

114 Sir Leo Pliatzky, interview with the author, 22 July 1998.

115 NAPRO, CAB 130/116, GEN 532 minutes, 23 July 1956.

116 Sir Leo Pliatzky, interview with the author, 22 July 1998.

117 NAPRO, MT 115/82, Watkinson, note, 23 July 1956.

118 For what follows see CTCC, *Proposed Withdrawal of Train Services from the Lewes–East Grinstead Branch Railway* (London: HMSO, 1958).

119 *Ibid.*

120 *Ibid.*

121 NAPRO, MT 115/306, Beamish–Nugent, 16 June 1958.

122 NAPRO, MT 115/306, Chambers–Bostel, 13 May 1958.

123 NAPRO, MT 115/3, CTCC minutes, 8 October 1957.

124 NAPRO, MT 115/82, Watkinson–Fraser, 31 January 1956.

125 Harold Watkinson, *Turning Points – A Record of Our Times* (Salisbury: Michael Russell, 1986), p. 67.

126 Quoted in Peter Hennessy, *Having It So Good – Britain in the Fifties* (London: Penguin, 2006), pp. 533–4.

127 NAPRO, MT 124/177, press release, 11 June 1958.

128 NAPRO, MT 124/177, cutting, 'Village in Secret fight for life', *Reynolds News*, 13 July 1958.

129 *Ibid.*

130 NAPRO, MT 124/177, Morgan–Windsor, 21 July 1958.

131 NAPRO, MT 124/177, press release, 11 June 1958.

132 NAPRO, MT 115/3, Munro–Goodison, 14 February 1958.

133 Hansard, HC Deb, 23 July 1958, vol. 592, col. 421.

134 Sir David Serpell, interview with the author, 3 April 1995.

135 NAPRO, T 230/353, Watts–Clarke, 29 June 1957.

136 NAPRO, T 234/562, Clarke–Stevenson, 22 May 1958.

137 Sir Geoffrey Wardale, interview with the author, 24 April 1998.

138 NAPRO, MT 115/279, 'The future position of the railways', 16 January 1959; Glover–Lang, 20 January 1959.

139 NAPRO, T 234/556, Ogilvy-Webb–Mark, 29 July 1959.

140 NAPRO, MT 115/280, Glover, note on BTC paper on 'The financial and economic effects of the plan for the modernisation and rationalisation of British Railways', July 1959.

141 NAPRO, T 234/522, Mark, 'The economic case for road building', 6 October 1959.

142 NAPRO, MT 115/280, note of meeting, 6 August 1959.

143 NAPRO, MT 115/77, Dunnett, 'The railway problem', 4 January 1960.

144 NAPRO, MT 132/11, Bird–Lang, 15 December 1959.

145 NAPRO, T 267/15.

146 Thomas, *Country Railway*, pp. 131–2.

147 NAPRO, MT 132/79, BTC, 'Fringe areas', 14 December 1959.

148 NAPRO, T 224/340, Vinter–Clarke, 14 February 1961.

149 NAPRO, T 234/558, Padmore–Lee, 18 February 1960.

150 David Gould, *Westerham Valley Railway* (Tarrant Hinton: Oakwood, 1974, 1981 reprint), pp. 4, 33.

151 http://thepeerage.com/e433.htm, accessed 17 August 2012.

152 NAPRO, AN 177/245, Kilmaine–Roberts, 21 November 1951.

153 NAPRO, AN 177/245, Kilmaine–Hopkins, 29 November 1951.

154 NAPRO, AN 177/245, CTCC minutes, 4 October 1960, appendix C.

155 NAPRO, AN 177/245, Hopkins–Assistant General Manager (Traffic), 6 December 1960.

156 NAPRO, AN 177/245, handwritten note to Hopkins.

157 Sampson, *Anatomy of Britain*, p. 542.

158 Geoffrey Freeman Allen, *British Railways Today and Tomorrow* (London: Ian Allan, 1962), p. 29; Faulkner and Austin, *Holding the Line*, p. 129.

159 Henshaw, *Great Railway Conspiracy*, pp. 10, 109–10, 115–7, 122–37.

160 Hansard, HC Deb, 10 March 1960, vol. 619, cols 522–3.

161 Richard Hardy, *Beeching – Champion of the Railway* (London: Ian Allan, 1989), p. 39.

162 Sampson, *Anatomy of Britain*, pp. 542–3.

163 NAPRO, PREM 11/3577, Marples–Macmillan, 9 August 1960.

164 Vicky cartoon, *Evening Standard*, 19 January 1961, reproduced in Lamb, *The Macmillan Years* (London: John Murray, 1995), endpapers.

165 Richard Stott, *Dogs and Lampposts* (London: Metro, 2002), pp. 166–71; Lamb, *Macmillan Years*, pp. 479–1; *Lord Denning's Report* (London: HMSO, 1963).

166 Sir James Dunnett, interview with the author, 11 April 1995; Sampson, *Anatomy of Britain*, p. 88.

167 Watkinson, *Turning Points*, pp. 67–92.

168 NAPRO, T 278/3, McAulay–Fraser, 16 September 1959.

169 NAPRO, MT 124/55, minutes of meeting between Marples and RHA delegation, 28 March 1960.

170 NAPRO, T 298/197, 'The motor industry in the 1960s: report by a group of officials', June 1960.

171 Booker, *Neophiliacs*, p. 132.

172 Mick Hamer, *Wheels Within Wheels – A Study of the Road Lobby* (London: Routledge and Kegan Paul, 1987), pp. 37–51.

173 Michael Robbins, *The Railway Age* (London: Routledge and Kegan Paul, 1962), p. 37.

174 Peter Catterall (Ed.) *Macmillan Diaries – Prime Minister and After, 1957–66* (London: Macmillan, 2011), p.270, 16 February 1960.

175 Hansard, HC Deb, 10 March 1960, vol. 619, cols 642–3.

176 NAPRO, T 298/174, draft, Marples 'Re-organization of the BTC: problem of appointments', September 1960.

177 NAPRO, MT 96/169, note of meeting, 3 May 1961.

178 Hansard, HC Deb, 19 October 1961, vol. 646, cols 528–30.

179 NAPRO, AN 177/246, WBRPA, open letter, 27 April 1962.

180 NAPRO, AN 177/246, note of WBRPA meeting, 7 April 1962.

181 NAPRO, MT 114/634, memo '25' to Scott-Malden (signature and date missing) circa July–October 1963.

182 NAPRO, PREM 11/4277, Woodfield–Robertson, 1 August 1962.

183 NAPRO, PREM 11/4277, Marples, 'Rebuilding urban Britain', 26 October 1962.

184 NAPRO, MT 124/658, Serpell–Heaton, 24 July 1962.

185 Gould, *Westerham Valley Railway*, pp. 32–3.

186 CAB 134/2426, Committee on the reorganization of railways, minutes, 13 March 1963.

187 Cromartie, letter, *The Times*, 3 April 1963, p. 15.

188 Sampson, *Anatomy of Britain*, pp. 537, 544, 631.

189 Gourvish, *British Railways 1948–73*, p. 309; Henshaw, *Great Railway Conspiracy*, pp. 122–9.

190   NAPRO, T 298/174, SAG recommendation five, 29 September 1960.

191   NAPRO, T 298/185, Lee, note for the record, 18 May 1960.

192   Serpell, interview with the author, 3 April 1995.

193   NAPRO, MT 124/664, note of meeting, 4 December 1962; Scott-Malden–Serpell, 5 December 1962.

194   NAPRO, MT 96/174, 'Interim report of the long-term transport policy steering group', 20 December 1962.

195   *Ibid.*

196   NAPRO, PREM 11/4548, Macmillan–Marples, 30 September 1962.

197   NAPRO, T 298/184, note of meeting, 10 November 1961.

198   Richard Pryke and John Dodgson, *The Rail Problem* (London: Martin Robertson, 1975), pp. 197–210.

199   NAPRO, AN 177/5, McKenna, 'Plan for closure and discontinuance of services', 10 April 1963.

200   NAPRO, MT 96/169, note of meeting, 3 May 1961.

201   *Financial Times*, 'How To Spend It', July 2008, quoted at http://www.burnhammarket.co.uk/Link.asp?Advert=74, accessed 13 July 2012.

202   http://www.mynorfolkguide.co.uk/index.php/directory/entry/the-railway-inn/ and http://www.thehoste.com/accommodation/railway-house/, accessed 13 July 2012.

203   Catterall (Ed.) *Macmillan Diaries, 1957–66*, p.550, 20 March 1963.

204   S. Brittan, *The Treasury Under the Tories 1951–64* (Harmondsworth: Penguin, 1964), pp. 267–8.

205   NAPRO, PREM 11/3930, text of Macmillan's speech to Cabinet, 28 May 1962.

206   Peter Hennessy, *The Prime Minister – The Office and its Holders since 1945* (London: Penguin, 2000), p. 285.

207   Hansard, HC Deb, 30 April 1963, vol. 676, col. 923.

208   NAPRO, T 224/1239, Lee-Vinter, 30 September 1964.

209   NAPRO, CAB 21/4813, Cary–Trend, 13 February 1963.

210   NAPRO, PREM 11/4548, two minutes from Macmillan to Marples, both dated 30 September 1962.

211   NAPRO, PREM 11/5166, Redmayne–Bligh, 17 May 1963.

212   Hansard, HL Deb, 20 June 1963, vol. 250, cols 1478–9.

213   NAPRO, MT 124/1234, Stonham–Marples, 28 October 1963; Serpell–Padmore, 31 October 1963.

214   NAPRO, CAB 134/2453, RRT minutes, 16 December 1963.

215   NAPRO, MT 124/725, Bull–Marples, 9 November 1963.

216   NAPRO, AN 177/5, south-eastern TUCC minutes, 18 March 1964.

217   NAPRO, T 319/342, Littlewood–Vinter, 23 July 1963.

218   NAPRO, CAB 134/2426, 'Report of the interdepartmental working party on the railways', 18 July 1963.

219   NAPRO, CAB/195/23, Cabinet Secretary's notebook, 17 January 1964.

220   NAPRO, T 319/343, Littlewood–MacDonald, 4 and 11 February 1964.

221   NAPRO, MT 124/725, Wells-next-the-Sea Urban District Council,
      'Statement accompanying resolution of protest of proposed closure of
      the Dereham–Wells-next-the-Sea branch line', November 1963.

222   NAPRO, PREM 11/4548, Marples–Macmillan, 19 February 1963.

223   *The Times*, 10 February 1964, p. 6.

224   NAPRO, MT 124/725, Haygreen–Baxter, 23 January 1964; BRB,
      Reshaping, pp. 54–5

225   NAPRO, PREM 11/5167, George–Douglas-Home, 6 January 1964.

226   NAPRO, MT 124/718, Stevenson–Castle, 1 March 1968.

227   NAPRO, MT 124/725 Baxter, note, 23 June 1964.

228   *Whitby Gazette*, 18 September 1964, pp. 1–2; 25 September 1964, pp. 1–2.

229   *Hull Daily Mail*, 14 October 1964, p. 4.

230   P. Howard Anderson, *Forgotten Railways: Volume Two, The East Midlands*
      (Newton Abbott: David and Charles, 1973, 1985 edition), pp. 80–81.

231   John Betjeman, *Great Central Railway – Sheffield Victoria to Banbury*,
      reproduced in John Healy, *Great Central Memories* (London: Baton
      Transport, 1987), p. 148.

232   NAPRO, AN 172/58, GCA, *Give this railway a new future*, undated
      leaflet c.1962

233   NAPRO, AN 172/58, BRB, *The Changing Role of the Former Great
      Central Main Line*, 1959.

234   NAPRO, AN 172/58, report of TUCC discussion, 15 February 1962.

235   Castle, *Fighting All the Way*, p.369.

236   NAPRO, T 319/344, Lee–Macdonald, 26 October 1964; T 319/347,
      Macdonald–Hunt, 24 August 1965; CAB 128/39, Cabinet conclusions,
      22 October 1965.

237   Hansard, HC Deb, 4 November 1964, vol. 701, cols 195–202.

238   NAPRO, MT 124/1132, Baxter–Scott-Malden, 8 February 1965.

239   Hansard, HC Deb, 9 February 1965, vol. 706, cols 210–11.

240   NAPRO, PREM 13/647, Fraser–Wilson, 26 February 1965 with Wilson's
      comments.

241   NAPRO, PREM 13/647, Wilson, note on ED(RR) committee minutes,
      15 February 1965.

242   Philip Noel Baker, MP, quoted in Gourvish, *British Railways 1948–73*,
      p. 445.

243   NAPRO, MT 124/1132, Baxter–Scott-Malden, 28 June 1965.

244   NAPRO T 319/344, cutting, Michael Shanks, 'The Beeching Line',
      Sunday Times, 27 December 1964.

245   Fiennes, *I Tried to Run a Railway*, p. 144; Hardy, *Beeching*, p. 100.

246   *Sunday Telegraph*, 'The derailing of Dr. Beeching', 27 December 1964.

247   NAPRO, MT 124/1131, Scott-Malden–Swingler, 8 March 1966.

248   NAPRO, MT 124/1132, Sanders–Fraser, 17 June 1965.

249   Anderson, *Forgotten Railways: East Midlands*, p. 11.

250   Barbara Castle, *The Castle Diaries 1964–76* (London: Papermac, 1990),
      p. 39.

251 Philip Bagwell and Peter Lyth, *Transport in Britain: From Canal Lock to Gridlock 1750–2000* (London: Hambledon and London, 2002), p. 216.

252 Henshaw, *Great Railway Conspiracy*, p. 186.

253 Castle, *Diaries*, p. 39, 21 December 1965.

254 *Ibid.*, 5 April 1968, p. 215.

255 NAPRO, MT 124/1173, Bailey–Scott-Malden, 21 July 1966; MoT press release, 20 September 1966.

256 NAPRO, PREM 11/4548, Marples–Macmillan, 19 February 1963; MT 124/1258, draft, Minister–Noel-Baker, covered by Custance–Minister, 29 December 1965.

257 NAPRO, T 319/839, cutting, *Financial Times*, 17 March 1967.

258 NAPRO, MT 124/1255, Baxter–Scott-Malden, 8 September 1966.

259 NAPRO, MT 124/1224, Hunt–Scott-Malden 12 August 1966.

260 NAPRO, PREM 13/2431, Thomas–Wilson, 25 July and 12 August 1968.

261 NAPRO, PREM 13/2431, White–Wilson, 30 July 1969.

262 Quoted in M. Weiner, *English Culture and the Decline of the Industrial Spirit, 1850–1980* (Cambridge: Cambridge University Press, 1981), p. 162.

263 NAPRO, MT 97/1055, Moore–Scott-Malden, 13 November 1970.

264 NAPRO, T 319/1779, Thomas–Peyton, 23 November 1971.

265 NAPRO, T 319/1779, Lazarus–Peeler, 14 September 1971.

266 NAPRO, T 319/1779, Peyton, draft paper, 'Railway closures and regional development Policy', September 1971; Peyton–Macmillan, 10 November 1971; CAB 134/3379; Walker and Macmillan, 'Review of grants for unremunerative rail services', 23 July 1971.

267 Letter, *The Times*, 11 June 1973, p. 15.

268 *The Times*, 9 October 1972, p.1; 12 October 1972, p. 5.

269 NAPRO, T 319/1771, Bowman–Elliott-Binns, 23 October 1973, original emphasis.

270 Terence Gourvish, *British Railways 1974–97: From Integration to Privatisation* (Oxford: Oxford University Press, 2002), p. 62, Appendix A, p. 455.

271 Hennessy, *The Prime Minister*, p. 333.

272 NAPRO, T 319/2114, draft Cabinet paper for Chief Secretary, May 1974.

273 *The Standard*, 21 January 1983, quoted in Philip Bagwell, *End of the Line? The Fate of the Railways Under Thatcher* (London: Verso, 1984), p. 125.

274 Roger Salmon, quoted in C. Wolmar, *Broken Rails – How Privatisation Wrecked Britain's Railways* (London: Aurum, 2001), pp. 71–2.

275 'Axe threatens local lines in rail reshuffle', *The Observer*, 3 October 2004, http://observer.guardian.co.uk/uk_news/story/0,,1318468,00.html, accessed 2 July 2005.

276 MoT paper, 'Examining railway figures: some useful concepts', September 1974 (author's collection).

277 Sir Peter Parker, *For Starters: The Business of Life* (London: Jonathan Cape, 1989), p. 272.

278 Jeff Vinter, *Railway Walks: GWR and SR* (Stroud: Alan Sutton, 1990), pp. xv–xvi.

279 Henry White, *Forgotten Railways* (Newton Abbot: David and Charles, 1986), pp. 10–12.

280 Stuart Maconie, *Blur 3862 Days – The Official History* (London: Virgin, 1999), p. 152.

281 Robert Hewison, *The Heritage Industry: Britain in a Climate of Decline* (London: Methuen, 1987), p. 38.

282 House of Commons Transport Committee, *Rail 2020*, Seventh Report of Session 2012–13, December 2012 (hereafter, HCSC, *Rail 2020*), pp. 34–9 (annex B)

283 Marchant, *Parallel Lines*, p. 306.

284 *Ibid.*, p. 135.

285 Catterall, *Macmillan Diaries 1957–66*, p. 421, 24 October 1961.

286 Alan Jackson, *London's Termini* (Newton Abbott: David and Charles, 1969; second edition 1985), p. 50.

287 Hansard, HC Deb, 29 April 1963, vol. 676, col. 742.

288 Hansard, HC Deb, 3 February 1955, vol. 536, col. 1328.

289 Keith Middlemas, *Power, Competition and the State, Volume Two: Threats to the Post-War Settlement 1961–74* (London: Macmillan, 1990), p. 30.

290 Meyer Hillman and Anne Whalley, *The Social Consequences of Railway Closures* (London: Policy Studies Institute, 1980), p. 118.

291 Fiennes, *I Tried to Run a Railway*, pp. 114–9.

292 Examples include: NAPRO, CAB 129/47, Barnes, 'Long-term financial Prospects of the British Transport commission', 10 September 1951; R. Marsh, *Off the Rails: An Autobiography* (London: Weidenfeld and Nicholson, 1978), p. 188; C. Wolmar, 'The spectre of cuts by stealth is stalking the railway', *Rail*, 22 June–5 July 2005, p. 29; HCSC, *Rail 2020*.

293 Middlemas, *Power, Competition and the State*, p. 28.

294 Faulkner and Austin, *Holding the Line*, p. 25

295 Hansard, HC Deb, 29 April 1963, vol. 676, col. 741.

296 Kenneth Glover (MoT official), letters to author, 22 March 2000, 1 August 2005.

Index

...plished
...brands,
...travel.

...ars our
...secrets
...world,
...ealth of
...experience ... ... travel.

Rely on Thomas Cook as your travelling companion on your next trip and benefit from our unique heritage.

Thomas Cook **pocket** guides

LISBON

Thomas Cook

Your travelling companion since 1873

Written by Louise Pole-Baker, updated by Anwer Bati

Published by Thomas Cook Publishing
A division of Thomas Cook Tour Operations Limited
Company registration no. 3772199 England
The Thomas Cook Business Park, Unit 9, Coningsby Road,
Peterborough PE3 8SB, United Kingdom
Email: books@thomascook.com, Tel: +44 (0) 1733 416477
www.thomascookpublishing.com

Produced by Cambridge Publishing Management Limited
Burr Elm Court, Main Street, Caldecote CB23 7NU
www.cambridgepm.co.uk

ISBN: 978-1-84848-439-9

© 2006, 2008 Thomas Cook Publishing
This third edition © 2011 Thomas Cook Publishing
Text © Thomas Cook Publishing
Maps © Thomas Cook Publishing/PCGraphics (UK) Limited
Transport map © Communicarta Limited

Series Editor: Karen Beaulah
Production/DTP: Steven Collins

Printed and bound in Spain by GraphyCems

Cover photography © Sergio Pitamitz

CONTENTS

SYMBOLS KEY

The following symbols are used throughout this book:

ⓐ address ☎ telephone ⓦ website address ⌚ opening times
ⓝ public transport connections ❶ important

The following symbols are used on the maps:

🇮 information office		▦ point of interest	
✈ airport		O city	
✚ hospital		O large town	
🛡 police station		○ small town	
🚌 bus station		═ motorway	
🚆 railway station		— main road	
Ⓜ metro		— minor road	
✝ cathedral		— railway	
❶ numbers denote featured cafés & restaurants			

Hotels and restaurants are graded by approximate price as follows:
£ budget price **££** mid-range price **£££** expensive

In addresses, 'Avenida' (meaning 'avenue') is abbreviated to 'Av'

❿ *The view over Rossio Square*

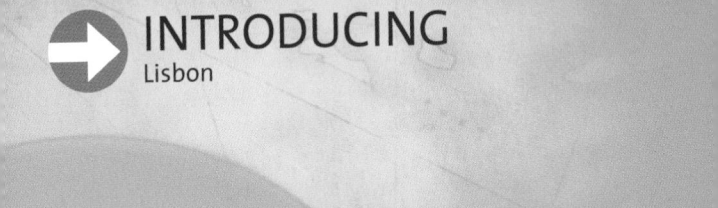

INTRODUCING
Lisbon

Introduction

The Portuguese capital is a city on a human scale, and its immediately likeable atmosphere is the gateway to a rich cultural background. History and politics are inscribed on its soul and written into its unique geography. Get up high on the Elevador de Santa Justa and look out over the cobbled, hilly streets and hotchpotch of roofs and alleyways that cover Lisbon's seven hills. At one end of the city you'll see the Castelo de São Jorge, towering over an area that forms a powerful historical and architectural reminder of the city's reclamation from the Moors. At the other end of Lisbon, the 1960s Padrão dos Descobrimentos is a monument to its maritime glories. The 25 de Abril Bridge and the modern Vasco da Gama Bridge – the longest bridge in Europe – link their most famous maritime hero to the modern European city of today. The ruins of the Convento do Carmo date back to the devastating 1755 earthquake; the rebuilt, earthquake-proof Baixa area is testament to the city's successful reconstruction.

Decorative blue *azulejos* tiles cover palaces, houses and even metro stations, telling the fascinating story of Portugal's social and cultural history. Inside the palaces, the opulent décor harks back to the wealth squandered by the royal family and ruling classes before the rise of Portugal's former dictator Salazar. Large parts of Lisbon's architectural landscape have been transformed since Portugal's transition to democracy – from the contemporary building and walkways of the Centro Cultural de Belém to the ambitious Parque das Nações, where everything is named after heroes from the past – and Lisbon's urban landscape continues to evolve.

Located at the mouth of the Rio Tejo (River Tagus), the city has a rich gastronomy influenced both by the sea and by its imperial history. In the streets you'll smell smoky, roasting chestnuts and freshly baked custard tarts, and in the restaurants you'll be served up salted cod or fresh sardines washed down with young *vinho verde* wine and fiery after-dinner *ginginha*.

Fado music and other sounds fill the air in the historic Bairro Alto. However you like to spend your days and evenings, immerse yourself in Lisbon's unique, enticing atmosphere and you're sure to find something to entertain you.

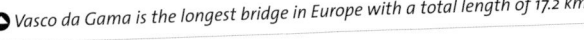

⬤ *Vasco da Gama is the longest bridge in Europe with a total length of 17.2 km*

When to go

Lisbon is a full-time fabulous destination. The weather is balmy all year round and there's no shortage of things to do, indoors and out.

SEASONS & CLIMATE

Located at the mouth of the River Tagus, Lisbon's southerly position gives it a Mediterranean feel, though there are around 100 rainy days a year. The river and the Atlantic mean it's not quite as hot here as it is in the Algarve or inland. Although the average temperature from May to September is 20°C (68°F), in July and August this can rise to 30°C (86°F) or more. There is some breeze due to the proximity of the river and the sea but summer is generally a good time to escape to your hotel swimming pool for some cooling off. On the other hand, the average temperature from October to April may only be 10°C (50°F), but it rarely drops below 5°C (41°F). During this time of year, you can expect a mixture of grey, rainy days and sunny days when the sky is an impenetrable blue.

ANNUAL EVENTS

There's a lot going on in Lisbon year-round. To help you to find out what takes place and where, here are some annual events and festivals. It's always a good idea to check with the tourist information office (see page 153) when you're planning your visit.

February

Carnival Colourful festivities in the city lead right up to Lent (which begins on 22 February in 2012 and 14 February in 2013), and the city develops a particularly Brazilian feel, with carnival floats, fancy dress and dancing.

March

Lisbon Half-Marathon The city shakes off its winter blues
with a half-marathon that sees thousands of athletes running
through the Parque das Nações (see page 110).
Ⓦ www.lisbon-half-marathon.com

Moda Lisboa Mode-maniacs devour the latest styles from
Portugal-based designers at the first of the city's annual fashion
shows. Ⓦ www.modalisboa.pt

May–June

Festas de Lisboa/ Festas dos Santos Populares The streets of the
Bairro Alto, Chiado, Baixa and Alfama come alive for the popular

⬤ *Lisbon's Christmas lights reflect in a fountain pool*

saints' days, which include special celebrations for St Anthony, St John and St Peter. These areas fill with parades, music and dance, and balconies are decorated with paper lanterns, streamers and coloured lights. Locals give each other gifts of basil pots and paper carnations.

Rock in Rio This popular music festival attracts big-name performers and bands to Lisbon (not Rio) for a five-day fest. Ⓦ www.rockinrio-lisboa.sapo.pt

Sintra Music and Ballet Festival A programme of chamber music and ballet by international performers and some of Portugal's finest talent.

July

Estoril Jazz Festival As the summer starts heating up, this jazz festival attracts plenty of top names.

Cascais Summer Festival A celebration of summer that lights up the area with fireworks and nightly entertainment.

August

Jazz em Agosto The Fundação Calouste Gulbenkian (Calouste Gulbenkian Foundation, see page 89) hosts this festival that brings contemporary sounds to the public. Ⓦ www.musica.gulbenkian.pt/jazz

October

Moda Lisboa Fashion hawks can once again check out cutting-edge creations by Portugal-based designers. Ⓦ www.modalisboa.pt

Trienal de Arquitectura de Lisboa Lisbon's prestigious architectural event – running from Oct–Jan and which started in 2007 – is held every three years in venues around the city. The next will be in 2013/14. Ⓦ www.trienaldelisboa.com

November
Arte Lisboa The capital's contemporary art fair sees artists and galleries from around the world descending on the exhibition centre in the Parque das Nações (see page 110). Ⓦ www.artelisboa.fil.pt

December
Lisbon Marathon This starts every year at the Praça do Comércio (see page 63) and fills the city with spectators. Ⓦ www.lisbon-marathon.com

Super Bock em Stock Contemporary music festival at venues in Avenida da Liberdade. Ⓦ www.superbock.pt

PUBLIC HOLIDAYS
New Year's Day 1 Jan
Shrove Tuesday 21 Feb 2012; 13 Feb 2013; 4 Mar 2014
Good Friday 6 Apr 2012; 29 Mar 2013; 18 Apr 2014
Easter 8 Apr 2012; 31 Mar 2013, 20 Apr 2014
Liberty Day 25 Apr
Labour Day 1 May
Corpus Christi 7 June 2012; 30 May 2013; 19 June 2014
Portugal Day 10 June
Assumption 15 Aug
Republic Day 5 Oct
All Saints' Day 1 Nov
Restoration Day 1 Dec
Day of Our Lady 8 Dec
Christmas Day 25 Dec

Many people in Lisbon also take St Anthony's Day (13 June) off.

Modern architecture

While Lisbon retains plenty of Moorish and Manueline (Portuguese late Gothic) architecture, it's the modern face of its urban furniture that is most captivating. It was after Portugal joined the EU in 1986 that the city really began to change. After the horrific fire in the Chiado in 1988, the area's reconstruction was given over to Portugal's greatest contemporary architect, Álvaro Siza Vieira, who redesigned many of the city's façades and interiors. The highlight of the renovation of the area was the Armazéns do Chiado shopping centre (see page 66).

Another project that changed Lisbon's architectural landscape was the Centro Cultural de Belém (see page 102), a landmark structure designed by architects Manuel Salgado and Vittorio Gregotti. It was controversial when inaugurated in 1992, as the boxy modern building was placed opposite the historical Mosteiro dos Jerónimos (see page 98), blocking its river access.

What really made an indelible imprint on modern-day Lisbon was the reconstruction of the city's neglected eastern waterfront, inspired by the Expo '98 that marked the 500th anniversary of Vasco da Gama's voyage to India. This decaying industrial zone was transformed into the modern and stylish Parque das Nações (see page 110), a social and cultural haven of museums, auditoriums, a conference centre, shops and restaurants, as well as the 17-km (11-mile) Vasco da Gama Bridge. The area's showcase buildings include the award-winning Gare do Oriente (see page 48) by the Spanish star architect Santiago Calatrava.

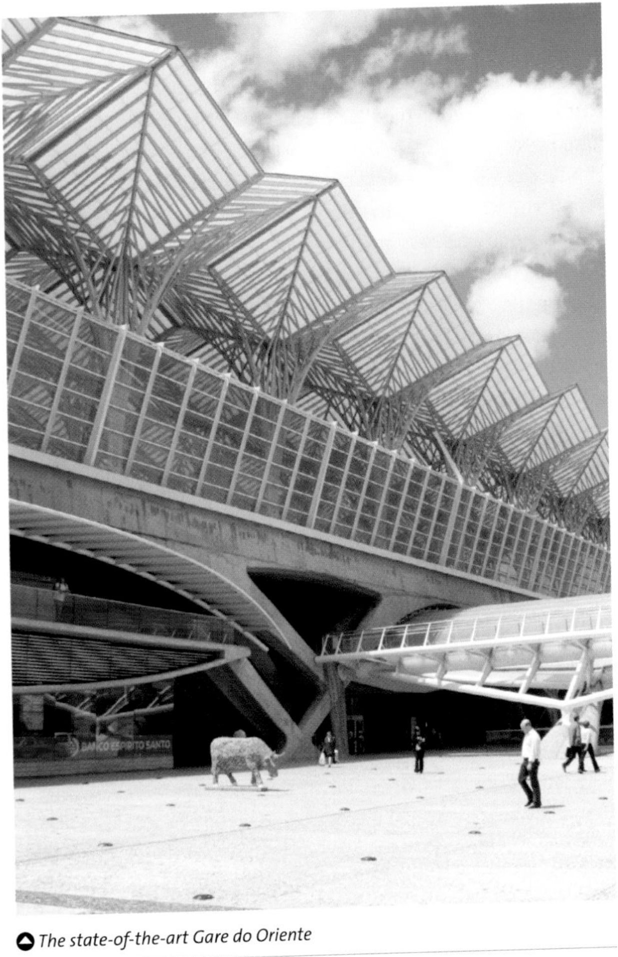

The state-of-the-art Gare do Oriente

History

Lisbon's turbulent past is full of invasions, occupations and war. When the Romans arrived in the 2nd century AD, they integrated the territory into the empire under the name of Felicitus Jullia, later Olissipo.

The city, which was also known as Lixbuna, Lizhboa and other variations, was taken by the Moors in AD 711. They built houses, mosques and a fortress on the site of what is now the Castelo de São Jorge (see page 74) in Alfama (then called al-Hamma). Arabic became the official language, Islam the official religion. Lisbon was reconquered by crusader knights in 1147.

Lisbon was made Portugal's capital in 1260 and, from the 14th to 16th centuries, Portugal's maritime explorers such as Bartolomeu Dias and Vasco da Gama pioneered routes to sail around the Cape of Good Hope and to the Americas. Gold was discovered in Brazil, and, while the Portuguese royal family grew rich from its colonial pickings, life on the city's streets wasn't so glorious. In 1506, around 2,000 Jews were massacred.

In 1580, Spain gained control of the country after Portugal's young king was killed in battle. Growing colonial unrest led to the Wars of Restoration, during which a group of noblemen laid siege to Lisbon in 1640. The Duke of Bragança was crowned King Dom João IV, but Spain would not recognise Portuguese independence until 1668.

It wasn't until 1755, when the Great Earthquake (and tsunami that followed) devastated the city, killing 90,000 people, that ideals began to change. After what became known as the first 'modern' disaster, the Marquês de Pombal rebuilt Lisbon by bringing the city centre into the Age of Enlightenment, though poor areas such as the Alfama remained medieval.

After suffering Napoleonic invasions and civil war during the 19th century, Portugal experienced a major turn of events when its king Dom Carlos I was assassinated in 1908. His successor, Dom Manuel II, lasted only until the Republican revolution of October 1910. The country remained unsettled until the 1926 coup d'état and the subsequent rise of Dr António de Oliveira Salazar to prime minister in 1932, who then led a 48-year dictatorship during which he imposed a somewhat repressive regime, called the Estado Novo (New State). Establishing the true nature of Salazar's dictatorship – and the extent to which it was good or bad for Portugal – is a vexed and shifting question. Although he voiced admiration for some far-right leaders of other countries, he prevented his own from drifting too far in that direction. The Estado Novo effectively ended in 1968, when serious illness finally caused Salazar to step down.

The 1960s had already seen unrest in the colonies, gradual liberalisation of the press, and socialist cultural movements. The highlight of Portugal's transition to democracy was a bloodless coup known as the Carnation Revolution. At 12.25 on 25 April 1974, the banned protest song *Grândola, Vila Morena* was broadcast on the radio and soldiers entered the streets of Lisbon with red carnations protruding from their tanks.

Since then Portugal has pulled itself out of the past and its capital has been transformed once again. Portugal joined the EU in 1986, and Lisbon was the European Capital of Culture in 1994. The city hosted Expo '98 and, in 2004, the European Football Championships. Although the economy still struggles, particularly in the wake of the international financial crisis which started in 2008, these events have led to massive investment and renewed confidence, and Lisbon is now a firmly established, magnificently attractive, city-break destination.

Lifestyle

A famous saying in Portugal is that 'Lisbon plays, Porto works and Braga prays'. While people in Lisbon also work and pray, it is a vibrant metropolis with a laid-back café culture and lively nightlife.

This is a capital city with a busy financial district where socialising is important. Rather than belonging to international café chains, the numerous coffee shops of Lisbon are individual. There are cafés where people spend an hour chatting to friends and sipping *um galão* (milky coffee in a glass) and others where they stand at the counter for a quick snack such as *pastel de nata* (Portuguese custard tart). There are also Internet cafés and coffee kiosks in the street.

Although there are sandwich bars in Lisbon, people can take two hours for lunch in order to eat properly, so you'll often find that the shops and some museums close at this time. Portions tend to be large, but don't be afraid of leaving a little on your plate – they'll take it as a compliment that they've fed you enough! In some places you can order a main course to share between two people.

Generally the Portuguese are very polite, so unless you're very familiar, you should say *bom dia* (good morning) or *boa tarde* (good afternoon) rather than *olá*. You're unlikely to see anyone taking their shoes off in a public place, except on the beach, as it's considered bad manners.

The Portuguese do like a drink and, in fact, have a very high national average of alcohol consumption. However, you're unlikely to see drunken Portuguese falling out of the bars as in some other countries. Even though locals tend to go out late at night, even the younger people can spend hours pondering over one drink before heading on to a club after midnight. It's all about taking your time and enjoying the food, wine, good company and surroundings more than the actual alcohol content. There's no rush – just enjoy yourself!

◆ *Stop and unwind at a café in leafy Parque Eduardo VII*

Culture

Fado remains at the forefront of Lisbon's musical identity. Whether you love or hate the melancholic sounds of *fado* music, it attracts thousands of tourists and locals to the restaurants and bars of the Bairro Alto and Alfama every year.

There are two forms of *fado*: one form developed among the privileged students of the University of Coimbra, while the other arose among the working classes in Lisbon and was sung by social outcasts. It was often called *fado do marinhero* (sailors' song), referring to the seafarers during the Golden Age of Discovery who yearned for their homeland.

Fado is sung by a solo vocalist and usually accompanied by a *viola* (Spanish guitar) and a *guitarra* (pear-shaped, 12-string Portuguese guitar). Lisbon's most famous *fadista* is Amália Rodrigues (see page 101), who rose to fame in the 1950s and 1960s, but others have followed in her wake.

Aside from *fado*, Lisbon is home to the Orquestra and Coro Gulbenkian (see page 20), has a thriving jazz scene, popular music venues and several music festivals (see page 10). There is plenty of dance in the city, too, from performances by the Companhia Nacional do Bailado to shows by contemporary dance groups.

The Baixa, Chiado and Bairro Alto were once the favourite haunts of artists and writers, and today you'll find monuments to Luís de Camões and Fernando Pessoa in these areas. Outside A Brasileira café (see page 68) in the Bairro Alto is a seated statue of Pessoa; he used to frequent the café, which is still popular with arty types who meet there for a daily chat.

When it comes to the visual arts, Lisbon boasts the Fundação Calouste Gulbenkian (Calouste Gulbenkian Foundation, see page 89),

◉ Mother and child statue in Parque Eduardo VII

the premier arts organisation in Portugal and home to the Orquestra Gulbenkian and Coro Gulbenkian, as well as the Museu Calouste Gulbenkian and Centro de Arte Moderna José de Azeredo Perdigão (see page 90). Beside that, Centro Cultural de Belém (see page 102), the largest and one of the most popular contemporary arts venues in the city, hosts regular exhibitions by international artists in its galleries, as well as putting on opera, ballet, classical music and jazz concerts in its Performance Centre. The Museu Nacional de Arte Antiga (see page 103) is considered one of the most important museums in the country. Located in a 17th-century palace, it showcases a stellar collection of 15th- to 19th-century Portuguese and European paintings. Museu do Chiado (see page 64) was Lisbon's first modern art gallery and has an impressive collection of works by Portugal's most representative 20th- and 21st-century artists.

For the performing arts, Teatro Camões (see page 114) in the Parque das Nações is one of the city's newest theatres, and is home to the Companhia Nacional do Bailado, the country's national ballet company. Teatro Nacional Dona Maria II (see page 65), historically one of the city's most important theatres, presents a programme of theatre, circus and performance art. Teatro Nacional de São Carlos (see page 66), with its stunning rococo interior, replaced the pre-1755 building that previously stood there. It has an extensive repertoire of opera, classical music and theatre.

● *Lisbon's famous blue tiles*

MAKING THE MOST OF
Lisbon

Shopping

Lisbon has an alluring profusion of boutiques, markets, regular street shops and large shopping centres. In the Baixa-Chiado area, particularly along the Rua Augusta, there's a mix of international chain stores, as well as small traditional shops selling leather goods, jewellery and handicrafts. For funky boutiques and offbeat fashions, check out the storefronts of Bairro Alto. Indulge your penchant for designer labels on the Avenida da Liberdade or opt for the traditional shopping area on the Campo de Ourique (see page 92). The downtown shopping centre of Armazéns do Chiado (see page 66), with a FNAC and a series of food outlets, is a favoured retail destination. **Amoreiras** (ⓦ www.amoreiras.com) and **Colombo** (ⓦ www.colombo.pt) are both popular shopping centres, but the newest is Centro Comercial Vasco da Gama (see page 114) in Parque das Nações, with 164 shops on four floors.

When it comes to what to buy, there's a good choice of leather goods, lace and linen. Look out for copper dishes, painted terracotta ceramics and *azulejos* tiles. From the supermarket you can pick up a selection of *presunto* (smoked ham) and *chouriço* (spicy sausage).

● *Souvenirs rule the roost here ...*

There are small, sometimes impromptu, markets dotted all around the city. The Feira da Ladra is a flea market in the Alfama, and if you like to rummage among gems and junk, it is open for action every Tuesday and Saturday. There's also a fish market in Cais do Sodré, selling everything from the wet pulp of octopus to *bacalhau* (salt codfish).

Consider investing in a Lisboa Shopping Card. This lasts for either 24 (€3.70) or 72 hours (€5.80) and can be purchased from the tourist office (Lisbon Welcome Centre, see page 153). It gives up to 15 per cent off in more than 200 shops in the Baixa, Chiado and Avenida da Liberdade.

USEFUL SHOPPING PHRASES

What time do the shops open/close?
A que horas abrem/fecham as lojas?
A kee orah abrayng/fayshown ash lohzhash?

How much is this?
Quanto custa isto?
Kwantoo kooshta eeshtoo?

Can I try this on?
Posso provar este?
Possoo proovahr aysht?

My size is ...
O meu tamanho (número) é ...
Oo mayo tamanyo (noomiroo) eh ...

I'll take this one, thank you
Levo este, obrigado
Lehvoo aysht, ohbreegahdoo

This is too large/too small/too expensive. Do you have any others?
Este é muito grande/muito pequeno/muito caro. Tem outros?
Aysht eh muingtoo grangdi/muingtoo pikaynoo/muingtoo kahroo. Tayng ohtroosh?

Eating & drinking

Eating in Lisbon is a real pleasure, as the Portuguese love their food; menus are full of variety and portions are generous.

Traditional Portuguese restaurants compete with a large number of international eateries. Try one of the Brazilian restaurants, which often have buffet menus that include cold meats and fish as well as hot meat from a spit. There are plenty of pizzerias, steak houses, Chinese and even a few Indian restaurants, as well as the usual choice of fast food and sandwiches. Vegetarians sometimes find it easier to eat in the international restaurants as the local diet doesn't regularly include options for non-meat eaters; a smattering of vegetarian restaurants does exist, though.

Lisbon's proximity to the sea means that fish and seafood feature high on the menu, but there are plenty of meat dishes as well. Soup is the mainstay of the Portuguese diet and you'll find it on many menus as a starter, particularly *caldo verde* (a delicious cabbage soup made from chicken stock and a slice of the spicy *chouriço* sausage), *sopa de legumes* (vegetable soup) or *Açorda*, a highly filling bread soup.

Bacalhau (salt cod) is a common local speciality and you'll often see it hanging up in the shops. The most popular salt codfish recipe is *bacalhau com natas*, salt codfish with cream and potatoes. *Lulas* (squid)

PRICE CATEGORIES

Restaurant ratings in this book are based on the average price of a two-course dinner for one without drinks:

£ up to €20   **££** €20–35   **£££** over €35

RESTAURANT CARD
The Lisboa Restaurant Card is valid for 72 hours and can be purchased from the tourist office (Lisbon Welcome Centre, see page 153). It offers discounts of 10 to 20 per cent in around 40 quality Lisbon restaurants.

is another staple and is often fried in batter – the larger ones in rings and the baby squid fried whole. Also look out for *camarão* (prawns), *gambas grelhadas* (grilled king prawns), *caldeirada* (fish stew), *lulas recheadas* (stuffed squid), *polvo grelhado* (grilled octopus), *sardinhas assadas* (grilled sardines), *robalo* (sea bass) and *sargo* (sea bream). These will often be served with *batatas* (potatoes), *batatas fritas* (chips), *salada mixta* (mixed salad) with *azeitonas* (olives) or vegetables such as *espinafres* (spinach).

Meat also features high on the menu and includes *bife tornedo* (a succulent, quite rare piece of beef), *bifes de Perú* (turkey steak), *cabrito assado* (grilled kid), *costeleta de vitela* (veal cutlets/chops),

⬤ *Traditional* bacalhau *is both widely available and delicious*

frango no churrasco (barbecued chicken), *leitão assado* (spit-roast suckling pig) and *lombo de porco assado* (roast pork).

Many of the desserts and cakes are made with eggs, including *pasteis de nata* or *pasteis de Belém* (custard tart), *papos de anjo* (egg-based pastry dish) and *pudim* (crème caramel).

Cafés are your best option for less formal dining; try one of the *cervejarias* (café/bar) for snacks such as *tosta mixta* (toasted cheese and ham sandwiches) or surf 'n' turf of steak with crab claws (they'll give you a hammer to crack them). Many restaurants will automatically put a basket of bread and cheeses or other items, such as ham or olives, in front of you, but unless you want to eat and pay for these, you should ask for them to be taken away.

There are many ways to drink coffee: *uma bica* (small coffee, like an espresso), *um meia de leite* (coffee with milk), *um garoto* (small coffee with milk) and *um galão* (milky coffee in a tall glass). You can also order *chá* (tea) but you'll have to ask for *leite* (milk). There are plenty of regional wines in Portugal, including those from the Estremadura region (around Lisbon), Beiras, Dão, Douro (where port

○ *You're never far from a good coffee shop in Chiado*

wine comes from) and the Minho (where the young, slightly tangy *vinho verde* is produced).

USEFUL DINING PHRASES

I would like a table for ... people
Queria uma mesa para ... pessoas
Kireea ooma mehza para ... pesoash

May I have the bill, please?
Pode-me dar a conta, por favor?
Pohd-mi dahr er kohngta, poor favohr?

Waiter/waitress!
Faz favor!
Fash favohr!

Could I have it well-cooked/medium/rare, please?
Posso escolher bem passado/médio/mal passado, por favor?
Possoo ishkoolyer bayng pasahdoo/medio/mahl pasahdoo, poor favohr?

I am a vegetarian. Does this contain meat?
Sou vegetariano/a. Isto tem carne?
Soh vezhetahreeahnoo/a. Ishtoo tehng kahrni?

Where is the toilet (restroom) please?
Por favor, onde são os lavabos?
Poor favohr, ohngdee sowng oos lavahboosh?

I would like a cup of/two cups of/another coffee/tea
Queria uma chávena de/duas chávenas de/outro café/chá
Kireea ooma shahvna di/dooash shahvnash di/ohtroo kafeh/shah

Entertainment & nightlife

There's no shortage of entertainment in Lisbon, but don't expect the Portuguese to be falling out of the pubs. They know how to have fun, but generally stay well in control. Part of the reason is that they eat well and drink slowly. Dinner can be taken around 20.00 or 21.00 and accompanied by music in a *fado* bar, or you can enjoy a drink before heading out to a club.

Clubs don't generally get going until midnight. You can wine, dine and dance all over the city but the labyrinthine streets of Bairro Alto, such as Rua Diário de Noticias and the adjacent alleys, are traditionally the most popular place to go out drinking and clubbing. The Alfama is less of a party area, with the exception of the city's most famous club, the Lux Bar (see page 83) by Santa Apolónia Station.

Two areas have transformed nightlife in Lisbon: the Parque das Nações (see page 110) and Alcântara. The first has a long line of riverfront restaurant-bars, some of which become clubs later in the evening. Alcântara and the former Docas (docks) by 25 de Abril Bridge include some of the city's trendiest restaurants, bars and nightclubs.

There are multiplex cinemas in the large shopping centres such as Amoreiras (see page 22) and Colombo (see page 22). Most films are shown in their original language with subtitles. **Londres** cinema (🅐 Av de Roma 7A 🕒 21 840 1313) and Cinemateca Portuguesa (see page 84) show arthouse films.

Lisbon offers a good choice of live music, including *fado* clubs where you can eat and drink, jazz clubs such as the Hot Clube de Portugal (see page 95), Speakeasy and Blues Café (see page 108), and larger venues, such as the Coliseu dos Recreios (see page 89) and Pavilhão Atlântico (see page 113), where international bands play. Coliseu dos Recreios is a frequent venue for both popular music and

⬥ *Balmy evenings in the Bairro Alto*

classical concerts. There are also open-air events throughout the year. The tourist office publishes *Follow Me*, a monthly magazine in English that highlights forthcoming live events and festivals.

Tickets for live events can be bought from FNAC bookshops (in most shopping centres), or online at Ⓦ www.fnac.pt or Ⓦ www.ticketline.pt

◗ *Evening dining and entertainment at the Casino Estoril (see page 122)*

Fado houses with live entertainment daily are dotted around the Bairro Alto (see page 69) and the Alfama (see page 81), and retain their popularity both with locals and tourists.

Theatre might not be the best live entertainment unless your Portuguese is particularly good. However, most of the large theatres in Lisbon also have a decent programme of classical concerts, opera and ballet (see Culture, pages 18–20).

Sport & relaxation

SPECTATOR SPORTS
Football
The Portuguese love football, whether it's played by an international outfit, a Superliga team or a local club. There are two Superliga teams in Lisbon: **Sport Lisboa e Benfica** (Ⓦ www.slbenfica.pt) and **Sporting Clube de Portugal** (Ⓦ www.sporting.pt). Benfica is based at the Estádio da Luz (see page 84), while Sporting Clube de Portugal is based at the **Estádio José de Alvalade** (Ⓐ Rua Professor Fernando da Fonseca Ⓣ 21 751 6000). While it can be difficult to get tickets for the larger matches, you might be able to buy a ticket on the day of the match from the stadium (see Ⓦ www.fpf.pt).

Racing
The **Estoril Race Track** (Ⓐ Av Alfredo Cesar Torres Alcabideche, Estoril Ⓦ www.circuito-estoril.pt) is a Formula One circuit and hosts car and motorbike racing throughout most of the year.

PARTICIPATION SPORTS
Horse riding
There are several places to go horse riding, including the **Quinta da Marinha** resort (Ⓣ 21 486 0100 Ⓦ www.quintadamarinha hipico.com), the **Manuel Possolo** school in the Parque Municipal de Gandarinha (Ⓣ 21 482 1720) and the **Centro Hípico da Costa do Estoril** (Ⓣ 21 487 2064 Ⓦ www.centrohipicocostaestoril.com).

Sailing & watersports
There are sailing and watersports schools dotted all along the beach from Cascais Marina to Oeiras, as well as on the Sintra coast further

north. The most popular sport among the younger crowd is surfing, and for this Carcavelos is one of the best places, along with Guincho and Colares. You can hire equipment and have lessons with **SuperWind** in Oeiras (❶ 21 469 4602), **Surfing Clube de Portugal** in São Pedro do Estoril (❶ 21 466 4516) and **Windsurf Café** in Carcavelos (❶ 21 457 8965), or catch a few waves on your own board. Most of these schools offer windsurfing and bodyboarding as well.

Tennis

Tennis can be played at the **Quinta da Marinha** resort (❶ 21 486 0180) and the **Clube de Ténis do Estoril** (❶ 21 466 2770) on Avenida Conde de Barcelona, which has 18 floodlit courts and often hosts international matches.

RELAXATION

Golf

Estoril has quite a concentration of top-notch golf courses, including the **Golf do Estoril** (❶ 21 466 0367), **Penha Longa** (❶ 21 924 9031 ⓦ www.penhalonga.com), **Quinta da Marinha** (❶ 21 486 0180 ⓦ www.quintadamarinha.com) and **Oitavos Golf** (❶ 21 486 0600 ⓦ www.oitavosdunes.com).

⬤ *Lisbon's Estádio José de Alvalade is known for its multicoloured seats*

Accommodation

Lisbon has a diverse range of accommodation, from luxury 5-star hotels with pools to mid-range 3-star hotels and *residenciais* (bed and breakfasts).

There is plenty of accommodation available around the Bairro Alto and Chiado, including some of the city's trendiest (and most expensive) hotels, alongside budget options. This area is ideal if you're after a party weekend as it won't be far to get back to your hotel from either the Bairro Alto or the Docas.

The hotels in the streets around Parque Eduardo VII and Amoreiras are favoured for business trips, but don't let this put you off if you want to be in a quieter part of town.

Parque das Nações (see page 110) is also popular for business with its easy access to the airport and the Feira Internacional de Lisboa (FIL), the city's conference centre. It is also good for children, as it features several attractions for kids, plus you are close to shopping, eating and drinking venues. However, if you are looking for some surf, you might prefer to stay out of Lisbon in Cascais or Estoril (see page 130), which have easier access to the beach. Here you'll find everything from camping and small hotels to resort and apartment hotels.

For romantic weekends, there are manor houses, historic and boutique hotels in Sintra, Chiado and Alfama. Portugal's *pousadas*,

PRICE CATEGORIES
The price symbols indicate the approximate price of a double room for two people, including breakfast:
£ up to €100   **££** €100–200   **£££** over €200

luxury hotels housed in converted historic buildings such as churches, palaces, monasteries and fortresses, are also popular. The nearest ones to Lisbon are in Queluz, towards Sintra (see page 142), and just outside Setúbal, so this is a better option if you are staying longer and want to go exploring. For ideas see Ⓦ www.pousadas.pt. Also look out for *estalagems*, state-run hotels.

You can easily book hotels online at a number of websites, many of which offer reasonable discounts. As well as Ⓦ www.expedia.com and Ⓦ www.hotels.com, try Ⓦ www.maisturismo.pt for a range of accommodation, Ⓦ www.heritage.pt for historic boutique hotels in Lisbon, Ⓦ www.solaresdeportugal.pt for manor houses and Ⓦ www.portugalvirtual.pt for *residenciais*. It can sometimes be cheaper to book directly. If you find yourself without accommodation, contact the tourist office (see page 153) or head to the Bairro Alto or Chiado area and try one of the *residenciais*.

HOTELS & GUESTHOUSES

Hotel Nacional £ A comfortable hotel within easy reach of the Praça do Marquês de Pombal, with private bathrooms, buffet breakfast room and a bar. ⓐ Rua Castilho 34 ⓣ 21 355 4433 Ⓦ www.hotel-nacional.com Ⓜ Metro: Marquês de Pombal; Bus: 22, 48

Residencial Dom Sancho I £ Conveniently located for the Bairro Alto and Alfama, this is a family-run hotel. Rooms have private bathrooms, there's a breakfast room decorated with *azulejos*, and room service. ⓐ Av da Liberdade 202 ⓣ 21 351 3160 Ⓦ www.domsancho.com Ⓜ Metro: Restauradores; Bus: 2, 9, 36, 44, 711, 732

Hotel Açores Lisboa ££ A contemporary hotel in the financial district, five minutes from the Praça do Marquês de Pombal and right by the metro station at Praça de Espanha. Facilities include a restaurant, bar, terrace, TV lounge, business centre and private indoor car park. ⓐ Av Columbano Bordalo Pinheiro 3 ⓣ 21 722 2920 ⓦ www.bensaude.pt ⓜ Metro: Praça de Espanha

Hotel da Estrela ££ One of Lisbon's newest design hotels (opened in late 2010) in a quiet area near the Basilica and Estrela park. The ultra-modern décor is combined with a school theme – inspired by the fact that the fine building it is housed in stands between two colleges. The very good restaurant has a terrace for outdoor dining. There is also a small garden. ⓐ Rua Saraiva de Carvalho 35 ⓣ 21 190 0100 ⓦ www.hoteldaestrela.com ⓜ Tram: 28

Hotel Miraparque ££ This hotel overlooks the Parque Eduardo VII and has a quiet location. It also has its own restaurant and bar. ⓐ Av Sidónio Pais 12 ⓣ 21 352 4286 ⓦ www.miraparque.com ⓜ Metro: Marquês de Pombal; Bus: 22, 48

Hotel Tivoli Oriente ££ A modern hotel in the Parque das Nações, opposite the Centro Comercial Vasco da Gama and ten minutes from the airport. There's a heated indoor pool, health club, bar and two restaurants. ⓐ Av Dom João II ⓣ 21 891 5100 ⓦ www.tivolihotels.com ⓜ Metro: Oriente

Sofitel Lisbon Liberdade ££ One of Lisbon's best hotels, in an excellent central location. The modern rooms (some with terraces) are very well appointed, the service is impeccable, and prices are competitive. The Ad Lib restaurant is one of the best in town, and the bar is a popular local meeting place. ⓐ Av da Liberdade 127 ⓣ 21 322 8300 ⓦ www.sofitel-lisboa.com ⓜ Metro: Avenida

🔺 *A modern suite in the Hotel Açores Lisboa*

Hotel Dom Pedro Palace ££–£££ Located opposite the Amoreiras shopping centre, this tall hotel in mirrored blue glass is close to the business centre. A modern de luxe hotel, it showcases stunning views across the city. ⓐ Av Engenheiro Duarte Pacheco 24 ⓣ 21 389 6600 ⓦ www.dom-pedro-palace-lisbon.com ⓜ Metro: Rato; Bus: 83, 718

As Janelas Verdes £££ Once the home of Portuguese writer Eça de Queiroz, this former 18th-century mansion still has a library on the top floor. It has pretty gardens and is located near the river by the Museu Nacional de Arte Antiga. ⓐ Rua das Janelas Verdes 47 ⓣ 21 396 8143 ⓦ www.asjanelasverdes.com ⓜ Tram: 15; Bus: 28, 706, 714, 727

Hotel Avenida Palace £££ The first palace hotel in the city, it is located by Praça dos Restauradores and is convenient to the Baixa,

Bairro Alto and Avenida da Liberdade. **a** Rua 1 de Dezembro 123
t 21 321 8100 **w** www.hotelavenidapalace.pt **m** Metro: Rossio

Bairro Alto Hotel £££ A stylish boutique hotel in the heart of the old
city, it has easy access to cultural attractions as well as shopping and
nightlife. All of its 55 rooms are kitted out with the latest technology
and swanky design; there's also a rooftop bar, restaurant, lobby
lounge and fitness room. **a** Praça Luís de Camões 2 **t** 21 340 8288
w www.bairroaltohotel.com **m** Metro: Baixa-Chiado

Hotel Britânia £££ Designed by famous Portuguese modernist
architect Cassiano Branco in the 1940s, this renovated boutique
hotel features Art Deco décor. Ideally located on a quiet street just off
the Avenida da Liberdade. **a** Rua Rodrigues Sampaio 17 **t** 21 315 5016
w www.hotel-britania.com **m** Metro: Restauradores

Hotel Jerónimos 8 £££ This design hotel at the heart of historic Belém
features ultra-stylish rooms with modern amenities and a swanky
bar. **a** Rua dos Jerónimos 8 **t** 21 360 0900 **w** www.jeronimos8.com
m Tram: 15; Bus: 714, 727, 751

Olissipeo Lapa Palace £££ A former aristocrat's palace built in 1870,
this luxury hotel is set on a hill amid tropical gardens with
spectacular views of the river and city. There are outdoor and indoor
heated pools and a spa. **a** Rua do Pau de Bandeira 4 **t** 21 394 9494
w www.lapa-palace.com **m** Tram: 25; Bus: 713

Palácio Belmonte £££ A 14th-century palace, this romantic
hotel is located in the Alfama by the Castelo de São Jorge. The
refurbishment has maintained the ancient beams and 18th-century

tiles. Each suite has been individually designed and named after a Portuguese personality. ⓐ Páteo Dom Fradique 14 ⓣ 21 881 6600 ⓦ www.palaciobelmonte.com Ⓝ Tram: 12, 18, 28; Bus: 37

Solar do Castelo £££ This delightful hotel in a historic mansion is located within the walls of the Castelo de São Jorge. Known as the Kitchen Mansion, it was constructed where the kitchens of the former Alcáçova Palace once stood. ⓐ Rua das Cozinhas 2 ⓣ 21 880 6050 ⓦ www.solardocastelo.com Ⓝ Tram: 12, 18, 28; Bus: 37

⬭ The sumptuous foyer in the Hotel Avenida Palace

THE BEST OF LISBON

You could easily fill a week with Lisbon's interesting sights, but if you just have a short time, here is the pick of the crop.

TOP 10 ATTRACTIONS

- **Castelo de São Jorge (Castle of St George)** See the castle's dry moat, towers, look-outs and squares for an idea of the city's history (see page 74).

- **Tram No 28 ride** A quick and easy way to see the Bairro Alto, Baixa and Alfama without a tour guide (see page 56).

- **Alfama district** A tangle of narrow streets; take in the cathedral, castle, Jewish quarter, museums and great city views (see page 72).

- **Torre de Belém (Belém Tower)** Superb example of Manueline architecture; look out for the stone ropes, heraldic motifs and carved rhinoceros (see page 101).

- **Mosteiro dos Jerónimos (Hieronymites Monastery)** Architectural masterpiece in historic Belém (see page 98).

- **Fundação Calouste Gulbenkian (Calouste Gulbenkian Foundation)** Modern art, lush gardens and musical history in the making (see page 89).

- **Elevador de Santa Justa** Ride the elevator for great views over the Baixa (see page 60).

- **Museu Nacional de Arte Antiga (National Museum of Ancient Art)** A green-shuttered 17th-century palace of art (see page 103).

- **Baixa district** Thrash that credit card into submission in this shopaholics' paradise (see pages 58 & 66).

- **Museu Nacional do Azulejo (National Tile Museum)** A 16th-century former convent with a superb collection of *azulejos* (see page 80).

The Padrão dos Descobrimentos with the Christ statue in the distance

Suggested itineraries

HALF-DAY: LISBON IN A HURRY

Jump on the vintage tram No 28 (see page 56), which clatters along the narrow streets through several key districts. There are *paragems* (stops) along the route in Campo Ourique, Estrela, Bairro Alto, Baixa, Alfama and Martim Moniz. Hop off at Alfama and visit Castelo de São Jorge (see page 74) to take in its spectacular city views. If you have time, stop for a coffee in the Largo das Portas do Sol before heading back.

1 DAY: TIME TO SEE A LITTLE MORE

Again, take tram No 28 up to the Alfama and visit the Castelo de São Jorge, but stop for lunch in or around the castle. Wind your way back downhill past the Jewish quarter and the **Casa dos Bicos** (❸ Rua dos Bacalhoeiros), then head along to the Baixa for a spot of shopping. If your feet are tired from Lisbon's hills, take the Elevador da Glória (see page 60) from Praça dos Restauradores up to the Bairro Alto and walk round to the Solar do Vinho do Porto (see page 71) where you can sink into an armchair with a well-earned glass of port.

2–3 DAYS: TIME TO SEE MUCH MORE

A little bit of extra time means that you can really explore the one-day options suggested above, and maybe linger in particular districts. Spend some time soaking up the atmosphere of the Bairro Alto and Chiado, visiting the Convento do Carmo (see page 58) and Museu do Chiado (see page 64) and making time for its cafés and for a very Portuguese evening of *fado*, before heading off to a club in the renovated Docas. A whole day is needed to take in the sights of Belém. The Mosteiro dos Jerónimos (see page 98) and Torre de Belém (see page 101) should be at the very top of your list, but make sure you don't miss the Centro Cultural de Belém (see page 102), and the Padrão dos Descobrimentos (Discoveries Monument, see page 99). Another day could easily be spent in the Parque das Nações (see page 110) with its superb Oceanário de Lisboa (Lisbon Oceanarium, see page 110), Teleférico (cable car, see page 112) and the huge Centro Comercial Vasco da Gama (see page 114), as well as plenty of riverside restaurants and bars.

LONGER: ENJOYING LISBON TO THE FULL

Visit the Fundação Calouste Gulbenkian (see page 89), find a retreat in one of the city parks, such as the lush Jardim Botânico (see page 86) and Parque Eduardo VII (see page 87), or take a boat trip on the River Tagus. Make time for a trip to Sintra (see page 132) to see the Castelo dos Mouros and the Palácio da Pena, or head to Cascais and Estoril (see page 120) for beaches, watersports, golf, a young crowd and plenty of vibrant nightlife.

● The gorgeously manicured gardens at the Fronteira Palace (see page 86)

Something for nothing

Exploring Lisbon on foot is a tiring but worthwhile experience. As it is built on seven hills – Castelo, Estrela, Graça, Monte, Penha de França, Santa Catarina (see page 63) and São Pedro de Alcântara – it gives you a vista of the city at no cost. At various points around the city, *miradouros* (belvederes or viewing points) have been built to enhance the view and let you relax as you take in the sights.

After climbing the steep Alfama streets to the Castelo de São Jorge (see page 74), you'll be rewarded with fabulous views from the first castle square across the Baixa and Chiado. Look out for the ruins of the Convento do Carmo (see page 58) and the domes of Igreja de Santa Engrácia (see page 74) and **Basilica de Estrela** (❸ Largo da Estrela) as well as the Parque Eduardo VII (see page 87) and the River Tagus. Just a walk downhill from the castle, you'll find two adjacent viewing points, Portas da Sol and Santa Luzia (see page 77), from where you can peer over the rooftops of the Alfama to the river. At Santa Luzia, look for the old *azulejos* tiles to see an image of Lisbon prior to the 1755 earthquake.

On the other side of the hill, on Largo da Graça, is another viewing point (see page 77) with similar views as the castle. It's much more romantic here and you can look up towards the castle, relax in the shade of the pine trees and gaze over the rooftops of the Mouraria quarter.

Walk to the top of the slanting Parque Eduardo VII to have a well-defined view of the park's formal gardens and straight down the Avenida da Liberdade.

From the *miradouro* at São Pedro de Alcântara (see page 63) in the Bairro Alto, there's a panoramic view of the castle, Baixa and Avenida da Liberdade. For a view in the opposite direction, head to

Santa Catarina (see page 63) at the other end of the Bairro Alto, from where you can see the Basilica da Estrela, the districts of Lapa and Madragoa and over the roofs to the port.

⬥ *There are priceless views from the city's* miradouros

When it rains

There are so many museums, cultural and historic sites and other attractions in Lisbon that you won't be short of things to do if it rains. Although the weather is generally fair, it does rain from time to time and you don't want to be caught slipping down the cobbled streets through Alfama (see page 72) or heading for the beach in Cascais (see page 126). With the help of the efficient metro system and trams, you can zip across the city from one attraction to the next.

The Museu Calouste Gulbenkian (see page 90) and the Centro de Arte Moderna (see page 90) are a good place to start. You could easily spend a day looking round them both – and there's a restaurant to stop for lunch. Then if it stops raining you can head straight outdoors to the lush Gulbenkian gardens or walk back to town through the Parque Eduardo VII (see page 87).

If you're caught in a shower in the Bairro Alto, head downhill to see the Museu do Chiado's modern art collection (see page 64) or immerse yourself in a long lunch at one of the area's numerous restaurants.

You could spend a few hours in the Museu Nacional de Arte Antiga (see page 103), where the collection of Portuguese painting will keep you intrigued. Also the Docas are not far away if you want to spend some time under cover eating and drinking until the rain stops.

Another option is Belém (see page 96). You can hop from the Mosteiro dos Jerónimos (see page 98) next door to the Museu Nacional de Arqueologia (see page 103) and the Museu de Marinha (see page 103), or nip over the road to the Centro Cultural de Belém (see page 102), with its contemporary exhibitions and restaurant.

Alternatively, spend the day indulging yourself in one of the shopping centres, which generally open from 10.00 until midnight – there are metro stations at Colombo and Centro Comercial Vasco da Gama (see page 114). You can stay for lunch here too, and this doesn't necessarily mean settling for fast food – there are quality restaurants alongside sandwich and coffee bars.

If you opt for the Parque das Nações (see page 110), you could see the wonders of the underwater world at the Oceanário de Lisboa (see page 110) and discover something scientific at the Pavilhão do Conhecimento (see page 112), a particularly good option if you're with children.

⬤ The Centro Comercial Vasco da Gama is a great place to spend a rainy day

On arrival

TIME DIFFERENCE

Portugal follows Greenwich Mean Time (GMT). During Daylight Saving Time (late Mar–late Sept), the clocks are put forward by one hour.

ARRIVING

By air

Aeroporto de Portela (☏ 21 841 3500 Ⓦ www.ana.pt), Lisbon's international airport, is located in the north of the city. You will find a tourist information booth in the arrivals terminal. If you want to take a taxi into the city centre, you should buy a voucher here. However, the quick and efficient AEROBUS runs every 20 minutes from the airport to Cais do Sodré via Saldanha, Marquês de Pombal, Avenida da Liberdade, Restauradores, Rossio and Praça do Comércio. Tickets can be purchased on board and cost €1.35 for a single with the Lisboa Card (see page 53) or €3.35 otherwise. There are also a few local buses, including the No 5 direct to Parque das Nações (see page 110), and an hourly Airport Shuttle Bus to Cascais/Estoril (€8.50). The red metro line is being extended to the airport and should be completed by late 2011 or early 2012. It should take around 20 minutes to get to the centre of town.

By rail

Portugal's Alfa-Pendular trains are the best ones to take if travelling long distances. Clean, fast and reasonably priced, these run to Faro in the south and Coimbra, Porto and Braga in the north, with a few stops in between. Long-distance trains leave from **Gare do Oriente** (ⓐ Av Dom João II) and **Santa Apolónia** (ⓐ Av Infante Dom Henrique) stations, while trains to Cascais/Estoril leave from **Cais do Sodré**

(🚇 Cais do Sodré) and to Sintra from **Entrecampos** (🚇 Rua Dr
Eduardo Neves). The phone number for all railway stations is
📞 21 318 5900. For more information, see the Portuguese railway site
🌐 www.cp.pt

By road

There are two main coach terminals in Lisbon, one in Gare do Oriente
in Parque das Nações (see opposite) and the other in **Sete Rios**
(🚇 Estrada de Benfica). For more information on coach transport,
see **Rede Expressos** 🌐 www.rede-expressos.pt

IF YOU GET LOST, TRY ...

Sorry, do you speak English?
Desculpe, fala Inglês?
Dishkoolper, fahla eenglaysh?

**Sorry, is this the right way to ... the cathedral/the tourist
office/the castle/the old town?**
Desculpe, é este o caminho certo para ... a catedral/o
departamento de turismo/o castelo/a cidade velha?
*Dishkoolper, eh aysht oo kameenyo sehrtoo para ... er katidrahl/
oo dehpartamehntoo deh tooreesmoo/oo kastehloo/
er seedahd vehlya?*

Can you point to it on my map?
Pode indicá-lo no meu mapa?
Pohd eendeecahloo noo mayo mahpa?

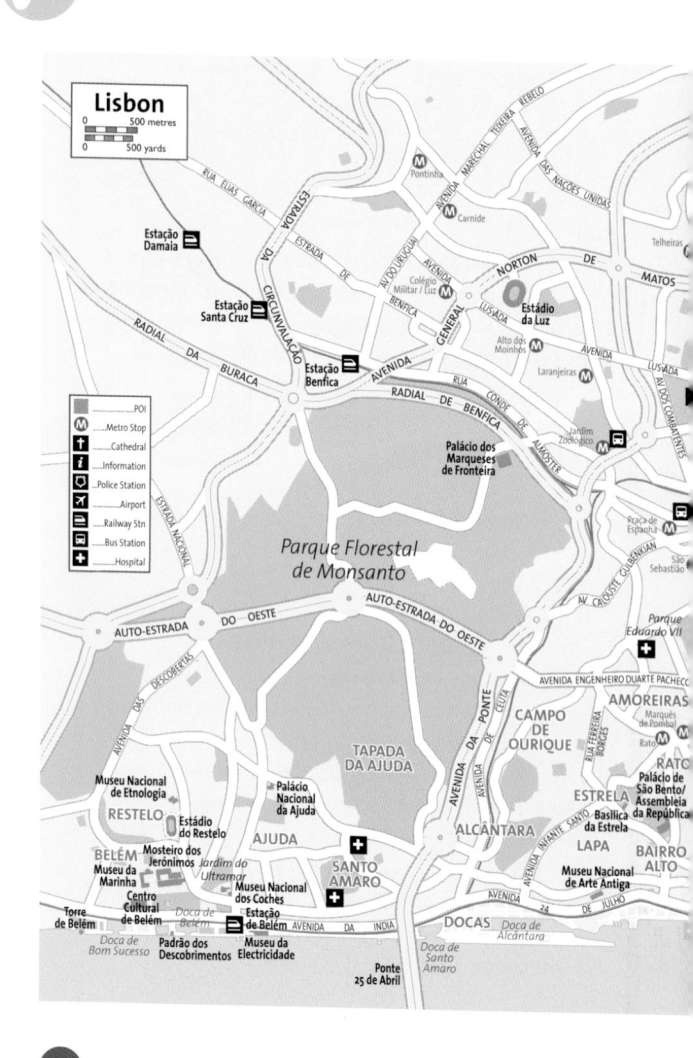

Lisbon

0 500 metres
0 500 yards

POI
Metro Stop
Cathedral
Information
Police Station
Airport
Railway Stn
Bus Station
Hospital

Estação Damaia

Estação Santa Cruz

Estação Benfica

RUA ELIAS GARCIA

ESTRADA DA CIRCUNVALAÇÃO

RADIAL DA BURACA

ESTRADA NACIONAL

Pontinha

Carnide

Colégio Militar / Luz

NORTON DE MATOS

Telheiras

Estádio da Luz

AV DO URUGUAI

AVENIDA GENERAL

AVENIDA BENFICA

Alto dos Moinhos

Laranjeiras

RUA CONDE DE ALMOSTER

AVENIDA

LUSÍADA

RADIAL DE BENFICA

Jardim Zoológico

Palácio dos Marqueses de Fronteira

Praça de Espanha

São Sebastião

AV CALOUSTE GULBENKIAN

Parque Eduardo VII

Parque Florestal de Monsanto

AUTO-ESTRADA DO OESTE

AUTO-ESTRADA DO OESTE

AVENIDA DAS DESCOBERTAS

AVENIDA DA PONTE DE CEUTA

AVENIDA ENGENHEIRO DUARTE PACHECO

CAMPO DE OURIQUE

AMOREIRAS

Marquês de Pombal

Rato

RUA FERREIRA BORGES

TAPADA DA AJUDA

Museu Nacional de Etnologia

RESTELO

Estádio do Restelo

Palácio Nacional da Ajuda

AJUDA

Jardim do Ultramar

SANTO AMARO

ALCÂNTARA

ESTRELA

Palácio de São Bento/ Assembleia da República

LAPA

Basílica da Estrela

AVENIDA INFANTE SANTO

RATO

BELÉM

Mosteiro dos Jerónimos

Museu da Marinha

Centro Cultural de Belém

Torre de Belém

Museu Nacional dos Coches

Estação de Belém

AVENIDA DA ÍNDIA

Museu Nacional de Arte Antiga

BAIRRO ALTO

DOCAS

AVENIDA 24 DE JULHO

Doca de Alcântara

Doca de Bom Sucesso

Padrão dos Descobrimentos

Doca de Belém

Museu da Electricidade

Ponte 25 de Abril

Doca de Santo Amaro

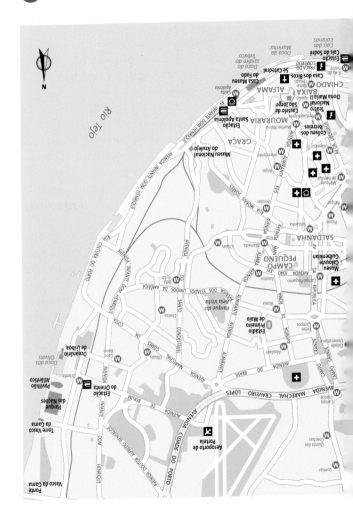

By water

Cacilheiros (small ferries) are used often here by locals travelling to and from work on the south side of the Tagus. The main ferry route is from Terreiro do Paço across the river, but tourist boats also operate between here and Parque das Nações (see page 110). For more information, see **Transtejo** Ⓦ www.transtejo.pt

FINDING YOUR FEET

You'll need a map to find your way through some areas of the city, but don't panic if you do feel lost as it will not be long before you will find a viewing point and be able to reorientate yourself. Lisbon's *bairros* (neighbourhoods) have distinct characteristics.

While Portugal's crime rate is lower than in some countries, tourists are often targeted by opportunists. There has been a rise in the number of pickpockets in the past decade, particularly on tram No 28. Also avoid walking home through dark streets in the Alfama and Bairro Alto late at night. You can always ask for a taxi from a bar or restaurant to your hotel.

ORIENTATION

Lisbon lies on the northeast bank of the mouth of the River Tagus and is built on seven hills: Castelo, Estrela, Graça, Monte, Penha de França, São Pedro de Alcântara and Santa Catarina. It's better known by its *bairros*. The easiest place to start is the Baixa, easily navigable because of its grid-like structure, starting from the Praça do Comércio on the riverside north of Rossio Square.

To the east of the Baixa is the Alfama, recognisable by its tangle of streets and crowned by the Castelo de São Jorge (see page 74). Beyond Alfama is the traditional neighbourhood of Graça, which boasts fabulous views of the city, and next door is Santa Apolónia on the riverside, the location of one of the major train stations. Further

TRAVEL CARD/LISBOA CARD

The **Lisboa Card**, available from tourist information outlets, gives free access to public transport, 26 museums, monuments and discounts at a large number of other attractions. A one-day card costs €17.50; two-day cards €29.50; three-day cards €36. If you don't want to be tied to seeing the attractions but would like to have the freedom of getting around the city, then you can also buy one-day passes for the metro. The **7 Colinas** rechargeable card lets you ride the buses, trams and metro.

northeast lie the Parque das Nações (see page 110) and the Vasco da Gama Bridge.

North of the Baixa and Rossio Square, the Avenida da Liberdade leads up to Praça Marquês de Pombal, a large roundabout with the Parque Eduardo VII to the north (see page 87). The main business areas of the city are located west and north of Pombal.

To the west of the Baixa are the lively old artistic districts of the Chiado and the Bairro Alto, and beyond lie the residential enclaves of Estrela and Madragoa. West along the river is the renovated dock area of Alcântara and the 25 de Abril Bridge, from where you can see the towering Cristo Rei (Christ the Redeemer) statue (although it is a miniature of the one in Rio de Janeiro). Westwards from the bridge is the historic area of Belém and the coastal road out of Lisbon to Cascais and Estoril.

GETTING AROUND

You will probably need to use the city's public transport system at some point, as Lisbon is both hilly and spread out. There is a comprehensive

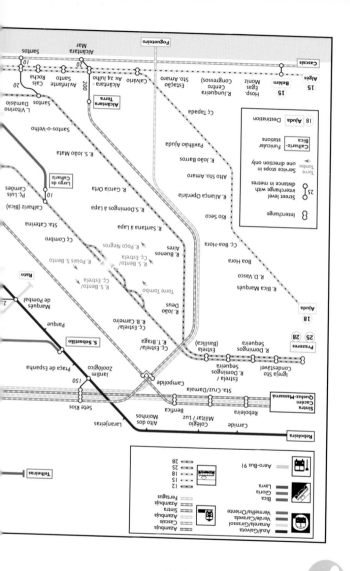

ON ARRIVAL

Style45 design
© Communicarta Ltd 2011 UDN5
Map user Ref:WZFG/PG/US
A Communicarta

Cais do Sodre [91]

Praça do Comércio

R. Alfândega [18] [25]

Corpo Santo

Av.24 de Julho (Conde Barão)

Conde Barão

R. S. Paulo

R.S.Paulo-Bça

Terreiro do Paço

R. Conceição

Lg. Belas Artes

R. Vitor Cordon ←

R.V. Cordon/ R. Serpa Pinto

Santa Apolónia

R. Conceição (R. Franqueiros)

Sé

Chiado

Baixa-Chiado

Bairro Alto

Rossio

Limoeiro

Pça Figueira [12] [15]

M. Moniz [28] [12]

Sta. Luzia

Miradouro

Lg. Portas Sol

R. Escolas Gerais

Cç. S. Vicente

R. Voz Operário

Graça

R. Graça

Sapadores

Socorro

S. Tomé ←

R. Lagares

Lg. Terreirinho

Martim Moniz

Restauradores

Pc. dos Restauradores

Avenida

R. Palma

Intendente

Largo da Anunciada

Rua Câmara Pestana

Igreja Anjos

R. Maria Andrade

R. Maria Fonte ←

Av. Liberdade

Av Fontes P. Melo

Marquês de Pombal

Anjos

Picoas

Saldanha

R. Angelina Vidal

R. Furno Tijolo

Rua Maria

Arroios

Alameda

Avenida República

Campo Pequeno

Entrecampos

Entre Campos

Chelas

Marvila

Olaias

Bela Vista

Chelas

Areeiro

Roma-Areeiro

Braço de Prata

Cabo Ruivo

Olivais

Oriente

Cidade Universitária

Roma

Alvalade

Campo Grande

Due to open end 2011

Lisboa Portela [91]

Quinta das Conchas

Odivelas

Azambuja Alverca Castanheira do Ribatejo

Lisboa Portela

city bus service in Lisbon run by **Carris** (Ⓦ www.carris.pt) and night buses run from Cais do Sodré (see page 48) through the main areas of the city. Tickets can be bought from the driver but it's cheaper to buy multiples or passes for a day or longer. Trams and funiculars are also a good option, depending on where you are going. The old tram No 28 is a good way of ascending to Castelo de São Jorge in Alfama, and it also travels between Ourique and Graça via Estrela, Bairro Alto and Baixa. Modern tram No 15 is the best way of getting to Belém from the old city and leaves from Praça do Comércio.

Lisbon's metro system (Ⓦ www.metrolisboa.pt) covers a wide expanse of city. As with the buses and trams, it may be worth buying a Lisboa Card for a day or more (see page 53). Otherwise you will need to buy a 7 Colinas or Viva Viagen card (€0.50) from a ticket machine at the metro station and charge it accordingly. The machines have instructions in English.

Car hire

Driving is only the best option if you're planning to explore some out-of-town places. Car hire in Portugal can be reasonable compared with other countries in Western Europe, but for the best rates it's better to book in advance. Several companies operate at the airport, including:

Auto Jardim ❶ 21 846 2916 Ⓦ www.auto-jardim.com
Avis ❶ 21 843 5550 Ⓦ www.avis.com.pt
Budget ❶ 21 994 2402 Ⓦ www.budgetportugal.com
Europcar ❶ 21 840 1176 Ⓦ www.europcar.com
Guerin ❶ 21 848 6191 Ⓦ www.guerin.pt
Hertz ❶ 21 843 8660 Ⓦ www.hertz.co.uk
Sixt ❶ 21 799 8701 Ⓦ www.sixt.pt

❶ Azulejo *tiles cover many façades in Lisbon*

The Baixa, Chiado & Bairro Alto

Part of the traditional old centre of the city and still very much a focal point for tourists, the Baixa, Chiado and Bairro Alto are visually quite distinct from the rest of Lisbon. Following the destruction of much of the area by the Great Earthquake of 1755, the Baixa (or Baixa Pombalina) was rebuilt by the Marquês de Pombal, who gave it the grid-like structure that can still be seen today. The streets are named after the traders and craftsmen based here since the Age of Discoveries. In the Bairro Alto, the ruins of the Convento do Carmo are testament to the earthquake's ferocity, but the area certainly isn't depressed by it. Along with the elegant Chiado, the more bohemian Bairro Alto is cosmopolitan and renowned for its artistic and literary connections.

SIGHTS & ATTRACTIONS

The pleasant and airy Baixa is easy to navigate from Praça do Comércio to Rossio and is a great place to start exploring the city.

Ascensor da Bica (Bica Funicular)

Descending from the edge of Bairro Alto towards Cais do Sodré through the scenic *bairro* of Bica, lined with funky bars and cafés, this funicular affords spectacular views of the Tagus below. ⓐ Largo do Calhariz to Rua de São Paulo ⓛ 07.00–21.00 Mon–Sat, 09.00–21.00 Sun ⓝ Metro: Baixa-Chiado; Tram: 28

Convento & Museu Arqueológico do Carmo (Carmo Convent & Archaeological Museum)

The skeletal ruins of this 14th-century convent church survived the 1755 earthquake. The archaeological museum that occupies the site

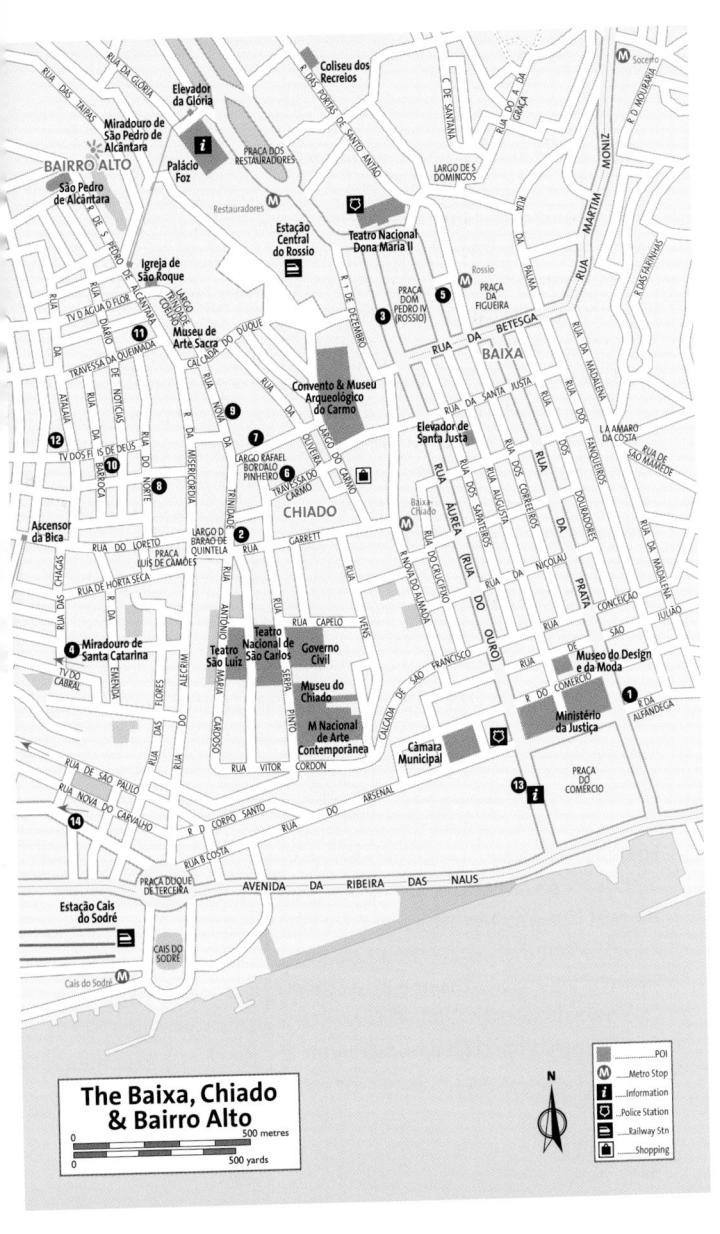

The Baixa, Chiado & Bairro Alto

today has an interesting and wide-ranging collection of artefacts dating back to the Visigoths and Romans, as well as fascinating pieces found in the Americas. ⓐ Largo do Carmo ⓣ 21 346 0473 ⓛ 10.00–18.00 (May–Sept); until 17.00 (Oct–Apr) ⓜ Metro: Baixa-Chiado; Tram: 28; Lift: Elevador de Santa Justa

Elevador da Glória

One of the funiculars built to cope with Lisbon's hills, the Elevador da Glória links Restauradores with the Bairro Alto and the Miradouro de São Pedro de Alcântara. It's just a short ride but a steep uphill walk, especially after a day's sightseeing. ⓐ São Pedro de Alcântara – Restauradores ⓛ 07.00–24.00 Mon–Thur, 07.00–00.30 Fri & Sat, 09.00–24.00 Sun ⓜ Metro: Restauradores

Elevador de Santa Justa

At the junction of Rua do Ouro and Rua de Santa Justa, the Elevador de Santa Justa is a dazzling iron structure. It links the Baixa with Bairro Alto and has a viewing tower and café at the top. Note that queues to go up can be long. ⓐ Largo do Carmo – Rua do Ouro ⓛ 07.00–21.00 (winter); 07.00–23.00 (summer) ⓜ Metro: Baixa-Chiado; Tram: 28

Igreja de São Roque

Initially constructed in the 16th century, this church was altered over the next few centuries, including the addition of the Chapel of São João (St John). Look out for the different artistic styles, such as the 16th-century *azulejos*, the *trompe-l'oeil* ceiling and paintings by Italian artists. ⓐ Largo Trindade Coelho ⓣ 21 323 5381 ⓛ 08.30–17.00 Mon–Fri, 09.30–17.00 Sat & Sun ⓜ Metro: Restauradores; Lift: Elevador da Glória

Beautiful city views from the Elevador de Santa Justa

▶ A view uphill in the Bairro Alto

Miradouro de Santa Catarina

Further on from the Praça Luís de Camões towards Estrela, the Santa Catarina viewing point is set in a green, tree-lined square. ③ Travessa de Santa Catarina ⓜ Metro: Baixa-Chiado; Tram: 28

Miradouro de São Pedro de Alcântara

At the top of the Elevador da Glória is one of the most pleasant viewing points in the city. ③ São Pedro de Alcântara ⓜ Metro: Restauradores; Lift: Elevador da Glória

Praça do Comércio

Located at the south entrance to the Baixa, locals sometimes call this wide-open square by its old name, Terreiro do Paço, because of the Paços da Ribeira royal palace that stood here before the earthquake of 1755. It also has the nickname of Black Horse Square, due to the bronze statue of Dom José I (king at that time) that stands in the centre. You'll find the Lisbon Welcome Centre here. ⓜ Metro: Baixa-Chiado; Tram: 15

Praça da Figueira & Rossio

At the northern end of the Baixa Pombalina is the Praça da Figueira, a plain Pombaline square with a statue of Dom João I at the centre. It's a good place to stop for coffee and cake. To the left is Praça Dom Pedro IV, whose statue is also at the centre. However, it's more commonly known as Rossio Square, after the train station on the left-hand side. ⓜ Metro: Rossio

Praça Luís de Camões

This small square is dedicated to one of Portugal's most renowned poets, Luís de Camões, author of *The Lusiads* (1572), whose narrative

FERNANDO PESSOA

Born in Lisbon in 1888, Fernando Pessoa is Portugal's most celebrated poet. He believed texts should be appreciated for themselves and not for the author, and so began to write under pseudonyms (as himself) and heteronyms (as an alter-ego). Much of his work remained unpublished until after his death in 1935. Lisbon was at the heart of his writing, including his major prose works, *The Book of Disquietude*, and *Lisbon: What the Tourist Should See* (1992). Other notable works include *Poesías de Alvaro Campos* (1944), *Odes to Ricardo Reis* (1946) and *Cartas de Amor* (1988).

follows the journey of Vasco da Gama. At the centre of the square is a large bronze statue of Camões. Tram: 28

CULTURE

Museu do Chiado

This former traditionalist museum was redesigned in 1994 by Jean-Michel Wilmotte. With neo-modern architecture of suspended walkways, floors and ceilings, the museum hosts temporary exhibitions and showcases an impressive collection of paintings, sculptures and drawings spanning 1850 to 1960. Rua Serpa Pinto 4 21 343 2148 10.00–18.00 Tues–Sun, closed Mon www.museudochiado-ipmuseus.pt Metro: Baixa-Chiado; Tram: 28

Museu do Design e da Moda (Museum of Design and Fashion)

One of Lisbon's newest (opened in 2009) and most exciting museums is housed in a former bank building near the Arco Triumfal

● *Pessoa sits outside a café in Bairro Alto*

(Triumphal Arch). Apart from the permanent collection at MUDE, as it's known, there are regular special exhibitions. The main collection was formerly housed at the Bélem cultural centre. ❸ Rua Augusta 24 ❶ 21 888 6117 ⓦ www.mude.pt ❹ 10.00–20.00 Tues–Thur & Sun, 10.00–22.00 Fri & Sat, closed Mon ⓝ Metro: Baixa-Chiado; Tram: 12, 28

Teatro Nacional Dona Maria II
The Teatro Nacional Dona Maria II was originally built in the 1840s by Italian architect Fortunato Lodi in a neoclassical style. It offers

guided tours and a programme of theatre, circus and performance art. ⓐ Praça Dom Pedro IV ⓣ 21 325 0835 ⓦ www.teatro-dmaria.pt ⓝ Metro: Rossio

Teatro Nacional de São Carlos

Located in the Chiado, the theatre was built in the 18th century as a replacement for the opera house that once stood here, and includes a neoclassical façade and elaborate rococo interior. It hosts a busy programme of opera, classical music and theatre. ⓐ Rua Serpa Pinto 9 ⓣ 21 325 3045 ⓦ www.saocarlos.pt ⓝ Metro: Baixa-Chiado; Tram: 28

Teatro São Luíz

Opened in 1894, this theatre was once frequented by the 'elegant classes' of the era. Today it presents a diverse range of dance, theatre and music. ⓐ Rua António Maria Cardoso 38 ⓣ 21 325 7650 ⓦ www.teatrosaoluiz.pt ⓝ Metro: Baixa-Chiado; Tram: 28

RETAIL THERAPY

The Baixa is one of the most traditional and pleasant shopping areas in the city, with international chains as well as a few local stores selling leather goods and jewellery. Look out for the names of the streets, which reflect the traders and craftsmen that worked here for hundreds of years. In the Praça do Comércio you'll also find a parade of shops, including some local crafts. Just round the corner in the renovated Chiado there are trendy clothes shops and large bookstores, such as FNAC, inside the **Armazéns do Chiado** shopping centre (ⓦ www.armazensdochiado.com). High-profile Portuguese fashion designers have their flagship stores in the Chiado-Bairro Alto area. Look out for creations by **Ana Salazar** (ⓐ Rua do Carmo 87

ⓦ www.anasalazar.pt) and **Fátima Lopes** (ⓐ Rua da Atalaia 36
ⓦ www.fatima-lopes.com).

TAKING A BREAK

Martinho da Arcada £–££ ❶ Going since 1782, and a listed local
institution. The small café and restaurant have separate entrances
but are united on the terrace in the arcade outside. The café is
cheap-ish and cheerful, and serves snacks and light lunches. The
restaurant, with decent cooking, is more formal and has an
extensive menu. Fish is a speciality. ⓐ Praça do Comércio 3 ❶ 21 887
9259 ❶ Café: 07.30–22.00 Mon–Sat, closed Sun; restaurant:
12.00–14.30, 19.00–21.30 daily ⓜ Metro: Baixa-Chiado; Tram: 15, 25, 28

⬤ *Stop by the Martinho da Arcada – a local institution*

A Brasileira (do Chiado) ££ ❷ This popular café is a must. ⓐ Rua Garrett 120–122 ❶ 21 346 9541 ⓛ 08.00–02.00 daily ⓝ Metro: Baixa-Chiado

Nicola ££ ❸ Opened in 1929 (the interior is still Art Deco) on the site of an 18th-century café, this is one of Lisbon's most popular meeting places, with tables on the square. The menu is varied, the food is good and the prices are reasonable compared with some of the more touristy places nearby. ⓐ Praça Dom Pedro IV 24–25 ❶ 21 322 3023 ⓛ 08.00–24.00 daily ⓝ Metro: Rossio

Noobai Café ££ ❹ Sip a health juice or an exotic tea while taking in splendid city views at this charming café. The light Mediterranean

⬤ *A Brasileira is an authentic Portuguese café*

fare is worth a try, too. ⓐ Miradouro de Santa Catarina ⓣ 21 346 5014
ⓦ www.noobaicafe.com ⓛ 12.00–21.00 Tues–Thur, 12.00–24.00 Fri
& Sat, 12.00–20.00 Sun, closed Mon ⓜ Metro: Baixa-Chiado; Tram: 28

Pastelaria Suiça ££ ❺ Great outdoor seating, and its cakes are
considered some of the best in Lisbon. ⓐ Praça Dom Pedro IV 96–104
ⓣ 21 321 4090 ⓦ www.casasuica.pt ⓛ 07.00–21.30 daily
ⓜ Metro: Rossio

Vertigo Café ££ ❻ This popular hangout with a retro vibe has a
great selection of teas and delicious snacks. ⓐ Travessa do Carmo 4
ⓣ 21 343 3112 ⓛ 10.00–23.00 daily ⓜ Metro: Baixa-Chiado

Royale Café £££ ❼ This elegant Chiado spot serves great organic
treats and a nice offering of coffees and teas. ⓐ Largo Rafael Bordalo
Pinheiro 29 ⓣ 21 346 9125 ⓦ www.royalecafe.com ⓛ 10.00–23.00
Mon–Sat, 10.00–20.00 Sun ⓜ Metro: Baixa-Chiado

AFTER DARK

RESTAURANTS & *FADO* HOUSES
Cantinho do Bem Estar £ ❶ This tiny storefront restaurant serves
tasty portions of Portuguese mainstays. ⓐ Rua do Norte 46
ⓣ 21 346 4265 ⓛ 12.30–14.30, 19.30–22.45 Tues–Sat, 19.30–22.45 Sun,
closed Mon ⓜ Metro: Baixa-Chiado

Cervejaria Trindade £ ❷ Relaxed and friendly, this cervejaria is great
for steaks and seafood. ⓐ Rua Nova da Trinidade 20 ⓣ 21 342 3506
ⓦ www.cervejariatrindade.pt ⓛ 10.00–02.00 daily ⓜ Metro:
Baixa-Chiado

Arcadas do Faia ££ ⑩ *Fado* house renowned for its authentic but expensive cuisine. ⓐ Rua da Barroca 54–56 ⓣ 21 342 1923 ⓦ www.ofaia.com ⓛ 20.00–02.00 Mon–Sat, closed Sun ⓜ Metro: Baixa-Chiado

Café Luso £££ ⑪ One of Lisbon's oldest *fado* houses, dating back to 1927, this basement venue has a restaurant and a nightly performance by a local folk group. ⓐ Travessa da Queimada 10 ⓣ 21 342 2281 ⓦ www.cafeluso.pt ⓛ 19.30–02.00 daily ⓜ Metro: Baixa-Chiado

Pap' Açorda £££ ⑫ One of Lisbon's most famous restaurants. Have a drink at the marble-topped bar before enjoying the menu from the Alentejo region, particularly shellfish. ⓐ Rua da Atalaia 57–59 ⓣ 21 346 4811 ⓛ 12.30–14.30, 20.00–23.00 Tues–Sat, closed Sun & Mon ⓜ Metro: Baixa-Chiado

Terreiro do Paço £££ ⑬ A sleek purveyor of updated local recipes. ⓐ Lisbon Welcome Centre, Praça do Comércio ⓣ 21 031 2850 ⓦ www.terreiropaco.com ⓛ 12.30–15.00, 20.00–23.00 Mon–Fri, 20.00–23.00 Sat, closed Sun ⓜ Metro: Rossio

Yasmin £££ ⑭ Creative fusion cuisine served in a beautifully designed space close to the waterfront. ⓐ Rua da Moeda 1A ⓣ 21 393 0074 ⓦ www.yasmin-lx.com ⓛ 12.30–15.00, 19.30–02.00 Mon–Sat (closed Sat lunch), closed Sun ⓜ Metro: Cais do Sodré

BARS & CLUBS

Bicaense A fun bar in Bica that's a boho hangout, with a small dance floor and excellent cocktails. ⓐ Rua da Bica Duarte Belo 42 ⓣ 21 015 6040 ⓛ 20.00–02.00 Mon–Sat, closed Sun ⓜ Metro: Rossio

Capela Housed in a former chapel, this bar/club is usually packed and plays electronic, dub and groove. ☎ Rua da Atalaia 45 ☏ 21 347 0072 🕐 22.00–04.00 Mon–Sat, closed Sun Ⓜ Metro: Baixa-Chiado

Clandestino This graffiti-covered bar is a Bairro Alto old-timer, still going strong. ☎ Rua da Barroca 99 ☏ 21 346 8194 🕐 22.00–04.00 Mon–Sat, closed Sun Ⓜ Metro: Baixa-Chiado

Clube da Esquina A laid-back corner bar with a DJ most nights. ☎ Rua da Barroca 30 🕐 21.30–02.00 daily Ⓜ Metro: Baixa-Chiado

Frágil Classic club that plays a mix of dance music, reggae, samba and drum 'n' bass. ☎ Rua da Atalaia 126 ☏ 21 346 9578 🕐 23.30–04.00 daily Ⓜ Metro: Baixa-Chiado

Ginjinha do Rossio A tiny bar that serves nothing but shots of *ginjinha* (a cherry-like fruit liqueur). ☎ Largo São Domingos 8 🕐 09.00–22.30 daily Ⓜ Metro: Restauradores

Majong This avant-garde Bairro Alto bar is a gathering spot for the upwardly mobile artsy crowd. ☎ Rua da Atalaia 3 🕐 20.00–02.00 Sun–Thur, 20.00–03.00 Fri & Sat Ⓜ Metro: Baixa-Chiado

Pavilhão Chinês One of Lisbon's most atmospheric bars. ☎ Rua Dom Pedro V 89 ☏ 21 342 4729 🕐 18.00–02.00 Mon–Sat, 21.00–02.00 Sun Ⓜ Metro: Restauradores

Solar do Vinho do Porto Sink into the comfy armchairs and select from 300 varieties of port. ☎ Rua de São Pedro de Alcântara 45 ☏ 21 347 5707 🕐 11.00–24.00 Mon–Sat, closed Sun Ⓜ Metro: Restauradores

Alfama & Graça

The Alfama is the oldest district in Lisbon, a clutch of ancient houses, churches, squares and narrow cobbled streets that clings to the hillside just east of the Baixa and sweeps down to the Tagus. It was the Moors that built the first fortified settlement in the city – the Castelo de São Jorge (see page 74) that crowns the Alfama. The Moors were driven away by Dom Afonso Henriques in 1147, and the district became home to royals and the aristocracy. Once they left, the Alfama fell into decline and has remained an area of patchwork buildings. Apart from the castle, the district miraculously survived the 1755 earthquake, though the poverty remained.

SIGHTS & ATTRACTIONS

The easiest way to access the Alfama is by jumping on a No 28 tram to the top of the hill. From there it's just a short stroll up to the Castelo de São Jorge. After your castle visit it's all downhill in the best possible sense, past the Museu de Artes Decorativas, the Santa Luzia viewing point and the Sé Catedral, through the old Jewish quarter and down to the Casa dos Bicos near the riverfront. If you circle round to the far side of the castle you can visit the Miradouro da Graça and then the Mosteiro de São Vicente de Fora and the Panteão Nacional.

Igreja da Conceição Velha

If you are walking back towards the Baixa after seeing the Casa dos Bicos, take a look at the doorway of this church. Built on the grounds of a former Jewish synagogue in the 16th century, the church was damaged, like so many buildings, in 1755. What survived and is most notable is the Manueline portal. Look out for the elaborate symbols of

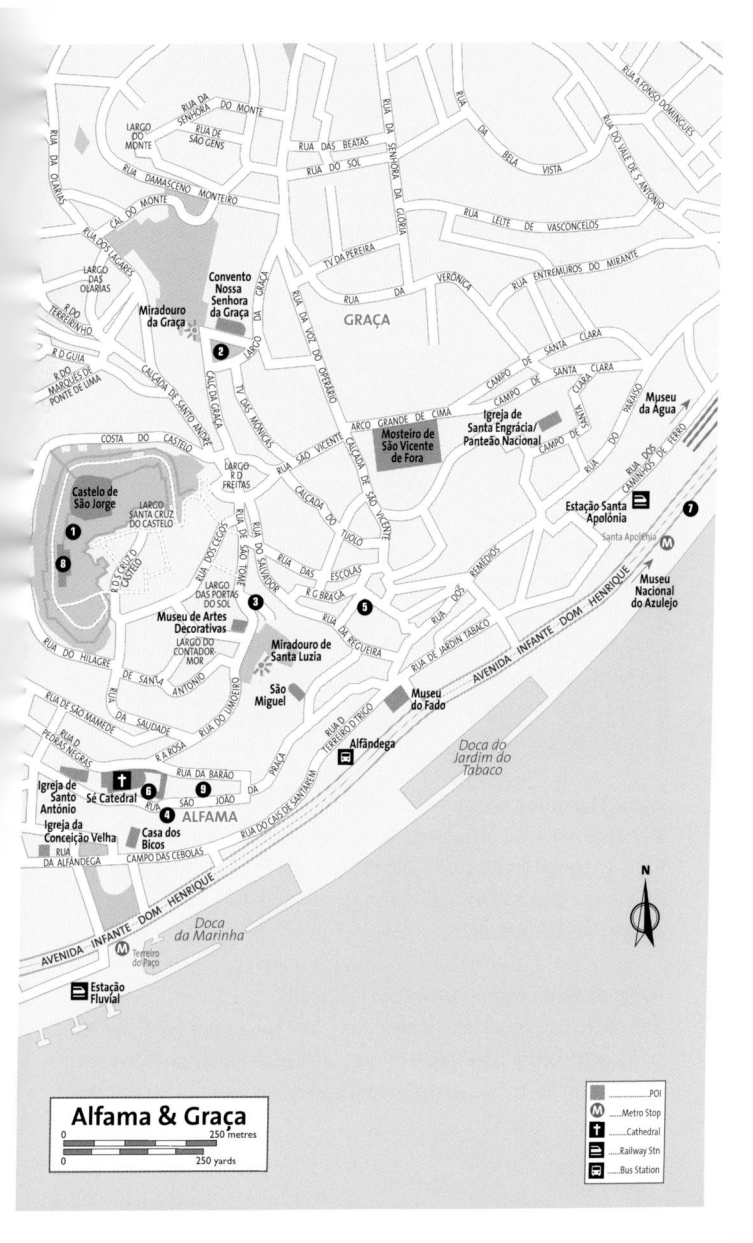

Alfama & Graça

RUA À AFONSO DOMINGUES
RUA DA SENHORA DO MONTE
LARGO DO MONTE
RUA DE SÃO GENS
RUA DAS BEATAS
RUA DA BELA VISTA
RUA DO VALE DE S. ANTÓNIO
RUA DO SOL
RUA DA SENHORA DA GLÓRIA
RUA DAMASCENO MONTEIRO
CAL. DO MONTE
RUA LELTE DE VASCONCELOS
RUA DOS LAGARES
TV. DA PEREIRA
LARGO DAS OLARIAS
R. DO TERREIRINHO
R. D. GUIA
Miradouro da Graça
Convento Nossa Senhora da Graça **2**
RUA DA VERÓNICA
RUA ENTREMUROS DO MIRANTE
R. D. MARQUÊS DE PONTE DE LIMA
CALÇADA DE SANTO ANDRÉ
COSTA DO CASTELO
GRAÇA
RUA DA VOZ DO OPERÁRIO
RUA DA GRAÇA
CAL. DA GRAÇA
TV. DAS MÔNICAS
ARCO GRANDE DE CIMA
CAMPO DE SANTA CLARA
CAMPO DE SANTA CLARA
CAMPO DE SANTA CLARA
Museu da Água
Castelo de São Jorge **1 8**
LARGO SANTA CRUZ DO CASTELO
R. DO CHÃO DO CASTELO
LARGO R.D FREITAS
RUA DE SÃO VICENTE
CALÇADA DE SÃO VICENTE
Mosteiro de São Vicente de Fora
CALÇADA DO TIJOLO
Igreja de Santa Engrácia/ Panteão Nacional
RUA DOS CAMINHOS DE FERRO
RUA DO PARAÍSO
Estação Santa Apolónia **7**
Santa Apolónia Ⓜ
RUA DOS CEGOS
RUA DE SÃO TOMÉ
RUA DO SALVADOR
RUA DAS ESCOLAS
R. G BRAGA **5**
RUA DA REGUEIRA
RUA DOS REMÉDIOS
RUA DO ...
Museu Nacional do Azulejo
LARGO DAS PORTAS DO SOL **3**
Museu de Artes Decorativas
LARGO DO CONTADOR MOR
Miradouro de Santa Luzia
São Miguel
RUA DE JARDIM TABACO
AVENIDA INFANTE DOM HENRIQUE
RUA DO HILAGRE
RUA DE SANTO AMARO
RUA DA SAUDADE
RUA DO LIMOEIRO
RUA D. TERREIRO TRIGO
Museu do Fado
RUA DE SÃO MAMEDE
R. DAS PEDRAS NEGRAS
R. A ROSA
RUA DA BARÃO
Alfândega
Doca do Jardim do Tabaco
Igreja de Santo António
Sé Catedral **4**
R. SÃO JOÃO **6**
ALFAMA
RUA DA PRATA
Igreja da Conceição Velha
Casa dos Bicos
RUA DA ALFÂNDEGA
CAMPO DAS CEBOLAS
RUA DO CAIS DE SANTARÉM
AVENIDA INFANTE DOM HENRIQUE
Doca da Marinha
Terreiro do Paço Ⓜ
Estação Fluvial

N

Alfama & Graça

0 ——— 250 metres
0 ——— 250 yards

POI
Ⓜ ...... Metro Stop
✝ ...... Cathedral
🚉 ...... Railway Stn
🚌 ...... Bus Station

CASTELO DE SÃO JORGE (CASTLE OF ST GEORGE)

One of the most prominent testaments to the city's history, the existing battlements of the castle were built by the Moors. When they were expelled, the castle became a royal residence, undergoing various additions, alterations and renovations. Partially destroyed by successive earthquakes, particularly the great one of 1755, it was classified as a National Monument in 1910 and underwent restoration in the 1940s and 1990s. Surrounded by a dry moat, it features a statue of St George at the entrance. Inside the first square, the Praça de Armas, look out for the statue of Afonso Henriques, the first king of Portugal, and take in the panoramic views of the city (take time to look at the *azulejos*, which give you an idea of what you are seeing). ❸ Castelo de São Jorge ❶ 21 880 0620 ❿ www.castelodesaojorge.pt ❺ 09.00–21.00 (Mar–Oct); 09.00–18.00 (Nov–Feb) ❷ Tram: 12, 18, 28; Bus: 37 ❶ Admission charge

state, religion, nature and discovery that characterise this architectural style, including the Portuguese coat of arms, the Cross of the Order of Christ and the armillary sphere. ❸ Rua da Alfândega ❶ 21 887 0202 ❺ 09.00–17.00 Mon–Fri, 09.00–13.00 Sat, closed Sun ❷ Tram: 18, 25

Igreja de Santa Engrácia/Panteão Nacional

The church was first built here in the 16th century, but was knocked down after being desecrated in 1630. The replacement church then collapsed after storm damage in 1681. Construction of the replacement

◗ *Dom Afonso Henriques stands tall in the Castelo São Jorge*

🔺 *Castelo de São Jorge – the crown jewel of the Alfama district*

wasn't completed until the mid-20th century. The octagonal structure, Baroque figurines and main church were designed by architect João Atunes. The dome was added in the 1960s and it was declared the National Pantheon in 1966. Today you can see cenotaphs dedicated

to Afonso de Albuquerque (first viceroy of Portuguese India), Henry the Navigator, Vasco da Gama, Pedro Alvares de Cabral (who discovered Brazil), Nuno Alveres Pereira (who secured Portugal's independence from Spain) and Luís de Camões (see page 63).
ⓐ Campo de Santa Clara ☎ 21 885 4820 ⏰ 10.00–17.00 Tues–Sun, closed Mon 🚊 Tram: 28; Bus: 35, 781, 782

Miradouro da Graça

This viewing point in Graça, on one of Lisbon's highest hills, offers one of the best panoramas in the city. Lined with pine trees, it is a relaxing and romantic spot with views of the castle behind and the city in front. There is also a café here, so you can stop for a rest (see page 81). ⓐ Largo da Graça, off Calçada da Graça 🚊 Tram: 28; Bus: 34

Miradouro de Santa Luzia

This viewing point is recognisable because of both the Santa Luzia Church and the tiled panel depicting Lisbon before the 1755 earthquake. A great place for a breather if it is sunny; if you are walking downhill, go down the steps on the far side of the church (Beco da Corvinha) – here you will see the remains of Moorish walls. ⓐ Rua do Limoeiro 🚊 Tram: 28

Mosteiro de São Vicente de Fora

Built in the 16th and 17th centuries, and partially damaged in 1755, the church is named after Lisbon's patron saint. You can easily spot its Italian façade and two white towers from the viewing points at the top of the Alfama. The real highlight is the cloisters; added in the 18th century, they are decorated with elaborate *azulejos*. ⓐ Rua de São Vicente ☎ 21 882 4400 ⏰ 09.00–12.30, 15.00–18.00 daily 🚊 Tram: 28; Bus: 34

Sé Catedral

After liberating the city in the 12th century, Portugal's Conquistador and first king, Afonso Henriques, ordered that the cathedral should be built. A mixture of Gothic and Romanesque styles, it didn't come out unscathed from the 1755 earthquake. It was renovated and today you can go inside and visit its small museum. ⓐ Largo da Sé ⓣ 21 887 6628 ⓛ Church 09.00–19.00 daily; museum 10.00–13.00, 14.00–17.00 Mon–Sat, closed Sun ⓝ Tram: 18, 25; Bus: 37

CULTURE

Museu da Água (Water Museum)

Housed inside the former boiler room, the permanent exhibit of this water museum traces the evolution of Lisbon's water supply from the Roman era until today. ⓐ Rua do Alviela 12, Santa Apolónia ⓣ 21 810 0215 ⓛ 10.00–18.00 Mon–Sat, closed Sun ⓝ Bus: 12, 35, 706, 794 ⓘ Admission charge

Museu de Artes Decorativas (Museum of Decorative Arts)

Housed in a former 17th-century palace, both the building and the collection were donated by banker and art collector Ricardo do Espírito Silva to the Portuguese state. Inside you can see an example of a typical 18th-century aristocratic residence and an important collection of Portuguese tiles, furniture and textiles. ⓐ Largo das Portas do Sol 2 ⓣ 21 881 4600 ⓦ www.fress.pt ⓛ 10.00–17.00 Wed–Mon, closed Tues ⓝ Tram: 12, 28; Bus: 37 ⓘ Admission charge

Museu do Fado (Fado Museum)

At the entrance to the Alfama, this museum and cultural centre dedicated to soulful *fado* features a permanent exhibition, temporary

⬥ *You might be glad of the No 28 to climb Lisbon's hills*

shows, a store, a small auditorium and a café. The museum showcases a wealth of *fado*-related artefacts including a collection of Portuguese guitars by famous *fadistas*, sheet music, posters, stage props and old records. ⓐ Largo do Chafariz de Dentro 1 ❶ 21 882 3470 ⓦ www.museudofado.pt ❷ 10.00–18.00 Tues–Sun, last entrance 17.30, closed Mon ⓝ Bus: 35, 39, 46, 59 ❶ Admission charge

Museu Nacional do Azulejo (National Tile Museum)

Located east of the Alfama along the riverfront, this museum in a former convent has one of the most important collections of *azulejos* in the world. Dating from the 15th century to the present, the tiles reflect both the cultural and political history of the city and the country, from the early geometric patterns of the Moorish tiles to the modernist ones found in the metro stations. ⓐ Rua da Madre de Deus 4 ❶ 21 810 0340 ⓦ www.mnazulejo-imc-ip ❷ 10.00–18.00 Wed–Sun, 14.00–18.00 Tues, closed Mon ⓝ Bus: 718, 742 ❶ Admission charge

RETAIL THERAPY

The Alfama is not renowned for shopping, but if you like rummaging for a bargain then head to Feira da Ladra market, which takes place every Tuesday and Saturday. The market is an array of household goods, bric-a-brac and the occasional antique. Go early so you can grab the best bargains.

TAKING A BREAK

With so many fabulous views of the city, the Alfama is an ideal place to stop for some refreshment.

Café do Castelo de São Jorge £ ❶ There is plenty of outdoor, shaded seating here, so you can rest your feet after a day of exploring the castle. ⓐ Castelo de São Jorge ❶ 21 880 0620 ❶ 09.00–21.00 daily (Mar–Oct); 09.00–18.00 daily (Nov–Feb) Ⓝ Tram: 28; Bus: 37

Café Esplanada da Graça £ ❷ Have a drink in the shade surrounded by pine trees, with a castle backdrop and views across to the Baixa and Bairro Alto. ⓐ Esplanada da Graça, off Calçada da Graça ❶ 10.00–02.00 daily Ⓝ Tram: 28; Bus: 37

Cerca Moura £ ❸ A favourite with locals, this offers great views over the Alfama rooftops to the Tagus. ⓐ Largo das Portas do Sol 4, off Rua de São Tomé ❶ 21 887 4859 ❶ 10.00–02.00 daily Ⓝ Tram: 28

Pois, Café £ ❹ A loungey Austrian-run café where it's easy to while away hours reading and sipping a coffee. ⓐ Rua São João da Praça 93–95 ❶ 21 886 2497 Ⓦ www.poiscafe.com ❶ 11.00–20.00 Tues–Sun, closed Mon Ⓝ Tram: 12, 28

AFTER DARK

Although not the main area for clubbing and dining in Lisbon, this zone still offers some excellent options.

RESTAURANTS & *FADO* HOUSES
Dragão de Alfama £ ❺ Serves typical Portuguese food such as fried squid and plates of *presunto* (smoked ham). Live *fado* music every Thursday, Friday and Saturday. ⓐ Rua Guilherme Braga 8 (by Largo de Sto Estevão) ❶ 21 886 7737 ❶ 08.00–24.00 daily Ⓝ Metro: Martim Moniz

Viagem dos Sabores ££ ❻ Cosy restaurant near the cathedral, with a cosmopolitan menu of well-executed dishes from all corners of the world. ⓐ Rua São João da Praça 103 ❶ 21 887 0189 ❸ 20.00–22.30 Mon–Thur, 20.00–23.30 Fri & Sat, closed Sun ⓝ Tram: 12, 28

Bica do Sapato £££ ❼ A warehouse conversion that attracts local celebrities. Overlooking the river, it serves Portuguese and international food and upstairs has a sushi bar. ⓐ Av Infante Dom Henrique, Armazém B ❶ 21 881 0320 ❿ www.bicadosapato.com ❸ 12.30–14.30, 20.00–23.30 Tues–Sun, 20.00–23.30 Mon ⓝ Metro: Olaias

Casa do Leão £££ ❽ With its superb location in the grounds of the Castelo de São Jorge, this restaurant is perfect for intimate dinners, and has great views over the city. ⓐ Castelo de São Jorge ❶ 21 888 0154 ❸ 12.00–15.00, 20.00–22.30 daily ⓝ Metro: Martim Moniz

Clube de Fado £££ ❾ This *fado* house is an old building with columns, arches and even a Moorish well in the corner. A very traditional way to enjoy good Portuguese food and hear some of the best *fado* in the area where it first emerged. ⓐ Rua São João da Praça 94 ❶ 21 885 2704 ❿ www.clube-de-fado.com ❸ 20.00–02.30 daily ⓝ Tram: 12, 28

BARS & CLUBS

Chapitô A creative space, a training school for performance arts, a theatre-cum-bar and a restaurant with a terrace. It's great for snacks but don't rely on the full menu always being on offer. ⓐ Rua Costa do Castelo 1–7 ❶ 21 885 5550 ❿ www.chapito.org ❸ 22.00–02.00 Wed–Mon, closed Tues

🔺 *The Lux Bar is a popular and trendy nightspot*

Lux Bar Cool, stylish and impressive bar, with large chairs and beds to slouch on as well as a roof terrace. Located in a converted warehouse near Santa Apolónia Station, its main bar, club and video bar have different DJs every Thursday, Friday and Saturday. 🅰 Av Infante Dom Henrique, Armazém A 📞 21 882 0890 🌐 www.luxfragil.com 🕐 22.00–06.30 Tues–Sat, closed Sun & Mon 🇲 Metro: Santa Apolónia

Onda Jazz This cavernous jazz bar hosts stellar jazz performers and freestyle jam sessions. 🅰 Arco de Jesus 7 📞 21 887 3064 🌐 www.ondajazz.com 🕐 20.00–02.00 Tues–Thur, 20.00–03.00 Fri & Sat, closed Sun & Mon 🇲 Metro: Baixa Chiado

North of the centre

This chapter covers the area from Praça dos Restauradores just north of the Baixa up to the Estádio da Luz football ground and the Colombo shopping centre, as well as from the Praça Duquade Saldanha west to the Parque Florestal de Monsanto. The tree-lined Avenida da Liberdade is one of the central arteries of the city and the Praça Marquês de Pombal is considered the 'very centre' of the city because other main roads radiate out from it. From Pombal to Amoreiras and north of Parque Eduardo VII (see page 87), the main focus is the business district, but there are also plenty of attractions, museums, palaces and gardens.

SIGHTS & ATTRACTIONS

Avenida da Liberdade

This attractive avenue, built in the style of a French boulevard, offers a pleasant walk from the Praça dos Restauradores to the Praça Marquês de Pombal. It is lined with elegant buildings such as the 1920s Tivoli cinema, the remodelled 1930s **Tivoli Lisboa Hotel** (ⓐ Av da Liberdade 185 ⓣ 21 319 8900 ⓦ www.tivolihotels.com) and the 19th-century **Cinemateca Portuguesa** just behind the hotel (ⓐ Rua Barata Salgueiro 39 ⓣ 21 359 6200 ⓦ www.cinemateca.pt). Designer shops are dotted along its length, along with restaurants and cafés in the shade. ⓜ Metro: Rossio/Restauradores/Avenida/ Marquês de Pombal; Bus: 12, 36, 44, 91, 709, 711, 732

Estádio da Luz (Stadium of Light)

This is the largest stadium in the country and the home ground for Sport Lisboa e Benfica (see page 32). The stadium also has facilities

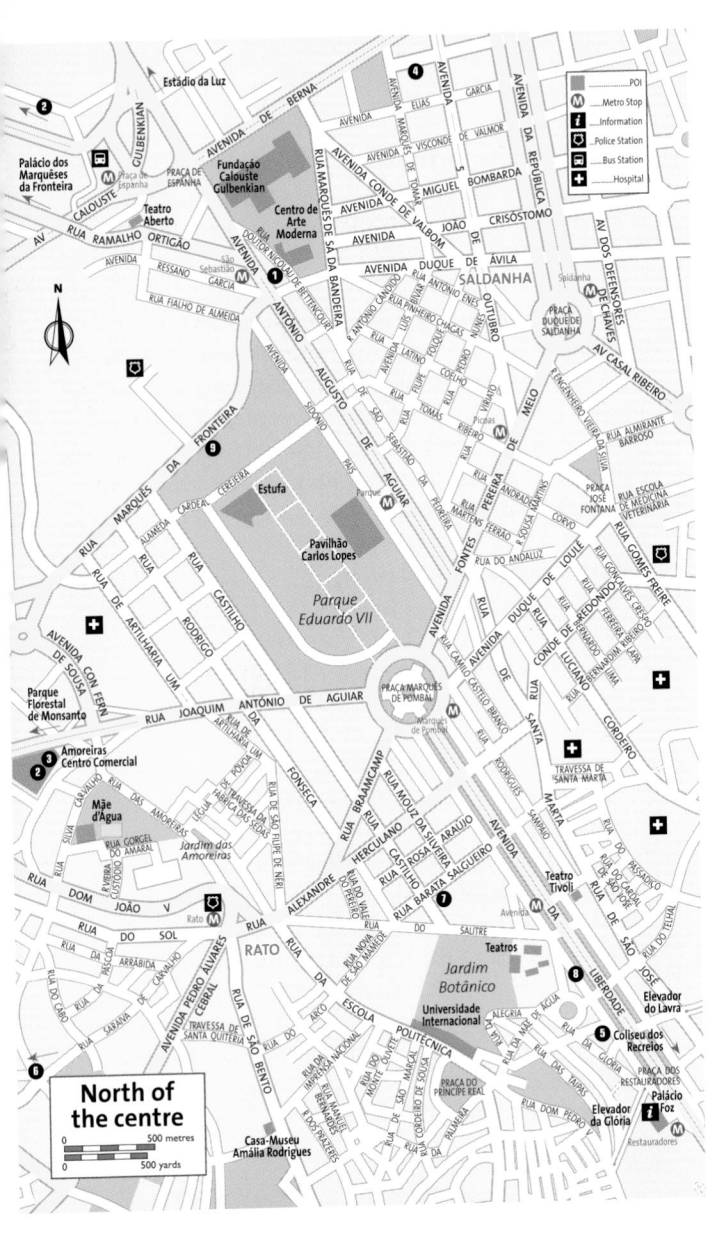

for basketball, roller hockey, volleyball, five-a-side football, billiards and badminton. ⓐ Av General Norton de Matos ⓣ 21 721 9520 ⓦ www.slbenfica.pt ⓝ Metro: Colegio Militar/Alto dos Moinhos; Bus: 54, 720, 750

Jardim das Amoreiras & Mãe d'Água (Amoreiras Gardens)

Inaugurated by the Marquês de Pombal in 1759, the Jardim das Amoreiras was filled with *amoreiras* – mulberry trees that were intended to boost the silk industry nearby. Today there are still some mulberry trees here, along with nine other species. At the back of the garden is the Mãe d'Água, a 19th-century reservoir decorated with *azulejos*. ⓐ Rua das Amoreiras ⓝ Metro: Rato; Bus: 12, 48, 74, 701, 711

Jardim Botânico (Botanical Gardens)

Located in the grounds of Lisbon University's Faculty of Sciences, these gardens have the largest number of tall palms (*cicas*) in the country, along with numerous rare tropical flora, from palms to cacti and other fleshy plants. ⓐ Rua da Escola Politécnica 58 ⓣ 21 392 1800 ⓦ www.jb.ul.pt ⓛ 09.00–20.00 Mon–Fri, 10.00–20.00 Sat & Sun (Apr–Oct); 09.00–18.00 Mon–Fri, 10.00–18.00 Sat & Sun (Nov–Mar) ⓝ Metro: Rato; Bus: 711 ⓘ Admission charge

Palácio dos Marquêses da Fronteira (Fronteira Palace)

This 17th-century palace displays Mannerist architecture, Baroque decoration and some fine 17th- and 18th-century tiles. The formal gardens are geometric in style and filled with fountains and ponds, statues and still more tiles – this time illustrated with mythological scenes. ⓐ Largo São Domingos de Benfica 1 ⓣ 21 778 2023 ⓛ Guided tours 10.30–12.00 daily (June–Sept); 11.00–12.00 daily (Oct–May) ⓝ Metro: Alto dos Moinhos; Bus: 54, 70, 729, 746

◯ *An avenue of tranquillity at Jardim Botânico*

Parque Eduardo VII

Named after the British king Edward VII, who visited Lisbon in 1903, this park lies on a slope at the top end of the Avenida da Liberdade. A network of pathways runs between green lawns, and you can visit the Estufa Fria and Estufa Quente, greenhouses with an array of exotic and rare plants. ◷ 09.00–19.30 daily (Apr–Sept); 09.00–16.30 daily (Oct–Mar) ◎ Metro: Marquês de Pombal; Bus: 12, 22, 36, 83, 91, 702, 711

Parque Florestal de Monsanto

This park is Lisbon's biggest green space and it is better to explore it by car, as it is not really appropriate to walk around, for reasons of both safety and size. Within the vast expanse of the park, there is a campsite, mini-golf, tennis courts, swimming pool, an amphitheatre, shops and a restaurant, as well as an exhibition centre and activities for children. ➌ Estra Barcal, Monte das Perdizes Ⓝ Metro: Jardim Zoológica; Bus: 714, 750

Praça Marquês de Pombal

Named after the man who rebuilt the Baixa following the 1755 earthquake, this double roundabout is the very centre of the city. From here main roads radiate out to different parts of the city, including south to the old quarters and the river, west to the business district and on to Sintra, and northeast towards the airport. Ⓝ Metro: Marquês de Pombal; Bus: 12, 22, 36, 44, 83, 702, 711

Praça do Príncipe Real

In this large, romantic square you can relax on the benches in the shade or have a drink in the café. There is also a children's play area and an underground museum, the **Reservatório da Patriarcal** (🕐 10.00–18.00 Mon–Sat, closed Sun). It is set in an antique water cistern, part of the Mãe d'Água (see page 86). Ⓝ Metro: Rossio; Bus: 36, 92, 758, 773, 790

Praça dos Restauradores

Just north of Rossio Square, this large open square is dedicated to those who fought in the War of Restoration. On the left-hand side of the square is a former palace, Palácio Foz, which now houses the Ministry of Culture as well as the tourist office and shop. Ⓝ Metro: Restauradores; Bus: 36, 44, 91, 709, 711, 732, 745, 759

CULTURE

Coliseu dos Recreios

The Coliseum was originally built in 1890 but renovated in 1994 when Lisbon was European City of Culture. You can see both classical and popular music concerts here. ⓐ Rua das Portas de Santo Antão 96 ☎ 21 324 0585 ⓦ www.coliseulisboa.com ⓑ Box office 13.00–19.30 Mon–Sat (closes half an hour before start time), closed Sun ⓜ Metro: Restauradores; Bus: 1, 36, 44, 92

Fundação Calouste Gulbenkian (Calouste Gulbenkian Foundation)

Portugal's most important cultural institution was conceived by Calouste Sarkis Gulbenkian in 1953. It comprises the country's most prestigious orchestra and choir, as well as museums, exhibition spaces, an auditorium, an arts library and lush gardens.

The Orchestra Gulbenkian has an annual season of concerts at home as well as touring internationally. The Coro Gulbenkian is a choir of more than 100 voices. It performs in a range of styles, from *a cappella* using a few choir members to large-scale performances in conjunction with the Orchestra Gulbenkian.

CALOUSTE GULBENKIAN

Calouste Sarkis Gulbenkian (1869–1955) was the son of a merchant family of Armenian origins, who made his own fortune through investments in a Turkish petroleum company. During his life-long passion for the arts he built up an impressive collection, which can now be seen in the Museu Calouste Gulbenkian.

The **Museu Calouste Gulbenkian** (Ⓦ www.museu.gulbenkian.pt) includes pieces collected by its founder throughout his lifetime. This is a real treasure trove, so you could spend quite some time here. The **Centro de Arte Moderna José de Azeredo Perdigão (CAMJAP)**, Gulbenkian's modern art museum (Ⓦ www.camjap.gulbenkian.pt), was founded in 1983 but its collection comprises work acquired by the Foundation since the 1950s. The most representative Portuguese artists from the 20th century are included, as well as some international modernist pieces. Highlights include works by Sonia and Robert Delaunay, Arpad, Pablo Gargallo, Henry Moore, Gilbert & George, and Antony Gormley. Ⓐ Foundation and museum: Av de Berna 45A; CAMJAP: Rua Dr Nicolau de Bettencourt Ⓣ Tickets 21 782 3700; museum 21 782 3461; CAMJAP 21 782 3474 Ⓦ www.gulbenkian.pt; on-line tickets: www.bilheteira.gulbenkian.pt Ⓛ 10.00–18.00 Tues–Sun, closed Mon Ⓜ Metro: São Sebastião/Praça de Espanha; Bus: 31, 718, 726, 742, 746 Ⓘ Admission charge

Teatro Aberto

Founded in 1982 by a group of theatre professionals, Teatro Aberto puts on fringe performances by its resident Novo Grupo de Teatro as well as companies from around the country and overseas. Ⓐ Praça de Espanha Ⓣ 21 388 0089 Ⓦ www.teatroaberto.com Ⓜ Metro: São Sebastião/Praça de Espanha; Bus: 726, 746

Teatro Tivoli

Designed by Paul Rino in a grand, classical style, the Tivoli was a cinema from when it opened in 1924 until 1988. Today it still has a screen but is primarily used for theatrical productions. Ⓐ Av da Liberdade 182–188 Ⓣ 21 357 2025 Ⓦ www.teatro-tivoli.com Ⓜ Metro: Avenida; Bus: 36, 44, 91, 207, 711, 732

RETAIL THERAPY

Avenida da Liberdade has plenty of designer boutiques. Amoreiras (see page 22) is one of the older shopping centres but handy if you are staying in the business district; it has around 250 quality shops, a ten-screen cinema, supermarket, restaurants and parking. For a full-on shopping day, take the metro to Colégio Militar for the Colombo shopping centre,

● *Sitting proudly outside the Museu Calouste Gulbenkian*

which has 400 wide-ranging stores with smart boutiques and trendier shops. For something more traditional, **Campo de Ourique** (ⓐ Rua Saraiva de Carvalho) has most of the international stores found in the shopping centres as well as local leather products and jewellery. There is a branch of the Spanish department store **El Corte Inglés** (ⓦ www.elcorteingles.pt) at Alto del Parque Eduardo VII, where you can find everything from clothes to stationery, as well as a supermarket.

TAKING A BREAK

You won't have to walk far to find a café along the Avenida da Liberdade or in Parque Eduardo VII. Many cafés have gardens and a play area for children nearby.

Cafetaria do CAMJAP (Gulbenkian) £ ❶ Great snacks, great surroundings: every box ticked, and reasonable prices. ⓐ Rua Dr Nicolau de Bettencourt ❶ 21 782 2751 ⓦ www.camjap.gulbenkian.pt ❶ 10.00–17.45 Tues–Sun, closed Mon ⓝ Metro: São Sebastião/Praça de Espanha

Shopping Centres £–££ ❷ All venues are a good option for lunch or coffee and a pastry: Colombo: ⓐ Av Lusíada ⓦ www.colombo.pt ❶ 10.00–24.00 daily ⓝ Metro: Colégio Militar/Luz; Amoreiras: ⓐ Rua Carlos Alberto da Mota Pinto, off Rua Joaquim António de Aguiar ⓦ www.amoreiras.com ❶ 10.00–24.00 daily ⓝ Metro: Avenida

AFTER DARK

There are some quality restaurants to be found along Avenida da Liberdade as well as around Parque Eduardo VII and Rato. There are also some decent eateries in the Amoreiras shopping centre – it is not limited to fast food.

RESTAURANTS

O Madeirense ££ ❸ This restaurant is popular for business lunches. Try some typical dishes from Madeira, including a *caldeira* (fish soup), tuna, swordfish and *espetada* (skewers of meat or fish). ⓐ Amoreiras Shopping Centre, Av Engenheiro Duarte Pacheco, off Rua Joaquim António de Aguiar ⓣ 21 383 0827 ⓦ www.omadeirense.pt ⓛ 12.00–16.00, 19.00–23.00 Mon–Sat, closed Sun ⓜ Metro: Amoreiras

Paladar Zen ££ ❹ One of Lisbon's best vegetarian options, this stylish eatery serves tasty food that ranges in flavour from

⬆ *Not just shops, but architecture and statues on Avenida da Liberdade*

Mediterranean to Asian. ⓐ Av Barbosa du Bocage 107C, off Av da República ① 21 795 0009 ⓦ www.paladarzen.pt ① 12.00–15.30, 19.30–23.00 Mon–Sat, closed Sun ⓝ Metro: Campo Pequeno

Sancho ££ ⑤ A friendly neighbourhood restaurant, popular with locals, serving fish, seafood and grills. The décor is rustic, the service is efficient and the wine list is sensibly priced. There is a section where you can smoke. ⓐ Travessa da Glória 14 ① 21 346 9780 ⓦ www.restaurantesancho.com.pt ① 12.00–15.30, 19.00–22.30 Mon–Sat (closed Sat lunch, Sun) ⓝ Metro: Avenida

Trempe ££ ⑥ A family-run neighbourhood restaurant in the area near the Estrela Basilica serving high quality Portuguese cuisine. A good selection of grills, fresh fish and wines, in a pleasant atmosphere with friendly service. ⓐ Rua Coelha da Rocha 11–13 ① 21 390 9118 ⓦ www.restaurantetrempe.com ① 09.00–22.00 Mon–Sat, closed Sun ⓝ Tram: 28

Varanda da União ££ ⑦ Panoramic city views over the rooftops to the river. The menu is mainly Portuguese with house specialities including stuffed codfish and veal with lobster. ⓐ Rua Castilho 14C, 7th floor ① 21 314 1045 ⓦ www.varandadauniao.com ① 12.00–15.00, 19.30–23.30 Mon–Fri, 19.30–23.30 Sat, closed Sun ⓝ Metro: Avenida/Rato

Ad Lib ££–£££ ⑧ One of Lisbon's best and most stylish restaurants (part of the Sofitel hotel, but with a separate entrance) serving essentially Portuguese cuisine with French flair and refinement – and imaginative presentation. The atmosphere is relaxing and the service both friendly and polished. Brunch is served on Sundays. ⓐ Avenida da Liberdade 127 ① 21 322 8350 ⓦ www.restaurante

adlib.com.pt ⏰ 12.30–15.00 Mon–Fri, 11.30–14.30 Sun, 19.30–22.30 Sun–Wed, 19.30–23.30 Thur–Sat Ⓜ Metro: Avenida

Eleven £££ ❾ The only Michelin-starred restaurant in Lisbon, Eleven has a prime location in the business district by the Amália Rodrigues Gardens. Modern and minimalist, the food is as internationally renowned as its chef, Joachim Koerper, with an innovative menu influenced by Mediterranean flavours. ⓐ Rua Marquês da Fronteira, Jardim Amália Rodrigues ☎ 21 386 2211 ⓦ www.restauranteleven.com ⏰ 12.30–15.00, 19.30–23.00 Tues–Sat, closed Sun & Mon Ⓜ Metro: Parque

BARS & CLUBS

Cinco Lounge This swish cocktail lounge by Principe Real attracts a trendy clientele for its wide variety of 100 cocktails and a relaxed yet stylish ambience. ⓐ Rua Ruben A Leitão 17A ☎ 21 342 4033 ⓦ www.cincolounge.com ⏰ 21.00–02.00 Tues–Sat, closed Sun & Mon Ⓜ Metro: Restauradores

Hot Clube de Portugal This is a legendary basement venue, the oldest jazz club in Portugal, with live music most nights. Next door there's a music school, which runs master classes and workshops. ⓐ Praça da Alegria 39 ☎ 21 346 7369 ⓦ www.hcp.pt ⏰ 23.00–02.00 Tues–Sat, closed Sun & Mon Ⓜ Metro: Avenida

Trumps Spread over two floors, this is the biggest and most popular gay venue in the city. There's a café with music and newspapers, while downstairs is split into a bar and club. ⓐ Rua da Imprensa Nacional 104B ☎ 21 397 1059 ⓦ www.trumps.pt ⏰ 23.45–06.00 Fri & Sat, closed Sun–Thur Ⓜ Metro: Rato

Belém & West Lisbon

Located on the banks of the Tagus, it was from Belém that many explorers set sail for Africa and the Americas. Many of its attractions are associated with or dedicated to them, including the Mosteiro dos Jerónimos (see page 98) and the Torre de Belém (see page 101). Belém has enough museums to keep you busy for several days, but the pick of the bunch is the Centro Cultural de Belém (see page 102), with its modern art museum.

Walk east along the river and you will come to the 25 de Abril Bridge, with the statue of *Cristo Rei* towering above it on the far side of the river. From the bridge onwards you come to the transformed Docas, the former docks that have now become one of the trendiest places to eat, drink and dance in the city.

Just east of the docks is one of Portugal's most important museums, the Museu Nacional de Arte Antiga (see page 103), and north is Estrela where you can see the domes of the Basílica da Estrela (see below) and the Palácio de São Bento (see page 101), where parliament now sits.

SIGHTS & ATTRACTIONS

Basílica da Estrela

This church was built on the orders of Dona Maria I (Queen Mary I of Portugal) in the late 18th century as thanks for giving birth to a son (José, Prince of Brazil). The Basilica can be easily spotted from various viewing points around the city, due to its large white dome and neoclassical façade. Inside it is decorated with Portuguese marble and has paintings by Italian masters. ⓐ Praça da Estrela ⓣ 21 396 0915 ⓛ 07.45–20.00 daily ⓝ Tram: 25, 28; Bus: 709, 713, 720, 738

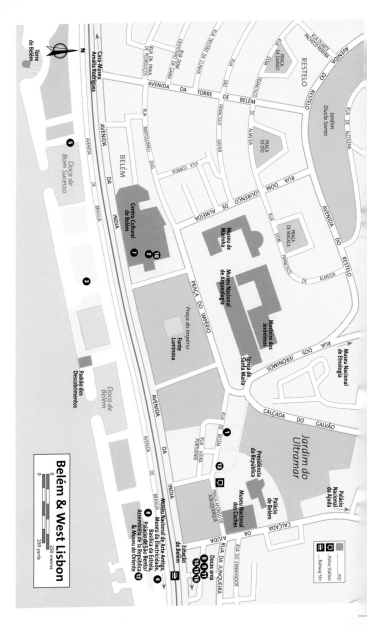

Belém & West Lisbon

0 250 meters
0 250 yards

N

Torre de Belém

Casa-Museu Amália Rodrigues

RESTELO

Jardim Ducla Soares

AVENIDA DA TORRE DE BELÉM

RUA DUARTE PACHECO PEREIRA
RUA DE BARÃO
AVENIDA DO RESTELO
RUA DE ALCOLENA

RUA DA PRAIA DE PEDROUÇOS
RUA DOM CRISTÓVÃO DA CUNHA
RUA TRISTÃO DA CUNHA
RUA SÃO FRANCISCO
RUA DOM FRANCISCO

PRAÇA DO BARÃO

RUA DOM FRANCISCO XAVIER
RUA DOM DIOGO
PRAÇA DE MALACA
VILA CORREIA
AVENIDA DO RESTELO
RUA DOM LOURENÇO DE ALMEIDA
PRAÇA DE MALACA
RUA DOM FRANCISCO DE ALMEIDA

AVENIDA DA BELÉM

AVENIDA DA ÍNDIA

BELÉM

RUA BARTOLOMEU DIAS

AVENIDA DE BRASÍLIA

Doca de Bom Sucesso ❺

Doca de Belém

Padrão dos Descobrimentos

Centro Cultural de Belém ❼ ❷ ⓫

❸

Museu de Marinha

Museu Nacional de Arqueologia

Mosteiro dos Jerónimos

Igreja de Santa Maria

Praça do Império

Fonte Luminosa

Museu Nacional de Etnologia

RUA DOS JERÓNIMOS

CALÇADA DO GALVÃO

Jardim do Ultramar

Palácio Nacional da Ajuda

Presidência da República

Palácio de Belém

Museu Nacional dos Coches

RUA DE BELÉM
RUA VIEIRA PORTUENSE
PRAÇA AFONSO DE ALBUQUERQUE

AVENIDA DA ÍNDIA
AVENIDA DE BRASÍLIA

❶ ⓭ ❻

CALÇADA DA AJUDA
RUA DA JUNQUEIRA
RUA DO EMBAIXADOR

Doca area ❾❿⓮⓯
Estação de Belém ❹

❽ Museu Nacional de Arte Antiga,
Museu da Electricidade,
Basílica da Estrela,
Palácio de São Bento/
Assembleia de la República
⓬ & Museu do Oriente

POI
Police Station
Railway Stn

GOLDEN AGE OF DISCOVERY

Portugal's seafaring success really began with Henry the Navigator, who led an expedition to North Africa in 1415. He was a leader in navigation and set up a school in the Algarve. Over the course of the next century, expeditions were sent to Africa, trade links were set up and islands were colonised – including the Canary Islands (later transferred to Castile), Madeira, the Azores, the Cape Verde Islands and São Tomé. Bartolomeu Dias eventually made it around the Cape of Good Hope in 1487, and Vasco da Gama opened up the spice trade route to India in 1498. João Cabral landed in Brazil in 1502 and trade posts were set up in Mozambique, Angola, Mombasa, Timor, China and Japan. The last leading maritime figure was Magellan, who circumnavigated the globe in 1522.

Mosteiro dos Jerónimos (Hieronymites Monastery)

At the heart of Belém, this former monastery was built on the grounds of a former church dedicated to the Virgin of Belém. It was later called the Mosteiro dos Jerónimos after the monks who lived there. Work began in 1501 on the orders of Dom Manuel I and took almost a century to complete. Highlights include the portals, which are adorned with statues and scenes from the life of São Jerónimo, the Church of Santa María with its cross shape, Manueline sculpting, the tombs of Vasco da Gama and Luís de Camões and the cloisters. ⓐ Praça do Império ❶ 21 362 0034 ⓦ www.mosteiro jeronimos.pt 🕐 10.00–17.00 (last entry 16.30) Tues–Sun, closed Mon (Oct–Apr); 10.00–18.00 (last entry 17.30) Tues–Sun, closed Mon (May–Sept) Ⓥ Tram: 15; Bus: 28, 714, 729, 751 ❶ Admission charge

⬤ *The Mosteiro dos Jerónimos, viewed from Padrão dos Descobrimentos*

Padrão dos Descobrimentos (Discoveries Monument)

This impressive building is 50 m (164 ft) high and dedicated to Portugal's Golden Age of Discovery. Built by architect José Cotinelli Telmo and sculptor Leopoldo de Almeida, it was inaugurated in 1960 to mark the 500th anniversary of the death of Henry the Navigator. Along the side of the building is a sculpture depicting a Portuguese *caravela* (boat) with the most renowned of the country's seafarers looking out to sea. Henry the Navigator is at the prow, with Vasco da Gama, Pedro Alvares Cabral and Ferdinand Magellan among the other figures. Inside there are exhibition rooms and you can take the lift to the top of the monument for panoramic views of the Tagus and the city. ⓐ Av de Brasília ⓣ 21 303 1950 ⓛ 10.00–19.00 daily (May–Sept); 10.00–18.00 Tues–Sun, closed Mon (Oct–Apr); last entry 30 mins before closing ⓥ Tram: 15; Bus: 28, 714, 727, 729, 751 ⓘ Admission charge

🔵 *Padrão dos Descobrimentos: a fitting tribute to Portugal's great explorers*

Palácio de Belém

Located behind the Museu Nacional dos Coches, this 16th-century pink palace can be seen from the main road. Today it is the official residence of the President of Portugal and can only be visited by prior arrangement. ⓐ Calçada da Ajuda 11 📞 21 361 4600 🕐 By appointment only 🚊 Tram: 15

Palácio Nacional da Ajuda

Take a detour towards the Parque Florestal de Monsanto to see this neoclassical palace, built for the royal family who occupied it from 1861 until 1910. It became a museum in 1938 and holds an important collection of decorative arts from the 15th to the 20th centuries, including pieces in gold, as well as jewellery, paintings, sculpture,

furniture, textiles and ceramics. ⓐ Largo da Ajuda ❶ 21 363 7095
🕐 10.00–17.00 Thur–Tues, closed Wed Ⓝ Tram: 18; Bus: 729, 742

Palácio de São Bento/Assembléia da República

This parliamentary building occupies a former convent. Once a month
there are guided tours to see parts of the convent church and the
refectory with its tiled panels, the grandiose official reception rooms,
plus the coats of arms and statues. Tours must be booked in advance.
ⓐ Rua de São Bento ❶ 21 391 9625 Ⓦ www.parlamento.pt 🕐 Tours
14.00 & 15.00 last Sat of the month Ⓝ Tram: 28; Bus: 706, 727, 773

Torre de Belém (Belém Tower)

This riverside tower was built between 1514 and 1520 as part of a
defence system for the River Tagus and as homage to Lisbon's
patron saint, São Vicente da Fora. It is also a symbol of Portugal's
maritime exploits and in 1983 was declared a UNESCO World
Heritage Site. You can see some of the best examples of Manueline
architecture here, particularly the stone ropes that encircle the
building, as well as the heraldic emblems, the cross of the Order of
Christ and the famous carving of a rhinoceros. If you climb the steps
to the top of the tower you will find fabulous city and river views.
ⓐ Av de Brasilia ❶ 21 362 0034 🕐 10.00–17.30 Tues–Sun, closed Mon
(Oct–Apr); 10.00–18.30 Tues–Sun, closed Mon (May–Sept) (last entry
30 mins before closing) Ⓝ Tram: 15; Bus: 729 ❶ Admission charge

CULTURE

Casa-Museu Amália Rodrigues

This small museum (see map on page 85) pays tribute to the
internationally famous *fado* diva Amália Rodrigues, who lived in this

house until her death in 1999. The interiors display the original decorations and furnishings as well as Amália's personal objects such as dresses, jewellery and shoes. ❸ Rua de São Bento 193 ❶ 21 397 1896 🕒 10.00–13.00, 14.00–18.00 Tues–Sun, closed Mon Ⓜ Metro: Rato

Centro Cultural de Belém

This modern cultural centre was completed in 1988 and comprises exhibition, performance and meeting centres. The meeting centre is a high-tech facility that caters for meetings and conferences and includes shops, a restaurant (see page 106), two bars and the CCB's administration centre.

The performance centre hosts some of the best performances of opera, ballet, classical music, jazz and theatre in the city. The exhibition centre comprises four galleries with temporary exhibitions by both Portuguese and renowned international modern and contemporary artists. The highlight of the museum is the collection of modern art compiled by tycoon José Berardo, running to thousands of pieces, and including works by many major 20th-century artists. ❸ Praça do Império ❶ 21 361 2400 Ⓦ www.ccb.pt 🕒 08.00–20.00 Mon–Fri, 10.00–19.00 Sat & Sun (until 02.00 when there are performances); exhibitions 10.00–19.00 daily (last entry 18.15) Ⓜ Tram: 15; Bus: 28, 714, 727, 729, 751

Museu da Electricidade (Electricity Museum)

The former Tejo Power Station houses a museum where you can admire the industrial beauty of this architectural landmark and learn about various electrical phenomena. ❸ Av de Brasília ❶ 21 002 8190 Ⓦ www.fundacao.edp.pt 🕒 10.00–18.30 Tues–Sun, closed Mon Ⓜ Tram: 15; Bus: 28, 714, 727, 729, 751 ❶ Admission charge

MANUELINO

While the Reconquest had led to the building of Gothic churches such as the Sé (see page 78), from 1480 to 1540 a new architectural style emerged. *Manuelino*, or Manueline architecture, named after Dom Manuel I, the king during this period, explored elaborate decoration reflecting themes of maritime voyages, heraldry and religion. Dom Manuel I commissioned numerous buildings, including the Mosteiro dos Jerónimos and Torre de Belém (see pages 98 & 101).

Museu de Marinha (Naval Museum)

Occupying two wings of the Mosteiro dos Jerónimos, it includes models of Golden Age Ships, royal, merchant, fishing and leisure boats. ❸ Praça do Império ❶ 21 362 0019 ❿ www.museu.marinha.pt ❻ 10.00–18.00 Tues–Sun, closed Mon (Apr–Sept); 10.00–17.00 daily (Oct–Mar) ❷ Tram: 15; Bus: 28, 714, 727, 729, 751 ❶ Admission charge

Museu Nacional de Arqueologia (National Archaeological Museum)

This museum has occupied the former monks' quarters at the Mosteiro since 1893. Here you can see displays of archaeology, ethnography, coins, jewellery, stone engravings, sculpture, mosaics and physical anthropology. ❸ Praça do Império ❶ 21 362 0000 ❿ www.mnarqueologia-ipmuseus.pt ❻ 10.00–18.00 Tues–Sun, closed Mon ❷ Tram: 15; Bus: 28 ❶ Admission charge

Museu Nacional de Arte Antiga (National Museum of Ancient Art)

This museum in Santos is also known as the Museu das Janelas Verdes (the Green Shutter Museum) because of the shutters on the former 17th-century palace in which it is housed. Highlights include the collection of Portuguese and European paintings from the 15th to the 19th centuries. Also look out for the pieces collected during Portugal's seafaring travels to Africa, India, China and Japan, dating from the 16th to the 18th centuries. ⓐ Rua das Janelas Verdes ⓣ 21 391 2800 ⓦ www.mnarteantiga-ipmuseus.pt ⓛ 10.00–18.00 Wed–Sun, 14.00–18.00 Tues, closed Mon ⓝ Tram: 15, 18; Bus: 28, 706, 714, 727 ⓘ Admission charge

Museu Nacional dos Coches (National Coach Museum)

Housed in a former royal riding school, this museum has a collection of coaches from the 16th to the 19th centuries, as well as a collection of oil paintings of the Portuguese royal family. ⓐ Praça Afonso de Albuquerque ⓣ 21 361 0850 ⓦ www.museudoscoches ⓛ 10.00–18.00 Tues–Sun, closed Mon ⓝ Tram: 15; Bus: 28, 714, 727, 729, 751 ⓘ Admission charge

⬤ *Crossing the Tagus; in the background, 25 de Abril Bridge and Cristo Rei statue*

Museu Nacional de Etnologia (National Ethnology Museum)

With a 30,000-strong collection of artefacts, this museum showcases a display on rural life in Portugal as well as items from the former Portuguese colonies, from sculpture to fabrics and paintings. ❸ Av Ilha da Madeira ❶ 21 304 1160 ❼ www.mnetnologia-ipmuseus.pt ❹ 14.00–18.00 Tues, 10.00–18.00 Wed–Sun, closed Mon ❹ Bus: 28, 714, 732 ❶ Admission charge

Museu do Oriente (Museum of the Orient)

Opened in 2008, this captivating museum celebrates Portugal's historical connection to Asia. The wide-ranging collection of art and artefacts is housed in a six-storey, former dried cod store. It was transformed by architect João Luís Carrilho da Graça. You can get some great views from the top-floor restaurant (there is also a café at basement level). ❸ Av de Brasilia, Doca de Alcantara Norte ❶ 21 352 7042 ❼ www.museudooriente.pt ❹ 10.00–18.00 Tues–Thur, Sat & Sun, 10.00–22.00 Fri (free entry 18.00–22.00), closed Mon ❹ Tram: 15, 18; Bus: 714, 727; Train: Alcantara ❶ Admission charge

TAKING A BREAK

This area offers a wide choice of places to stop for lunch. If you fancy a walk along the river, just east past the 25 de Abril Bridge is the renovated Docas with a large number of cafés, open-air terraces and restaurants.

Antiga Confeitaria de Belém £ ❶ Belém's most famous café. Try their *pasteis de Belém* (custard tart). ❸ Rua de Belém 84–92 ❶ 21 363 7423 ❼ www.pasteisdebelem.pt ❹ 08.00–23.00 Mon–Sat, 08.00–22.00 Sun (Oct–May); 08.00–24.00 daily (June–Sept) ❹ Tram: 15

⬤ *Take a tour bus around Belém*

Cafeteria Quadrante £ ➋ Inside the Centro Cultural de Belém, it overlooks the river. ➌ CCB, Praça do Império ☎ 21 362 2888 ⓦ www.ccb.pt ⌚ 10.00–22.00 Mon–Fri, 10.00–21.00 Sat & Sun 🚋 Tram: 15

Belém Bar Café ££ ➌ Stylish bar, café and restaurant with a terrace and great river views. ➌ Av de Brasília, Pavilhão Poente ☎ 21 362 4232 ⓦ www.belembarcafe.com ⌚ 12.00–15.00, 20.00–02.00 Tues–Fri, 12.00–15.00, 20.00–05.00 Sat & Sun, closed Mon 🚋 Tram: 15

Café In ££ ➍ A well-known café and restaurant serving coffee, tea, croissants, cakes, toasted sandwiches and light lunches as well as full meals, including good fish. ⓐ Av de Brasília 311 ❶ 21 362 6248 ⓦ www.gastronomias.com/cafe-in/ ❷ 10.00–03.00 daily Ⓝ Tram: 15

Vela Latina ££ ❺ Serves both Portuguese and international food. Good for a light lunch. ⓐ Doca do Bom Sucesso ❶ 21 301 7118 ⓦ www.velalatina.pt ❷ 12.30–15.00, 20.00–23.30 Mon–Sat, closed Sun Ⓝ Tram: 15

AFTER DARK

RESTAURANTS & BARS

Alentejo nas Docas £ ❻ This three-storey restaurant with a terrace offers traditional dishes from the Alentejo region. ⓐ Doca de Santo Amaro ❶ 21 390 8024 ⓦ www.alentejodocas.com ❷ 12.00–15.30, 19.30–23.30 daily Ⓝ Tram: 15; Bus: 714

Bar do Terraço £ ❼ Almost every evening during the summer you can come and listen to live jazz and other concerts. Nice nibbles, too. ⓐ CCB, Praça do Império ❶ 21 361 2613 ⓦ www.ccb.pt ❷ 12.30–20.00 Mon–Fri, 12.30–19.00 Sat & Sun

Já Sei £ ❽ This terraced riverside restaurant has plenty of seafood and fish on the menu, as well as peppered steak and roast lamb. ⓐ Av de Brasília 202 ❶ 21 301 5969 ❷ 12.30–15.30, 19.30–23.00 Mon–Fri, 12.30–15.30 Sat & Sun

Tertulia do Tejo £ ❾ Spread over two floors, this relaxed restaurant serves typical Portuguese dishes such as *caldo verde*. Its *pratos do dia* (daily specials) are good value. ⓐ Doca de Santo Amaro ❶ 21 395 5552 ⓦ www.tertuliadotejo.com ❷ 12.15–16.00, 19.45–23.30 daily

A Commenda ££ ❿ Located inside the Centro Cultural de Belém, this sophisticated restaurant is renowned for its privileged position overlooking the river. ⓐ CCB, Praça do Império ❶ 21 364 8561 Ⓦ www.ccb.pt ❶ 12.30–15.00, 19.30–22.30 Mon–Sat, 13.00–16.00 Sun

Blues Café ££ ⓫ This mixture of restaurant, bar and club serves Cajun food and has four bars. ⓐ Rua da Cintura do Porto, Edifício 226, Armazém H ❶ 21 395 7085 Ⓦ www.bluescafe.pt ❶ 20.00–03.30 Tues–Thur, restaurant service until 01.00; 20.00–05.00 Fri & Sat, closed Sun & Mon

Piazza di Mare ££ ⓬ You'll find all the old favourites from pizza to pasta to Parma ham and mozzarella and tomato salad – and it won't break the bank. ⓐ Av de Brasília, Pavilhão Poente ❶ 21 362 4235 Ⓦ www.piazzadimare.com ❶ 12.30–16.00, 20.00–00.30 daily

Rosa dos Mares ££ ⓭ The restaurant is named after a legend that tells of sailors who saw roses floating in the sea. Today the restaurant even has a codfish dish named after the 'sea roses', as well as splendid *arroz de mariscos* (shellfish rice). ⓐ Rua de Belém 2–6 ❶ 21 362 1811 Ⓦ www.rosadosmares.com ❶ 12.00–15.00, 19.00–22.00 daily

Speakeasy ££ ⓮ Serving Portuguese and international food until the club starts, there's music most nights. ⓐ Rocha do Conde de Óbidos, Cais das Oficinas, Armazém 115 ❶ 21 396 4257 Ⓦ www.speakeasy-bar.com ❶ 20.00–03.00 Mon–Thur, until 04.00 Fri & Sat, restaurant service until 23.00, closed Sun

Uai! ££ ⓯ Brazilian restaurant with a menu that includes fried cassava (manioc), spare ribs, black beans and stuffed pumpkin, as well as *caipirinhas* (a Brazilian cocktail made with *cachaça*, limes, sugar and ice). **ⓐ** Rocha do Conde de Óbidos, Cais de Oficinas, Armazém 114 **ⓣ** 21 390 0111 **ⓦ** www.uai.pt **ⓛ** 13.00–15.00, 20.00–23.00 Tues–Sun, closed lunch Tues & Wed, closed dinner Sun, closed Mon

Alcântara Café £££ ⑯ A 1920s-style restaurant decorated in wood, leather and velvet, this place serves a mixture of Portuguese specialities and French cuisine. Fish features highly on the menu. **ⓐ** Rua Maria Luísa Holstein 15 **ⓣ** 21 362 1226 **ⓦ** www.alcantaracafe.com **ⓛ** 20.00–03.00, restaurant service until 01.00 Mon–Sun

BARS & CLUBS

Dock's Club Late-night club that's popular with the younger crowd. It has theme nights and ladies' nights. **ⓐ** Rua da Cintura do Porto de Lisboa 226 **ⓣ** 21 395 0856 **ⓛ** 23.00–06.00 Tues–Sat, closed Sun & Mon

Indochina Club with a Vietnamese-Oriental theme that's one of the trendiest on the Docas. Most popular for a mix of pop and the latest dance tunes. **ⓐ** Rua da Cintura do Porto de Lisboa, Armazém H **ⓣ** 21 395 5875 **ⓛ** 23.00–06.00 Tues–Sat, closed Sun & Mon

Kremlin A favourite for dance music, this club starts late and stays open until breakfast. **ⓐ** Rua das Escadinhas da Praia 5 (Av 24 de Julio) **ⓣ** 21 395 7101 **ⓦ** www.grupo-k.pt **ⓛ** 24.00–08.00 Wed–Sat, closed Sun–Tues

Queens The décor of this club with an enormous dance floor is distinctly 1970s. It has three bars and views of the river. **ⓐ** Rua da Cintura do Porto de Lisboa, Armazém H **ⓣ** 21 395 5870 **ⓛ** 23.00–06.00 Tues–Sat, closed Sun & Mon

Parque das Nações

The Parque das Nações was built for Expo '98 and is a showcase of modern architecture. Stretched along a 3-km (2-mile) length of the River Tagus in east Lisbon, it doesn't have a crumbling building in sight (though it does have a tall one – the former Vasco da Gama Tower). Just a ten-minute bus ride from the airport, and with a major train station, it is here that Portugal travels into the 21st century.

SIGHTS & ATTRACTIONS

The easiest way to get to Parque das Nações is the short metro ride to Oriente. You arrive by the shopping centre and once outside you will see the cable car along the riverfront with the Vasco da Gama Bridge at one end and the Oceanário at the other. In front are the Pavilhão Atlântico (see page 113) and the Doca dos Olivais.

Oceanário de Lisboa (Lisbon Oceanarium)

Located at the southern end of the Doca dos Olivais, the Oceanário is well worth the pricey ticket. Inside are four areas representing coastal habitats of the North Atlantic, Antarctic, temperate Pacific and tropical Indian Oceans, connected by a central tank to create the illusion of a single ocean. The Global Ocean is 49 m (160 ft) high and is the centrepiece of the exhibition. You can come face to face with sharks, rays and barracuda, conga eels, giant grouper and tuna, puffins, penguins, seals, seahorses, sea urchins, anemones, corals and jellyfish, to mention just a few. ⓐ Esplanada Dom Carlos I ⓣ 21 891 7002 ⓦ www.oceanario.pt ⓛ 10.00–19.00 daily (Apr–Oct); 10.00–18.00 daily (Nov–Mar); last entry 1 hour before closing ⓜ Metro: Oriente; Bus: 25, 28, 44, 708, 750, 759 ⓘ Admission charge

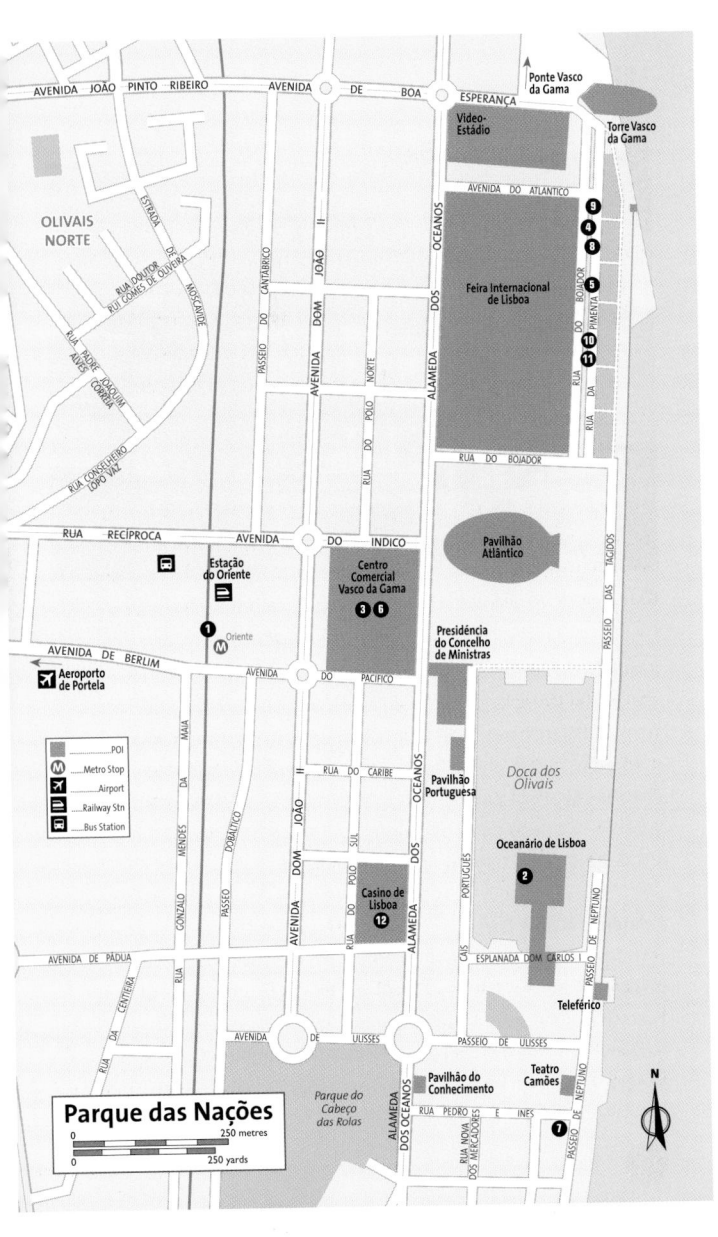

🔺 *The largest oceanarium in Europe is in the Parque das Nações*

Pavilhão do Conhecimento (Knowledge Pavilion)

This is an interactive science and technology museum that aims to make science available to all. Highlights include displays on mathematics, the 'Flying Bicycle' and nanotechnology. ❸ Alameda dos Oceanos ❶ 21 891 7100 Ⓦ www.pavconhecimento.pt ⏰ 10.00–18.00 Tues–Fri, 11.00–19.00 Sat & Sun, closed Mon Ⓜ Metro: Oriente; Bus: 25, 28, 44, 708, 750, 759 ❶ Admission charge

Teleférico (Cable Car)

If you get a thrill from heights and you don't want to walk the distance between the Oceanário and the Vasco da Gama Tower, then the cable car is a suitable option. You'll also get a bird's-eye view over the park as you pass the Pavilhão Atlântico concert venue, the huge Exhibition Centre, restaurants and the former Vasco da

PARQUE DAS NAÇÕES CARD

This card (€17.50 adults; €9 children under 12, adults over 65) includes a visit to the Oceanário and Pavilhão do Conhecimento, a single or return trip on the cable car, unlimited rides on the tourist train that travels around the park, 20 per cent off bicycle hire at Tejo Bike (see page 148) and 15 per cent off at some restaurants. You can purchase the cards from the Oceanário or the Parque das Nações Information Desk.

Gama Tower. ⓐ Doca dos Olivais, Parque das Nações ⓣ 21 895 6143 ⓛ 11.00–19.00 Mon–Fri, 10.00–19.00 Sat & Sun ⓜ Metro: Oriente; Bus: 25, 28, 44, 708, 750, 759 ⓘ Admission charge

CULTURE

Casino Lisboa

Here, aside from the slot machines, roulette, blackjack and poker, there's also an auditorium that plays host to live international and Portuguese music and dance and theatre productions, as well as a lounge bar with live music, several bars linked to the gaming rooms, and three restaurants. ⓐ Alameda dos Oceanos ⓣ 21 892 9000 ⓦ www.casino-lisboa.pt ⓛ 15.00–03.00 Sun–Thur, 16.00–04.00 Fri & Sat ⓜ Metro: Oriente; Bus: 25, 28, 44, 708, 750, 759

Pavilhão Atlântico

One of the city's major concert and sports venues, this state-of-the-art pavilion is easy to find on the riverfront. ⓐ Rossio dos Olivais ⓣ 21 891 8409 ⓦ www.pavilhaoatlantico.pt ⓜ Metro: Oriente; Bus: 25, 28, 44, 708, 750, 759

Teatro Camões

Home of the National Ballet of Portugal, this theatre's calendar also focuses on dance performances by other leading companies.
ⓐ Passeio de Neptuno ❶ 21 892 3470 Ⓦ www.cnb.pt Ⓝ Metro: Oriente; Bus: 25, 28, 44, 708, 750, 759

RETAIL THERAPY

Centro Comercial Vasco da Gama (ⓐ Av Dom João II ❶ 21 893 0600 Ⓦ www.centrovascodagama.pt ⏰ 09.00–24.00 daily Ⓝ Metro: Oriente) is the main shopping area. Spread over four floors, it includes fashion stores such as Zara, Mango, Cortefiel, Massimo Dutti, Lacoste and Bershka, as well as shoe, sports, gift, music, furniture, jewellery and perfume shops. There is also a cinema and a huge supermarket.

There are a few outlets along the Alameda dos Oceanos and Rua da Ilha dos Amores, offering car hire, art galleries, stationery, furniture and toys. There is also a craft shop along Rua da Pimenta.

TAKING A BREAK

There are several cafés and boutique-y places for coffees and snacks, and plenty of bars if you fancy a gin and tonic with a river view.

Baskin-Robbins £ ❶ In Oriente Station, and just right for a snack and a cuppa. ⓐ Estação Oriente, Loja G103 ❶ 21 941 9575 ⏰ 08.00–21.00 daily Ⓝ Metro: Oriente; Bus: 28, 44

Il Caffè di Roma £ ❷ By the Oceanário, one of an Italian chain of boutique cafés that serve good coffee – you can have it with cream,

● *The Teleférico takes you from the Oceanário to the Vasco da Gama Bridge*

ice cream or alcohol. ❷ Edificio Oceanário de Lisboa, Esplanada Dom Carlos I Ⓦ www.ilcaffediroma.pt Ⓛ 10.00–20.00 daily Ⓜ Metro: Oriente; Bus: 28, 44

Centro Comercial Vasco da Gama £ ❸ There is no shortage of places to stop for refreshment and a rest from tiring shopping (see opposite).

AFTER DARK

There is a wide range of restaurants and bars all along the riverfront between the Pavilhão Atlântico and the Vasco da Gama Tower.

RESTAURANTS

100 Norte £ ❹ A restaurant by day and bar-club by night, there is a large terrace and indoor seating. The menu includes steaks, pizza, pasta, fish and sandwiches as well as a children's menu. The bar-club has karaoke and ladies' nights. ❹ Rua do Bojador 107 ❶ 21 895 8248 ❷ 12.00–05.00 Tues–Sun (Oct–Apr), closed Mon & Nov–Mar ❷ Metro: Oriente

Café da Palha £ ❺ Caters for large groups and serves traditional Portuguese food. It is particularly good for steaks, grills and salads. They have karaoke and club nights until the early hours of the morning. ❹ Rua da Pimenta 75–79 ❶ 21 895 5915 ❷ 16.00–05.00 Sun, Mon, Wed & Thur, 11.00–05.00 Fri & Sat, closed Tues ❷ Metro: Oriente

Cervejeira Lusitana £ ❻ Portuguese steak chain restaurant, specialising in Portuguese beers such as Pilsener Checa, with a tasty children's menu. ❹ Centro Comercial Vasco da Gama, 3rd floor ❶ 21 896 8162 ❿ www.lusitana.com ❷ 11.00–24.00 daily

Mestre Doce £ ❼ Small family-style restaurant, serving home-cooked Portuguese cuisine such as prawn rice and steaks, as well as good desserts. ❹ Passeio de Neptuno 3 ❶ 21 894 6043 ❷ 08.00–24.00 daily ❷ Metro: Oriente

🔺 *Groundbreaking architecture in the Parque das Nações*

El Tapas ££ ❽ Typically Spanish restaurant serving tapas, paellas and other Iberian specialities. It is located by the former Torre de Vasco da Gama. ❷ Rua da Pimenta 99–101 ❶ 21 896 6900 🕐 12.00–01.00 Mon–Fri, 12.00–03.00 Sat & Sun Ⓜ Metro: Oriente

Havana ££ ❾ Typically Cuban restaurant looking out on to the former Vasco da Gama Tower and Bridge. Specialities include steak Che Guevara, fried prawns and Caribbean salad. ❷ Rua da Pimenta 115–117 ❶ 21 895 7116 🕐 12.00–04.00 daily Ⓜ Metro: Oriente

Passeio do Oriente ££ ⑩ With a large terrace and two floors inside, this restaurant serves traditional Portuguese lunches, dinners and snacks, German beers, sangria, *caipirinhas* and shots. There is also live music, karaoke and Spanish dancing. ⓐ Rua da Pimenta 51 ❶ 21 895 6147 ❷ 12.00–02.00 Sun–Tues & Thur, until 04.00 Fri & Sat, closed Wed Ⓝ Metro: Oriente

Senhor Peixe ££ ⑪ Specialises in fish dishes, such as shrimps with garlic to start, shrimp soup, fish stew, lobster rice, grilled squid, grouper or langoustines. They also serve vegetable soup and steaks. ⓐ Rua da Pimenta 35–37 ❶ 21 895 5892 Ⓦ www.cidiarte.pt/senhorpeixe ❷ 12.00–15.30, 19.00–22.30 Thur–Sun, closed Mon–Wed Ⓝ Metro: Oriente

Spot Lx ££ ⑫ Grills are the thing at this elegant restaurant inside Casino Lisboa. ⓐ Alameda dos Oceanos ❶ 21 892 9043 Ⓦ www.casino-lisboa.pt ❷ 19.30–24.00 daily

BARS & CLUBS
Peter Café Sport This bar is a replica of the famous bar in Faial, Azores, where sailors would stop to pick up their messages and have a gin and tonic. If you want something to eat, try the Steak Peter or a toasted sandwich. ⓐ Rua da Pimenta 39–41 ❶ 21 895 0060 ❷ 12.00–02.00 daily Ⓝ Metro: Oriente

---

❷ *Enjoy a walk in Cabo da Roca, Europe's most westerly point*

OUT OF TOWN
trips

Cascais & Estoril

Just 24 km (15 miles) west of Lisbon, the seaside resorts of Estoril and Cascais provide the perfect beach and golf locations within easy reach of the capital's culture and attractions. The popularity of the Estoril coast began in 1889 with the opening of the train line from Lisbon.

Today surfing and sailing are popular and there are several first-class golf courses (see page 33), a race track (see page 32), a marina and a casino. Popular with kids and the young crowd because of the beach, surfing and clubs, Estoril also features plenty of cultural activities: picturesque museum-mansions, cultural centres, open-air entertainment and the famous Casino Estoril (see page 122) – as well as the relaxing atmosphere, good seafood and fresh sea air.

The Estoril Coast Tourism website covers the region west of Oeiras and south of Sintra, and includes Estoril and Cascais, as well as various coastal and inland towns and villages.
Ⓦ www.estoril-portugal.com Ⓦ www.cascais.net

GETTING THERE

By rail

The Cascais train line runs from Cais do Sodré along the coast via Alcântara Mar and Belém. The journey from Cais do Sodré to Cascais takes 33–40 minutes, from Alcântara 24–31 minutes and from Belém 28–50 minutes, depending on whether you take a fast or slow train. Estoril is two stops before Cascais, so you can deduct about five minutes from the journey time. You can check the exact schedule at Ⓦ www.cp.pt

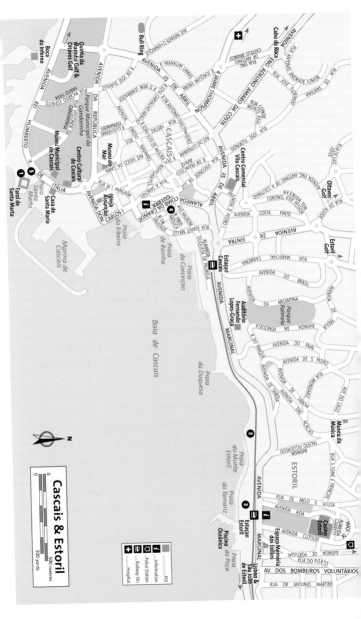

SIGHTS & ATTRACTIONS

Boca do Inferno (Mouth of Hell)

This is a 150-million-year-old cavern with steep sides and deep gouges made by the turbulent sea. When it is windy and the sea fairly choppy, it is quite a spectacular sight to see the Boca turn into a mass of bubbling white water. You can reach it by walking west along the coastal road, but be careful of going too close, as some people have been swept away. **ⓐ** Av Rei de Italia, Cascais **Ⓝ** Train: Cascais

Cabo da Roca

West of Cascais, and connected by regular buses (it's about 20 minutes away), this is the most westerly point in continental Europe. As well as containing a lighthouse, tourist office and other facilities, this is a great spot for walks and wild and dramatic views. **ⓐ** Cabo da Roca, Azóia

Casa de Santa Maria

Built by architect Raúl Lino in the early 20th century, this is a romantic combination of Mediterranean mansion and Moorish revivalist style. Look out for the 17th-century *azulejos* taken from an old chapel (which depict some quite horrific scenes), the elaborate ceilings and the view from the patio. **ⓐ** Estrada do Farol de Santa Marta, Marina de Cascais **ⓣ** 21 481 5382 **ⓛ** 10.00–13.00, 14.00–17.00 Tues–Sun, closed Mon **Ⓝ** Train: Cascais

Casino Estoril

The largest casino in Europe, this has a theatre-auditorium, restaurants, art gallery and shops, as well as gaming rooms. It is strictly smart

⬛ *Boca do Inferno is just outside Cascais*

dress only (men with a jacket and tie). ➌ Praça José Teodoro dos Santos ☎ 21 466 7700 ⓦ www.casino-estoril.pt 🕓 15.00–03.00 daily Ⓜ Train: Estoril

Espaço Memória dos Exílios (Estoril Post Office Museum)
This is a modernist building designed by Portuguese architect Adelino Nunes and opened in 1942. As Estoril was a haven for many exiles during World War II, the first floor of the post office now has a permanent exhibition on this theme. ➌ Av Marginal 7152A ☎ 21 481 5930 🕓 10.00–18.00 Mon–Sat, closed Sun Ⓜ Train: Estoril

Igreja de Nossa Senhora da Assunção

Built in the 16th century, this church includes gilt-work on the wooden altar, panels of *azulejos* and the 17th-century paintings of the Annunciation by Josefa de Obidos. ⓐ Largo da Assunção 🕒 09.00–13.00, 17.00–20.00 daily Ⓝ Train: Cascais

Marina de Cascais

Cascais Marina is a hub of social and sporting activity. Modern and well equipped, it has 650 moorings for boats as well as commercial space. Sailing races and regattas regularly start from here, and the sailing school **Escola de Vela Tuttamania** (ⓦ www.tuttamania.com) runs courses. The races are run by the **Clube Naval de Cascais** (ⓦ www.cncascais.com). There are also a few shops, restaurants and cafés here. ⓣ 21 482 4857 ⓦ www.marina-cascais.com 🕒 09.00–18.00 daily (winter); 09.00–19.00 daily (summer) Ⓝ Train: Cascais

Museu do Mar (Museum of the Sea)

Here you can discover the town's links with the sea and learn something about natural history and underwater archaeology. One of the most interesting parts of the museum includes models of boats and treasure salvaged from shipwrecks found off the coast. ⓐ Rua Júlio Pereira de Mello, Cascais ⓣ 21 481 5906 🕒 10.00–17.00 Tues–Sun, closed Mon Ⓝ Train: Cascais ❶ Admission charge

Museu Municipal de Cascais/Palácio dos Condes de Castro Guimarães

Housed in the 20th-century former mansion home of Jorge O'Neill, this place has fabulous ocean views. Sold to the Condes de Castro Guimarães in 1910, it underwent some alterations and today reflects the owner's penchant for acquiring art and furniture from various eras, including a neo-Gothic organ. The count died in 1927 and left

 *The marina at Cascais*

the house to the local authorities, who turned it into a museum. Officially opened in 1931, there is a rich collection of *azulejos*, porcelain, furniture and a fine library of historic books. ❸ Av Rei Humberto II de Itália, Parque Municipal da Gandarinha ❶ 21 482 5401 ❶ 10.00–17.00 Tues–Fri, 10.00–13.00, 14.00–17.00 Sat & Sun, closed Mon ❷ Train: Cascais ❶ Admission charge (except Sun)

ESTORIL COAST BEACHES

Most beaches along the Estoril Coast have been awarded a blue flag, in recognition of the water quality as well as the nearby infrastructure.

There are beaches and a promenade all the way from Cascais to Estoril. Praia da Ribeira by Cascais old town is a focal point because of the fishing boats that arrive here and the craft stalls and music performances, but it is not really a place to go swimming. Conceição, Rainha and Duquesa are small sandy beaches where you can hire sunbeds and grab a drink at one of the nearby bars. In Estoril the beaches include Monte Estoril, by the **Mirage Cascais Hotel** (ⓐ Av Marginal 8554 ❶ 21 006 0600 ⓦ www.cascaismirage.com), and Tamariz, which is popular with children, as there are pools of seawater. Further east is Poça, a calm and pleasant long beach, but the biggest stretch of sand and best place for watersports is Carcavelos near Oeiras. Popular with surfers, particularly in spring and autumn, it has volleyball and beach football pitches and a roller-skating rink. All have nearby cafés and restaurants.

For something a little more remote, you will have to drive west to Cabo da Roca (see page 122), then head north to Guincho. Naturally wild, it has a large area of sand dunes, long stretches of sand, and, because of the Atlantic wind, is good for surfing, bodyboarding and windsurfing.

Parque Municipal da Gandarinha

This large, leafy park stretches from the Condes de Castro Guimarães Museum (Municipal Museum) to the Boca do Inferno.

Traditional houses in Estoril

It is a pleasant place for a leisurely walk, faces the seafront and is filled with statues, ponds and palms, as well as the Cascais Sports Pavilion and the Manuel Passolo riding school. ❸ Av Rei Humberto II de Itália ❽ Train: Cascais

CULTURE

Auditório Fernando Lopes-Graça

Named after one of the 20th century's famous Portuguese composers, this open-air auditorium is used for orchestral concerts, jazz, theatre and *fado* groups. ⓐ Parque Palmela, Avenida Marginal ❶ 21 482 5447 Ⓝ Train: Cascais

Centro Cultural de Cascais

Located on the site of a former 17th-century convent, the buildings were rebuilt by architect Jorge Silva as an art museum and exhibition centre. There is also an auditorium here, which is used for concerts. ⓐ Av Rei Humberto II de Itália ❶ 21 484 8900 ⓛ 10.00–18.00 Tues–Sun, closed Mon Ⓝ Train: Cascais

Museu da Música/Casa Verdades de Faria (Music Museum/Verdades de Faria House)

Wealthy arts patron Mantero Belard left this house to the town as a house-museum and gardens, and dedicated it to his mother. Decorated with painted stucco, glass and 17th-century tiles, today it houses a collection of Portuguese instruments bought from the Corsican ethnomusicologist Michel Giacometti. ⓐ Av de Sabóia 1146B, Estoril ❶ 21 481 5904 ⓛ 10.00–13.00, 14.00–17.00 Tues–Sun, closed Mon Ⓝ Train: Estoril

RETAIL THERAPY

There are craft stalls on the beaches, traditional shopping in Cascais old town, and a weekly market next to the bullring, where you can find good-quality leather goods and jewellery. There is an open-air crafts fair during July and August by Casino Estoril, selling crafts from all over the country, including ceramics, tiles and woodcarvings.

There is a large shopping centre, **Cascais Shopping** (ⓦ www.cascaishopping.pt), located out of town towards Sintra on the EN9 road. You can catch buses 406, 417 and 418 from Cascais Station.

AFTER DARK

Cascais and Estoril have a good range of cafés and restaurants – many with outdoor seating areas – from traditional Portuguese tavernas to international cuisine. Watch out for touristy prices; there are reasonable places to be found. In Largo Luiz de Camões and Rua Frederico Arouca there are several bars and a few *fado* clubs. There are also a lot of bars around Cascais Marina, and Carcavelos Beach is also a popular choice.

RESTAURANTS
Coconuts Club £ ❶ A restaurant/club noted as much for its delicious nibbles as it is for its dancing. ⓐ Av Rei Humberto II de Itália 7 ❶ 21 484 4109 ❺ 23.30–05.00 Tues–Sat, closed Sun & Mon (summer); 23.30–05.00 Fri & Sat, closed Sun–Thur (winter)

Jonas Bar £ ❷ Located on the edge of Tamariz Beach, this is a fast-food restaurant-bar where you can have burgers for lunch or stop for a beachfront drink in the evening. ⓐ Paredão, Praia do Tamariz, Estoril ❶ 21 467 6946 ❺ 08.00–02.00 daily (May–Sept); 08.00–18.00 daily (Oct–Apr)

Restaurante Praia do Tamariz £ ❸ This beachside Spanish restaurant is good for tapas and paella. ⓐ Praia do Tamariz, Estoril ❶ 21 468

1010 Ⓦ www.restaurantepraiatamariz.com Ⓛ 09.00–02.00 daily (summer); 09.00–17.00 daily (winter)

Restaurante Cervejaria Luzmar ££ ❹ A typical Portuguese surf 'n' turf restaurant where you should also try the seafood rice option (*arroz de marisco*). ❸ Alameda dos Combatentes Grande Guerra 104, Cascais ❶ 21 484 5704 Ⓦ www.luzmar.dcsa.pt Ⓛ 12.30–16.30, 19.00–24.00 Tues–Sun, closed Mon

Restaurante Rosa Maria £££ ❺ This restaurant located inside the Farol Design Hotel serves Mediterranean fusion cuisine and has excellent sea views. ❸ Av Rei Humberto II de Itália 7, Cascais ❶ 21 482 3490 Ⓛ 12.30–15.30, 19.30–23.30 daily

ACCOMMODATION

Being a coastal resort area, the Estoril coast has no shortage of accommodation. For more options try Ⓦ www.secretplaces.com & Ⓦ www.estoril-portugal.com

Clube do Lago £ This hotel in Monte Estoril offers apartment-style units with kitchenettes and has a well-equipped health club on the premises. ❸ Av do Lago 4 ❶ 21 464 7597 Ⓦ www.hotelclubedolago.com Ⓝ Train: Estoril

Estalagem Muchaxo £ Located on Guincho Beach, just a short distance west of Cascais, this is a typical Portuguese hotel with restaurant, breakfast room, bars, anti-stress centre, sauna and seawater pool. ❸ Estrada do Guincho ❶ 21 487 0221 Ⓦ www.muchaxohotelcascais.com Ⓝ Train: Cascais

Farol Design Hotel ££ This boutique hotel combines a 19th-century mansion with 21st-century interior design. It is located next to the marina and it has restaurants, bars and a saltwater swimming pool. Av Rei Humberto II de Itália 7 21 482 3490 www.farol.com.pt Train: Cascais

Hotel Cidadela ££ Just 500 m (1/3 mile) from the beach, this modern hotel has a bar, restaurant, swimming pool, poolside bar and barbecue. Av 25 de Abril 21 482 7600 www.hotelcidadela.com Train: Cascais

Hotel Estoril Eden ££ A large hotel with guest rooms and apartments, it also has indoor and outdoor swimming pools, jacuzzi, sauna, massage service, sunbeds, restaurant and poolside snack bar. Av de Sabóia 209 21 466 7600 www.hotelestorileden.pt Train: Estoril

Hotel Inglaterra ££ This grand Estoril hotel in a converted mansion has a great location near the beach and steps from the casino. Rua do Porto 1 21 468 4461 www.hotelinglaterra.com.pt Train: Estoril

Hotel Albatroz £££ Situated on the bay, this is one of Portugal's top boutique hotels. A privately owned residence, each of its rooms has a unique character. Rua Frederico Arouca 100 21 484 7380 www.albatrozhotels.com Train: Cascais

Hotel Quinta da Marinha £££ Perched on the cliff tops facing the sea and with views of the Sintra hills, this resort hotel has two pools, a golf course, tennis courts, restaurants and bars. Quinta da Marinha 21 486 0100 www.quintadamarinha.com Train: Cascais

Sintra

Sintra is great to see if you have more than a couple of days in the Lisbon area. Surrounded by the green and rocky hills of the Serra da Sintra, its palaces, castle, houses and museums are among the country's top attractions. A UNESCO Heritage Site since 1995, the Romans, Moors and Portuguese royal family all adored it here, and with the advent of the Lisbon–Sintra railway in the 19th century it became a summer resort for the middle classes. You can easily walk around the Vila Velha (historic centre), dominated by the Palácio Nacional, but it is easier to take a bus or car to see the Palácio da Pena and some of the other attractions.

Each year Sintra hosts one of the most famous music festivals in the country, and the Centro Cultural Olga Cadaval (see page 138) hosts a string of exciting concerts and performances.

Getting around Sintra is easy – a bus (434) runs every 20 minutes from the train station to the historic centre and the Palácio Nacional, the Castelo dos Mouros, Palácio da Pena and back to the station. A rover ticket allows you to hop on and off where you please. Alternatively you can ride in one of the horse-drawn carriages that operate between Sintra and the Serra – you will see these in front of the Palácio Nacional.

Sintra's local authority website covers all aspects of tourism and culture in the area. Ⓦ www.cm-sintra.pt

GETTING THERE

Rossio Station in Lisbon is the most central station for reaching Sintra; trains run regularly (every ten minutes) and the journey only takes 40 minutes. There are also trains from the Oriente and

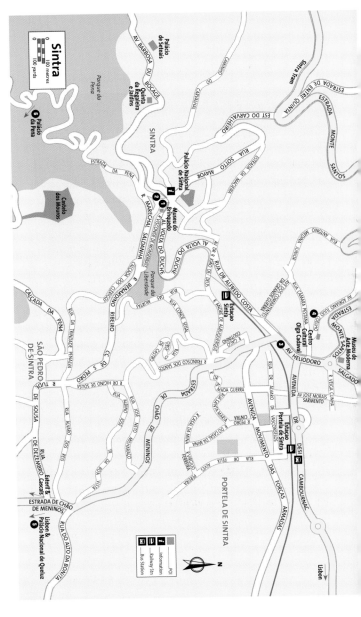

Entrecampos stations which stop at Queluz on the way to Sintra. Trains leave every half hour and take 75 minutes from Oriente to Sintra; 39 minutes from Entrecampos.

SIGHTS & ATTRACTIONS

Castelo dos Mouros (Moorish Castle)

Originally built by the Moors around the 8th and 9th centuries in dramatic surroundings on two hills in the Serra de Sintra, the castle was conquered by Dom Afonso Henriques in the 12th century and

● Sintra's Castelo dos Mouros is a worthy reminder of Moorish style

PALÁCIO NACIONAL DE QUELUZ
(QUELUZ NATIONAL PALACE)

This pink palace is located between Lisbon and Sintra, so you might like to stop off for a tour. It is often referred to as a 'little Versailles' for its elegance and formal gardens filled with Baroque statues. Today the East Wing is the official residence of foreign dignitaries invited by the Portuguese state. Highlights include the façade of the palace, the Music Room, the Throne Room, the collection of Portuguese furniture and the gardens. ⓐ Largo do Palácio de Queluz ❶ 21 434 3860 ⏰ Palace: 09.30–17.00 Wed–Mon, closed Tues; gardens: 10.00–18.00 Wed–Mon, closed Tues (summer); 10.00–17.00 Wed–Mon, closed Tues (winter) Ⓝ Train: Queluz ❶ Admission charge

rebuilt by Dom Fernando in the 19th century, when the walls were restored. The walls and turrets of the castle can be seen winding their way around the ridges of the hills. Look out for the chapel built by Dom Afonso with its Romanesque doorways, tracings of paintings and medieval tombs, as well as the Moorish cistern and the 'royal tower'. ⓐ Rua da Pena ❶ 21 923 7300 ⏰ 09.30–20.00 daily (Apr–Sept); 10.00–18.00 daily (Oct–Mar); last admission one hour before closing Ⓝ Train: Sintra; Bus: 434 from Sintra ❶ Admission charge

The impressive Parque da Pena is a 200-hectare (494-acre) garden surrounding the palace.

Palácio Nacional de Sintra (Sintra National Palace)

As you approach Sintra, look out for the unmistakeable white chimneys of the National Palace, also known as the Paço Real or Palácio da Vila.

A mixture of mudejar (Arabic-style), Gothic, Manueline and Renaissance styles, it is a national monument.

You cannot fail to admire the stunning mudejar *azulejos* that cover the walls of various halls, patios and the royal chapel. Renaissance style was added during the reign of Dom João III (1521–57), who built the Sala dos Cisnes, where you can see various royal portraits. The Sala dos Brasões contains 18th-century tiles by the best masters of the time. ❸ Largo Rainha Dona Amélia ❶ 21 910 6840 ● 09.30–17.30 Thur–Tues, closed Wed (last entry 17.00) Ⓝ Train: Sintra; Bus: 434 from Sintra ❶ Admission charge

Palácio da Pena (Pena Palace)

Located in the Serra da Sintra on the peak of a rocky hill, this 19th-century palace was built on the orders of Dom Fernando II. The former monastery had been severely damaged by the 1755 earthquake, but around the remaining Renaissance altar of the chapel, a palace of Moorish, Gothic, Manueline and Renaissance pastiche was built, influenced by the European castles of the time. Don't miss the original 16th-century Manueline cloisters, the odd-shaped sentry boxes, the 18th-century tiles, period furniture and the murals, as well as impressive views across the park and surrounding area. ❸ Estrada da Pena ❶ 21 910 5340 ● 09.45–17.30 daily (summer); 10.00–18.00 daily (winter) (last entry 17.00) Ⓝ Train: Sintra; Bus: 434 from Sintra ❶ Admission charge

Quinta da Regaleira e Jardins (Regaleira Estate & Gardens)

This fascinating palace and gardens are worth a visit if you are interested in mystery, mythology and fantasy. It is a beautiful combination of architectural styles, built at the beginning of the 20th century. Look out for the neo-Gothic, neo-Manueline carved

● *You can't miss the unmistakeable chimneys of the Palácio Nacional in Sintra*

stone motifs, the labyrinthine gardens, statues, grottoes, waterfalls and lakes, as well as the dry well with the Templar's cross, eight-pointed star and a chapel. Underneath is a crypt that leads into a gallery connecting it to the palace. You can visit the palace and gardens, but if you want a guided visit you should book ahead.
ⓐ Av Barbosa du Bocage ⓣ 21 910 6650 ⓛ 10.00–17.30 daily

(Nov–Jan); 10.00–18.30 daily (Feb, Mar & Oct); 10.00–19.00 daily (Apr–Sept) Ⓝ Train: Sintra; Bus: 434 from Sintra ❶ Admission charge

Sintra tram

Hop on this tram for a relaxing ride to the wine-growing town of Banzão, near Colares, and on to Praia das Maças, where you will find the best-known beach on the Sintra coastline. The tram is near the Museu de Arte Moderna in Sintra. ❶ 21 923 8789 Ⓛ Fri–Sun (summer only): first tram leaves Sintra at 10.00, last tram leaves Praia das Maças at 16.45

CULTURE

Centro Cultural Olga Cadaval

This cultural centre was restored and updated after it was damaged by fire in 1985. Today it hosts concerts, theatre and performing arts events. ⓐ Praça Dr. Francisco Sá Carneiro ❶ 21 910 7100 Ⓦ www.ccolgacadaval.pt Ⓛ 13.30–19.00 Tues–Fri, 10.00–13.00, 14.00–18.00 Sat, closed Sun & Mon; booking office closes one hour before event starts Ⓝ Train: Sintra; Bus: 434 from Sintra

Museu de Arte Moderna (Museum of Modern Art)

This museum is a treat for 20th-century art lovers. It houses an interesting collection of European and American art. The Berardo Collection, as it is known, includes works by Pablo Picasso, Miró, Max Ernst, Man Ray, George Segal, Andy Warhol and Roy Lichtenstein. Many of the finest works are now to be found at the Cultural Centre in Bélem, on permanent loan. ⓐ Av Heliodoro Salgado ❶ 21 924 8170 Ⓦ www.berardocollection.com Ⓛ 10.00–18.00 Wed–Sun, 14.00–18.00 Tues, closed Mon Ⓝ Train: Sintra; Bus: 434 from Sintra

● *One of many interesting exhibits from the toy museum*

Museu do Brinquedo (Toy Museum)

Here you can see the toy collection of João Arbués Moreira, gathered together over the course of 50 years, from teddy bears and carousels to soldiers and Dinky toys. ⓐ Rua Visconde de Monserrate 26 ❶ 21 910 6016 Ⓦ www.museu-do-brinquedo.pt ⏱ 10.00–18.00 Tues–Sun, closed Mon Ⓝ Train: Sintra; Bus: 434 from Sintra ❶ Admission charge

RETAIL THERAPY

Don't expect large state-of-the art shopping centres in the middle of Sintra. Wander the tangle of streets of the Vila Velha and you are bound to find some treasures, from local crafts, traditional instruments and antiques to books, pottery and wine. The **Loja do Arco** (ⓐ Rua Arco do Teixeira 2) is a treasure trove of Portuguese music, from *fado* to classical and contemporary, as well as books and sheet music. It also has Internet access. For hand-painted Portuguese ceramics try Sintra Bazar and A Esquina (both in Praça da República), head to **Almorábida** (🄐 Rua Visconde de Monserrate 12–15) for lace, and **Casa Branca** (🄐 Rua Consiglieri Pedroso 12) for linens and embroidered silks.

TAKING A BREAK

There are several cafés in the Old Town area, including some by the station and tram, in case you have to wait. While in Sintra you should try a *queijada*, a tasty local cake made from cheese, eggs, sugar, flour and cinnamon.

A Piriquita £ ❶ Great for pastries. 🄐 Rua das Padarias 1–5, off Rua Visconde de Monserrate ❶ 21 923 0626 ❶ 09.00–22.00 daily

⬤ *Enjoy outdoor dining at a restaurant in Sintra*

Vila Velha £ ➋ Good for a quick snack. Stop by for a salad, sandwich or *caldo verde*. It is located along the narrow alleyway opposite the Palácio Nacional. ➌ Rua das Padarias 8, off Rua Visconde de Monserrate ➊ 21 923 0154 ➍ 08.00–19.00 daily

AFTER DARK

RESTAURANTS & BARS

Tirol de Sintra £ ➌ A good basic place for lunch or dinner, this restaurant has outdoor seating and serves traditional Portuguese cuisine. Specialities include roast leg of lamb, pork meat with clams, pizzas, home-made breads and *queijada*. ➌ Av Heliodoro Salgado 5 ➊ 21 923 0505 ➍ 07.00–20.30 daily

Casa Orixás ££ ➍ This Brazilian restaurant has a choice of buffet or à la carte menu with food from various regions, as well as tropical gardens and a lively ambience. ➌ Av Adriano Julio Coelho 7 ➊ 21 924 1672 ➎ www.orixasclub.com ➍ 16.00–24.00 Tues–Thur, 16.00–01.00 Fri, 11.00–01.00 Sat, 11.00–24.00 Sun, closed Mon

Cozinha Velha £££ ➎ Located in the former palace kitchen at the Palácio Nacional de Queluz (see page 135), this superb restaurant offers fine dining in luxurious surroundings. ➌ Largo do Palácio ➊ 21 435 6158 ➍ 12.30–15.00, 19.30–22.00 daily

Restaurante Palácio Nacional da Pena £££ ➏ You can dine on traditional Portuguese cuisine at the restaurant inside the Palácio Nacional, but you will pay for the pleasure. ➌ Estrada da Pena ➊ 21 923 1208 ➍ 12.00–16.00, 19.00–22.00 daily

ACCOMMODATION

Casal da Carregueira ££ Small guest house set in enclosed gardens near Queluz, dressed in period furniture and with a bar, comfortable sitting room, sauna and barbecue area. ⓐ Belas ❶ 21 432 1474 ⓦ www.portugalvirtual.pt ⓝ Train: Sintra

Hotel Tivoli Sintra ££ Located in the centre of Sintra, this hotel has a bar and restaurant with panoramic views of the valley. ⓐ Praça da República ❶ 21 923 7200 ⓦ www.tivolihotels.com ⓝ Train: Sintra

Quinta de São Thiago ££ On the lower slopes of the Sintra hills, this 16th-century house has been modernised but has retained its chapel, old tiles, library and music room. There is also a swimming pool and tennis court. ⓐ Estrada de Monserrate ❶ 21 923 2923 ⓦ www.portugalvirtual.pt ⓝ Train: Sintra

Penha Longa Hotel & Golf Resort £££ Large resort hotel with three restaurants, beautiful gardens, two golf courses, spa, health club, indoor and outdoor pools, tennis courts and a jogging track. ⓐ Estrada da Lagoa Azul, Linhó ❶ 21 924 9011 ⓦ www.penhalonga.com ⓝ Train: Sintra

Pousada de Queluz – Dona Maria I £££ Located by Queluz National Palace, 5 km (3 miles) from Lisbon. Comfortable rooms with mini-bar and satellite TV. ⓐ Largo do Palácio ❶ 21 435 6158 ⓦ www.pousadas.pt ⓝ Train: Queluz-Belas

---

❶ *Trams on the busy Praça do Comércio*

PRACTICAL
information

Directory

GETTING THERE

By air

Several airlines currently operate from the UK to Aeroporto da Portela, Lisbon's international airport. Schedules are liable to constant change, so do check the websites of the following carriers while planning your journey:

Air Berlin ☎ 0871 500 0737 🅦 www.airberlin.com

British Airways ☎ 0844 493 0787 🅦 www.ba.com

easyJet ☎ 0871 244 2366 🅦 www.easyjet.com

TAP Portugal ☎ 0845 601 0932 🅦 www.flytap.com

easyJet is one of the most convenient choices in terms of price, choice of airport and arrival times.

From North America, TAP Portugal (see above) and **Continental** (🅦 www.continental.com) are the only airlines that offer non-stop flights from New York. Most major US airlines offer flights, but with a change of planes somewhere in Europe.

From Australia, British Airways (see above) offers flights via London. Most other airlines, like **Qantas** (🅦 www.qantas.com.au) and **Cathay Pacific** (🅦 www.cathaypacific.com), fly to Lisbon but with a stopover somewhere in Asia (like Singapore or Hong Kong) and in Europe. From New Zealand, **United Airlines** (🅦 www.united.com) offers flights via Los Angeles and London.

Many people are aware that air travel emits CO_2, which contributes to climate change. You may be interested in the possibility of lessening the environmental impact of your flight through the charity **Climate Care**, which offsets your CO_2 by funding environmental projects around the world. Visit 🅦 www.jpmorganclimatecare.com

By rail

To reach Lisbon by rail you will have to be prepared for a long haul and a few changes, but this might be an option if you are buying a multi-country train pass with stops along the way. From London you can take one of the frequent Eurostar services to Paris Gare du Nord station. From there you should transfer to Paris Montparnasse or Austerlitz and take a train to Hendaye/Irún. Overnight trains run direct from here to Gare do Oriente (see page 48). It takes at least 24 hours to make the journey non-stop. See Ⓦ www.railpass.com or call ❶ 0844 848 4064 for exact connections and tickets.

Eurostar ❶ 0870 518 6186 Ⓦ www.eurostar.com

Rail Europe ❶ 0844 848 5848 Ⓦ www.raileurope.co.uk

SNCF (France) Ⓦ www.voyages-sncf.com

ENTRY FORMALITIES

Citizens of EU countries can enter Portugal with either a valid identity card or passport. Citizens of Canada, the United States, Australia and New Zealand must travel with their passport but do not need a visa if staying for less than 90 days. Citizens of South Africa require a visa.

Travellers to Portugal are currently entitled to bring the following duty-paid goods into the country for their own personal use: up to 800 cigarettes, 10 litres of spirits, 90 litres of wine (60 litres of sparkling wine), and 110 litres of beer. However, if you are questioned by customs officials and cannot satisfy them that it is not for commercial use, it could be seized and not returned.

If you are travelling to and from non-EU countries, you still have a duty-free allowance of 200 cigarettes or 50 cigars or 250 g of tobacco; four litres of wine or one litre of spirits; plus 50 g of perfume, 250 ml of *eau de toilette* and gifts worth up to 430 euros.

MONEY

Portugal adopted the euro in 2002, and its former currency, the escudo, was withdrawn from circulation. Euro notes are available in denominations of 5, 10, 20, 50, 100, 200 and 500 euros; coins are available in 1, 2, 5, 10, 20 and 50 cents plus 1 and 2 euros. One side of the coin is common throughout the EU but the flipside is individual to the country where it was minted. However, all currency can be used throughout the EU countries where the euro is used.

You can change money and traveller's cheques, but be prepared to pay a commission – traveller's cheques should be in US dollars, pounds sterling or euros. However, with so many ATMs around, it is more likely that you will prefer to withdraw money as and when you need it. Most cards are accepted and the instructions are multilingual. Credit cards are also accepted at most places.

HEALTH, SAFETY & CRIME

Citizens of the EU are entitled to reduced-cost and sometimes free medical treatment on production of a European Health Insurance Card (EHIC). You can apply for this online from the UK Department of Health (ⓦ www.dh.gov.uk). The card lasts for three to five years and covers medical treatment in the case of emergency or accident. Also make sure you take identification with you as well as your EHIC. As this may not cover all your medical needs it is better to have your own private travel insurance to pay for repatriation, should you need it. Insurance also usually covers you if you are a victim of crime, but check your policy carefully before you travel.

Although Lisbon does not have a high crime rate compared with some cities, there has been a rise in violent crime in the past couple of decades. In general, Lisbon is safe, but tourists are easy targets for opportunists. Watch out for pickpockets in crowded areas, particularly where there is a high concentration of tourists, such as on tram No 28 (see page 56). Be careful when travelling back to your hotel late at night, especially in the dark, narrow streets of the Alfama, Bairro Alto and Chiado. If you are unlucky enough to be the victim of a crime, contact the tourist police in Praça dos Restauradores (☏ 21 342 1634). For lost property, ask the tourist police where you can find the nearest *Guardia Nacional da República* (GNR, National Guard).

OPENING HOURS

Most shops tend to open 09.00–13.00 and 15.00–19.00 Mon–Fri. On Saturday some shops only open 09.00–13.00. However, the large shopping centres are open 09.00–24.00 Mon–Sat. Banking hours are generally 08.30–15.00 Mon–Fri, but some branches in Lisbon reopen from 18.00 until 23.00. Most museums are open 10.00–18.00 Tues–Sun, but this can vary – some also close for lunch.

TOILETS

There are public toilets in shopping centres, department stores, in most museums and in the main railway stations. Cafés and bars have toilets but it is always better and more polite to buy something first.

CHILDREN

Most Portuguese are very good with children, and families regularly go out together to eat in the evening, even late at night. Children are welcome in most places except late-night bars and clubs. Depending on the age of the children, some museums and historic attractions might not be exciting enough for them. They might like to climb up the towers of the Castelo de São Jorge (see page 74), the Torre de Belém (see page 101) and ride on the trams and elevators. Parque das Nações (see page 110) has various suitable attractions, including the Pavilhão do Conhecimento (see page 112), the Oceanário (see page 110), and the Teleférico (see page 112).

At **Lisboa Zoo** (ⓐ Estrada de Benfica 158–160 ⓣ 21 723 2900 ⓦ www.zoolisboa.pt) there is a wide range of animals, from big cats and camels to tropical birds and reptiles. Feeding time is a good time to take the children, and there are numerous rides as well. There are various activities for children in the Parque Florestal de Monsanto (see page 88), and the beaches of the Estoril coastline are also close enough to take a day trip. They are easily reached by train from Cais do Sodré.

You can hire bicycles in the Parque das Nações – there are many safe routes here, and **Tejo Bike** (ⓐ Rossio dos Olivais or Sony Plaza ⓣ 21 891 9333 ⓦ www.tejobike.pt) is very reliable. There is a discount of 20 per cent if you have a Parque das Nações Card (see page 113). If you do go for the card, you'll also be able to use the Tourist Mini Train to travel round the Parque das Nações. The route begins and ends at Alameda dos Oceanos in front of the Pavilhão Atlântico.

COMMUNICATIONS
Internet
Internet cafés include:

Lisbon Welcome Centre ⓐ Praça do Comércio ⓣ 21 031 2810
ⓛ 09.00–20.00 daily
Net Centre Café ⓐ Rua Diário de Noticias ⓛ 16.00–02.00 daily
Peter Café Sport ⓐ Rua da Pimenta, Parque das Nações
ⓛ 11.00–01.00 daily

Phone
Many people prefer to take their mobile phones abroad these days rather than use a public phone. Before you go remember to contact

Belém Tower is right on the River Tagus

your mobile provider to make sure your phone is activated for international use. Also check that your existing handset will work in Portugal and ask how much the charges for calls and texts will be. You will often have to pay for receiving calls while abroad and texts can be charged twice, depending on the provider. Phone providers in Portugal include **Vodafone** (🌐 www.vodaphone.com) and **Optimus** (🌐 www.optimus.pt).

TELEPHONING PORTUGAL

To call Portugal from abroad, dial the international access code (00), then the country code (351), then the phone number, which should be nine digits long.

Lisbon telephone numbers start with 21, followed by seven digits. When calling from anywhere in Portugal (including Lisbon), dial all nine digits.

TELEPHONING ABROAD

To call abroad, dial 00, then the country code and city/local code, minus the first 0, then the phone number you require. You can also make calls at post offices and pay for the call at the end.

The country code for the UK is 44, for Ireland 353, for the USA and Canada 1, for Australia 61, for New Zealand 64 and for South Africa 27.

Telephones in hotels are also convenient but tend to be quite expensive for anything other than a local call. A list of charges should be provided in your room. If they aren't, ask at reception.

Using a public telephone box is quite easy, and direct dialling in Lisbon is not a problem. Public phones can be found in cafés and bars as well as stations and in the street. Phones take euro coins in denominations of 2 cents up to 2 euros.

Alternatively, phone cards can be bought from newspaper kiosks, the post office or other retail outlets – ask for a CrediPhone – and they come in units of 50, 100 or 150.

◢ The very bright Palácio da Pena in Sintra

Post

Post office (*correios* Ⓦ www.ctt.pt) opening times can vary in the larger cities. The main post offices in Lisbon, Cascais, Estoril and Sintra can be found at:

ⓐ Praça dos Restauradores, Lisbon Ⓛ 08.00–22.00
ⓐ Aeroporto, Lisbon Ⓛ 24 hours
ⓐ Avenida Marginal, Lote C, Cascais Ⓛ 09.00–18.00
ⓐ Avenida Nice 1, Estoril Ⓛ 09.30–19.30
ⓐ Praça Don Afonso Henriques 7 Ⓛ 08.30–18.00

ELECTRICITY

Voltage is 220 V using standard continental Europe two-pin sockets. To use American appliances, a 220-V transformer should be used, together with an adapter plug.

TRAVELLERS WITH DISABILITIES

Lisbon's cobbled streets and hilly geography make it rather a challenge for wheelchair users or anyone with a physical disability. However, access for travellers with disabilities is improving gradually and some hotels now offer adapted rooms and bathrooms. Modern buildings are generally fairly accessible, but wherever you go it is a good idea to call in advance and be clear about your needs.

For general advice on accessible travel contact:

RADAR The principal UK forum for people with disabilities.
ⓐ 12 City Forum, 250 City Road, London EC1V 8AF Ⓣ (020) 7250 3222
Ⓦ www.radar.org.uk

SATH (Society for Accessible Travel & Hospitality) advises US-based travellers with disabilities. ⓐ 347 Fifth Ave, Suite 605, New York, NY 10016 Ⓣ (212) 447 7284 Ⓦ www.sath.org

TOURIST INFORMATION

There are three main tourist offices in Lisbon:

ⓐ Airport **ⓣ** 21 845 0660 **ⓛ** 07.00–24.00 daily. In the arrivals hall, it has maps and information on hotels and main attractions. You also need to go here to pick up a taxi voucher that takes you to the city centre.

ⓐ Palácio Foz, Praça dos Restauradores **ⓣ** 21 346 3314 **ⓛ** 09.00–20.00 daily. You can pick up information here; there is also a shop.

ⓐ Praça do Comércio **ⓣ** 21 031 2810 **ⓛ** 09.00–20.00 daily. This is the main tourist office, the Lisbon Welcome Centre, and provides detailed information on hotels, attractions, tours, discount cards and travel cards. It also has a café, Internet access and a shop.

Lisbon's tourist office website covers both the city and Estoril, Leiria/Fatima, Costa Azul, Sintra, Templarios, Oeste, Ribatejo and other places close by. **ⓦ** www.visitlisboa.com. Also try **ⓦ** www.askmelisboa.com

The Lisbon local authority website also has a good tourist information section. **ⓦ** www.cm-lisboa.pt

There are tourist offices in Cascais (**ⓐ** Rua Visconde da Luz 14 **ⓣ** 21 486 8204 **ⓛ** 09.00–19.00 Mon–Sat, 10.00–18.00 Sun), Estoril (**ⓐ** Arcadas do Parque **ⓣ** 21 466 3813 **ⓛ** 09.00–19.00 Mon–Sat, 10.00–18.00 Sun) and Sintra (**ⓐ** Praça de Republica 23 **ⓣ** 21 923 1157 **ⓛ** 09.00–20.00 June–Sept, 09.00–19.00 Oct–May).

BACKGROUND READING

Lisbon by Paul Buck. An interesting insight into the city. A cultural and literary companion, the book provides factual information on the city's history and sights, often through the views of artists and writers.
The Last Kabbalist of Lisbon by Richard Zimmler. A crime thriller set in the 16th century, during the time of Jewish persecution.

Emergencies

For police, ambulance and fire services, the number is 🛈 112

MEDICAL SERVICES

In an emergency you should go to the nearest public hospital, which will provide emergency treatment. EU citizens with a European Health Insurance Card (see page 146) are entitled to reduced-cost, and sometimes free, basic treatment. Medical insurance is advisable for EU citizens and essential if you are a non-EU visitor.

If you can get to a hospital yourself, head for *urgências* or a 24-hour public health clinic. *Farmácia* (pharmacies) can help you with a list of emergency clinics, doctors and dentists.

British Hospital ⓐ Rua Tomás da Fonseca 🛈 21 721 3400

Clinica Internacional de Saúde de Cascais ⓐ Rua João Infante, Lote 1 r/c A, Alto das Flores, Bairro do Rosario, Cascais 🛈 21 486 5946 ⓦ http://cis-cascais.pai.pt

Hospital Santa Maria ⓐ Av Prof Egas Moniz 🛈 21 780 5000; Urgencias: 21 780 5111 and 21 780 5222 ⓦ www.hsm.min-saude.pt

Doctors

Dr David Ernst ⓐ Clínica Médica Internacional de Lisboa, Av António Augusto Aguiar 🛈 21 351 3310

Dr Andrew French ⓐ International Health Centre, Rua do Regimento Dezanove 67, 2nd floor 🛈 21 484 5318

Dentists

Dr Francis Haley B.D.S. and Dr D B Skinner ⓐ Av 25 de Abril, Edificio Grei 184, 1st floor, Cascais 🛈 21 486 3011

POLICE
The tourist police are located in Praça dos Restauradores
(🕿 21 342 1634).

EMBASSIES & CONSULATES
Australian Embassy 🅐 Av da Liberdade 200, 2nd floor 🕿 21 310 1500
🅦 www.portugal.embassy.gov.au
Canadian Embassy 🅐 Av da Liberdade 198–200, 3rd floor 🕿 21 316 4600
🅦 www.portugal.gc.ca
Irish Embassy 🅐 Rua Imprensa-Estrela 1, 4th floor 🕿 21 392 9440
New Zealand Consulate 🅐 Rua do Periquito, Cascais 🕿 21 370 5779
South African Embassy 🅐 Av Luís Bívar 10 🕿 21 319 2200
🅦 www.embaixada-africadosul.pt
UK Embassy 🅐 Rua de São Bernardo 33, Lisbon 🕿 21 392 40 00
🅦 www.ukinportugal.fco.gov.uk
US Embassy 🅐 Av das Forças Armadas 🕿 21 727 3300
🅦 http://lisbon.usembassy.gov

EMERGENCY PHRASES

Help!	**Fire!**	**Stop!**
Socorro!	Fogo!	Pare!
Sookohrroo!	*Fohgoo!*	*Pahreh!*

Call an ambulance/a doctor/the police/the fire brigade!
Chame uma ambulância/um médico/a polícia/os bombeiros!
*Shami ooma angboolangsya/oong medeekoo/a pooleesseeya/
oosh bombehroosh!*

ACKNOWLEDGEMENTS

Thomas Cook Publishing wishes to thank the photographers, picture libraries and other organisations, to whom the copyright belongs, for the photographs in this book.

Anwer Bati, pages 5, 21, 61, 68 & 117; Axel Buhrmann, pages 30–31; Sergio Calleja, page 39; Dreamstime.com (Episousa, page 112; Peter Szucs, page 119); Alan Grant, page 151; Graham Hoggarth, pages 40–41 & 143; istock photo (oiartzuar, page 127); Jorge, page 9; Jo McLure, page 65; Martin Röll, page 37; Massimiliano Ruggieri, page 33; John Saxenian/BigStockPhoto. com, page 123; Pedro Simões, page 140; SXC.hu (Attila Iván, page 7; Rui Lousão, page 149; Carlos Paes, page 104); Turismo de Portugal, pages 29 & 83; Christopher Holt, all others.

For CAMBRIDGE PUBLISHING MANAGEMENT LIMITED:
Project editor: Jennifer Jahn
Copy editor: Paul Hines
Layout: Paul Queripel
Proofreaders: Ceinwen Sinclair & Sarah Loker

Send your thoughts to
books@thomascook.com

- Found a great bar, club, shop or must-see sight that we don't feature?
- Like to tip us off about any information that needs a little updating?
- Want to tell us what you love about this handy little guidebook and more importantly how we can make it even handier?

Then here's your chance to tell all! Send us ideas, discoveries and recommendations today and then look out for your valuable input in the next edition of this title.

Email the above address (stating the title) or write to:
pocket guides Series Editor, Thomas Cook Publishing, PO Box 227, Coningsby Road, Peterborough PE3 8SB, UK.

WHAT'S IN YOUR GUIDEBOOK?

Independent authors Impartial up-to-date information from our travel experts who meticulously source local knowledge.

Experience Thomas Cook's 165 years in the travel industry and guidebook publishing enriches every word with expertise you can trust.

Travel know-how Thomas Cook has thousands of staff working around the globe, all living and breathing travel.

Editors Travel-publishing professionals, pulling everything together to craft a perfect blend of words, pictures, maps and design.

You, the traveller We deliver a practical, no-nonsense approach to information, geared to how you really use it.

Useful phrases

English	Portuguese	Approx pronunciation
BASICS		
Yes	Sim	*Seem*
No	Não	*Nown*
Please	Por favor	*Poor favohr*
Thank you	Obrigado/a	*Ohbreegahdoo/a*
Hello	Olá	*Ohlah*
Goodbye	Adeus	*Adayoosh*
Excuse me	Com licença	*Cong lisensah*
Sorry	Desculpe	*Dishkoolper*
That's okay	Está bem	*Istah bayng*
Do you speak English?	Fala Inglês?	*Fahla eenglaysh?*
Good morning	Bom dia	*Bohm deea*
Good afternoon	Boa tarde	*Boha tahrd*
Good evening	Boa noite	*Boha noyt*
Goodnight	Boa noite	*Boha noyt*
My name is ...	Chamo-me ...	*Shamoo-mi ..*
NUMBERS		
One	Um	*Oong*
Two	Dois	*Doysh*
Three	Três	*Traysh*
Four	Quatro	*Kwahtroo*
Five	Cinco	*Seengkoo*
Six	Seis	*Saysh*
Seven	Sete	*Set*
Eight	Oito	*Oytoo*
Nine	Nove	*Nov*
Ten	Dez	*Desh*
Twenty	Vinte	*Veengt*
Fifty	Cinquenta	*Seengkwayngta*
One hundred	Cem	*Sayng*
SIGNS & NOTICES		
Airport	Aeroporto	*Aehrohportoo*
Smoking/ No smoking	Fumadores/ Não fumadores	*Foomadohrsh/ Nown-foomadohrsh*
Toilets	Lavabos	*Lavahboosh*
Ladies	Senhoras	*Sinyohrash*
Gentlemen	Homens	*Omayngsh*